MORE
MERRY-GO-ROUND

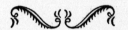

By the Authors of

WASHINGTON
MERRY-GO-ROUND

1932

LIVERIGHT, INC., PUBLISHERS

NEW YORK

Published August, 1932
Second printing, August, 1932

TO THOSE WHO PAY
FOR THE RIDE

CONTENTS

MORE MERRY-GO-ROUND

CHAPTER ONE

DANCE OF THE DEPRESSION

*E*ARLY on the morning of July 11, 1864, General Jubal
A. Early led a ragged army of 20,000 Confederates up Seventh
Street toward the capitol of the United States. They had come
up through the Shenandoah Valley and across Maryland, tak-
ing Washington completely by surprise and cutting it off from
Baltimore, Philadelphia and its communication with a friendly
North.

The city, basking in the usual somnolence of midsummer,
was thrown into confusion. President Lincoln, who had spent
the night at his summer residence—the Soldiers' Home—was
brought back to town and a ship assigned to carry him down
the Potomac. The War Department made frantic preparations
to defend valuable stores of arms, ammunition, clothing and
gold bullion. Only an untrained local militia defended the
capital and it looked as if the city would be ransacked and
burned.

General Early, however, did not know that Washington
was defenseless. He halted his men halfway up Seventh Street
to reconnoiter. Just ahead and within clear sight was the
capitol. The sun burned down with impartial severity upon
its shining dome and the dusty invaders. The latter had come a
long way, many of them without shoes. They had been living
on the country.

It was just before noon when Early halted his advance. An hour later two divisions of the Sixth Corps of the Army of the Potomac arrived at the Potomac wharf. Early dared not risk a battle and retreated over the road by which he had come.

The capital was saved; the North awakened.

*

WASHINGTON, in the third winter of Herbert Hoover, slept just as peacefully as on the morning of July 11, 1864. The city was, of course, aware that it was the third year of the depression, and that prosperity, despite Mr. Hoover's repeated promises, had not been just around the corner. This realization, however, did not penetrate poignantly.

The capital, for the most part, had its head in the sand. There were, of course, many whose incomes were hurt by passed dividends and had to let out one or two servants. There were even some, like the staff of the Spanish Embassy, whose government refused longer to buy gold braid for diplomatic uniforms and who were forced to appear at the capital's dinner parties more modestly attired than in the heyday of Coolidge prosperity. There were even one or two protestants from the depression-ridden world outside who insisted upon disrupting the serenity of the capital's existence by placing their troubles on the very doorstep of the White House.

But for the most part they made little impression. When an army of hunger marchers, 1800 strong, began on December 3 to converge upon the city, President Hoover sent word that he would not see them.

That night he held his first Cabinet dinner. It was a gorgeous affair, even if some of the guests did complain that they received their invitations only a week in advance, whereas it had been the punctilious practice of Calvin Coolidge to send out his cards thirty days in advance at the minimum. Despite the last minute notices, sixty-eight guests reneged on other invitations in order to have the honor of reading their names

in the papers as guests of the White House. Pink chrysanthe-
mums—Mrs. Hoover's favorite—together with pink snap-
dragons and stevia decorated the long table. Edward Johnson,
a tenor imported from New York, and Mischa Levitzki, his
accompanist, relieved the monotony of after-dinner conversation. All of the members of the Cabinet were there, including
William Nuckles Doak, Secretary of Labor, who had been
struggling diligently for some months to get accustomed to
"state occasions"; his predecessor, Puddler Jim Davis, whose
ten years in the Cabinet has given him a blasé manner about
White House dinners, which he completely lacked when he
first arrived from the coal regions of Pennsylvania; and Ruth
Wilson Hurley, whose husband, the Secretary of War, was
more proud than ever of her golden hair, and who was most
solicitous of the happiness of Andrew W. Mellon, oldest and
only unmarried member of the Cabinet.

In order to strengthen the weakening political allegiance of
other important personages, the Hoovers had invited a large
sprinkling of non-Cabinet guests, most of them a trifle too
overwhelmed with the unexpected honor to be at ease. This,
however, was not true of Governor Douglass Buck, who
strutted about the East Room as if it were the back porch of
the Governor's mansion at Dover, Delaware; nor of "Silk
Stocking" Congresswoman Ruth Pratt, whose Standard Oil
millions had thrown more luxurious parties than the Hoovers
had ever dreamed; nor of Edna Ferber, who regaled several
Cabinet members with the story of how she got her nose
Gentilized. When the party broke up, Mrs. Hoover was told
that it was one of the best of the entire administration.

While the Cabinet dined, the hunger marchers bumped
toward the capital in motor trucks. They were a motley crew,
some obviously cajoled by communist organizers into making
the trip, but all unemployed, bewildered, many desperate. They
wore arm bands identifying themselves as members of the
hunger army and followed with childish precision the direc-
tions of Brigadier General "Happy" Glassford, chief of the
Washington police force. When Herbert Benjamin, their gen-

eralissimo, asked to carry a petition to President Hoover, he was rebuffed at the White House gates, and thereupon quietly led his cohorts back whence they had come.

The march stirred not a ripple on the calm of Washington's social season. On the day before the hunger marchers arrived, Mrs. Hoover was entertained at luncheon by Mrs. Charles Francis Adams and other Cabinet ladies; Secretary of State and Mrs. Stimson were entertained by the Belgian Ambassador; the Ogden Millses returned from a vacation at Pinehurst; while Dolly Curtis Gann, Mrs. Stimson and Mrs. Adams held their usual at-homes.

On that day also the White House sent out invitations to the Diplomatic reception. It took place four days later and was one of the outstanding events of the season. In gold braid, medals, high boots, glittering jewelry—the Roumanian and Peruvian military attachés even wearing corsets—the entire Corps was present.

Diamonds were the symbol of the depression. They glittered everywhere. Countess Szechenyi, once Gladys Vanderbilt, blazed a fat diamond pendant with almond earrings to match. Lady Lindsay set off a pale pink gown with a diamond stomacher. Mrs. Herridge, wife of the Canadian Minister and sister of Canada's prime minister, featured a diamond tiara and diamond bracelets. Signora de Martino, wife of the Italian Ambassador, lent the regal touch with a diamond coronet. Sesostris Sidarouss Pasha, large-mustached Egyptian minister, varied the picture by wearing a red fez as he danced. Pink-cheeked Sir Ronald Lindsay towered above every one in a marine uniform with a military belt, provoking curiosity from the admirals. Count Szechenyi, in the uniform of a Hungarian cavalry officer, wore a black cape, black boots, a black patch over his eye and a heavy silver chain around his neck. The Japanese Embassy staff, all nineteen of them, dressed in plain evening clothes. They bowed low and said: "Good evening, Mr. President. Very pleased. Very much honor."

One incident only marred the complete perfection of the occasion.

War between Bolivia and Paraguay had been threatening. Not many of the guests who danced in the East Room or ogled each other's makeups were any more aware of this than they were that the capital recently had been visited by an army of workless men. But standing in the line of guests to the reception that night were delegates of both these countries invited by the State Department to meet in Washington to prevent impending war.

Lacking diplomatic status, however, the delegates stood not in the line of diplomats but in the much less privileged line of outside guests. And they had to stand a long time. Especially long was the wait of Señor Juan José Soler of Paraguay and his colleague Señor César A. Vasconsellos. Slowly, six inches at a time, they moved toward the point where President and Mrs. Hoover stood solemnly, shaking hands. No place in the line, however, could they espy their Bolivian colleagues. The Paraguayans became nervous.

Finally, as the line approached the Mecca of their pilgrimage, Señores Soler and Vasconsellos were nonplussed to see standing among the diplomats who already had shaken hands with the President, Señor Eduardo Diez de Medina and Señor Enrique Finot, delegates of Bolivia. Both were decked out in resplendent uniforms and looked as if they had just swallowed a canary. Medina exhibited the blue, red and yellow sash of the Venezuelan order of Busto de Los Andes. Finot flaunted the great green order of the Condor de Los Andes. Having jumped the silken cords which separate the diplomats from the hoi polloi, they had shaken hands with the President long before, and now were wandering with complete abandon around the sanctuary reserved only for the Diplomatic Corps.

Señores Soler and Vasconsellos stepped out of line. They called for their wraps and went home.

The next morning a formal protest arrived at the State Department. Paraguay was sorry that its delegates had had to forgo the pleasure and privilege of shaking hands with the President of the United States, but to have done so after that act already had been performed by the Bolivian delegates would have been a slight to national honor which the Paraguayan government could not tolerate. Was it not a fact, the Legation of Paraguay asked the State Department, that lots had been drawn at the start of the negotiations and it was decided that Paraguay, not Bolivia, should have precedence in all social matters?

It looked for a time as if the chances of war between Paraguay and Bolivia, instead of being removed by American conciliation, had been materially enhanced. In the end, however, the State Department sent a formal note of apology, explaining that a White House naval aide, Lieutenant Raymond R. Waller, in an effort to be courteous, had moved the Bolivians into the Diplomatic guest line.

No such *faux pas* marred the harmony of the reception to the Judiciary one week later, nor any of the other official social gatherings. During the Christmas holidays, Washington was as gay as ever and when Father James R. Cox, of Pittsburgh, led another army of the unemployed upon the capital it made no more of a ripple than the first. On January 6—the day the new army arrived—Mrs. Hoover attended Mrs. Lawrence Townsend's morning musicale, Mrs. Walter Brown, wife of the Postmaster General, sitting in her box. The next day President Hoover, having become slightly worried over these repeated appeals to Washington, found it expedient to receive the Pittsburgh priest. That evening the Hoovers entertained in honor of the Vice-President and Mrs. Gann. Mr. Gann also was there. So was a galaxy of social and political satellites whom the President found it profitable to honor—among them General and Mrs. J. G. Harbord, head of the Radio Corporation; Colonel Henry W. Anderson, Republican boss of Virginia; Mr. and Mrs. Joseph Frelinghuysen of New Jersey, former crony of President Harding; Mr. and Mrs. Rufus Dawes, brother of the former Vice-President; Mr. and Mrs.

Kermit Roosevelt; Mr. and Mrs. Albert D. Lasker, whom Herbert Fleishhacker got appointed chairman of the Shipping Board to have some of the best Pacific routes turned over to his Dollar Line; Harvey Firestone, whose rubber plantations the State Department had protected in Liberia despite their use of forced labor; together with Kent Cooper of the Associated Press and Rollo Ogden of the New York *Times,* whose support Mr. Hoover needed dearly.

Pink carnations, baby primula and adiantum decorated the table. While the guests were enjoying Hulda Lashanska, soprano, and Paul Shirley, viola d'amore, other crowds in drabber parts of the city were listening to a different form of entertainment.

"The United States is not the firm of Herbert Hoover, Limited," announced the rasping voice of Father Cox, shortly after his visit at the White House.

"I am the mayor of Shantytown. That is a town in the heart of Pittsburgh—in the shadows of the skyscrapers owned by one of the richest men in America—Andrew W. Mellon. The men in my town want work but can't get it. So they live in huts and hovels....

"If the Pilgrim Fathers came back here to-day, would they be satisfied? They came here to give us a country. Now it has been taken away. Who owns it now? The Andrew Mellons. The bankers—500 of them—while the rest of us starve.

"Herbert Hoover has spent billions aiding the bankers and big business, but not one cent helping the working man.

"Abraham Lincoln told us we had a government of the people, for the people and by the people. Now it is a government of the bankers, for the bankers and by the bankers. Are we going to be so weak that 120,000,000 red-blooded workers will allow 500 millionaire bankers to tell us what we eat and when we eat it?"

Talk of this kind was somewhat worrying even to a somnolent Washington, intent upon its social successes; so Andrew W. Mellon was approached regarding the idea of paying the transportation of the unemployed army back to the city from which both he and Father Cox came. Mr. Mellon obliged,

*

FROM that time on, little disturbed Washington's blissful concentration on the Dance of the Depression. There were, of course, some wallflowers who sat on the side-lines and, either because they were not invited or because they did not know how to dance, merely looked on. There were one or two who emitted discordant notes and warned of the calamity. Finally, there were a few who either stumbled, trod on their partners' toes or from sheer exhaustion had to drop out. But the vast majority danced enthusiastically, if a little blindly, and enjoyed themselves.

In addition to Herbert and Lou Henry Hoover, the chief fox-trotters in Washington's Dance of the Depression were:

> Secretary of State Stimson, whose retention of a military aide to handle his lengthy dance list caused the House of Representatives to insert an amendment in the army bill abolishing military aides for civilian officials of the government;
> George "Long Live Linen" Marshall, Washington's premier laundryman, who papers his bathrooms with risqué pages from *La Vie Parisienne* and who posts a notice over his chaise longue "No Children Allowed";
> Dolly Curtis Gann, the big bassoon of the Hoover Administration, who, with the retirement of Alice Roosevelt Longworth from the ring, enjoyed her hard-fought position as Second Lady of the Land more than ever;
> Secretary of War Patrick J. Hurley, who, after patient practice before a mirror, has become a hail-fellow-well-met to every one, and who pirouetted with equal ease at a barbecue for newspaper men or a White House reception;
> The Patten Sisters, to whom all Washington caters, and who once bullied meek Senator Arthur Capper into putting traffic lights around DuPont Circle so they might walk across with equanimity;
> The débutantes, who were as pretty as ever and had just a little less realization than usual of what it was all about;

Eleanor Medill Patterson, who, while editing the capital's most interesting morning newspaper, made her parties the most fascinating, albeit the most bizarre in Washington.

*

FOR Cissy Patterson it was a big year. For the first time in her life she found herself doing something more useful than ordering servants around, hunting big game in the Rockies or taking the Herbert Swopes down to Florida in her private car "Ranger." With no journalistic experience and only the blind belief that the granddaughter of the founder of the Chicago *Tribune* could edit any newspaper, Cissy had cajoled, stormed and goaded the staff of the Washington *Herald* into putting out a first-class sheet. It suffered from the handicap of carrying all the "canned" editorials and other pet features of William Randolph Hearst which so overburden his papers, but at the same time it showed flashes of the genius of a woman who has spent all her life groping for an opportunity to do just exactly what she is doing now.

Having finally found her life's work, Cissy went at it whole-hog. She got the thrill of her life dressing up as a homeless woman and bumming the streets at night looking for a job. Many others got a thrill reading Cissy's account of her wanderings, especially the description of the embroidered crêpe de chine peach-colored sheets which decorated the bed which she left to go out into the cold, cold world.

Among these was Ralph Palmer, managing editor of the Washington *News,* afternoon rival of the *Herald.* He got a much greater thrill, however, when the lady in question flounced into his office and, using language which would have brought blushes from a stevedore and which stopped every typewriter in the city room, proceeded to lambast George Abell, witty social satirist of the *News.* Mr. Abell had picked up a social note from the New York *Herald Tribune* to the effect that Mrs. Patterson was going to spend the winter at her Port Washington, Long Island, home, and the insinuation

that editorial duties were to be neglected caused the editor of
the *Herald* acute pains of anguish. The chief result of the
incident was a fast and ripening friendship between Mr.
Palmer, managing editor of the *News,* and Mrs. Patterson,
editor of the *Herald*.

Mr. Palmer was one of those who had read of Mrs. Patterson's embroidered peach crêpe de chine sheets. Mr. Palmer also
was one who did not suffer from suppressed desires. He called
Mrs. Patterson up and told her of his great admiration for
any woman with her command of profanity and of his overwhelming curiosity to come into closer contact with those embroidered crêpe de chine sheets. Mrs. Patterson in turn invited
him to come to a Christmas party.

When he arrived he pulled his hostess to one side.

"I have come," he said, "both prepared and determined to
enjoy the exquisite luxury of those sheets."

Whereupon he pulled up his trousers, exhibiting underneath
a silken cerise pajama leg.

Cissy was convulsed. She took her latest arrival over to
Senator Capper of Kansas.

"Mr. Palmer has come to sleep with me," she announced,
assisting in the ceremony of pulling up the trouser leg.

Senator Capper, just a moment before, had had one shock
and was not at all prepared for another. Having been handed
a large flat package from which other gentlemen guests ex-
tracted handkerchiefs, the aged widower pulled from his box
a pair of ladies' underpants. They were made of black trans-
parent lace and on a card inside was written: "To Rose Nano."

The lady in question, wife of the Roumanian chargé
d'affaires and most bewitching beauty in the Diplomatic Corps,
is famous for the scantiness of her attire.

The Senator, however, was not an experienced man in these
matters. Not at all sure what it was he had unearthed, he held
it up for the world to see.

Although a widower, the Senator, after all, comes from
Kansas. Also he is a very mild man. So with the climax of

Cissy's latest confidence, he quietly got his hat and went home.

Much later, Mr. Palmer also went home, but without satisfying his curiosity regarding the embroidered peach crêpe de chine sheets. However, he came again. And although he came frequently and had many amusing talks with the charming editor of the *Herald,* his curiosity still remained unsatisfied. On one of these visits his hostess was scheduled to get home early from a dinner party. Palmer also left a dinner in order to arrive punctually at nine-thirty. He was ushered into a library. But the wait seemed interminable, and finally Palmer rang for the butler and asked what time it was.

"Is there anything I can do for you?" the butler asked.

"Yes, bring me a highball."

The butler obliged. Eventually he brought four. But even they did not relieve the monotony of the wait.

"For God's sake sit down and talk to me," Palmer finally commanded.

Again the butler obliged. But after a half hour of mutual reminiscences, he suggested that his duties required him to be about early in the morning and excused himself.

Time dragged on. Finally Ralph remembered that frequently he had seen his hostess come down the stairway from what he supposed was her own room above, and he decided to explore. Now was the time, if ever, at least to see those famous embroidered peach crêpe de chine sheets.

Upstairs he found a bedroom. It had high ceilings, ornate dressing tables and a chintz-covered chaise longue. Near the middle was a double bed, over which hung a green canopy. On it lay a pair of green silk pajamas and a green negligée. The sheets were turned down, but alas, although embroidered and crêpe de chine, they were not peach, but green—to match the canopy.

Palmer sat down and renewed his vigil. The wait seemed interminable. Finally, for the sake of comfort, he removed his coat and lay down on the bed. Then his collar started gouging

his neck, so he took it off. Next he began thinking how funny
he must look with a starched bosom, no collar, tie or coat.
This preyed on his mind; so he took off his pants and shoes.
Then he realized that any one entering the room suddenly—
especially at that time of night—would be taken slightly aback
at the sight of a gentleman lying on a lady's bed, clad only in
his B.V.D.'s. So he decided to make a thorough job of it.

He took off the last remaining vestige of his clothes and
slipped into the green negligée. It would not quite reach round
his rotund tummy, but he made it do the best he could, and
lay down upon the outside coverlet. To slip in between those
embroidered crêpe de chine sheets, uninvited and unan-
nounced, was not the right thing to do, Palmer reasoned.

How many hours elapsed, Ralph never knew. He awoke
to hear a woman's voice. It was pitched in high key, obviously
irate.

"This is the Countess Gizycka's room."

The voice of two men, in lower key, replied:

"Yes, madame."

"We'll get him out."

And they did.

The embroidered crêpe de chine sheets, both peach and
green, retained their pristine purity.

*

At the opposite pole of Washington's Dance of the Depression
was Henry Lewis Stimson. The Secretary of State can trace
his ancestry back to the seventeenth century and is never able
to forget it. For him it is more important to uphold the
prestige of ancient Stimson tradition than to get to his office
in the morning, and to this end his $800,000 estate at Woodley
was the scene of an interminable series of garden parties,
dinners and luncheons, all as punctilious as Cissy Patterson's
were bizarre. The right people were there. They arrived at the
right time. They left at the right time. They said the right

thing. And all of them sent their footmen to the Stimsons' front door with cards between four and six the next day.

It was deadly serious business for both host and guest, but for none more so than young Captain Eugene Regnier, first military aide in history to a Secretary of State. Captain Regnier, having little else to do, took over the Stimson social activities in toto. He made it his life's work. After garden parties at Woodley he brought the calling cards down to the State Department in a shoe box, spread them out on the table and spent hours going over them to see who had been present and who had spurned the invitations. On the basis of this scrutiny and of the whim of young Captain Regnier were drawn up the Stimsons' dinner and luncheon lists—lists which always were released to the press with an air of great importance and which displayed modestly at the bottom the name of Captain Regnier as one of the chosen few.

It was Regnier who devised the idea of a military demonstration as a part of the New York welcome of Ramsay Mac-Donald, expelled from Belgium during the War as a pacifist and ostracized for his convictions by the town of Lossiemouth where he lived. It was Regnier also who helped sell Stimson the idea of spending his vacation in the capitals of Europe during the summer of 1931—a trip which he, Regnier, took at government expense. And it was Regnier finally who nearly gave the State Department heart failure during the visit of Dino Grandi, Fascist foreign minister of Italy, to the United States.

The Grandi reception was in the hands of Warren Delano Robbins, arbiter of protocol for the White House and State Department. And it was something of a responsibility. Several weeks previous, when it became known that Pierre Laval, Premier of France, was to come to Washington, Ambassador de Martino had trotted down to the State Department with the suggestion that Premier Mussolini might come too. To this Secretary Stimson was distinctly cool. The chief of all Fascists, he indicated, probably would not receive a cordial reception when he docked in a city where there are more Italians than in Rome, many of them exiles from Mussolini's iron rule. As a compromise, therefore, it was decided to send Grandi.

But even Grandi, young and inoffensive as he was, immediately provoked anti-Fascist plots to bombard him with over-ripe tomatoes during the triumphal tour up the grand canyon of Lower Broadway.

It was to circumvent this that Robbins arranged for Grandi to take a tug straight from his boat in the lower harbor to Jersey City, where a special train would speed him on to Washington. The hostile crowds of Manhattan were to be left holding the bag.

After several days of effort every detail of this program had been worked out, when young Captain Regnier gave birth to a brilliant idea.

He proposed to fly Grandi from New York in the new Pan-American Airways plane, *The American Clipper*. Colonel Lindbergh, he said, would pilot the ship. All hostile demonstrations would be avoided; Grandi would get to Washington quicker, and the stunt would make page one of every newspaper in the country. Robbins remonstrated that *The American Clipper* was a new plane not adequately tested and that the weather might be bad. Regnier, however, had the approval of his chief and was adamant.

"Cancel the special train," he commanded, "and leave the rest to me."

That night it rained. The next morning it was misty.

"Did you cancel that special train?" Regnier asked Robbins.

"You told me to, didn't you?"

"Yes, but Pan-American Airways have just telephoned that they can't possibly make the trip. It's too foggy. Grandi's ship will be in quarantine in an hour. What are we going to do?"

"Well, you'll find the special train waiting at Jersey City," Robbins assured him. "I knew we'd need it."

As long as Regnier remained a glorified social secretary for the Stimsons he was safe enough, but he kept getting ideas about bigger and better things. One of these was the press. After several times watching his Secretary of State squirm and dodge under a cataclysm of embarrassing questions, Regnier decided to reform press relations.

That was the beginning of his end.

Stimson had been skating on dangerous ground in retaining Regnier. In addition to his military aide, he had four personal secretaries—more than Congress had granted President Hoover and three more than his predecessors, Charles Evans Hughes and Frank B. Kellogg. Moreover, each of these secretaries had one or more assistants, and one of them—G. Harold Keatley—was placed on the government pay-roll at $3,400, merely for the purpose of handling Stimson's personal checks. Actually he spent most of his time studying for a law degree at George Washington University.

In days of alleged government economy, this was difficult even for such an exalted person as a Secretary of State to get away with; and when the War Department Appropriation Bill was made public, Mr. Stimson was somewhat surprised to read that no part of its funds should go toward the support of a military aide for any civilian member of the government.

Washington society tittered audibly. It increased its mirth to ill-concealed guffaws when Stimson began pulling every possible wire to get the provision stricken from the bill. At first he thought William R. Castle, Jr., his Under Secretary, who dislikes Regnier, had inspired the bill and so sent Assistant Secretary Carr to Capitol Hill to prevail upon Representative Ross Collins in charge of the appropriation. Collins was adamant. Then he went to Brigadier General C. H. Bridges, the adjutant general. Bridges explained that the law was the law and, if passed, the War Department would have to live up to it. Finally, Stimson appealed to the Secretary of War, himself.

The army, however, was all with Congress and the public. For three years brigadier generals had had to take social orders from a high-handed young cavalry captain and they were all for sending him to Marfa, Texas, or Fort Meade, South Dakota, the two worst cavalry posts in the army. So Stimson got nowhere, even with Hurley.

Finally, Stimson found a friend in David Aiken Reed, senior Senator from Pennsylvania, who struck the provision from the War Department bill when it reached the Senate.

The military aide of the Secretary of State was saved. But his baptism of publicity had relegated him to the realm of calling cards and dinner lists, in which he excels, and from which he never should have strayed.

*

PRESIDENT HOOVER took his social duties so seriously during the depression that he recalled from the diplomatic service Warren Delano Robbins—a full-fledged minister at a salary of $10,000 a year—and set him up as Protocol Officer for the White House. Mr. Robbins' duties are to present ambassadors to the President when they arrive with their credentials, to fix the dates of White House dinners and receptions, and to rule upon that all-important problem of who shall sit where. In order to justify recalling a career minister for work of this kind, Secretary Stimson also appointed Robbins as chief of the Division of Protocol of the State Department. It is the duty of this division to meet visiting potentates at the Union Station, decree whether top hats or derbies shall be worn on formal occasions and write letters of congratulation or condolence when a son is born to a reigning monarch or an earthquake devastates a foreign land.

Prior to the depression, all of these painstaking niceties were left in the capable hands of one Charles Lee Cooke. With Mr. Cooke duty always came first—so much so that in carrying a gold-framed autographed portrait of Herbert Hoover across the Mediterranean as a coronation present to the Emperor of Abyssinia he guarded the gift so assiduously that his own pocket was picked for $300.

To Mr. Cooke, during the many years he handled all the knotty social problems of the capital, the State Department paid an annual stipend of $3,800. In the second year of the depression, when the increased yearning of the Hoover Administration for intense social activity caused the creation of the Division of Protocol, its salaries alone cost $33,300 annually.

Within his circumscribed field Warren Delano Robbins operates with precision, a sense of humor and a healthy disregard for certain conventions. He has, for instance, no time for those who maintain that cuffs cannot be worn on trousers in afternoon dress or that white waistcoats clash with a cutaway. This does not outrage New York tailors nearly as much as some of the more meticulous-minded members of the career service who are all in favor of American diplomats decking themselves in the gold-braid-and-lace uniforms of their European confrères.

Hanford MacNider, Hoover's Minister to Canada, is one of these. MacNider wore the full-dress regimentals of a colonel while presenting his credentials to a country with which the United States has boasted 3,000 miles of demilitarized border for more than one hundred years. His propensity for display aroused considerable discussion. There were some career diplomats who pointed to the fact that Benjamin Franklin, first American Ambassador, appeared at the court of Louis XVI wigless and carrying a crabapple cane. This precedent, they said, had been made a part of American policy by William L. Marcy, Secretary of State, 1853-57, who issued an order that American diplomats adopt the "simple dress of an American citizen."

"The simplicity of our usages and the tone of feeling among our people," decreed Marcy, "is more in accordance with the example of our first and most distinguished representative at a royal court than the practice which has since prevailed. It is to be regretted that there was ever any departure in this respect from the example of Dr. Franklin."

Other diplomats pointed to the furore which this decree had aroused in Europe and the edict given the American Minister to Sweden by the Royal Chamberlain that "his appearance at court in plain clothes would have been likely to be regarded by the Swedish Government in the light of a spirit of a revolutionary propagandism."

Besides, they said, consider the embarrassment of an American minister who presents his credentials in full evening dress at ten o'clock in the morning and who invariably is mistaken either for a head waiter or a derelict who forgot to go home the night before.

In reply to all of which, Mr. Robbins continues to wear white waistcoats and cuffs on his trousers when and where he wishes.

*

EVEN before the days when the late Mrs. Thomas F. Walsh and old Mrs. Eleanor Patterson brought their millions to Washington to build palatial mansions along Massachusetts Avenue and launch their daughters in society, the capital has been the Mecca of débutantes. There is good reason for this. Few cities offer better chances of snagging a promising young official, a titled embassy attaché or a wealthy, if slightly decadent, bachelor than the gilded and fast-moving social life which pulses in the nation's capital.

It is true that from the standpoint of quantity production there is a scarcity of males, frequently resulting in the desk clerk of the Mayflower Hotel or a Georgetown student being drafted for the evening. But the golden rewards for the select débutantes far transcend this disadvantage and every year fond mothers bring forward their entries, hope springing eternal in the matronly bosoms.

The Dance of the Depression did not change this ambient. If anything it intensified the competition. Gowned by Patou

and jeweled by Cartier, the entries for the race during the
years of Herbert Hoover were just as lovely, just as blasé
and just as expensive as in the days of Coolidge prosperity.

Perhaps because Washington danced with such abandon
it attracted to it parasites who found blood-sucking difficult
in other depression-ridden cities. Among these was one Baron
Wrangel who worked in collaboration with local talent as a
salesman for European tours, advertising a whirl in Paris society, a stay at the exclusive apartment of his mother and a
shot at one or two eligible noblemen, all thrown in for the
price of the trip.

The Baron had a most naïve way of going at things. Penned
by one of his female assistants, the following letter turned up
one morning on the breakfast tray of a well-endowed young
lady:

"Dear Sally:
"Two young men and myself were more than disappointed
that for some reason or other we did not make connections last
Saturday at the Willard. We had the best-looking Packard
which one could even enjoy in the rain. After waiting until
one-thirty, we took lunch at Pierre's, which did lend an atmosphere of Paris. Mr. Myers is very interested in the summer's
trip with Baron Wrangel prior to his studies at Oxford. Need-
less to say, it is he who has the roadster.

"Can you believe that there are still castles with designing
mothers looking for American heiresses who will renovate property in exchange for a son and a title? Are you in the market?
Although I am having the opportunity of arranging a most
romantic wedding in Rome for a Baltimore girl while we are
all there, I have been asked to seek a proper wife for a young
and proud Czecho-Slovak Baron.

"Here's hoping that we will not slip up next time and that
I shall be seeing you very soon."

Yet the Baron got customers.

He did not, however, get nearly as many customers as another individual who appeared on the depression horizon in a
new rôle and was promptly christened "The Débutante's Delight." That individual was Brigadier General Pelham D.

Glassford, U. S. A. retired, and the rôle which he assumed was that of Chief of Police.

"Happy" Glassford is one of those rare officers who managed to sandwich into thirty years of army life a summer as a San Francisco reporter, a few months as a day laborer and a tour with a traveling circus. Despite this, he was, after thirty years' service, fed up with martial inactivity and retired. Now he has all the activity he wants. In addition to policing one of the least law-abiding capitals of the world, Glassford is constantly called upon to protect speeding diplomats or the indiscreet wives of Congressmen, the latest, Mrs. George Huddleston, wife of an ardent Alabama dry, being threatened by the wife of a traveling salesman with whom she was speeding when arrested for driving while intoxicated.

Glassford is a straight shooter, has the respect of his men, is partial to blondes and once let Evelyn Walker persuade him not to delete from the film "Scarface" the business of gangster-striking-match-on-policeman's-badge. Socially he is in great demand, his only mistake being that of leaving a sporty-looking roadster with the familiar license number 778 in front of the homes of his feminine admirers until too late an hour.

*

For two whirlers in the Dance of the Depression, the third winter of Herbert Hoover saw the zenith of their careers. Both had come up from humble beginnings. One had done her own cooking and on occasion bent over her own washtub in Topeka, Kansas. The other had done the same in Uvalde, Texas. The first, when she became hostess for the Vice-President of the United States had moved her somewhat retiring husband and her hitherto-unsocial half-brother from a modest vine-covered house in Cleveland Park to a palatial suite in the Mayflower Hotel and waged a battle which astounded the world over her right to take social precedence over every one except Mrs. Hoover. The second had become so accustomed to slaving for John Nance Garner, before a never-failing capacity for winning at poker and a canny instinct for investment made him wealthy, that she continued to darn his socks, sort out his laundry and run his office, even after he became Speaker of the House of Representatives, the second most powerful political position in the land.

Nor was Ettie Garner merely a salary-drawing name on the congressional pay-roll. She earned her monthly $325. Moreover she installed a small electric stove in one of the rooms on the first floor of the capitol, commandeered for her own suite, where, much to the horror of more socially minded ladies of Congress, she cooked favorite dishes for Jack when she was not too busy with office work.

A lot of people remarked that no wonder the Garners saved money; and when the sudden turn of a Chicago convention nominated her husband as the Democratic choice for the Vice-Presidency, a lot more were consumed with curiosity to know whether, if successful in November, this wallflower would go social *à la* Dolly Gann.

Immediately after the convention she showed no signs of social stampede. Notified of the honor conferred upon her husband, she sat down on a pile of the Speaker's speeches, which she was about to frank to his constituents, and remarked that she guessed she'd go back to Texas after Congress while Jack went to Albany to confer with Roosevelt, although she really should go with him—"he's such an infant."

Efforts to enlist political support for her own down-trodden sex also failed. When a delegation from the National Woman's Party called to point out the iniquities of the economy bill backed by her husband, which they said would cause the dismissal of many married women from government service, she replied:

"Government employees spend too much anyway. I know one that spent as much as $12 for a pair of shoes. They should economize. Why don't they buy their food at the Sanitary, the way I do?"

"But, Mrs. Garner, don't you realize that this bill will result in many young government workers who are planning to get married dispensing with the legal ceremony?"

"That's nothing new," replied the wife of the Speaker. "That's going on all the time anyway."

Perhaps in contemplation of possible havoc in the political upheaval of November, Dolly Curtis Gann meanwhile made the most of her opportunities. Thanks to her strident claims of three years before, she was a lone lioness rampant on a social battlefield, with no enemies to conquer. Her victory, however, was an empty one. Alice Roosevelt Longworth, her former rival, was in mourning and removed from the field by the death of the late Speaker, while Ettie Garner would rather cook in the capitol than go out to dinner, and didn't care who knew it.

Nevertheless, Dolly seemed to enjoy her empty honor and fought desperately to retain it for another four years. When the Republican convention opened in Chicago she was there in full force—Mr. Gann being also present—to do battle for the renomination of Curtis.

"All newspaper talk," was the way she described reports that Republican leaders did not want her brother on the ticket. "The reporters have nothing else to write about."

And during three hectic days she buttonholed and bosomed perspiring delegates in lining up the vote for Charley.

When the balloting finally came and the first State chairman sang out "Alabama 16 for Curtis," a relieved smile spread over Dolly's face.

"It's all over, I congratulate you," said Silas Strawn, as he walked over to Mrs. Gann's box.

"Connecticut 17 for Harbord," continued the convention clerk.

Mrs. Gann released his hand and began to drum on the rail of her box.

"New York, 95 votes for Harbord."

Mrs. Gann's drumming fingers came to a standstill.

A little later when the tally stood 570 for Curtis and Pennsylvania announced that it had changed unanimously in his favor, Mabel Walker Willebrandt rushed over and clasped Dolly in her arms. Alice Longworth in a nearby box remained seated. So also did Dorothy Mills, wife of the Secretary of the Treasury, Ruth Wilson Hurley, wife of the Secretary of War, and Katharine Brown, wife of the Postmaster General. Their box was close by, but the social feud cut deep and bitter lines.

Both before and after the Chicago convention, Mrs. Gann boomed forth as the Big Bertha of the Hoover Administration. And she was effective. The Republican National Committee, dubious at first, tried her out and then came back for more. They found, however, that Dolly had one drawback. She was over-optimistic. In Chicago one day she "called off the depression." She announced it was past history.

After that her speeches were rigorously censored. Either Walter Brown or the President himself went over them, and on one occasion before a speech to be made in Detroit, she was called to the White House three times in one day.

When Dolly told a Chicago audience that the depression was over, she was probably sincere about it, because in the ball rooms and at the dinner tables from which Dolly views the world, few traces of the depression can be seen. And although there are some people who appear to begrudge Dolly her triumph, they can hardly have been among those who heard her describe her social whirl over the radio in an interview with Mrs. Frances Parkinson Keyes, wife of the junior Senator from New Hampshire.

Mrs. Keyes: "Mrs. Gann, won't you begin by describing some of the details of your Wednesdays at home at the height of the season?"

Mrs. Gann: "Yes, Mrs. Keyes, I think that's the logical way to begin, for those weekly receptions constitute a very important part of my schedule. I average more than 1,000 visitors on each of my days at home, which begin at 4 and end about 7."

Mrs. Keyes: "I realize what careful planning all this takes because I know how much you are out, Mrs. Gann."

Mrs. Gann: "Well, naturally, we are out to dinner almost every night except Sunday.... Many evenings are spent in going the rounds of embassies and legations alone. Then there are the countless American households, both official and non-official, to which we are constantly and cordially invited, and besides the dinners to which I go with my brother and husband, there are frequent ladies' luncheons to which I go as guest of honor."

Thus Dolly dances through the depression.

There were many who danced just as vigorously as Dolly but lacked either her luck or her bounce. They had not, for instance, her capacity for ignoring the titters of the gallery when they stumbled, but either continued in the shuffle, blushing to the eyebrows, or retired to the ante-room. Among these were:

Robert P. Lamont, Secretary of Commerce, whose fortune dwindled from a round million to his meager salary as a Cabinet officer, but who at Mr. Hoover's request kept on dancing just the same. Finally, however, the pace proved too fast and he resigned;

Evalyn Walsh McLean, who dropped $104,000 into the hands of Gaston B. Means, notorious swindler, with the idea she was recovering the Lindbergh baby, but who at the same time forced her husband to drop his control of the Washington *Post;*

Charles G. Dawes, who resigned from the chairmanship of the Reconstruction Finance Corporation just in time to receive $80,000,000 of the corporation's government money;

Mrs. Tom Mix, who dropped from the Klieg lights of Hollywood into the comparative obscurity of marriage to an attaché of the Argentine Embassy;

Major William D. Herridge, Canadian Minister, who went to a Harvard Commencement celebration and remained missing for two weeks during which time the only clew a worried Legation staff had of his machinations was a note received from Fred A. Delano, usually known for his sobriety, which read:

"Dear Mr. Minister:

"Not until I got home did I realize that I had your coat on. It is being sent to you by insured parcel post, and I hope none the worse for the events of the evening.

"Sincerely,

"Fred A. Delano."

John Franklin Carter, who after writing an article, "We Need a War," which attracted the attention of the Japanese Embassy, was advised to retire from the State Department and thereupon announced the organization of an American Fascist party;

Christian Channing Gross, who, dropped from the Diplomatic Service for being four months absent without leave, declared himself the protector of the American home and threatened to take legal action against the State Department;

Andrew W. Mellon, the Secretary of the Treasury, who stayed too long.

*

AMONG those who took their retirement from the dance floor with the greatest degree of dejection was Uncle Andy. He had been proud of his record of remaining Secretary of the Treasury longer than any other man, with the possible exception of Albert Gallatin, and he wanted to remain long enough to clinch that record definitely. Also he enjoyed keeping his hand on many of the details of his vast department and even took time to censor personally the radio addresses of his Public Health Service after the meat packers had complained that it was advising the public to eat vegetables rather than meat in the summer; although he did not, despite some critics, have anything to do with the work of his Customs Bureau in attempting to censor the book of Dr. Marie Stopes, *Married Love*. This case, when the Treasury Department filed suit against the publishers, was listed on the court docket as "United States versus Married Love."

But as much as anything, Uncle Andy loved the quiet poker parties held in his apartment, usually attended by Alice Longworth, Ogden Mills, Trubee Davison, Bob Bacon and Dick

Aldrich, at which it was not unusual to see several thousand dollars change hands in an hour. At the close of the poker sessions of the 1932 season Representative Ruth Pratt had increased her Standard Oil fortune by $11,000.

Probably Uncle Andy could have stayed on in the Treasury Department almost *ad infinitum,* but for three things: The first was the fact that he frequently opposed Mr. Hoover and made statements which subsequently the White House either asked him to retract or else retracted for him. The second was the fact that after his brother, R. B. Mellon, had conferred with other Pittsburgh bankers in an effort to rescue the Bank of Pittsburgh, Andy refused to take action and allowed the Bank of Pittsburgh to go to the wall, together with thirty-six other banks, while the Mellon institution stayed open until ten each night taking in the deposits transferred from them. The Mellons may have profited, but Mr. Hoover did not. It was the first big bank failure of the Administration.

Immediately on top of this occurred the final incident which later sent Uncle Andy into exile.

It was a state dinner that caused it all. The Secretary of the Treasury, charming of personality and stately of mien, was always in great demand as a dinner guest, and June 4, 1930, found him at the table of Secretary of State Stimson, seated by the side of Enrique Olaya, recently elected President of Colombia. During the course of the dinner conversation, President-elect Olaya asked Secretary Mellon what he thought Colombia needed to make it prosperous and got the reply that if Colombia would untangle its dispute with American oil companies, the banks would then lend it money.

President Olaya went back to Colombia and in a message to his Congress quoted Mellon to this effect. He then started to untangle the difficulties surrounding the Barco concession, richest oil reserve in Latin America, claimed chiefly by the Mellons' Gulf Oil Company. Simultaneously, and just as Uncle Andy predicted, Colombia got credit from New York bankers.

The only difficulty was that when the Colombian Congress

held up final approval of Mellon's award of the Barco and when the banks simultaneously held up final credits, Secretary Stimson intervened. And when all of this was published, a tremendous furore arose, which eventually resulted in Uncle Andy's being called to the White House—just after he had paid the expenses of Father Cox's unemployed back to the shadows of the Mellon banks—and awarded the honor of representing the United States in knee breeches and silken stockings at the Court of St. James.

*

THE exit from official society of the preceding Ambassador to that Court was not quite so sorrowful. Instead of borrowing money to pay his income tax, as Mellon's friends claimed for him, ex-Ambassador Charles G. Dawes was given a tidy sum by the Reconstruction Finance Corporation to bring cheer and sunshine into his retiring years.

Dawes has always been a believer in the bizarre in his social life. He has also practiced the unusual in his financial life. In London he hired Leon Errol to play the part of a drunken waiter and spill cold lobster in the lap of the Duke of Norfolk. In Chicago he once handed his friend William Lorimer a check for $1,250,000 of his depositors' money in order to help the LaSalle Street Bank get by the examiners.

Therefore after Dawes resigned as chairman of the Reconstruction Finance Corporation, those who knew him were not surprised to learn that he had received a loan of $80,000,000 for his Central Republic Trust Company. It was the largest sum ever advanced by the R. F. C. and with $15,000,000, borrowed from other institutions, exactly covered the amount of deposits in the Dawes Bank—which led many to believe that those deposits had pretty well evaporated.

Not so fortunate was Robert Patterson Lamont, also of Chicago. At the time President Hoover drafted him as Secretary of Commerce, Lamont was a wealthy man. He rated with Adams, Hurley, Stimson, Mellon and Brown as a millionaire Cabineteer. In his house on Kalorama Road he entertained on a commensurate scale. His money was invested in such apparently rock-ribbed securities as American Radiator, International Harvester, Montgomery Ward, Illinois Bell Telephone, Armour and Company and Dodge Brothers. He was even able to present his Alma Mater, the University of Michigan, with an astronomical observatory in South Africa.

All this, however, was before the Hoover depression. With the slump in stocks, Mr. Lamont's fortune gradually dwindled. When on several occasions he echoed his chief's prediction that prosperity was just around the corner, he was giving voice to a genuine, almost desperate hope. The Riggs Bank complained about renewing his notes. In order to take them up, he endeavored to take out a $100,000 life insurance policy with the Mutual Benefit Life Insurance Company of Newark, but was rejected, on account of high blood pressure. Later when the adjournment of Congress restored his health, he negotiated a policy of $50,000 with the Northwestern Mutual Life Insurance Company, plus $25,000 with the Mutual Benefit, which partially eased the acuteness of his financial pangs.

But on the whole, Lamont kept a stiff upper lip and remained in step with the dance music. He golfed in the afternoon, dined out in the evening and rode up to his office every morning in a private elevator requiring the full-time services of one operator for an average of four trips a day. There at a spacious desk in a high-ceilinged chamber Mr. Lamont endeavored to guide the laboring destinies of American business and the scattered details of the vast and ornate $17,500,000 office building planned by a Secretary of Commerce with more grandiose ideas than Mr. Lamont, and which the Chicago *Tribune* once christened "Hoover's Folly."

*

NOT so tragic were the missteps of other fox-trotters in this Dance of the Depression.

There was, for instance, the greeting extended to Madame Sacasa by Mrs. Ben Fuller, wife of the Commandant of the Marine Corps, whose men are coöperating with Minister Sacasa of Nicaragua in wiping out the revolutionary activities—and men—of General Sandino. Mrs. Fuller considers herself a big shot socially and nearly passed out when friends told her that in shaking hands with Madame Sacasa, she had said:

"How do you do, Madame Sandino?"

There was also the look of disappointment and chagrin on the face of Nobile Giacomo de Martino, Ambassador of Italy, when, upon opening a consignment of gold-sealed champagne, just arrived in bond from Baltimore, he discovered he had proposed a toast to Benito Mussolini—in sea water. Hijackers had tampered with his liquor en route.

There was also the resignation of Dr. Luis Debayle as chargé d'affaires of the Nicaraguan Legation, all because Carlos Morales, special 250-pound envoy of President Moncada to secure the State Department's permission for his reëlection, failed in that mission and in doing so made himself famous by buying several dozen pairs of green silk pajamas, getting into a dispute with the manager of the Shoreham Hotel for charging him eighty-five cents for two bananas which he said was enough to buy two bunches in Nicaragua, and by blocking traffic by a fall on the ice in a downtown shopping district. To cap this climax, the photograph of Señor Morales' 250-pound hulk was published in the Washington *News*, despite specific instructions by the motivator of that hulk against release of the photograph.

Debayle resigned when Morales claimed that he had upset the *ambiente* for his negotiations, but was reinstated when he proved that Louis J. Heath, 250-pound reporter of the United Press, had inveigled the photograph from Dr. Leo S. Rowe, director general of the Pan-American Union and chief harmonizer of Pan-American relations.

None of these, however, so intrigued the capital as the missteps of Edward Beale McLean and his estranged wife, Evalyn.

There was a day when the McLeans were a power in Washington politics and society. There was a day when Ned was called in for consultation at the White House, when the editorials of the Washington *Post* were read by every diplomat and congressman and when the Easter breakfast parties given at "Friendship," the McLean estate on the edge of the city, were the Mecca of every person of power and prestige in the capital.

Those days are now over.

The winding driveways of "Friendship" are overgrown with weeds. The windows are shuttered, the paint peeling, the statues which lined the walk, once the promenade of ambassadors, are green with moss.

The end came when the McLeans decided to get the goal each wanted most. Ned wanted Rose Davies, sister of Marion, the movie star. Evalyn wanted the power that went with the Washington *Post*. They got neither. Evalyn consistently thwarted Ned's efforts to get a divorce in Mexico and when a red-ribboned package arrived on Christmas Eve marked "Merry Christmas," containing notice of a Latvian divorce suit, Evalyn raised the question of contempt of court.

Ned, in turn, thwarted his wife's attempt to get control of the *Post* long enough for that paper to lose much of its former value and for Evalyn to lose most of her money.

It was Mrs. McLean's insatiable desire for the *Post* that led to her amazing gift of $104,000 to Gaston B. Means, notorious racketeer, and a fruitless trek through South Carolina and Texas in the blind belief that she was on the trail of the Lindbergh baby—a story which few people could have believed were there not a court record on the case and did they not know Evalyn McLean. Mrs. McLean was motivated by genuine sympathy for the Lindberghs. She has never quite recovered from the loss of her oldest son who was killed by an automobile, despite the fact that he was guarded night and day by both

a nurse and a detective. But more than this, she had in mind
the effect on her chances to obtain the *Post* if she could publish
in it the scoop of a lifetime—the story of the return of the
world-famous baby for which two continents had been looking
ever since he was whisked down a ladder from his crib in one
of the most merciless mysteries of the century.

Instead of this scoop, her coveted paper was even beaten on
the arrest of Gaston B. Means in Mrs. McLean's efforts to recover the $100,000 ransom. The afternoon papers got it first.

And now the value of the *Post* has shrunk from millions to
mere thousands. But so also has the estate of Evalyn's father,
the late Thomas F. Walsh. And so she cannot afford to
acquire the long-cherished paper, despite the fact that McLean
has relinquished his control—although not until October 1,
when his contract with Secretary of War Hurley for Hoover
Administration control expires.

*

THERE were many wallflowers during the Dance of the Depression who looked on disconcertedly and tried to change
the tune. Mr. Hoover once termed them calamity howlers.
Among them was Colonel Arthur Woods, drafted by the
President in the summer of 1930 to solve unemployment.
Colonel Woods in turn called upon Irving Fisher, Edwin R.
Seligman, Wesley C. Mitchell and other economists for an
indication of the length of the depression. They reported that
prosperity was not just around the corner—that the country
was in for a long siege. On the basis of this, Colonel Woods
prepared a program of road building, public works construction and reforestation which would have cost a billion dollars,
and urged Hoover to put it up to Congress in his annual
message.

Mr. Hoover refused. He said the depression had hit the bottom and the upturn was in sight.

That was in December 1930. Simultaneously, Woods made

a survey of unemployment and reported to the President that the total out of work was between 4,000,000 and 5,000,000. Hoover pooh-poohed the idea. The figure could not possibly be that large, he said. However, on Colonel Woods' insistence he agreed to let the Metropolitan Life Insurance Company make a survey and to accept its figures. A month later the Metropolitan reported 5,000,000 out of work. Woods was in the act of publishing the report when he got a telephone call from the White House. Under no circumstances must the figures be made public, the President ordered.

Then the Senate passed the Wagner bill, creating a Federal employment agency. It resembled proposals made by Hoover as Secretary of Commerce and as candidate for President. Despite this, he told Woods he would veto it. Colonel Woods thereupon brought his big guns into play. Senators Fess and Watson, staunch Republican leaders, called upon the President and urged approval. Julius Barnes, close personal friend, also called. And finally Dwight Morrow. On his way back from the White House, Senator Morrow stopped in to see Woods.

"I am afraid the President is going to veto that bill," he said, "and the only reason is his personal prejudice against Wagner."

The President did.

By this time Colonel Woods had decided the part of a wall-flower was not only futile but boring. He had been blocked all along the line. When he sent Frank Bane, one of his assistants, to Knoxville, Tennessee, to coöperate with the Post Office Department in selecting a site for a new post-office building and in speeding construction, he subsequently received a letter from Postmaster General Brown that work could commence in nine months.

Mr. Bane replied:

"What we want is a post-office, not a baby."

So, shortly after the veto of the Wagner bill, Colonel Woods resigned.

President Hoover then turned to Walter Sherman Gifford,

chairman of the American Telephone and Telegraph Company. Gifford came to Washington and listened patiently while the President outlined the work he wanted him to do. Mr. Gifford replied that the obligations of his company were vast and his responsibility was to that company.

"But if you fail me, to whom can I turn?" the President said, almost with tears in his voice.

Gifford was touched. After a prolonged debate with himself, while en route to New York, he decided to accept.

What President Hoover wanted Gifford to do was raise money throughout the country by which each community could feed its own unemployed. Gifford's campaign for funds was a thorough one. He put into it all of the organizing genius which has made his company so successful. But before two months had elapsed, he informed Mr. Hoover it was all a mistake. Unemployment relief must be handled by the government rather than by private or local agencies, he said. This was what Senators LaFollette and Costigan had been arguing for months. This was what President Hoover, six months later, accepted—one day after Senator Robinson of Arkansas and other Democratic leaders had launched a relief program twice as large as that proposed by Colonel Woods nearly two years before.

But Mr. Gifford at that time could not budge the President, and so he, like Colonel Woods, slipped quietly into the background.

*

THERE were many other wallflowers upon whom Mr. Hoover called for advice and counsel during the dance. Among them were some of the foremost newspaper publishers of the country. They assembled at the White House one evening after dinner and listened while the President, in a tired voice, outlined his troubles. Then he asked for suggestions. One by one the publishers replied, most of them saying:

"What we need, Mr. President, is leadership."

The President sat patiently, a little dejected, trying to twist his plump face into a smile. Once, with a pathetic note in his voice, he said:

"Well, I spank Congress every once in a while, but they always spank me right back, and so do you sometimes."

Eventually he called upon Clark Howell, editor of the Atlanta *Constitution*. Howell had had dinner with Roy Howard, of the Scripps-Howard newspapers, and had promised that if called upon by the President during the evening he would "give him the works." Howard had planted his chair directly across from that of the Georgia editor so that he could look him in the eye and make him keep his word. But it was unnecessary.

"Mr. President," he said, in a slow Southern drawl, "your request for ideas on how to bring back prosperity and save the country reminds me of an episode which occurred recently in Atlanta. One of our citizens went into a ladies' dress shop and in a sort of embarrassed way asked for a pair of ladies' underpants. The young lady who waited on him said all right and asked him if he wanted any particular color.

"'No, any color will do,' he said.

"'What kind of material do you want?' she asked.

"'What kind do you recommend?' he wanted to know.

"'Silk is really the best,' she told him, 'although rayon is cheaper.'

"So he said rayon would be all right.

"Then she asked:

"'Do you want them to open up the front or up the side?'

"'It doesn't make any difference,' he replied, 'they're for a corpse.'"

*

It was at about this time that those who led the Dance of the Depression began to get a feeble realization that Washington could not dance indefinitely. The realization was very faint, however, and, for the most part, Washington kept its head in the sand.

Cissy Patterson at that time was advocating boxing to relieve the monotony of life; delegates were preparing to go to the Chicago convention to receive engraved cards on sheet gold giving them the freedom of a bankrupt city; Secretary of the Interior Wilbur told a Philadelphia audience that the depression was good for children; Representative Cable of Ohio had introduced a bill which he said would keep "these society janes from stealing the cooks of the diplomats"; Mrs. Hoover gave a ladies' Cabinet luncheon at which she called the guests together by blowing a Girl Scout whistle; and the Emperor of Abyssinia, unwittingly but perhaps not incongruously, addressed President Hoover as "Your Majesty."

About this time Washington got a jolt comparable to that received on the morning of July 11, 1864, when General Jubal A. Early marched up Seventh Street.

Along that same street from Chicago and the West, across the Key Bridge from Virginia and the South, up Rhode Island Avenue from Baltimore and the North, came an army of 20,000 World War veterans. As ragged as their Confederate predecessors, without previous organization, without funds, without anything save a determination to rebel against continued unemployment, they came in a spontaneous pilgrimage toward the Mecca of their hopes. Where a mere handful of men started from Oregon, four hundred arrived in Washington. Where a dozen left Houston, a battalion was formed en route. The movement was like a rolling snowball. It attracted unemployed veterans throughout the country. Some brought their children, some their wives, some not even a bandanna full of belongings.

And after they had arrived, they paraded up Pennsylvania Avenue to the capitol, reversing the route so many of them had taken when they stepped jauntily past the White House, eyes left, on their way to France fifteen years before. Many processions of all sorts and sizes and at many different times have marched along this historic parade route of the nation, but never one which equaled this. There was, for instance, the funeral of the Unknown Soldier, when the most distinguished citizens of the country walked bareheaded behind the coffin of a fallen warrior. There was also the inauguration of Herbert Hoover, when the nation was at the height of its prosperity and rallied its most blatant bands, its shiniest limousines and its tallest silk hats to demonstrate that fact.

But this parade! How different! Gone were the pomp and pageantry. Gone also were the reviewing stands, the President and his Cabinet, the silken flags, the guns, the bayonets, the bands, the martial music, and the person of General John J. Pershing, who once had led the veterans overseas and eleven years before had walked bare-headed behind the coffin of their unknown comrade.

It was an army that marched in the same trousers and overalls, the same blue denim shirts it had worn when it left home three weeks before. It was an army of blind hope, lost hope—an army that forgot it was a mere infinitesimal fraction of 12,000,000 unemployed—an army that killed its effectiveness by its own self-seeking—an army of bewilderment that turned to the government which once had clothed and fed it—the Army of Despair.

And after it had staged its demonstration along Pennsylvania Avenue, this army of 20,000 proceeded to encamp on the sprawling mudflats of the Anacostia River. Here they erected an amazing city of tin cans, boxes, junked automobiles, dugouts roofed with wall-paper, egg crates covered with murdock leaves—anything that could be twisted into some form of shelter. Even the weeds once so profuse around the river were at a premium, being gathered in armfuls to be woven through old bed springs or chicken wire.

Not all resorted to ingenuity, however. Some tired of incessant exposure to rain and heat and took possession of five houses owned by the government. The buildings were to be razed to make way for the capital's beautification program, and the Treasury, which is charged with transforming Washington into the model city of the world, notified the police to evict the veterans.

"To hell with the Treasury," replied the veterans.

The capital's beautification program had to wait.

Official Washington began to get uneasy. A mine-sweeper was brought up the river and tied opposite the camp, its guns trained on the sprawling huts. White House guards practiced throwing tear gas bombs. Trucks were held ready to bring troops up from Fort Washington.

There had been, of course, other invasions of the capital. In addition to that of General Jubal A. Early, there had been the invasion of Rear Admiral Sir George Cockburn, who led a body of British blue-jackets into the House of Representatives in 1814, and plumping his muddy boots upon the rostrum, hammered the Speaker's gavel:

"Shall this harbor of Yankee Democracy be burned? All for it say aye!"

The vote was unanimous.

But these were external enemies. What aroused the capital over the march of the war veterans was that they were 100-per-cent Americans. Yet they mixed 100-per-cent Americanism with political doctrines which had caused European governments to totter and crumble. And here they were bivouacked within striking distance of the White House, the capitol, the millions of gold bullion in the Treasury, the supplies of the War Department, the tapestries of Larz Anderson, the portraits of Charles Francis Adams, the Chinese porcelains of Eugene Meyer, the wine cellar of Ned McLean and all the mansions of Washington's élite, most of them carpeted with rugs far softer than anything the veterans had slept upon in months.

Washington for the first time took its head from the sand.

Like the forces of General Early, the army was destined to failure. The selfish nature of its plea made defeat inevitable. But it achieved something bigger than the bonus. It hastened general unemployment relief. And more important, it awoke the capitol.

The climax in its bonus crusade on Congress came on the night of June 17. The Senate was in session about to ballot on the bonus. The future of all veterans hung upon that vote. The army decided to see it cast. Police authorities had anticipated such a move and had worked out war plans for the siege of the city. Three drawbridges separated the suburb of Anacostia from the rest of Washington, and these were raised. Pandemonium broke loose. Traffic was held up for blocks. Commuters stormed. The veterans stood in packed crowds, sullen, silent.

Finally, fearful of fanning resentment to a white heat, the police yielded. The drawbridges were lowered. The army advanced on the capitol. The plaza in front of the Senate was jammed. The men sat on the long flight of steps from which the President of the United States takes his oath of office. Some of them lay in the corridors inside the building. The police dared not touch them. The silence was ominous.

Silent also was the chamber of the United States Senate. The debate dragged. Occasionally a Senator tiptoed out to a window, to come back shaking his head.

The vote was overwhelmingly against the army. But it did not move. The silence continued oppressive. The commander-in-chief made a speech. The men about-faced and marched into the night.

"This marks a new era in the life of our nation," mused Senator Hiram Johnson. "The time may come when this folderol—these trappings of government will disappear—when fat old men like you and me will stop making speeches to sleepy galleries and be lined up against a stone wall."

But Hiram Johnson's worries were unfounded—at least for the moment. He was to be "saved," and by none other than his "old friend" Herbert Hoover.

As the last days of the Seventy-first Congress wore on, demonstrations before the capitol became almost continual, and those who occupied the White House and the Vice-Presidential suite became more fidgety. Hoover already had clashed with General Glassford regarding the eviction of the veterans. He had sent word through the Commissioners of the District of Columbia that the army was to be evacuated. It made no difference what methods were used—persuasion, threats or force—the army was to go. Glassford received this ultimatum in silence. Returning to his office he wrote a letter to the Commissioners. He said: "I shall be glad to carry out your orders and evict the Bonus Expeditionary Force by any means at my command, immediately upon receiving from you written orders to this effect."

The written orders never came.

The veterans continued their picketing of the capitol. Back and forth they moved, day and night, in drenching rains and scorching sun, an unending line of defeated men—a mute appeal—a "Death March."

The dreary monotony of their presence got on the nerves of Charles Curtis, Vice-President of the United States. One day he called out the Marines. They were rushed to the capitol in taxi-cabs, where their appearance aroused the ire of General Glassford. He informed the Vice-President that he, alone, with the exception of the President, was responsible for the maintenance of law and order in the District of Columbia. Then Senator Bingham telephoned the White House on behalf of Glassford to ask if Hoover wanted to take responsibility for calling out the Marines. Mr. Hoover said he did not.

Congress adjourned a few nights later after a final and tumultuous demonstration of five thousand men in front of the capitol and a much milder and more orderly parade of eighty men in front of the White House. The latter occurred at about 9:45 P.M., just as the President was about to go to the capitol to follow customary procedure in signing the last-minute bills turned out by Congress. His secret service men and their automobiles waited several hours. The President never left.

Instead, every policeman and detective in the city was called out. Hundreds patrolled the streets in front of the Executive Mansion. Traffic was barred from an area extending one block on each side of the White House. President Wilson, during the War, had stationed Marines in front of the White House and barred the grounds to the public, but never before in history had such extreme precautions as Mr. Hoover ordered been taken.

The next morning, with Congress adjourned, Mr. Hoover was left with the bonus army sitting almost at his front door. Their ranks had dwindled, but their belligerency had increased. So had the President's nervousness. For days press reports told the story of how the White House gates were chained every time a handful of the veterans tried to approach it. Hoover felt that he was being made to look foolish. Finally he decided to act.

During lengthy consultations, the General Staff worked out war plans for the evacuation of the veterans. All leaves and transfers of officers at Fort Myer and neighboring military establishments were cancelled. Men were given additional practice with tear gas. No detail of preparation was overlooked.

Then the order was given by the Treasury for the veterans to evacuate the abandoned buildings along Pennsylvania Avenue which were to be torn down for the capital beautification program. This property had been abandoned and undeveloped for weeks. The Supervising Architects' office had no plans for buildings on it, but suddenly the Treasury announced that work must be started in order to care for unemployed.

The veterans, however, refused to move. There were threats and counter-threats. Finally W. W. Waters, self-styled National Commander of the Bonus Expeditionary Force, ordered his men out. Some obeyed, others refused. Simultaneously General Glassford, having received written orders for the evacuation of the property, started to evict the men. The eviction was accompanied by a battle of bricks, during which several veterans and policemen were badly hit, but in the end Glassford succeeded in clearing one area and roping it off. An hour later, however, a scuffle occurred between a policeman and a veteran, during which the officer fired point blank, killed his man and wounded another, who later died.

Glassford said his officer had lost his head. But it was too late. The President had been waiting for just such an incident as this. At 2:50 he telephoned his Secretary of War. At 2:55 Secretary Hurley handed an order to his Chief of Staff. At 3:10 General MacArthur had his cavalry on the Ellipse at the south of the White House.

All this time, Theodore Joslin, Presidential Secretary, was denying that troops had been called.

It had all been carefully planned—except for one detail. Hurley's letter to MacArthur had been written in advance. The troops were awaiting marching orders. But MacArthur had forgotten his uniform. So he sent to Fort Myer for it and later in the afternoon was riding down Pennsylvania Avenue in glistening riding boots—three rows of medals on his bosom—four blocks in the rear of six tanks, six hundred infantrymen and two troops of cavalry.

The first engagement lasted only thirty minutes. At one and the same time it was gruesome, awful and amusing.

A Negro veteran seized a big American flag. "Oh, Lord, who done make dis country come and save it now," he sang out and paraded the flag in front of the cavalry.

Two troopers brought their sabres to salute. Others stood at attention. An officer gave a command. The Negro was ridden down.

One group of veterans dared a column of infantry to fire on an American flag. The soldiers finally took it from them.

The troops advanced, bayonets fixed. Spectators booed. The troops hurled gas bombs. Veterans ran, streaming from the dilapidated buildings. The crowd of spectators on the other side of the avenue scurried for cover. Senator Hiram Bingham, in white Palm Beach and Panama hat, ran, a handkerchief to his eyes. The cavalry charged the crowded sidewalks, filled entirely with spectators. They were forced back into the doors of shops. Many kicked and struck at the horses.

A crowd of veterans hurled taunts at a squad of cavalry.

"Bring on Bismarck!"

"Hoover's cossacks!"

"Where were you during the Argonne?"

"He's only got fuzz on his face!"

One trooper whirled, came down with his sabre on a veteran's head. An ear was slashed off.

Three blocks away General Douglas MacArthur sat in his limousine in the middle of Pennsylvana Avenue. A group of photographers approached.

"Point down to the troops, General," they commanded.

MacArthur, having stepped out of his limousine, obeyed.

"Now salute, General."

The General saluted.

"Now stand beside your horse."

The mount of the Chief of Staff was brought forward.

A policeman saluted.

"I couldn't help overhearing some of the ladies in the crowd, General, remark on what a fine figure you make in that uniform."

Meanwhile the troops had pushed spectators and veterans relentlessly south until, three blocks from Pennsylvania Avenue, they organized for the rout of the next bonus camp.

The advance continued on into the night. The vast encampment at Anacostia, home of several thousand veterans and their families, was the last to fall. Infantry threw bombs into every hovel. Pieced together after weeks of scavenging for bits of wood and weeds and iron, they went up in one great burst of flame. Children carried out by their fathers, stared wonder-eyed at the troops, the flames, the hurrying shadows in the night. Mothers wondered where they would sleep next. One veteran dashed into a shack already burning. He came out with a small sailboat.

In the Lincoln study of the White House, Herbert Hoover stood with Henry M. Robinson, Los Angeles banker, and Seth Richardson, of the Department of Justice. Out of the window they could see the flames which spelt the defeat of the veterans throw into bold relief the shipping in the Potomac, the airplane hangars at Bolling Field, the squalid surroundings, the hurrying figures of the bonus camp.

On the edge of the camp, although not discernible from the White House, stood General Glassford watching the veterans shoulder their packs and file off into the night.

"The army has put them on the street," he said. "They will still be on the police but not so well handled."

In the hospitals were one veteran dead, another dying, one baby almost dead of tear gas.

In the War Department across from the White House, General MacArthur announced the victory of the Bonus Offensive.

"I have entered villages in war time which have been in the grip of the enemy for three years," he said, striding up and down the office of Secretary Hurley, "and I know what their gratitude means. But never have I seen, even in those days, such expressions of gratitude as from the crowds to-day."

General MacArthur was the recipient of many letters and telegrams after that, most of them bitter in their denunciation—some commendatory.

One letter read:

"Dear General:

"You have done a great job and I am going to see that you are rewarded. When Congress reconvenes I am going to write my Congressman and have him take steps to give you another medal. This medal will have a ribbon on it, down the middle of which will be a broad streak of yellow, with a piece of bologny on the end."

Thus ended the Dance of the Depression.

CHAPTER TWO

NINE OLD MEN

*I*N the long and tunnel-like corridor of the capitol just north of the Dome there is a little black door, its edges covered with felt. Beside it all day long sits an aged Negro. Around him is an atmosphere of decadent repose and he dozes peacefully. On certain days, however, he wakes up enough to pull a cord attached to the door, which swings back and forth with noiseless solemnity.

Walking past this door one Monday morning, Andrew Furuseth, President of the International Seamen's Union of North America, gnarled warrior of a hundred labor battles, suddenly turned to a friend and exclaimed:

"Bill, you want to see God?"

The friend, somewhat startled, offered no objections. Andy took him by the arm and led him to the little black door. The aged Negro pulled the cord. They found themselves inside. There they faced a heavy screen which shut off from view a high-ceilinged chamber. But another Negro motioned them to a row of benches against the wall and the two men tiptoed to seats.

The same atmosphere of decadent repose pervaded the chamber. There was no sound except the droning of a man, dressed in cutaway coat and pin-striped trousers who stood before a raised reading table, making a quiet-voiced plea.

Around him were little desks and attendants, all in formal morning attire.

And looking down upon this awed and respectful assemblage from a long mahogany dais were nine old men. Some of their faces were benign and beautiful. Some were hard and cadaverous. All were set with age. The solemnity of the occasion was increased by the black gowns which draped their shoulders as they waggled back and forth, some of them seemingly half dozing, in their high-backed chairs.

Andy waited until his friend had taken in the scene. Then, leaning over and surreptitiously pointing to the bench, he whispered:

"The Supreme Court of the United States—that is God."

Andy was not joking. He and his friend were in the presence of the supreme arbiters of the nation. The one hundred and twenty-odd million people of the United States through their elected representatives, Congress, the forty-eight State legislatures, and the hundreds of municipal and county agencies, may propose; but these nine old men, appointed to their positions and holding them for life, have the final power to dispose.

The economic, social and political dictum of the land is what they say it is, or rather, what five of them, a bare majority of one, may dictate. Decades of laborious effort and millions of dollars may be expended to enact a statute sweeping aside a barbarism, but if the innovation runs counter to the hardened prejudices and obsolete theories of a majority of these nine then the taboo of "constitutionalism" is invoked and the statute is outlawed.

No matter how strong the popular demand, how powerful the legislative action, or how numerous and imposing the approval of the lower judiciary, if a majority of these old men say No, then progress stops. Only a revision of the Constitution, a super-human task, can overcome the dead hand of their disapproval.

In 1894, Congress enacted a law placing a two per cent tax

on incomes above four thousand dollars. It was the first income tax act, and it was adopted only after years of popular demand that wealth be made to bear its just share of the cost of government. The law was predicated on the fundamental right of the government to levy taxes, a right it had exercised without challenge since the founding of the Republic. But by the vote of one old man, who mysteriously and without a word of explanation reversed himself on the final decision, that right was abrogated. It took the nation eighteen years to enact an amendment to the Constitution restoring to itself, through the instrumentality of Congress, the right to impose an income tax.

In few other civilized countries are children as cruelly exploited by a ruthless and rapacious industrial system as in America. After fifty years of public outcry, the Senate in 1906 finally took up the discussion of child-labor legislation. During ten years a bitter struggle was waged in Congress before a measure striking at this evil practice was enacted. When the bill finally was passed, the vote was fifty-two to twelve in the Senate and three hundred and thirty-seven to forty-six in the House.

Despite this overwhelming endorsement by the elected representatives of the people, and the approval of President Wilson, the Supreme Court tore the law from the statute books, pronouncing it "unconstitutional." When Congress in 1919, under the spur of widespread public indignation, passed a second measure, the court again ruled against it. To-day, there is no Federal law prohibiting the exploitation of children in factories, mills and mines. So far as the national government is concerned they may toil their pitiful lives away, stunted in body and mind, because a few old men, long since gone to their graves, did not like the economic philosophy embodied in the legislation.

In the unending struggle to better the lot of the worker, a signal victory was won in Oregon in 1914. The legislature enacted a minimum-wage law which the seven members of the Oregon Supreme Court twice unanimously upheld. When the act reached the United States Supreme Court no final decision was reached. The court tied four to four on the issue, with Justice Brandeis, who had recently taken his place on the bench, not voting, as he had been counsel for the legislation in Oregon. This quirk of chance excluding the enlightened jurist was to prove fatal to the final outcome.

On the strength of this stalemate, which technically upheld the legislation without finally determining its constitutionality, a number of States followed in Oregon's progressive footsteps. In the next few years Massachusetts, Minnesota, Arkansas and Washington adopted minimum-wage laws which were upheld by their Supreme Courts. Twenty-seven State jurists sitting in deliberate judgment found the legislation constitutional, and only two disapproved it.

But in 1919 Congress passed a minimum-wage act for the District of Columbia. When it reached the District Supreme Court it was upheld by a two to one vote. But here again chance intervened and struck death to the legislation. Instead of the issue going immediately to the United States Supreme Court—a majority of which at that time unquestionably would have upheld the act—a technicality was invoked to force a re-hearing by the District Supreme Court.

This delay was fatal to the measure, for by the time it reached the United States Supreme Court that body had undergone important changes. Justice George Sutherland and Justice Pierce Butler, ultra-conservatives, corporation lawyers, had been installed on the bench by President Harding. When the District act reached the court on March 14, 1923, they made short shift of it. Three weeks later, by a vote of five to three—Justice Brandeis again not acting—the court held minimum wage legislation unconstitutional.

By one stroke, five men, their average age sixty-seven, had undone the work of decades, set at naught the votes of hundreds of elected legislators, and rejected the solemn judgment of thirty State jurists. That a literal interpretation of the Constitution had anything to do with the decision of these five old men is, of course, out of the question. Their decision was the result of a series of accidents and was prompted entirely by the fact that several of them had spent their lives as corporation lawyers.

What leading legal authorities of the country thought of the decision of these five old men, written by Justice Sutherland, was indicated by the sharp dissents of Chief Justice Taft and Justice Oliver Wendell Holmes. Thomas Reed Powell, professor of constitutional law at Harvard, had this to say of Sutherland's labored opinion: "As a flagrant instance of insufficient reasons and of a judgment widely regarded as an indefensible judgment, the minimum-wage decision has few if any rivals."

Not even the complete collapse of the economic system of the country and a world-wide struggle for a saner and happier order has won any concession from the time-hardened views of a majority of these nine old men. In 1932, with twelve millions out of employment, industry and agriculture prostrate, thousands of banks closed, and men and women the land over struggling with the colossal problem of bringing about fundamental changes in the bankrupt economic system, a majority of these old men grimly thrust the dead hand of their medievalism athwart the path of progress and in the name of the Constitution struck it down.

The people of Oklahoma through their elected legislators decided that unrestrained competition in the ice business was a menace to health and economic well-being. To safeguard themselves and their children they enacted a law designed to introduce some measure of regulation in the icemaking business of the State. It was not a revolutionary act. It was a simple regulatory provision requiring ice producers to obtain certificates of public convenience and necessity from a State agency. Apparently the people of Oklahoma thought they had a right to determine for themselves what was best for their health and happiness.

But they were wrong. Six justices of the Supreme Court of the United States, removed by two thousand miles of space and two centuries of ideas, held that such social consciousness was "unconstitutional" and cannot be tolerated.

So the ice business of Oklahoma has gone back to the chaotic and destructive system of uncontrolled competition—and the people of Oklahoma, even though their health and pocket-books may suffer, have the satisfaction of knowing that at least in the eyes of six justices of the Supreme Court they are once more constitutionally pure and anointed.

The United States is the only country in the world that permits the judiciary to subordinate the legislative branch of the government. There are other countries which have written constitutions, but none has ever permitted a judicial oligarchy to set itself up as the supreme arbiter of what shall or shall not be enacted.

It was tried only once in England. As a result, Chief Justice Tresillian was hanged and his associates exiled for life. In the constant extension of their jurisdiction the Federal courts of the United States are fond of citing English legal precedent. But on the question of the right to pass on legislation, no word of English precedent is to be found in their lengthy arguments. Obviously, what happened to Lord Tresillian and his fellow jurists is not a good example.

This right to pass on legislation assumed by the Federal courts is a self-arrogated power. There is no word or sentence in the Constitution which gives the judiciary such authority. When James Madison in the constitutional convention proposed giving the courts such power in limited form, the motion four times was decisively rejected. Even those who favored such provision in the Constitution admitted that it could not obtain ratification from the States.

But what the Fathers of the nation dared not do and what no legislative act has ever done, the United States Supreme Court has consummated by stealthy encroachment. As a result, economic, social and political truth in the United States is that which elicits the approval of a majority of the nine old men appointed for life and unaccountable to popular will.

The first step in this historic usurpation of power was taken in 1803 by Chief Justice John Marshall, an arch-Federalist, in the famous case of *Marbury* vs *Madison*. In a majority opinion, Marshall enunciated the principle, although it was not germane to the decision, that the Supreme Court had the right to nullify statutes. But even Marshall was cautious in proclaiming this theory. He carefully explained that the courts could only void legislation that was "repugnant to the Constitution"—a far cry from declaring unconstitutional an Oklahoma ice regulation, a Baltimore street-car fare, a minimum-wage law, a bakers' hours-of-labor act, or a village zoning ordinance.

Guarded as was Marshall's oligarchical pronouncement, it provoked a storm of protest. Jefferson bitterly denounced it, and for forty-eight years the Supreme Court did not again dare to intrude itself in the legislative processes. Then, in 1856, came the historic Dred Scott decision, the result of which was to precipitate a national cataclysm, the Civil War. So strong was the distrust and animosity against the Supreme Court at this period that a tenth seat was created. This place was later allowed to lapse when feeling over the court subsided.

Out of the great struggle between the States came the Fourteenth Amendment, enacted to safeguard the rights of the newly enfranchised Negroes and to insure—so its authors thought—the supremacy of Congress. Certainly, the last thing that was in the mind of Representative Thaddeus Stevens, of Pennsylvania, the leader of the Radical Reconstructionists who fathered the Amendment, was to increase the power of the Supreme Court. An all-dominant and domineering Congress was the objective of the crabbed, implacable enemy of the South, who, upon the assassination of Lincoln, became the ruler of Washington.

To-day, as a result of a long process of "interpretation,"

the Fourteenth Amendment has been metamorphosed by the Supreme Court into the greatest bulwark of the nation's vast and bankrupt *laissez faire* economic system. Successive majorities on the court have not only completely submerged the original intent of the Amendment, but by numerous decisions have subjugated the States and every branch of the Federal Government to their rule. And finally, in the practically unknown *Mugler* vs *Kansas* decision, the court completed the epochal revolution by setting itself up in the place of the Constitution.

How the court wrought this great usurpation of power is one of the least-known but most far-reaching and important phases of American history. The Fourteenth Amendment was enacted in 1868, but it was not until 1873 that it became officially known to the Supreme Court. A few years later the Amendment was no longer recognizable to its creators. The stand of the court in *Mugler* vs *Kansas* was gradual in its evolution and did not come to a head until 1887.

In 1873, the butchers of New Orleans started court action against a Louisiana statute which set up a slaughter-house corporation and gave it a monopoly of butchering in the city. The Supreme Court upheld the State act, ruling that it could not, without explicit language in the Constitution, degrade States and that the Fourteenth Amendment applied only to privileges and immunities of citizens of the United States as opposed to privileges and immunities of citizens of several States. This was a smashing victory, indeed, for States' rights and had this original interpretation prevailed it is entirely possible that the whole course of American economic history might have been different.

But by 1885, the personnel of the court had completely changed. Modern industrialism in the United States was in its first full stride. It was the day of the promoter, the exploiter, the entrepreneur, of tariffs, monopolies and trusts. The cry was for unrestricted competition, for government to keep its hands off and not to intrude, interfere or regulate,

When States attempted to do so, the economic rulers of the day turned to the Supreme Court—and they did not turn in vain.

The court at first proceeded warily. It did not reverse its predecessors in one fell swoop. In the Mississippi Railroad Commission case the Supreme Court of 1885 still upheld the earlier view of the dominance of the State, but in doing so laid down an entirely new and profoundly significant doctrine. The court declared that while States could take measures to protect themselves against discriminatory rates, they could not enforce, what it pleased to call "unreasonable rates." In other words, the Supreme Court laid down the dictum that there were good rate-regulatory measures and bad rate-regulatory measures and that *it* would determine which were which.

With this groundwork laid, the court proceeded rapidly to erect the full structure of its overtowering authority. Two years later, it completed the job in the *Mugler* vs *Kansas* decision. This case involved a State law prohibiting the manufacture of liquor for personal use. The defendant claimed the act violated the provisions of the Fourteenth Amendment which declare that "no State shall...abridge the privileges or immunities of citizens of the United States: nor shall any State deprive any person of life, liberty, or property without due process of law...."

The Supreme Court upheld the Kansas law on the ground that there is nothing in the Fourteenth Amendment limiting the exercise of "police power" by the States. But having made this gesture to established theory the court proceeded to stab it in the back by declaring that not every statute designated an exercise of police power would be accepted by it as such. In other words, the Supreme Court laid down the doctrine that while the Fourteenth Amendment does not prohibit States from exercising police authority it would examine into the object of such authority and determine whether the purpose was a "proper" one. That is to say, the court declared that State laws setting up economic restrictions were unconstitutional, unless, in its opinion, they were measures which should be enacted.

Thus by this deft pronouncement the court booted the Fourteenth Amendment out of the window and substituted its own omniscient wisdom in its place.

In 1890 in the case of *C. M. & St. P. Railroad* vs *Minnesota,* the Supreme Court no longer made any bones about the matter and openly proclaimed itself the supreme arbiter of the land. In holding the Minnesota act unconstitutional, the court flatly reversed its decision of three years previous in *Munn* vs *Illinois,* in which the right of States to regulate utilities was affirmed. Justice Bradley, assailing the court's position in a dissenting opinion in the Minnesota case, declared that its action meant that it was setting itself up as the "final arbiter in the regulation of fares and freights of railroads and the charges of other public accommodations."

Having already swallowed the Constitution, the court now set itself up as a body of economic experts and from that day on it has legislated as such, its decisions determined not by "law" but by what the economic views and prejudices of a majority of the court happen to be on a particular issue.

Thus this court, created by the Founding Fathers as a tribunal of law, has spent its latter days in deciding whether acts regulating Chinese laundries, Johnson grass on railroad rights of way, the manufacture and sale of oleomargarine, unripe lemons, bird shooting by aliens, oyster planting by non-residents, stock exchanges, private schools, trading stamps, cemeteries, ticket scalping in New York, kosher meat, boric acid, window screens in soft-drink parlors, street-car fares, railroad rates, utility profits, chain stores, junk dealers, prostitutes in New Orleans, chiropractors, sheep grazing in Idaho, importation of Texas cattle into Missouri, the size of bread in Chicago, Greek-letter fraternities and hundreds of other similar measures are sound economic practice.

This autocratic usurpation of legislative power by the court has not been consummated without challenge. Throughout its history, members of the court have inveighed against this assumption of authority. As early as 1796, seven years before the *Marbury* vs *Madison* decision, Justice Chase repudiated the right of the court to pass on legislation. In 1838 Justice Story echoed this view. In 1878, in the Sinking Fund cases, Justice Waite started a long line of notable dissents which have increased as the court extended its scope and jurisdiction. In recent years these dissents have become so significant and have aroused so much popular enthusiasm that they overshadow the majority opinions of the court in popular attention.

Twice in the last quarter of a century have great political leaders raised the issue of judicial legislating in national campaigns. Theodore Roosevelt made the demand for restraints upon the Supreme Court one of the major planks in his third-party platform of 1912, proposing a plan for the popular recall of judicial decisions and had not the World War intervened, public opinion, aroused over the danger of a paramount judiciary, probably would have forced drastic limitations on the court.

In 1924 the elder Senator Robert M. LaFollette renewed this demand. In his third-party campaign of that year, LaFollette, voicing widespread public indignation, current over two crushing blows the Supreme Court had directed against the child-labor and minimum-wage laws, proposed far-reaching constitutional limitations on the whole Federal judiciary.

In the last two years this deep-seated hostility and fear of the court was again manifested in the great interest with which the country followed the sensational fights in the Senate against the confirmation of Chief Justice Hughes and Judge John J. Parker. The White House claimed that the protests against the men were based on personal grounds. Unquestionably there were some in the Senate who felt that Hughes and Parker were not qualified to sit on the court. But the underlying motive of the opposition was predicated on a far more fundamental objection than this. The issue that

Senators Borah, Norris, Johnson, Glass, Walsh (Montana) and other outstanding leaders raised was the court's overweening power and the relation of the two appointees to that moot question. It was this viewpoint that Senator Connally of Texas expressed when he told the Senate: "The real issue before the people of the country to-day is whether government should regulate and control vast aggregations of wealth, or whether they through the Supreme Court shall dominate and run government. "

It was Connally also who calmed Senator Morris Sheppard, author of the Eighteenth Amendment, when the latter excitedly rushed up with the information that Hughes was a "big Baptist" and he feared voting against him. "Hell, Morris," said Connally, "you are not voting for a Moderator. You are voting on a Justice of the Supreme Court."

That the United States to-day has fallen so far behind European countries in the development of social legislation is the fault not so much of the individual States but of the Supreme Court which has blocked them. Many of the States have been willing to experiment with such measures but their efforts have been thwarted by the court.

During the last decade North Dakota has undertaken a program of practical State socialism; Kansas proposed compulsory arbitration of labor disputes; Arizona forbade labor injunctions; Oklahoma endeavored to restrict competition in the ice industry; Tennessee acted to regulate the price of gasoline; New Jersey sought to control fees that private agencies charged those looking for work; and a number of States moved to limit utility profits. But with the partial exception of the North Dakota acts, every one of these steps to mitigate the rigors of a ruthless competitive system, has been declared illegal by the Supreme Court.

They were stricken off the statute books not because of legal incompatibility with the provisions of the Constitution, but because the court disapproved the economic and social philosophy they embodied.

Seventy-five years ago Abraham Lincoln stirred the soul of the North with the declaration: "No nation can exist half slave and half free." That great dictum holds true in these tragic times. No nation can exist nine-tenths pauper and one-tenth rich. The greatest problem facing the American people to-day is the task of recasting the economic system so as to bring about and maintain an equitable distribution of wealth. The American citizen believes he has an inalienable right to an honest livelihood to keep himself and his loved ones in decency and comfort. "Rugged individualism" in the form of bread-lines, hunger marches, evictions, bankruptcies, foreclosed farms and starvation doles are not the American way and cannot long endure.

To-day more than any other time since the Civil War forces throughout the country are demanding vital economic changes. Economists, enlightened industrialists, liberal social and political leaders are discussing widely such sharp deviations from the established economic system as economic planning, unemployment insurance, nationalization of basic industries, and taxation of tax-exempt government securities. During the 1932 session extensive hearings were held in the Senate on the first two proposals. Under the spur of Governor Philip LaFollette the Wisconsin legislature enacted an unemployment insurance plan.

But what will happen when any of these measures having passed all the hazards of legislative obstacles and executive vetoes finally reach the supreme test—the nine old men seated on the bench of the Supreme Court of the United States? It is true they will encounter no barrier in the person of Louis D. Brandeis, who has spent a lifetime fighting for human rights and individual liberty; nor in the person of Harlan Fiske Stone, who although once a partner in the law firm representing J. P. Morgan, preserves the strictest impartiality toward all corporate questions; nor from Benjamin Nathan Cardozo, one of the great philosophers of American judicial life.

Probably also they may get an even break from Owen J. Roberts, baby member of the court, who despite a career as a Philadelphia corporation lawyer is groping to preserve a humanitarian detachment on the supreme bench—and occasionally finds his way to such a view.

But what will happen when they reach the hands of Charles Evans Hughes, who abandoned an early liberalism to become the highly paid counsel for some of the most monopolistic vested interests in the country? When they reach the hands of George Sutherland, product of the early Utah colonization days and an economic era long since shattered—a man who began his career on the court by outlawing the minimum-wage acts? What is to be hoped from a Pierce Butler who spent early years arguing before the Interstate Commerce Commission for higher rates and greater profits for his railroad clients and recent years as a member of the Supreme Court writing these corporation arguments into the law of the land? Or what will happen when they reach a Willis Van Devanter, seventy-three years old, whose active life revolves around the politics and feudal economics of territorial Wyoming? Or, finally, what can be expected from a James Clark McReynolds, irascible product of Tennessee fundamentalism, whose most notable dissent was against the majority opinion which upheld New York State in compelling publicity for the Ku Klux Klan?

Confronted by this galaxy of grim, unmovable defenders of reaction the outlook for attainment of fundamental reforms by peaceful legislative processes is bleak indeed.

It is true several of them are ailing, and a year or two may see them pass from the scene. But what then? They will be replaced by other old men of their kind. And if, miracle of miracles, an enlightened President or Senate should fill their places with liberals, still nothing would be changed, fundamentally.

Precedents of a century cannot be quickly overturned. And a few years may see a new President, a different-tempered

Senate, who would plug up other vacancies with "safe" appointees and the old march of exploitation would be resumed. It is a simple matter for the court to reverse itself. It has done so repeatedly in the past. A restored reactionary majority would unquestionably do so again in the future.

No real or lasting progress in reshaping the economic system can be achieved in the United States without a fundamental reconsideration of the controlling rôle held by the Supreme Court. Unless that is done, then no matter what changes and reforms the mass may force through Congress and the State Legislatures, nine old men on the Supreme Court will have the final say as to whether they shall stand or not.

*

THE SYSTEM by which the Supreme Court of the United States arrives at decisions which may mean dividends to corporations or shortened lives for mill workers is a matter of simple routine. The court convenes the first Monday in October and continues until the last Monday in May. During this period its procedure is to sit two or three weeks, hearing arguments, and then recess two or three weeks for deliberation and the preparation of opinions, the ratio during the 1931-32 session having been sixteen weeks of arguments against nineteen weeks of deliberation.

It is during these weeks of deliberation that the real work of the court is done. The Justices meet in their private room off the Supreme Court chamber, usually on Thursdays, and discuss the individual cases. Each of them has had an opportunity to study in advance the stenographic report of the oral argument, and on the basis of this advance study Chief Justice Hughes calls the roll, beginning with the most recent appointment to the court—now Justice Cardozo. Each Justice not only votes in the affirmative or negative, but also usually explains the reasons for his position. The Chief Justice always votes last, and, taking advantage of this during the last two terms, Mr. Hughes has shown a decided tendency to throw his weight with the majority.

Debate over a case sometimes is long and vigorous. Justice Butler has been known to become grouchy and irritable. Justice McReynolds often makes little effort to check his temper. Justices Van Devanter and Sutherland, hard-boiled reactionaries, are always calm and sweet-tempered but immovable. Chief Justice Hughes is the great pacifier. More and more he has assumed the rôle of harmonizer between the conservative right, above-mentioned, and the liberal left, consisting of Brandeis, Stone, Cardozo and occasionally Roberts.

This is a new rôle for a Chief Justice of the Supreme Court. In the past some Chief Justices, notably Taft, took great pride in the efficiency of the court, but made no effort to create an impression of internal harmony. Mr. Hughes, however, has become the greatest harmonizer in the court's history. He hates dissent. He hates it almost as much as he hates to be on the minority side in a dissenting opinion. Recently, therefore, he not only has been careful never to write a dissenting opinion, but to throw his persuasive influence against dissenting opinions by other Justices. And with the conservative group he has had notable success.

During the 1931-32 court term, here is his record of accomplishment:

Hughes—twenty-four majority opinions; no dissents.

Sutherland—twenty-one majority opinions; one dissent.

Roberts—twenty majority opinions; one dissent.

Butler—nineteen majority opinions; two dissents.

McReynolds—thirteen majority opinions; one dissent.

Van Devanter—one majority opinion; no dissents.

But with the liberal Justices, Hughes' efforts to curb individual opinion and preserve an outward appearance of harmony have been a complete failure. Here is their record:

Stone—twenty-one majority opinions; six dissents; one concurring opinion.

Brandeis—fourteen majority opinions; three dissents.

Cardozo—ten majority opinions; two dissents.

*Holmes—five majority opinions; one dissent.

After a case has been discussed and the vote taken, the Chief Justice assigns one of the majority to write an opinion, although frequently in cases where the decision is unanimous no assignment is made. During the 1931-32 term forty-eight of the two hundred and thirty-two decisions were handed down without written opinions.

When an opinion is assigned the justice writing it may take as much time as he desires. Dissenting opinions are not assigned, but are wholly voluntary statements by the dissenting justices. Sometimes it happens that several justices will dissent on the same case on entirely different grounds, and each will prepare a separate presentation of his views.

After the opinions are written, they are sent to the Pearson Printing Company, which has the unique record of handling the court's work for more than fifty years without a leak. Advance information regarding some decisions would be worth millions to stock-market manipulators, but only once in the history of the court has there been a leak. This occurred in the office of the late Justice McKenna and was followed by the dismissal of his secretary.

Galley proofs of the opinions are circulated to each of the justices, on the margin of which he marks "I agree" or "I disagree," or else makes a notation regarding a change which he believes might be made in the opinion. Suggestions of this kind are rare, however, since the opinion already has been thoroughly discussed; so that when the court meets privately on the Saturday prior to announcement of decisions on Monday, the work of passing upon the final opinions is chiefly one of formality.

In addition to his rôle as harmonizer, Chief Justice Hughes takes great pride in the speed with which opinions are handed down and the court docket kept up to date. In this he has car-

* Prior to his resignation in the middle of the term.

ried out a reformation which has won the praise of every lawyer practicing before the court. The reform was started by the late William Howard Taft, who when he became Chief Justice found that the court was two and three years behind in its docket. In order to remedy this, he asked Congress to give the court discretionary power to determine for itself which cases it considered of sufficient importance to review. Under this act, Taft, before he died in 1930, had settled hundreds of long-delayed cases.

Chief Justice Hughes has carried this even further. Taft was never able to clear the court docket entirely and always had many cases held over when court recessed in May. Hughes, however, has developed such a mania for speed that sometimes the docket has been cleared even before the periods set for hearing cases expired.

Mr. Hughes' perpetual rush has aroused some resentment on the part of his more meticulous colleagues, and also it has had the distinct disadvantage of cutting down the number of cases the court is willing to hear.

Although there are seven channels through which cases may reach the Supreme Court, by far the most prolific channel is that of writs of certiorari. Writs of certiorari are orders by a higher court to a lower court to send up the record in a case for review, in order to determine whether the higher court will take jurisdiction. No oral arguments are heard, and the petition for review must be brief. Hundreds of these cases flood the Supreme Court every year and hundreds of them also are turned down, the record for the 1931-32 term being five hundred and ninety-seven writs of certiorari rejected out of eight hundred and eighty-three cases disposed of. In addition thirty-nine pleas were dismissed on the ground of lack of jurisdiction and twenty-four other cases were dropped or withdrawn. The court heard arguments in two hundred and twenty-three cases and rendered written opinions on one hundred and seventy-five of them.

Decision to accept jurisdiction and to hear an argument is

not determined by a majority vote. If three or four justices express the view that a case should be heard, it is the practice of the court to place it on the calendar to await its turn for oral argument by opposing counsel. Under the Taft-Hughes system, this usually takes from one to three months.

One of the criticisms most frequently expressed by lawyers practicing before the court is the hard-boiled attitude it takes in rejecting cases. This results in frequent conflict between circuit courts of appeal, especially on tax cases. A circuit court in Alabama, for instance, will interpret a tax law one way and a circuit court in Illinois will interpret it another, so that tax-payers in the two States find themselves paying on a different scale, with the Supreme Court refusing to iron out the conflict unless there is a large amount of money involved.

With his reform of the docket, Chief Justice Taft also persuaded Congress to appropriate funds for a new building, and in a few years the Supreme Court will blossom forth in the splendor of its own home, now being erected across from the capitol. Some of the justices resent this, despite the fact that for years the court has been the step-child—from a housing point of view—of the Federal Government. Prior to 1860, when the Senate and House wings of the capitol were completed, the court sat in a small dark room on the ground floor of the capitol. But after 1860, the original House Chamber was converted into Statuary Hall—otherwise known as the Chamber of Horrors, where every State in the Union can place statues of two favorite sons—while the Senate Chamber was turned over to the Supreme Court.

Taft put across the imposing new judiciary building, despite the fact that Justice Brandeis and some of his friends felt that to remove the court from its cramped quarters in the historic capitol to a glistening marble palace was to add another link to its aloofness from the people. The new building, in addition to an elaborate chamber for the open sessions of the court, will be equipped with extensive archives, libraries, conference rooms and offices for the Justices.

For Justice McReynolds, however, the new building will have a handicap all of his own. It will be a ten-minute walk to the Senate lunch room across the Plaza, and Justice McReynolds has come to depend very much on this Senate lunch room. All the other justices lunch together in the robing room directly across the hall from the court chamber. There, during a brief half-hour recess at two o'clock on hearing days, their Negro messengers bring them lunch. Most of the justices eat frugally. Milk and crackers or soup and sandwiches are their favorite diet, Justice Brandeis bringing two sandwiches with him from home. But Justice McReynolds never deigns to eat with his colleagues. No one knows exactly why, and no one ever has had the temerity to ask. But at two o'clock, McReynolds hurriedly slips off his gown, goes down to the Senate lunch room and then hurries back again.

*

To the eye, Charles Evans Hughes might be any one of the Twelve Disciples, or even Andy Furuseth's description of the Supreme Court. He has a lordly and righteous mien, a beard, and a sonorous voice.

But his feet are of clay—a very common variety of clay.

Hughes has spent a lifetime of oscillation back and forth between serving himself and serving his country, and he has done both well. But the oscillation has been so rapid that he cannot always remember which he is serving.

Hughes began his career as a clerk in the office of Chamberlain, Carter & Hornblower, of New York, one of the most reactionary law firms in the country. In 1888 he organized his own law firm with Paul D. Cravath, for many years the confidential agent of Thomas F. Ryan, multi-millionaire utility and insurance operator, whose corporations were notorious for corrupting legislatures. From this, Hughes jumped to the work of prosecuting big utility and insurance companies. He became counsel for the Stevens Committee of the New York Legis-

lature investigating gas rates, then was made counsel for the
Armstrong Committee investigating insurance companies.
Both investigations he pushed with such industry and courage
and with such sensational disclosures that he was elected Republican Governor of the State for two terms.

But even while running for Governor as an anti-corporation
man, big business did not seem to fear Hughes, or else it was
because they did fear him that they contributed so generously
to his campaigns. J. P. Morgan gave $20,000, Andrew Carne-
gie and J. D. Rockefeller, Jr., gave $5,000 each, Harvey Fisk
& Sons, Chauncey M. Depew, J. & W. Seligman & Company,
Kuhn, Loeb and Company, contributed $2,500 each, and many
other bankers gave one to two thousand dollars.

As Governor, Hughes reflected both his strict Baptist background and his apprenticeship in representing big business.
With a considerable clatter of moral indignation he attacked
race-track gambling, and yet vetoed measures affecting large
corporation interests, such as a two-cent railroad fare bill. He
launched a program of utility regulation and then abandoned
it in the very thick of the fight, in order to accept an appointment to the Supreme Court suddenly offered by President
Taft.

Here Hughes, for six years at least, shook off his old corporate surroundings and preserved an attitude of genuine detachment. On the court he found an old friend in Louis D.
Brandeis, who had worked for Hughes in the Armstrong
investigation. Hughes privately did everything he could to
further Brandeis' cause when big business tried to block his
confirmation and when the Senate finally approved the appointment Hughes was the first to welcome the new Justice.

Having served his country faithfully on the Supreme Court,
Hughes made a categorical declaration in 1916 that he would
continue that service and was not a candidate for the Republican Presidential nomination. "Under no circumstances"
would he permit his name to be used, he announced, and even
if used he would "not accept the nomination."

In that same year—1916—Hughes accepted the nomination.

In those days the present Chief Justice was the acme of self-confidence and political ignorance. Angus McSween, political writer of the Philadelphia *North American,* was his chief adviser and insisted that the Republican candidate remain in New York and shun a swing around the circuit.

"No one has ever been elected who toured the country as against a candidate who stayed at home," McSween argued.

But Hughes was adamant. He maintained that he had led a cloistered life. The American people knew him legally but not personally, he said.

"Well, what will you talk about?" McSween asked.

"Why, the *Titanic* and the necessity of reorganizing the Coast and Geodetic Survey to prevent similar disasters," Hughes replied.

"All right, what else?" McSween persisted.

"I think I shall also talk on the importance of the Civil Service."

McSween gulped, but continued:

"What else?"

"I have not thought that out yet, but probably I can repeat some of these speeches."

McSween pointed out that in the modern days of telegraph and newspapers, repetition was impossible. He also pointed out the almost certain factional fights which would result and into which Hughes would be dragged.

"I am a candidate for the Presidency, not for State office," Hughes replied with all his dignity.

But exactly what McSween had predicted took place. Hughes found it next to impossible, despite his tremendous energy, to maintain a sufficient freshness in his speeches. The Old Guard Republicans took charge of his train, refusing to let the remnants of Roosevelt's Bull-Moosers get near him. Hughes was made the goat and lost four out of the five States he visited.

On election night, however, Hughes retired believing himself the next President of the United States. A little after midnight a newspaper man called at his house to tell him that California had gone Democratic.

"The President cannot be disturbed," young Charles Hughes, Jr., announced.

The newspaper man persisted.

"You will have to come back in the morning; the President cannot be disturbed."

"Well, just tell him when he wakes up that he isn't President," the reporter replied.

Hughes never got over that defeat. At first he could not believe that he had been defeated and waited several days before sending the customary telegram of congratulations to President Wilson. The telegram was worded in such unsportsmanlike language that it shocked the country. Several years later he repeated this partisanship, when Wilson, early in 1918, appointed Hughes as special Federal investigator of the wartime aviation industry which the United States was heavily subsidizing. Wilson had named Hughes with the hope of getting an impartial and non-partisan investigation, but for months Hughes conducted his inquiry in secret, carefully holding up his findings until November 1st, when on the eve of crucial congressional elections he made public a report which was of a most damaging nature politically. He charged Colonel Deeds, chief Government representative in the aviation industry, with "highly improper conduct," and recommended court martial. In substantiation of his accusation Hughes quoted four telegrams exchanged between Deeds and former business associates.

Two months later the War Department, after investigating Hughes' charges, completely vindicated Colonel Deeds and disclosed the fact that in publishing four telegrams Hughes suppressed a fifth which would have exonerated the aviation officer.

After his defeat for the Presidency, Hughes' life pendulum swung back to private law practice. The one-time crusader against public and private corruption became the darling of big business and his first case was in defense of a notorious Tammany graft contract.

Hughes made money, but at the same time he kept his eye on the football of politics, and brought his commanding oratory and prepossessing appearance into full play on behalf of Warren Gamaliel Harding in 1920, with the result that he was appointed Secretary of State. As such he sat for several years alongside Harry M. Daugherty, Albert B. Fall, and Edwin Denby, never raising his voice against their depredations. But compared with his contemporaries, Hughes was an excellent Secretary of State. He was vigorous, forceful, with an amazingly efficient command of all the details of his vast office.

But again his strict Baptist background clashed with a lifetime of private practice for big corporations. Hughes pushed the principle of peace at the Washington Arms Conference and in many negotiations with Latin-American countries, withdrawing the Marines from Santo Domingo and Nicaragua. At the same time he waged a stupendous battle for the programs of big corporations abroad, especially the oil interests, and in Turkey was charged by the American-owned Turkish Petroleum Company with discrimination in favor of the Standard Oil interests which later retained him as attorney.

Hughes performed a remarkable but little-noticed job in dispelling much of the bitterness which Latin-American nations had harbored against the "Colossus of the North." He took this mission most seriously, and, in 1924, made a goodwill pilgrimage to Rio de Janeiro to open the Brazilian Exposition and to dedicate the laying of the cornerstone of a monument given the city of Rio by the American colony.

Since leaving the State Department, Hughes has given unsparingly of his time and energy to aid Pan-American friendship. He spent three months at the sixth Pan-American Conference in Havana in 1928, where he served as chief of the American delegation and steered a reasonably harmonious course through the multitudinous pitfalls of Pan-American politics. Again in 1929, he abandoned his law practice to serve on the Pan-American Arbitration Conference and helped to draft the fairest arbitration and conciliation treaties ever approved by the Senate. Again in 1932, he acted as neutral arbitrator for the long-smoldering boundary dispute between Guatemala and Honduras and remained in Washington through most of the summer's heat, working on the case. For this and similar services he refused to take any honorarium, informing the State Department, which offered to remunerate him:

"The Justices of the Supreme Court should take care of these little judicial jobs as a patriotic duty."

It was while attending one of these Pan-American conferences four years after his trip to Rio de Janeiro that Franklin Adams of the Pan-American Union approached Mr. Hughes with a sad tale of woe.

Mr. Hughes, at the time, was looking exceptionally pleased with himself, having just scored a diplomatic victory for the United States.

"Mr. Hughes, do you remember that good-will pilgrimage of yours down to Rio de Janeiro?" Mr. Adams asked.

"Of course," replied Mr. Hughes, looking even more pleased. "I have a distinct recollection of that event. It was a great occasion. It did much to promote harmony between the United States and Latin America. There should be other such occasions."

"And do you remember, Mr. Hughes, the cornerstone you laid for the monument to be erected by the American colony in honor of Brazilian-American friendship?"

"Ah, I do indeed," replied Mr. Hughes, almost bursting with pride. "That also was a great occasion. Other Secretaries of State should go South and get acquainted with our Latin-American neighbors and dedicate more monuments to our friendship."

"But do you know what's happened to that monument?"

"No. I trust nothing of an untoward nature."

"It's still in a warehouse waiting to be erected, and all the Brazilians are wondering what's become of it," replied Adams. "You see, you only laid the cornerstone, and afterward the American colony found they would have to spend $30,000 on a marble pedestal which they had forgotten about. But about that time the price fell out of the coffee market and they have never been able to finish it."

So Mr. Hughes, perpetual apostle of Pan-American peace, dug down into his jeans and helped contribute toward the cost of finishing the monument which he had dedicated to Brazilian-American friendship.

Charles Evans Hughes resigned from the State Department on the excuse that he had to recoup his personal fortune. It was true that the money he had raked in as attorney for big business had dwindled almost to the vanishing point, but he recouped with astonishing celerity. Along with John W. Davis, former American Ambassador to the Court of St. James, Hughes was singled out as the chief Supreme Court attorney of the country. Scores of cases flocked to his office. And he lost most of them. True, this was to be expected. Most of the cases which came his way already were lost, and were put in his hands on the last lone chance that a man with his prestige, as a former justice of the Supreme Court and a former Secretary of State, could win.

Hughes developed a reputation during these days of hectic big corporation arguments for being slip-shod and careless in his legal preparation. This was not, perhaps, entirely his fault. He handled so many cases that obviously it was a physical impossibility for him to be thoroughly familiar with all of them, and his delivery gave the appearance of having taken a brief handed him by an underling in his law office and memorizing it on the train en route from New York.

Hughes has a photographic mind which can grasp and retain every detail with a few minutes' glance, after which his delivery is as automatic as a phonograph. If a member of the court knocked him off the beaten track of his speech with a question, Hughes came right back to the exact word and sentence where he deviated from the text, and, without looking at the manuscript or even having it in his hand, picked up the sequence again. This photographic mind, his persuasive voice, his beard, his prepossessing appearance combined to make Hughes a powerful pleader before any court, and once Justice Cardozo, then on the New York Circuit Court of Appeals, remarked of Hughes: "When I am listening to that man I say to myself: how can I ever decide against him?"

But as a special pleader before the Supreme Court after his resignation from the State Department, Hughes got distinctly in wrong with his former colleagues. They felt that he was taking advantage of his former position on the bench, that he was not giving enough attention to the legal points of his cases, and as a result his former colleagues appeared to go out of their way to pick up and challenge every slip he made. And there was one occasion when Mr. Hughes stood flushed and embarrassed while an attorney, arguing a case in which Hughes' clients were interested, said:

"I have ten minutes of my time left and if it please your Honors I should like to relinquish this to Mr. Charles Evans Hughes whose clients share our position."

"We will proceed to the next case," ruled Chief Justice Taft, looking straight through Hughes.

In 1928 Hughes shared honors with William Edgar Borah as the chief political ballyhoo agent of the Hoover Presidential campaign and got as his reward the appointment as Taft's successor on the Supreme Court. Hughes' record as special corporation pleader had so prejudiced him with the Senate, however, that, much to the President's surprise, twenty-six votes were rolled up in opposition, and he was confirmed only after four days of debate and a vigorous use of the party lash on Administration Senators. After the fight was over, the new appointee settled down to mold a career as Chief Justice which at first surprised all his critics. During his first term he frequently sided with the liberal minority and concurred in such dissenting opinions as the McIntosh case in which a Canadian professor of philosophy at Yale sought American citizenship without taking the oath to bear arms in defense of the United States.

Hughes' independence, however, was short-lived. During his second term he sided consistently with the four irreconcilable conservatives whose passion in life is to set their large and heavy feet squarely in the path of progress. Hughes was not always like this. When he served as Associate Justice from 1910 to 1916 he was a liberal and independent thinker, and the number of his dissents was greater than those of Justice Oliver Wendell Holmes. He disagreed thirty-one times as against twenty-four for Holmes, and in these dissents he lined up with the liberals on such basic questions as anti-trust laws, labor measures and government regulation of utilities.

But two changes had taken place since then. In the first place, Hughes had aged, and during the advance of the years he had spent many in the employ of vested interests whose point of view he had come to share and to be in the habit of defending. In the second place, Hughes was no longer an Associate Justice, but Chief Justice of the Supreme Court of the United States. And he felt his responsibility. All through his public life, Hughes has been a pacifier and harmonizer. So as Chief Justice, he began to exercise those earlier instincts more than ever before. He felt that so great and august a body as the Supreme Court should be above dissent; that when the law of the land was interpreted for an expectant public, that public should be made to feel that the law was a sacred thing regarding which all learned men, especially the Justices of the Supreme Court, were as one.

So all of the austere eloquence and sonorous pontification in which Mr. Hughes is supreme have been directed toward that end. But he has accomplished nothing. Both the conservatives and the liberals dislike his efforts, and Hughes, in an apparent effort to justify his position, has handed down some opinions in which he almost contradicts himself. The more he writes the more he flounders in a sea of redundancy.

This was especially true in the decision on the Longshoreman's and Harbor Workers' Compensation Act. In this opinion Hughes devoted twenty-two pages to upholding the constitutionality of the act—which was not involved—and then in the last two pages, stabbed the measure in the back by interpreting its administrative features in such a manner as to make it inoperative.

Hughes' colleagues on the Supreme Court bench like their Chief Justice and there is no exception to this rule. He even gets along with the surly McReynolds. But they do resent his sometimes circuitous efforts to bring them together, and not infrequently they joke at the expense of his opinions.

"The Chief's getting concise," remarked Justice Stone, after reading Hughes' lengthy verdict in the Longshoreman's and Harbor Workers' Compensation Act. "Whenever I read one of his opinions, I feel as if I've been through a cyclone with everything but the kitchen stove flying in my face."

*

JUSTICE WILLIS VAN DEVANTER is one of the most reactionary and at the same time one of the most useful members of the Supreme Court.

No matter what his views may be, no matter how radically they may differ from those of other justices, whatever he says commands their respect and attention. He is one of the ablest members of the court, and one of its hardest workers. He has an active and analytical mind. He knows every case thoroughly. The entire court defers to him on questions of jurisdiction. He is an excellent trial judge, keeps every detail of oral argument in his mind like a photograph, so that when a lawyer gets his own case badly twisted, Van Devanter has been known to lean forward and straighten him out.

And yet Van Devanter seldom writes an opinion.

During the entire term of 1931-32, he wrote only one. This is not unusual. The most he has ever written is two or three. Hughes, Stone, Roberts, Butler—all write twenty or more, but Van Devanter, one, two or three.

Justice Brandeis once remarked that if a stenographer could be present in the private conferences when cases are being discussed and could take down what Van Devanter says, the court would get as able an opinion as any he takes six months to write. But when Van Devanter sits down to put his thoughts on paper he flounders for weeks. He writes and re-writes. In the end he turns out an extremely able opinion couched in the best literary style—but the birth pangs are prolonged and prodigious.

However, all his decisions, beautifully as they are written, have never deviated from a rigid impervious reactionarism, a hangover from the antiquated economic system which ruled the Territory of Wyoming, to which he migrated as a young lawyer of twenty-five, whose laws he helped to frame, and whose vast virgin land he helped to open as attorney for the Union Pacific Railroad.

Van Devanter was a power in Wyoming in those days and he was boosted up the ladder of political achievement by another power, Senator Francis E. Warren, for many years chairman of the Senate Appropriations Committee. As Warren's henchman, Van Devanter served as chairman of the Republican State Committee and later was elected Chief Justice of the Wyoming Supreme Court, an honor which he found to be empty compared with the lucrative rewards which the Union Pacific Railroad subsequently offered him as its attorney. After an extensive apprenticeship in corporation practice, Senator Warren had Van Devanter appointed an Assistant United States Attorney General and put him in the Interior Department—a strategical position for a State whose primary interest was public lands. Some years later,

Roosevelt appointed Van Devanter to the Circuit Court and Taft elevated him to the Supreme bench.

With this background, Van Devanter's opinions are understandable—and, although he writes few of them, those which he does manage to put down on paper are among the most important in the records of the court, especially on prohibition, regarding which he is a fanatical dry. It was Van Devanter who in 1920 rendered the court's decision upholding the Eighteenth Amendment—by the extraordinary procedure of giving no reason for the conclusions reached. It was Van Devanter again who decreed that a liquor prosecution in a State court following one in a Federal court for the same offense did not violate the constitutional ban on double jeopardy.

Van Devanter also is the author of the opinion in the famous Dr. Lambert case which confirmed the right of Congress to set itself up as a medicinal authority. Dominated by the dry clerical hierarchy, Congress enacted a law limiting medicinal prescriptions of whisky to one pint per patient for every ten days. Van Devanter held this was sound medical judgment.

It was Van Devanter also who pronounced the patriotic doctrine that the Constitution did not permit Congress to tax the salaries of Federal judges. As a result of this, the judiciary to-day is not affected by the Federal pay cut.

Equaling the fervor of his dry fanaticism is Van Devanter's hostility to State regulation and control of industry. He has written little on the subject, but he always votes against State authority. The few opinions he has written are among the most reactionary in the history of the court. In the case of *Pennsylvania* vs *West Virginia,* Van Devanter invoked the Fifth Amendment, the so-called commerce clause, to crush the attempt by the people of West Virginia to obtain priority in the use of natural gas, one of the State's greatest resources.

Through the State legislature, the people of West Virginia enacted that no natural gas was to be exported until their own needs had been met. This would seem reasonable legislation, but the Supreme Court viewed it as a sinister interference with the free flow of interstate commerce.

The oldest member of the Supreme Court in years of service and himself seventy-three years old, Van Devanter has been frail in health during recent years.

He is one of the most charming members of the court and maintains the pleasantest relations with his colleagues, both reactionary and conservative. On the Wyoming bench during the rough and ready days of territorial justice, Van Devanter had a reputation for being just the opposite. On one occasion he fined a recalcitrant witness one hundred dollars for contempt of court.

"That's easy," the witness remarked. "I've got that in my hip pocket."

"And I also sentence you to thirty days in jail. See if you can find that in your hip pocket," shot back Van Devanter.

*

JUSTICE SUTHERLAND and Justice Van Devanter have much in common. Both are extremely conservative and both owe their conservatism to a Western pioneer era which molded their youth. Both are ardent prohibitionists. Both are Old Guard Republicans. Both are courteous, likable gentlemen and both, in contrast to some of their reactionary colleagues, get along perfectly with the liberal justices with whom they are in frequent legal disagreement.

But there is an outstanding difference between the two men. Van Devanter has brains. Sutherland has not. Van Devanter contributes a great deal to the life and discussion of the court. Sutherland does not.

Sutherland is rather an attractive and scholarly looking person. Tall and slender, with a neatly trimmed gray beard covering a mild face, he is a sweet human character. Once during a summer recess—which are filled with much work for the justices through the receipt of hundreds of writs which must be reviewed in preparation for the fall opening of the court—Sutherland was the only member of the Supreme Court in the city, and the attorney for a youngster convicted in Chicago for violation of the Prohibition Act sought him out. The attorney wanted Sutherland to grant a petition for writ of error which would serve as a period of delay. Sutherland took the petition and spent three minutes looking it over. Then he handed it back.

"I'm sorry I can't grant this," he said. "I only wish I could. It is the most courteous request ever made to a court. If lawyers only realized that we were busy and would write what they have to say in two pages instead of ten ... I really wish I could grant this. I should like to bring this petition to court to show the bar the real way to present a case to court. But you haven't a leg to stand on, and my opinion is fixed. I should be glad to have you see the other justices, however, and they may view the case differently. You can reach Justice Brandeis, the nearest, at Chatham, Massachusetts, and Justice Holmes is near him in Beverly Farms. The others are much farther away."

Sutherland maintains this agreeable manner through all court debates. He never gets irritated as does Butler. He never sulks as does McReynolds. He never tries to influence another Justice. He retains his poise no matter what happens. But to change Sutherland's set conviction on any economic question one might just as well talk to the moon.

He has pronounced hypochondriacal tendencies and constantly talks about medicine and his ailments. In 1930, his secretary, having taken a law degree, told the Justice that he wanted to resign, in order to establish a law practice of his own, but Sutherland asked him to stay on another year, at the end of which time he said he planned to retire. But if his activity in handing down opinions is any criterion, the Justice will remain a member of the Supreme Court for many years to come.

Sutherland is now seventy, but he is old even beyond his advanced years. He was old when he first came to the Supreme bench. He has spent all his life in a past generation, a past age that is no more—the frontier. He went West to practice the law of the West, the law which concerns itself with the land and mineral rights, which favored the railroads, the exploiters, those who got in and opened things up.

And Sutherland—his manner of thinking, his law still dates back to those days that are dead and gone.

Born in Buckinghamshire, England, Sutherland's family took him to Utah, where, after a law degree at the University of Michigan, he aligned himself with the Mormon-Old Guard Republican machine and in 1901 was elected to the House of Representatives, from which he retired voluntarily after one term. Later Sutherland returned to Washington as Senator and remained there for twelve years until defeated by Senator King, a Democrat, in 1917. In the Senate, Sutherland was known for his inoffensive good nature, his extreme conservatism, his unswerving party regularity, and his long dreary dissertations upon the Constitution, to which no one paid any attention, with the exception of one man. He was Warren Gamaliel Harding, a senatorial colleague, who, perhaps because he rarely listened and because he himself knew little of such things, thought the scholarly appearing Utahan a very erudite man.

Sutherland was a member of the Senate Judiciary Committee when Louis D. Brandeis came up for confirmation as Associate Justice. Sutherland heard that Brandeis was at one time retained by Louis K. Liggett in a case contending that chain drug stores did not violate the Sherman Anti-Trust Act. Sutherland considered this inconsistent with Brandeis' anti-trust views and although the committee had held extended hearings on Brandeis' appointment asked that the matter be reopened. This was done, but the committee after hearing one witness sent the appointment back with a renewed recommendation that it be confirmed.

After his senatorial defeat in 1917, Sutherland returned to a highly remunerative practice of corporation law, until, in 1920, he became the personal adviser of the one man in the Senate who had genuine esteem for his speeches on constitutional law. Sutherland spent several months at the home of the Republican Presidential nominee in Marion, Ohio, and Harding, who always took care of his friends, appointed Taft to the first vacancy on the Supreme Court and Sutherland to the second.

During the years that have followed, Justice George Sutherland has done as much to cripple labor legislation and block State efforts to control business as any man in the history of the United States. It was Sutherland who wrote the opinion outlawing the minimum wage. It was Sutherland who wrote the opinion making unconstitutional the child-labor law. It was Sutherland who, in the 1927 Journeymen Stonecutters' case, granted employers an injunction against union stonecutters because they refused to work on stone shipped into their territory. It was Sutherland who, in the Baltimore Street Railway case of 1930, ruled that a fare fixed by the State permitting the utility a 6¼ rate of return was "confiscatory" and that the company was entitled to a return of 7½ per cent or more. It was Sutherland who, during the tragic depression days of 1932, handed down the majority opinion outlawing Oklahoma's attempt to establish order in the ice industry. It was Sutherland also who checked Oklahoma's attempt to use the power of taxation to promote coöperative farming. The State legislature passed an act providing that cotton gins owned by individual operators had to have licenses to operate, while cotton gins owned by coöperatives did not. Sutherland declared such legislation to be unwarranted discrimination against the individual capitalist. Finally, it was Sutherland who handed down the opinions in the MacIntosh and Bland cases denying these two distinguished foreigners citizenship because they were conscientious objectors.

According to Professor Powell; "Justice Sutherland is a very able man."

He adds: "An old lady at the Chevy Chase Club told me so."

*

ALL HIS life Justice Pierce Butler has striven zealously to promote the power and glory of the Holy Roman Church and the power and profits of big business—and for a mediocre man he has done very well both for himself and his spiritual and material masters.

Son of poor Irish parents settling in Minnesota in the days when that State was in the heyday of its expansion, Pierce Butler was raised in a strict religious environment and early in life fixed his eyes on the goal of corporation law. And he got there. Not only did he spend thirty-five years fighting the battles of the companies to which he had dedicated his life, but he continues the fight on the Supreme Court of the United States. The only difference judicial robes have meant to Pierce Butler is that as an attorney he pleaded for special privilege and as a judge he creates special privilege.

There is only one other institution which Butler champions as zealously as he does his corporate friends. That is the Roman Catholic Church.

Butler's activities on behalf of the Church are carried on in such an energetic manner that he has won for himself the title of "Papal Delegate to the Supreme Court."

It was Butler the devout Catholic who alone dissented from the court's decision upholding the Virginia statute providing for the sterilization of imbeciles. It was in this decision that Justice Holmes, speaking for the court, declared:

"Three generations of imbeciles are enough."

To which Professor Powell, reading the opinion to a Harvard law class, added: "Mr. Justice Butler dissenting."

Some time ago Butler gave instructions to his secretary not to let any divorce cases come near the office. He said they were "contaminating." As a reward, Butler is formally entertained at least once a year by the Minister of the Irish Free State.

Butler's fanatical devotion to big business in every case appearing before the Supreme Court is understandable. He spent most of his life as a railroad lawyer, and Minnesota, in which he practiced, has, with the exception of Virginia, the most liberal laws of any State in the Union as far as personal injury suits are concerned.

No matter what the type of accident or where it happened, the plaintiff usually can get a verdict out of a Minnesota jury —almost even to stubbing a toe on a railroad platform. Butler spent a lifetime fighting such suits, so that now when a railroad attempts to appeal to the Supreme Court a negligence case in which it is contended a jury has soaked a road under the Federal Employees' Liability Act, Butler is ever alert to see that the case is heard, and the railroad favored.

Prior to his appointment by President Harding in 1922, Butler never had held public office. He jumped from a corporation law office, where for years he was the partner of Attorney General William D. Mitchell, straight to the Supreme Court. This reactionary background, added to a naturally narrow mind, has resulted in a unique record on the bench.

It was Butler who wrote the decision in the Nebraska Bread-Weight case, setting aside a law enacted by the legislature to protect consumers from dishonest bakers. The statute fixed a minimum and maximum weight for bread twenty-four hours after baking, and was to safeguard buyers from short weights and honest bakers from crooked competitors. Large baking corporations attacked the act as arbitrary and unreasonable, so Justice Butler accommodatingly declared it unconstitutional.

When Pennsylvania sought to protect immigrants unfamiliar with the language and customs of the country from being cheated by crooked steamship agents, it was Butler who struck the law down. An agent arrested for violating this act set up the defense that it ran counter to the commerce clause of the Constitution, which gives Congress exclusive jurisdiction over interstate and foreign commerce. Butler upheld him, thus leaving the helpless immigrants to be victimized.

And it was Butler, the corporation lawyer, who, in the Panhandle Oil Company case, established the farthest legal outpost ever attained by corporations in governmental immunity. Butler ruled that the company did not have to pay a tax to the State of Mississippi on gasoline sales to the United States Coast Guard located there because such sales made it a *Federal instrumentality*.

During the World War, Butler took an active part in suppressing free speech in Minnesota and has continued that policy on the bench. He wrote the opinion denying Rosika Schwimmer citizenship because she refused to promise to bear arms—a decision which set the precedent for denying citizenship to Professor MacIntosh and Miss Bland for the same reason. Butler also joined enthusiastically in the decisions affirming the conviction of Benjamin Gitlow and Anita Whitney under the New York and California syndicalism laws.

Large and bull-like of build, Butler is a slow and ponderous thinker. His decisions are dull, uninspiring and written in a slovenly manner. He is inclined to be sullen, and when a case goes against him sometimes takes no pains to conceal his resentment toward the other Justices. He lacks the force, the intelligence even of Sutherland. His decisions are actuated by prejudice rather than reason, and he is way over on the wrong side every time.

Once Butler was called upon to judge a debate at a St. Paul high school. The question was: "Resolved, that compulsory military education should be abolished."

There were three judges, Justice Butler presiding. One judge favored the affirmative, the other the negative. Faced with casting the deciding ballot, Justice Butler rendered his opinion thusly:

"The debate has been closely argued. In the clearness of

its presentation and weight of argument the affirmative has been superior. But no good American citizen should hold such a view, and therefore I cast my vote for the negative."

*

SEVERAL clerks and attendants of the Supreme Court once got into an argument as to who was the stupidest justice on the bench. The debate narrowed down to Butler and McReynolds. Finally it was decided in favor of the latter, although one point never definitely was determined, namely, whether McReynolds is chiefly stupid or lazy.

Apparently, however, he is both.

Some years ago, McReynolds scarcely wrote an opinion during several terms of the court. Years passed with practically no legal output from him. Finally, however, criticism in legal circles, which reached McReynold's ears, and the Taft-Hughes speed-up system forced him to bestir himself and he now turns out a moderate quota of work.

This, however, has not changed the fact that his opinions are sloppily written and that occasionally, in the middle of an oral argument before the court, McReynolds will stop the attorney and ask for an explanation of some point which is perfectly intelligible to every other Justice.

Indirectly McReynolds owes his appointment to the Supreme Court to Brandeis, yet when the first Jewish Justice took his seat no other member treated him with more disdain.

Woodrow Wilson had appointed Brandeis as Attorney General in his Cabinet, and almost immediately after started for a vacation in Bermuda, leaving behind a furore of protest led by the Boston Bar Association. Wilson, afraid to face the criticism, wrote Brandeis a letter asking that, as a personal favor, he withdraw. Then with the date of his inauguration approaching and the office of Attorney General unfilled, Wilson turned to William Gibbs McAdoo for advice. McAdoo recommended his old friend and fellow-Tennessean, James Clark McReynolds.

About all McReynolds had to recommend him for the position was his friendship with McAdoo, and Wilson soon found it out. Son of a small-town Kentucky doctor, McReynolds had spent thirty years in more or less insignificant law practice, during which his only claim to fame was four years as an Assistant United States Attorney General and a minor part in Roosevelt's trust-busting campaign.

Having discovered his mistake, Wilson got rid of McReynolds at the first opportunity by kicking him upstairs to a vacancy on the Supreme Court. McReynolds therefore landed in the Cabinet in place of Brandeis, and on the court ahead of him.

McReynolds, however, must be given due credit. For a man of his sheer ugliness of disposition he has come far.

When Justice Stone first came to the bench from the Department of Justice, McReynolds would deliberately get up and leave the conference-room when Stone discussed a case. When Cardozo's appointment was being pressed on Hoover, McReynolds joined with Butler and Van Devanter in urging the White House not to "afflict the court with another Jew." When Cardozo was sworn in, McReynolds read a newspaper. When Justice Brandeis read his famous dissent in the Oklahoma ice case to a crowded and intense court room, McReynolds pretended to be busy with his papers. When former Justice John H. Clarke retired from the Supreme Court, he told friends that one of his reasons for retiring was that he could not stand McReynolds.

McReynolds does not confine his rudeness to his colleagues of the court. Once, however, he got a salutary lesson at the Chevy Chase Club of which he is a member, and at which he plays a slow and atrocious game of golf. Despite the fact that he was almost constantly in the rough, McReynolds made it a practice of refusing to let any one play through him. The result was whenever McReynolds was on the greens

there was always sure to be a long line of irate players behind
him, forced to take hours to finish nine holes.

On one occasion McReynolds, playing with Howland
Chase, son of a former Supreme Court Justice, added to his
usual insults by standing on the fifth tee directing the caddy
where to find a lost ball and refusing to move off the tee or
allow a member to play through him until the ball was re-
covered.

That was the climax. A group of members filed a complaint against McReynolds and demanded that Morven
Thompson, chairman of the Golf Committee, call the Supreme Court Justice to account. Thompson, who had witnessed the scene, did so.

"Well, I've been a member of this club a good man
years," McReynolds replied, "and no one around here h s
ever shown me any courtesy, so I don't intend to show ̄ ̄y
to any one else."

Thompson, who had ' ̄en deferential, now becam ̄ indignant.

"Mr. Justice," ̄ ̄ said, "you couldn't be a member of this
club if it wasn't for your official position. The members of
this club have put up with your discourtesy for years, merely
because you are a member of the Supreme Court. But I'm
telling you now that the next time there is a complaint against
you, you'll be suspended from the privileges of the golf
course."

Since then, McReynolds has stepped aside.

On the bench, McReynolds is a queer mass of contradictions. For the most part, his opinions run true to form, and
he lines up as one of the four definite reactionaries. But on
rare occasions a gleam of the past, when he was a trust-
busting attorney for Roosevelt, stirs the old man's soul and
he comes out as a champion of human rights. Later he sinks
back into the slough again.

For instance, he touched off a pyrotechnic display of rhetoric
regarding the sacredness of the Bill of Rights in dissenting

from the majority opinion in the Carroll case. This held that
an automobile can be searched for liquor without a warrant.
Then he reversed himself completely by joining with the
majority in the Olmstead case, which permitted prohibition
agents to tap telephone wires.

Again McReynolds personally wrote the opinion in the
case which held that Massachusetts could not tax income from
patent royalties, on the ground that patents and copyrights are
granted by the Federal Government, only to turn round and
support a decision giving authority to tax income from copyrights to the State of New York.

For the most part, however, McReynolds has been faithful
to his Tennessee fundamentalism. In the Jensen case, he ruled
that an injured stevedore could not recover damages under
the New York Workmen's Compensation Act, on the ground
that his work was of a maritime nature and therefore under
the exclusive jurisdiction of the Federal Government. As this
jurisdiction was not then exercised, the stevedore was left
unprotected. But when Congress sought to overcome this
technicality by enacting a statute making compensation laws
applicable to dock workers, McReynolds led the court in holding that Congress had no authority thus to transfer Federal
power. Later he wrote the decision in a Pacific Coast case
which laid down the doctrine that injured longshoremen could
not secure damages in the absence of an act of Congress
specifically applying to them. Again in the 1931-32 term, Mc-
Reynolds joined in the Hughes opinion which nullified the
administrative features of the Longshoreman's and Harbor
Workers' Compensation Act, which Congress had passed in
an effort to overcome the court's persistent obstruction.

McReynolds also has joined enthusiastically in the State-
rights obstructions thrown up by his conservative colleagues.
He wrote the decision annulling the Wisconsin law which
taxed gifts made by rich donors within a certain time of their
death, and also the opinions outlawing the Minnesota and
Missouri acts taxing bonds and bank accounts of non-resi-

dents. These last two decisions reversed a previous ruling of the court written by Justice Holmes.

Several years ago McReynolds told some of his colleagues that he would retire from the bench when he reached the age of seventy. That deadline arrived in 1932, but with no indication that the Justice intended following out his promise. The reason for this is simple. On the court McReynolds is a personage; once he is off, his name will only be a matter of record in the *World Almanac*.

McReynolds is a bachelor, tall, slender of build and has a face with such a Satanic look that in it there is a certain charm. It has a definite appeal for women, and in his quiet way, the Justice is quite a ladies' man.

No matter what his record on the court, McReynolds will always go down in history as the Attorney General who checked the use of the Mann Act for blackmail purposes. While he was serving in the Wilson Cabinet, F. Drew Caminetti, son of the Commissioner of Immigration in the Labor Department, happened to escort a woman from California across the border to Nevada, and subsequently v s charged with violation of the Mann Act. Although the case patently was what Professor Powell described as "non-pecuniary interstate fornication," Caminetti was convicted and the conviction was sustained in the Supreme Court. Almost immediately afterward a woman in Pittsburgh attempted to blackmail a male escort under somewhat the same circumstances. McReynolds, then Attorney General, took personal charge of the case, had the woman herself up for blackmail and convicted her. There has been no attempted blackmail since.

Although McReynolds has many enemies, he numbers among his friends former Justice Oliver Wendell Holmes. Hardly a week passes but McReynolds does not stop in at the Holmes' house on I Street or go for a walk with the aged jurist.

No matter how much he may be disliked, McReynolds con-

ceals underneath his scowling exterior a real streak of human
kindness which few people have penetrated. One day, while
riding to his office on a Pennsylvania Avenue street car, a
man got aboard in the last stages of intoxication. When the
car lurched around a corner a moment later, he fell out in
the aisle. McReynolds picked him up, helped him back to his
seat and said:

"My friend, I see you are not feeling well. I'll just sit here
and see if I can help you."

The Justice sat beside his charge until they reached the top
of Capitol Hill, when he inquired where the man wanted to
get out, and left him only after giving explicit instructions to
the conductor.

*

IF Owen Josephus Roberts does not ossify he may become
one of the great Justices of the Supreme Court. In robust
health and an outdoor enthusiast, he should have many years
of service before him. What the record of that service will be
is still in doubt.

Son of moderately well-to-do parents, Roberts was born and
reared in Pennsylvania, where he attended the University of
Pennsylvania law school, later taught there as a professor of
law, and for thirty years practiced in Philadelphia as a member of a conservative firm. All his associations, all his training
tend to make Roberts just as reactionary as a Van Devanter
or a Sutherland. But he is not.

For many years Roberts served as the attorney for the
Philadelphia Rapid Transit Company and the Pennsylvania
Railroad, defending them in perhaps a thousand jury cases
where persons were injured by street cars or railways. During
that period Roberts thoroughly convinced himself that the
trials and tribulations of big business in fighting battles against
the people are not what they are supposed to be. One of the
cases which he tried was that of a German baker, who had
his wagon smashed by a street car, and claimed to have an

injured leg, but refused to show the leg in court. The doctors for the Philadelphia Rapid Transit Company claimed the injury was faked. Despite the baker's refusal, the jury sustained the claim and awarded him $3,500.

Illustrative of Roberts' astuteness in conducting trials and the never-failing quality of his memory, he was confronted with a similar case several years later, when a woman claimed injury when she fell from a street car after it had started suddenly. She also refused to show her leg. Roberts had before him a strike list of jurors who had been in similar accident cases and saw that five had crosses beside their names. Roberts had, however, only four strikes. So glancing at the jury he recognized the old baker who, long before, also had refused to show his injured limb. Working on the theory that jurors will never let others get away with practices which they themselves got away with, Roberts let the old German remain on the jury. He won his case.

With this background of constant struggle to defend the rights of big business it is almost a miracle that Roberts should not fall into line immediately with the definite reactionaries of the court. He started out, however, by siding with Holmes, Brandeis, Stone and Hughes in the O'Gorman case upholding the New Jersey Act regulating fire insurance rates, and again in the Indiana chain-store tax case, in which the same group declared valid a State tax on chain stores. Later, however, he switched to the conservatives, voting with them on the Oklahoma ice case and also on the MacIntosh and Bland citizenship cases.

Roberts' stand on the latter two is partially understandable. During the War he acted as Special Deputy United States Attorney General and prosecuted hundreds of cases arising under the vicious espionage acts in force at that time. Apparently he developed something of a mania on the question of patriotism, for when John W. Davis was arguing Professor MacIntosh's case, Roberts turned to Butler and asked why Davis was slopping over. Davis was making his plea in a most impassioned voice, wringing his handkerchief and occasionally dabbing his eyes. Roberts thought it was stage play; but Butler leaned over to whisper that Davis' father had been a clergyman with a great sense of religious liberty and that Davis felt very keenly on the subject.

Roberts later learned that Davis accepted no fee for arguing the case and was convinced of his sincerity.

Before the case opened, Mrs. Thomas D. Thacher, wife of the Solicitor General, who appeared against MacIntosh on behalf of the government, jokingly called Roberts aside and expressed the hope that he would vote against her husband. The interpretation Roberts had placed upon patriotism in his former rôle as an espionage prosecutor swayed him more than anything else, however, and he voted with the reactionaries.

No matter what his future record on the Supreme Court may be, Roberts has carved out for himself a prominent niche in contemporary history for his outstanding work in the prosecution of Albert B. Fall and Harry F. Sinclair in the oil scandals. Although he was assisted in this work by Atlee W. Pomerene, actually Roberts did practically all of the work, even advancing money out of his own pocket to pay for the expenses of the prosecution. The fact that Fall and Sinclair were sent to jail, even though for brief intervals, is entirely due to Roberts' diligence in uncovering evidence and his masterful court presentation. His experience with juries in the District of Columbia, which time after time acquitted the oil scandal culprits, despite the preponderance of evidence against them, has made Roberts a little bitter about Washington juries. He claims they are among the lowest type of jurors in the country and, instead of being responsible citizens, they are selected from telephone books or from court hangers-on who need $3.00 a day.

Roberts is an accomplished horseman, is fond of fox hunting and enjoys gardening. Near Valley Forge he has united six small farms into a large one which is now cultivated by a New York firm. Roberts can hardly wait each spring to get away from court sessions to the peace and quiet of his country place, where he keeps a watchful eye on the blooded cattle which make up his dairy herd.

To this farm he took the members of the German-American Mixed Claims Commission, of which he is serving as neutral chairman. Like Chief Justice Hughes, he refuses to accept remuneration for his work.

A tremendous worker, opinions roll off from Roberts' precise and agile mind in just as great number as from Chief Justice Hughes', but without the same juridical verbiage. Because he is young—the baby of the court—and has such unquestioned intellectual and legal ability, Roberts has a most important future before him. And provided he can maintain the same degree of impartiality evidenced during his first term on the bench, it is not improbable that he may become its Chief Justice.

*

NOT LONG after Benjamin Nathan Cardozo was appointed an Associate Justice of the Supreme Court, a friend asked how he liked his new work. The Justice replied with a note of discouragement in his voice.

"My chief job," he said, "is trying to find out what was in a Congressman's mind when he wrote certain legislation."

And it is a fact that compared with the variety and humaneness of the cases which he heard on the New York Court of Appeals, the Supreme Court suffers from suffocating legal stuffiness.

In the one hundred and forty-four years that the Supreme Court has been in existence, however, few men have been better qualified to bring it fresh legal atmosphere, or a better endowment in ability and experience than the latest Justice to join the court.

Despite the opposition to his appointment on racial grounds of his "early American" colleagues—McReynolds, Van Devanter and Butler—actually Justice Cardozo's lineage in this country goes back to the early seventeen hundreds. Of English-Portuguese extraction, the great grand-uncle of the Justice participated as Rabbi in the inauguration of George Washington. Another great grand-uncle was the first Jew to be made a trustee of Columbia University.

With this background, Justice Cardozo was started on his judicial career in 1914, literally at the demand of the judges of the New York Court of Appeals. The law of the State permitted appointment of a temporary judge when the court's calendar was overcrowded, and as this was the case that year, Governor Glynn asked the court whom it wanted. The court unanimously recommended Cardozo, a practicing attorney before it.

The request was contrary to precedent. It was the established rule that the temporary judge for the Court of Appeals be chosen from the Appellate Division of the New York Supreme Court. Glynn called this fact to the court's attention and submitted a list of names he favored. But the court insisted on Cardozo; and Glynn named him.

Three years later, Cardozo was elected on a non-partisan ticket to a full term on this bench, and in 1926 he was elected Chief Justice for a fourteen-year term.

Cardozo was a youngster just out of law school when he first appeared before the New York Court of Appeals. Practice before this court is one of the most important in the country, its decisions being cited more frequently than any other except the United States Supreme Court. Always diffident and shy in manner, Cardozo was in an agony of nervousness while awaiting his turn. He feared he would falter and make a spectacle of himself. But so brilliantly did he present his case that afterwards the Chief Justice sent him a note in his own handwriting, commending him for the brevity and clarity of his statement.

Cardozo soon won a wide reputation for his ability to argue difficult points of law before this court and his practice eventually consisted almost entirely of this super-legal work. Other attorneys employed him to handle this phase of their cases.

On the Court of Appeals, Cardozo's colleagues regarded him with a mixture of awed reverence and fatherly protection. They would gently chide him for his arduous labors and secretly conspire to take him away for a few hours of recreation.

Cardozo has a rare capacity for winning and holding the affection of people, and his former colleagues on the New York bench, and the hundreds of lawyers who have practiced before him, all speak of him in the warmest terms of admiration.

Cardozo is a bachelor. Until her death a few years ago, he lived with his sister. Nellie Cardozo was a brilliant and charming woman who devoted her life to her brother. Their mother died when he was nine years old and she reared and took care of him and their old family home on West 75th Street, Manhattan, during the remainder of her life. Between the brother and sister there was a deep and abiding love; and when in the last years of her life she became bed-ridden, Cardozo gave up his few simple pleasures, an occasional play or musical comedy, to spend all his leisure with his sister.

Cardozo is one of the most liberal men on the Supreme Court except on one point—morality. Due chiefly to the influence of his sister, the new justice will not even go as far as the pious Senator Smoot from Utah in admitting slightly risqué pictures and sexy literature into the United States.

Cardozo spends his summers on the Jersey coast where he lives in a rented house. In Washington he lives in a small suite in the Mayflower Hotel. Directly above him in the same type of suite is Count Marchetti, counselor of the Italian Embassy. Immediately below is Faik Kanitza, the Albanian Minister. All three are bachelors. The new Justice eschews formal society, but is a charming, gay and witty companion in a small gathering. He is especially fond of young people, and has many friends among them. A few years ago he took up golf on the demand of his doctor, but remains one of the worst golf players in his club. He has no hobbies, is monkish in his habits, rises early, and adheres to a rigorous schedule of work that includes night hours. In the few months that he took part in the work of the Supreme Court during the 1931-32 term he wrote ten decisions and two dissents, a number almost equal to those turned out by McReynolds for the full term.

Cardozo's appearance is striking. He dresses informally and very quietly, but his lean, ascetic face, shock of white hair falling across his fine, high brow, his dark eyes, and strong jutting jaw draw all eyes and hold them. Above all, there is an inherent dignity about him that comes only from aristocracy of blood and brains.

His greatest admiration and enthusiasm is for engineers. "A bridge builder can't guess," is a favorite saying of his. In his own work he exemplifies this love for the exact in his genius for seizing upon essentials no matter how involved and obscure and propounding them in brilliant, fluid and lucid language. He is one of the greatest literary stylists in American jurisprudence, and the author of an essay on the *Style of Judicial Opinions*. When Cardozo taught law at Columbia, a professor of English said of him: "He writes the most powerful English since Alexander Hamilton."

Cardozo reads omnivorously, and likes nothing better than to spend an evening with a volume of Latin or Greek. He has a prodigious memory and is always astounding his friends and associates with its seemingly limitless capacity. Charles Evans Hughes, Jr., then Cardozo's secretary, was asked if the job was a difficult one.

"It is the grandest in the world," he answered, "but you might as well be secretary to an encyclopedia."

*

JUSTICE HARLAN F. STONE is always right the second time.

A New Englander by birth and upbringing and of conservative views, his sturdy open-mindedness, scrupulous fairness and genuine humanity in the long run always lead him to liberal conclusions. But it takes time.

His first reaction is usually toward conservatism. But because he is open-minded, eager to learn and wants to take an enlightened stand, Stone slowly but surely finds his way to such a position.

Unquestionably one of Stone's chief weaknesses is the fact that most of his legal career was spent as a teacher of law. For years at Columbia he was a beloved and progressive educator, but his academic work restricted his experience and he lacks the rough and tumble work of the court room. This is not entirely a shortcoming because most of the other Justices are trial lawyers, and Stone, therefore, supplies a missing link. Conscious of this handicap, however, he has labored earnestly and tirelessly to overcome it. How successfully he has done so is strikingly attested by his magnificent record of impartiality on the bench.

A controlling factor in Stone's "education" as a liberal judge has been the example and friendship of two great colleagues, former Justice Holmes and Justice Brandeis. The big, democratic New Englander lacks the intellectual brilliance of his two friends, but the broad humanitarian philosophy of Holmes and the passionate crusading righteousness of Brandeis have found a ready response in his heart and mind. Each year of his close association with them has added to his stature and given a firmer tone to his liberalism.

Stone was born in New Hampshire in 1872 and graduated from Amherst, one class ahead of Calvin Coolidge and Dwight Morrow. He was admitted to the New York bar in 1898 and for twelve years practiced there and taught law at Columbia Law School. In 1910 Stone was made dean of the Law School and continued in this position until 1924, when his old college friend, then become President of the United States, selected him to succeed Harry M. Daugherty as Attorney General.

As 1924 was an election year, Coolidge was compelled to choose an Attorney General whose integrity and character were above suspicion, and not connected with business interests. But after the elections were over it was another matter. The new Attorney General's decisive steps against the copper trust alarmed Coolidge, and a few months after his reelection and less than a year after Stone's appointment to the Cabinet, Coolidge got rid of him by putting him on the Supreme Court. As his successor in the Justice Department, Coolidge tried to install Charles Beecher Warren, corporation lawyer and sugar lobbyist. When the Senate refused to confirm Warren, Coolidge then turned to a complete nonentity, John Garibaldi Sargent, of New Hampshire, whom the Senate accepted.

While a member of the Coolidge Cabinet, Stone got acquainted with Herbert Hoover and the warm personal friendship that grew up between them has continued unbroken ever since. It has continued despite the fact that Stone since then has become increasingly liberal, while Hoover has intensified his reactionism.

As a member of the medicine-ball Cabinet which exercises with the President before breakfast each morning in the rear of the White House, Stone has no illusions about Hoover's ability. He agrees that he has made many mistakes, has missed numerous opportunities to display broadgauged statesmanship. But he is personally fond of the President.

Stone makes no effort to volunteer advice. But when Hoover, in the course of the informal conversation of the early morning gatherings, asks his opinion, Stone speaks frankly. It was in the course of one of these chats that he warned the President that he would encounter trouble on his appointment of Judge John J. Parker to the Supreme Court. After the Senate rejected Parker, Hoover paid more attention to Stone's advice.

After Justice Holmes retired there was widespread public demand that Cardozo succeed him. Senator Borah—who in

1916 had opposed Brandeis—repeatedly urged Hoover to appoint the brilliant New Yorker and on one occasion the question was discussed at a White House reception which Borah attended. Hoover explained that he hesitated naming Cardozo because of geographic considerations. Two New Yorkers, Hughes and Stone, were already on the bench, he said, and he feared that other sections of the country would complain.

To this Borah replied: "Mr. President, the man you appoint to the Supreme Court represents every State, Idaho as well as New York. If you appoint Judge Cardozo you will be winning the applause of the whole country and not merely one part."

Still Hoover hesitated. Apparently he had other reasons for not wanting to name Cardozo and started a lengthy search for a conservative who might hope to get by the Senate. Finally he settled on three names: Senator Joseph T. Robinson of Arkansas, Democratic leader of the Senate, who was anxious to get the post and secretly expected it; James Grafton Rogers, able and hard-working Assistant Secretary of State; and Orie L. Phillips of Albuquerque, a Judge of the Circuit Court of Appeals.

Subsequently Hoover asked Stone what he thought of these men and went over their chances of getting Senate approval. Stone said nothing about their qualifications as compared with Cardozo, but laid stress on the fact that while it might be possible to obtain the votes to put any of them through, the naming of Cardozo not only would bring instantaneous confirmation, but would receive tremendous national applause. The argument convinced Hoover.

Justice Stone is one of the friendliest men in high public office in Washington. He loves to have people about him and is a chatty and delightful companion. He is fond of young people and is devoted to his former students. He follows their careers with fatherly interest and when any of them call on him, welcomes them with great enthusiasm.

*

"I cannot believe that the framers of the Fourteenth Amendment, or the States which ratified it, intended to leave us helpless to correct the evils of technological employment and excessive productive capacity which the march of invention and discovery has entailed. There must be power in the States and nation to remold through experimentation our economic practices to meet changing social and economic needs. . . . Denial of the right of such experimentation may be fraught with serious consequences to the nation."

This clarion declaration of militant economic democracy voiced by Justice Louis Dembitz Brandeis in his great dissent in the Oklahoma ice case epitomizes his character, philosophy and position in American affairs—the nation's affairs because Justice Brandeis is more than a powerful enunciator of legal doctrine.

There have been other enlightened and brilliant jurists on the Supreme Court—among the greatest of them, Brandeis' close friend Justice Holmes. But they were concerned above all else with propounding principle and law. Brandeis is not content with such a rôle.

He is the crusader of a social order, the defender, formulator and philosopher of economic democracy. There is nothing revolutionary about Brandeis' economic philosophy. He is an American economic fundamentalist, and the economic system he propounds is rooted deep in American tradition and history. He believes in competition, in the little fellow, in his right to a job, in his right to share the fruits of his labor and the wealth he produces.

But Brandeis is not content to remain on the sidelines, aloof from the turmoil of the political and economic struggle, merely upholding the right of a people to experiment to gain these rights. Holmes, gallant and stately knight that he is, proclaimed with reverberating voice the right of man to seek change. But having laid down that principle he stopped. He entered no camp; he remained removed from the fray always.

Not so Brandeis. To him, merely to proclaim the doctrine of liberty is not enough. He holds not only that people have a right to experiment, but he propounds a concrete program for them to follow. There is a profound distinction between the two positions. The first is that of the philosopher; the secon that of the crusader.

It is this historic rôle that Justice Brandeis fills in the life of the nation. It was as a crusader that he came to the Supreme Court over the bitter opposition and protests of entrenched wealth, and it is as a crusader that for sixteen years he has carved his mighty place as a jurist.

As a crusader and a great artist in the art of law, Brandeis is always the economic expert. His is the passion for concrete details, facts, facts, and ever more facts. Where the politician denounces with words, he annihilates with figures and logic. In the battles he waged for two decades against the financial wreckers of the New York, New Haven and Hartford Railroad, and for protective measures for labor, he fought not with invective but facts. He sought not the political platform, but the courts and legislatures. And he had the facts. He was ruthless in every case. He never gave quarter nor asked it. He was the most terrible cross-examiner of his time. When he finished with Sam Rea of the Pennsylvania Railroad, and Alfred H. Smith of the New York Central, in the famous Eastern Advance Rate case before the Interstate Commerce Commission, they left the stand hardly knowing their own names.

That was why, when President Wilson named Brandeis to the Supreme Court in 1916, the Elihu Roots, the Tafts, the Lowells held up their hands in horror and warned: "Dangerous radical."

Once before they had raised that cry when Wilson apponted Brandeis as Attorney General. And Wilson had withdrawn the appointment before their attack. But this time Wilson faced a difficult campaign for reëlection and he needed the Jewish vote. To get it he promised Louis Marshall, Samuel Untermyer and Charles R. Crane to appoint Brandeis to the Supreme Court. From this he could not recede.

The fight over Brandeis' confirmation was an epic struggle.

Every living former president of the American Bar Association opposed him. Taft publicly assailed the appointment. As the Senate approached the vote the outcome was in doubt. It was at this point that the Chicago *Tribune* carried a front-page story drawing a deadly parallel between Brandeis' legal career and that of the leaders of the bar who fought him. The article charged that every one of these men was motivated by a personal grievance. It showed that they had been arrayed against Brandeis in important cases, and had gone down to defeat before him.

The late Senator Oscar Underwood, Democrat from Alabama, had only recently come to the upper chamber from the House. He was a conservative, but of rigid impartiality and open-mindedness and because of this carried great weight with his colleagues. Underwood was still debating his position on the appointment when Elisha Hanson, then a member of the Washington staff of the *Tribune,* came to him with his paper's article.

Underwood was deeply impressed by the facts it presented. He asked Hanson to order ninety-six copies of the issue, and when they arrived he placed one on the desk of every member of the Senate. The result was that a number of Senators, who, like Underwood, were uncertain as to how they would vote, became convinced that the outcry against Brandeis was tainted, and voted for him.

One vote on this roll-call which aroused most comment was the unexpected "No" by Senator William S. Kenyon of Iowa. Kenyon, a militant Progressive, was one of the first to endorse Brandeis when his appointment was announced. The story of how he came to change his mind is this:

The Anti-Saloon League was one of the organizations which joined in the attack on Brandeis, charging him with being a "tool of the liquor interests." Its hostility arose from the fact that some years before, Brandeis had been employed as an attorney by Massachusetts brewers to put an end to a system of blackmailing which had grown up in the Legislature. It had become the practice of grafting law-makers to introduce drastic dry measures and threaten to press them unless bought off. These depredations finally became so onerous that the brewers refused to pay tribute longer, and secured Brandeis to make their fight. He exposed the system, drove the guilty legislators to cover, and put an end to the grafting.

Because of this connection, the drys, led by the Anti-Saloon League, attacked Brandeis; and Kenyon, a fanatical dry, was prevailed on to disregard his previous endorsement, and vote shoulder to shoulder with the reactionaries of the Senate against Brandeis' confirmation.

When President Wilson first offered the Supreme Court appointment to Brandeis, he had asked whether or not the jurist would accept it. And Brandeis, remembering how he had been forced to withdraw from the proffered attorney-generalship four years before, replied that he would answer that question after his confirmation.

So when the Senate fight was over, Brandeis slipped quietly up to the Senate at three-thirty in the afternoon and took the oath of office without even going through the formality of a reply to President Wilson.

Justice Brandeis once bemoaned the fact that William D. Mitchell, one of the best solicitors ever to appear before the Supreme Court, had become Attorney General, where he was doing a second-rate job. But probably Brandeis does not realize that he himself was chiefly responsible for Mitchell's appointment to the Cabinet.

It happened that Hoover, when the time approached for him to enter the White House, found himself in the same predicament Wilson had been in when he had withdrawn Brandeis' name as Attorney General. March 4th was approaching and he needed to complete his Cabinet. It happened also that in the previous summer Elisha Hanson was handling a Supreme Court land-grant case between a county and a

State, in which the attorney for the county wanted more time to file his brief, and which made it necessary to see one of the Justices of the Supreme Court to get an extension of time. Hanson wired Chatham, Massachusetts, asking if he could see Brandeis, and got a one-word reply: "Yes."

Brandeis granted the petition immediately, and then during the course of the ensuing conversation said he thought Mitchell was the best Solicitor General the country had ever had. He pointed out that Mitchell was brief and fair. He never wasted the court's time and he told the court when he thought the government was wrong.

Justice Holmes once told Mitchell: "I have always appreciated your fairness to your opponents."

Then as Mitchell's chest swelled, he added:

"Candor I have always thought was the best form of deception."

Early in February 1929 Hanson ran across George Akerson, Hoover's secretary, waving a telegram from Hoover at Miami asking for a list of nine prominent jurists from whom he might select his Attorney General. Hanson drew up the list. In sending it he took pains to stipulate why each candidate was listed, and after the name of William D. Mitchell he made a notation of the high praise given him by Justice Brandeis.

A day or two later Hoover announced the appointment of Mitchell as Attorney General.

Justice and Mrs. Brandeis live simply and rarely go out in the evening; but their modestly furnished apartment is visited by leaders in many walks of life who come for advice, counsel and inspiration.

Justice Brandeis is consciously and deliberately a teacher, particularly with young people, who adore and revere him. Always kindly and patient, he definitely seeks to pass on to the younger generation a point of view, a philosophy of life that may help them deal with personal and public problems in the future.

Each autumn Brandeis takes a new secretary from the graduating class of the Harvard Law School recommended to him by Professor Felix Frankfurter; and each spring he lets him go. These young men become disciples. A friend of the Justice not long ago remonstrated with him for putting himself to the trouble of breaking in a new secretary each year, but Brandeis brushed the personal inconvenience aside, observing: "It's good for me. It keeps me from getting lazy."

Through his friendships with hundreds of men and women in public and private life, Brandeis in his quiet and unobtrusive way wields a wider influence than any other Justice on the court.

Now seventy-five years old, Brandeis is tall, thin, slightly stooped but still strong, and he works as hard and indefatigably as ever. During the terms of the court he labors in a two-room suite on the floor above his apartment in the Brighton. He writes his opinions in pencil, correcting and rewriting a great deal, drawing not only on an exhaustive knowledge of the law, but on a vast fund of general information. When he has finished an opinion it is letter perfect, in forceful, clear English and in statement of fact. Justice Brandeis never has been tripped up on an error of law. Those who disagree with him must do so on point of view. They cannot do so on the facts.

During the summer, the Justice and Mrs. Brandeis reside at Oyster Pond, near Chatham on Cape Cod, not far from their dear friend Justice Holmes. The ties between the two men are close. When Holmes was on the bench they went to and from the capitol together every day and on walks in the late afternoon when the weather permitted. Since Holmes' retirement Brandeis visits him frequently and often accompanies him on his automobile rides and brief walks.

For years Brandeis urged Holmes to read more along economic and social lines. Holmes is a prodigious reader, but his tastes run to the classics and general literature. One of his favorite diversions is paper-backed French novels which he reads by the score, heaping them in piles on the floor of his library as he consumes them. So, to counteract this "low" literary taste, Brandeis once informed Holmes that he would send some worth-while material for summer reading.

Several weeks later a large box sent by the Library of Congress reached Holmes at his Massachusetts home. He had his servant open the lid and scanned the upper layer of books. They dealt with workmen's compensation acts, insurance laws, labor codes, and similar subjects. Holmes read the titles.

"Bob, put this box down in the cellar," he ordered his servant, and returned to the paper-backed novels. In the fall the box of books was returned to the Library.

Although no longer one of them, Justice Holmes still plays an important part in the lives of the Nine Old Men. He is a focal point, a common meeting ground, some one they all love, even two such diametrically opposite characters as McReynolds and Brandeis. They all come to see him, even Mrs. Mahlon Pitney, wife of the late Justice Pitney, who once told the aged friend of her husband about a burglary in her home. The robber had backed a truck up to the rear door and taken all the furnishings out in a most thorough manner. But the police caught him, Mrs. Pitney said, and put him in jail. There she went to visit him in his cell.

Mrs. Pitney talked at great length to Justice Holmes about the incident.

"I tried to find out how ever he had embarked on a career of crime," she explained. "I tried to point out the error of his ways and I hope I have done some good. I think I must have talked to him for two hours."

"Poor man, poor man," nodded Justice Holmes sympathetically.

For the first time in his ninety-odd years, Justice Holmes says he really is enjoying life. While on the court he complained that he had to work too hard. Once when he was about to drive out to Winchester, Virginia, to see the famous apple blossoms, a court messenger arrived with an opinion to be read.

"The God damned fertility of my colleagues will kill me," he said, and cancelled his trip.

Now he has plenty of time to read, to see the buds and the flowers which are his most absorbing interest every spring, and to reminisce about Civil War days. After he was wounded, Holmes tells his friends, life was much easier. When he returned to the front he did not want to oust the man who had taken his place, so he joined the General Staff, where he said you could have all you wanted to drink and where they passed around great big cocktails to start you off every morning. The General Staff also got champagne, at least it looked like champagne, and Holmes always gave it the benefit of the doubt.

As for prohibition:

"I don't know that it's a good thing," Holmes told some friends, "but we have started with it, and it would be a bad thing to change now. For my part I'm willing to wait a hundred years before it is changed."

He was then ninety-one.

Thus the old Justice radiates the joy of life.

Another fast friendship on the court in recent years was that between Brandeis and Chief Justice Taft. This was not always so.

As counsel in the famous Ballinger case, Brandeis had disclosed how Taft, then President, had deliberately lied to protect his political henchman. Brandeis did not attack Taft, he merely revealed the facts; but Taft harbored a bitter resentment against him and vigorously opposed his appointment to the court.

Not until the two men met in a pouring rain did they become reconciled. In his early years on the Supreme Court Justice Brandeis lived in a downtown apartment. Every day, just before dinner, served punctually at seven, he was in the habit of taking a brisk fifteen-minute walk. One rainy, misty evening he was hurrying back to his home when, in turning a corner, he bumped into a large, portly gentleman who also was walking hurriedly.

Brandeis looked up, but before he could say anything the other man held out his hand and said:

"Isn't this Mr. Brandeis? I am Mr. Taft. I once did you a great injustice, Mr. Brandeis. I am sorry."

"Thank you, Mr. Taft."

"Good night, Mr. Brandeis."

"Good night, Mr. Taft."

CHAPTER THREE

THE WIZARDS OF RECONSTRUCTION

OGDEN L. MILLS and Eugene Meyer are the right and left bower of the Hoover Administration. They are the President's two financial trumps. They excel at almost everything except the ability to win tricks. In this they do not harmonize. Mills is a jack of clubs; Meyer a jack of diamonds. Their chief can play one suit or the other; he cannot trump with both.

If the game were poker, it would be another matter. Mills and Meyer would make perfect openers and give the President something to draw on. But Mr. Hoover is not good at poker. He does not know how to bluff and he lacks a poker face. So much of the effectiveness of his two jacks is wasted.

This does not detract from the fact, however, that Mills and Meyer are two extremely capable gentlemen and that most of the financial thinking of the Hoover Administration has come from them. And although the President cannot trump with both, both, strangely enough, have much in common.

One a Jew the other a Gentile, both recognize only money as their god—and their god can do no wrong. Ambition is the key to the character of both men. Both come from families which base their tremendous fortunes on the old boom days of California. Both took their bearings in their early twenties and set a life course from which they have never deviated. And what has held both of them to that course is the conviction that their god can do no wrong; that the Mellons, the Millses and the Meyers are dedicated to the cause of guiding the financial destinies of the nation regardless of the fact that in so doing their own great fortunes amass greater volume like a snowball rolling downhill.

One a Yale man, the other Harvard, both are leaders in the Dance of the Depression. Both give large dinner parties and large sums to charity. Both are passionately devoted to their families. Both have the utmost contempt for Congressmen, than whom, in their opinion, there is no lower species of humanity. Both are hard fighters, cold-blooded, calculating. Both have played an important part in Mr. Hoover's chief economic moves—the Moratorium, the Relief of Big Business, and Reconstruction. Both have offered the same financial wizardry for Reconstruction—increased credit to private industry in order to stimulate production. And both forgot the fundamental fact that increased production is useless as long as the man at the bottom lacks the wherewithal to buy the stuff which the factories produce.

Despite all these common denominators, Mr. Hoover has not been able to use his two financial trumps in the same game. Working together, they do not quite click.

*

One evening during the height of the Dance of the Depression, Paul May, Ambassador of Belgium, entertained at dinner. Son of a prominent family of jewelers, and the only Jew in Belgium's diplomatic service, May is a gentleman of taste, culture and a none too subtle sense of humor. After dinner, some of the guests danced; others played bridge. Among the bridge players, but at separate tables, were May and Eugene Meyer. Presently the shift of winners brought the two men together at the same table.

"Now, Eugene," said May gleefully, "we'll show them what two Jews can do."

Eugene forced a laugh, but it was very forced, for there is nothing he likes less than being reminded of his Hebraic origin. And yet the fact that he is a Jew probably is responsible for the two things which count most in Eugene Meyer's life. One of these is happiness of his family life; the other is the success of his work.

Meyer's family had its origin in Alsace, and like some of the great Jewish banking families—Kuhn, Speyer, Schroeder—is equally at home in Germany, France, England or the United States.

One of Meyer's great uncles was Grand Rabbi of Paris. His father was a Jewish merchant who came to California via the Isthmus and a mule's back, settled in Los Angeles when it was little more than a village, married a woman who had sailed round the Horn, and later became the San Francisco and New York representative of that great firm of French Jewish bankers, Lazard Frères.

Behind the family, as with most Jewish families, was a long history of struggle and persecution which had planted in the Meyer blood a dogged determination, which with the typical shrewdness of the race, surmounted all obstacles and marched grimly toward its chosen goal. Behind the Meyers, also, as with most Jewish families, was a tradition of happy marriages, of devotion between parents and children.

Eugene Meyer profited from both of these. Early in life he selected one goal, and having achieved it, he selected another. The first goal was that of a successful investment banker, and he prepared for it with foresight and precision. Transferred from the University of California to Yale when his family moved to New York, Meyer went to Europe after graduation and spent two years in the counting houses of his father's relatives in Paris, London, Berlin and Frankfurt, learning all that generations of experience in international banking could give him. Then after four years of apprenticeship in the New York office of Lazard Fréres, he left the parental roof and set up business as Eugene Meyer, Jr. and Company, investment bankers.

Some seventeen years later, Meyer disclosed to Gutzon Borglum the second goal of his life.

"If you want to get ahead in politics," he advised, "keep out until you have made your pile. That's what I did. Once you have money, everything opens to you."

Meyer by that time had made his fortune as an investment banker, resigned all his directorships in big business, and had come to Washington as an advisor to the War Industries Board. Borglum, who later achieved even greater fame in his skirmishes with the State of Georgia over the Confederate memorial on Stone Mountain, was at that time achieving modest notoriety as an investigator of war-time aircraft scandals and enjoying it so much that he thought of abandoning art for politics.

Meyer and Borglum had known each other for many years. In fact it is to Borglum that Meyer chiefly owes his marriage to Agnes Elizabeth Ernst. He met her at one of Borglum's art exhibits. One of the most beautiful women in New York, many of her friends were skeptical regarding her marriage to a Jew and many continued to be skeptical even afterwards. But Borglum was not, and egged the couple on.

Eugene Meyer would have been an excellent husband and father no matter whom he had married. Family instincts run strong in his blood. When his younger brother Edgar was lost with the *Titanic,* Mrs. Edgar Meyer, who for a long time refused to leave him to take to a lifeboat, was left an estate of $185,063. Eugene was not as wealthy then as he is now, but he increased it to $513,063.

And as time has passed and Meyer's own family has increased to four daughters and a son, he has become prouder and fonder, and his wife almost as beautiful as in her younger days, until the happiness of the Meyer family has come to be something of a tradition in Washington society; so that well-meaning mothers-in-law hold them up to difficult sons-in-law with the discouraged sigh: "Now if you could only be like the Meyer family."

Social Washington has not always been as hospitable to Eugene Meyer as it is now. It has never listed him in the Social Register and there was a time when it was much too busy to notice a gauche young Jewish banker just down from New York. Eugene is inclined toward pomposity, is decidedly argumentative, so discreet in his conversation that he is boring, and loves to answer questions by asking others in return. Washington will tolerate this from the Governor of the Federal Reserve Board, but not from a young Jew just starting to get ahead in political life, even if he does have a charming wife and millions of dollars. So it fell to old Mrs. James Wadsworth, to whom Eugene was introduced by the everpresent Gutzon Borglum, to be his social godmother in those first days in Washington.

To-day the Meyers entertain frequently and lavishly. They entertain for their children and also because Eugene still suffers slightly from the inferiority complex common to his race and loves the feeling of social security inspired by a seven-course dinner, a sprinkling of ambassadorial guests and champagne. All Washington scrambles for opportunities to entertain the Meyers now. In fact those whom Eugene once had difficulty in getting to listen to him now hang on every word the chairman of the Federal Reserve utters—even about himself.

Eugene's love of his family is the key to what few activities he enjoys outside his home and office. One of these is the Madeira School where his daughters were educated. He is the institution's chief director and one of the heaviest contributors to its endowment. Busy as he is, he can always find time for anything concerning the school's welfare.

Some time ago, Mrs. Lucy Wing, who even more than Eugene Meyer, is responsible for its success, was endeavoring to raise enough money to transfer the school from Washington to a site on the upper Potomac just a few miles from the city. Her chief director fully approved, but insisted that she go at the thing in a businesslike way, raising the money by selling a $300,000 bond issue. And every two or three days he would telephone, urging her to get busy and sell the bonds, until this got to be a sort of parent-and-child nagging act. Mrs. Wing, greatly harassed and much discouraged, finally unearthed a broker who would take over the entire bond issue, but at a discount of twelve per cent.

Calling a meeting of the directors, she explained her complete failure to sell the bonds except through the agency, and announced that if the directors did not like her failure she would pay the discount herself or else resign.

Very quietly at this point spoke up the director who had hounded her for weeks:

"Lucy, I'll loan you the $300,000," he said. "I don't want you to pay twelve per cent."

Meyer had known all along that as a last resort he would put up the money, but true to the banking instincts which amassed his family fortune he wanted every possible effort expended before he got into action.

Eugene Meyer likes to affect a culture which he never actually has had the time to acquire. He does this partly because of his desire to be preëminent in all things, and partly to keep up with his wife, who goes in for such out-of-the-way cultural activities as Chinese art and Mayan architecture. Eugene's struggle frequently results in the most incongruous friendships and the most amusing incidents. One of the Meyer friends, for instance, is Theresa Helburn, of Theatre Guild fame. Another is Felix Frankfurter. Meyer goes in for the first because his eldest daughter, Elizabeth, seeks fame on the stage. He goes in for the second partly because he has underneath, an almost completely smothered, but still discernible streak of the same outlook on life that made Felix Frankfurter champion Sacco and Vanzetti. Even if this were not true, however, Meyer would cultivate Frankfurther because he thinks it is the cultured thing to do.

One day Frankfurter introduced Meyer to a young man whom he described as an ardent admirer and student of Alexander Meiklejohn, former president of Amherst.

"My boy," said Meyer, putting his arm around the young man's shoulder, "you must never lose the things President Meiklejohn gave you."

It developed later that Meyer scarcely had an inkling of what Meiklejohn stood for, but it was the right thing to say and the right time to say it; so he spoke with all the fervor and enthusiasm of one who had fought a death battle with those two former Amherst graduates, Calvin Coolidge and the late Dwight Morrow in preventing Meiklejohn's dismissal.

On another occasion, he was seated around an open fire with his wife and a close friend when the conversation turned to the Biblical character, Rebekah. Eugene launched forth with a diagnosis of the lady in as learned a manner as his great uncle, the Grand Rabbi of Paris. His wife restrained her mirth as long as she could and then burst into hoots of laughter. Eugene, in mock wrath, ordered her from the room.

"Now Eugene Meyer," reproved the friend, "you know that nine cases out of ten you don't really know anything about what you're saying. You just like to make people think you do."

It would be unfair, however, to give the impression that Eugene Meyer's only forte is finance. He has an excellent ear for music. He is not bad on the tennis court and cuts a very sportsmanlike figure on a horse. But where he really excels is at dominoes. And on the Congressional Limited en route to his large and robust family at Mt. Kisco you are almost sure to find Eugene Meyer every summer week-end seated beside a little table playing dominoes.

*

Aside from his family, Eugene Meyer lives only for his work. Regarding this, he is as cold and calculating as his opaque and glittering eyes. And he is as hard-boiled in government service as he was in private business. Perhaps more so. Five Senators once came to Meyer to urge the retention of a stenographer who was to be discharged, but Meyer dismissed him just the same.

Government service has become a fetish with Eugene. Having spent sixteen years amassing millions, he has definitely dedicated his life to public service. He does not care particularly whether he serves Republicans or Democrats. His first public office was in a Democratic Administration, and if he gets the opportunity he will serve under one again. His only ambition is to serve.

Therefore, having helped Calvin Coolidge in mopping up various complicated and embarrassing financial problems in the agricultural South and West, and having done what he could to bring about the election of his friend Herbert Hoover, Meyer was irked, to put it mildly, when the newly elected President failed to take advantage of Meyer's financial ability and his perpetual availability for public office.

Eugene was not only irked, but his pride was hurt. One of the most penetrating keys to his character is pride. He wants to be preëminent in all things, his children, the school they attend, his wife, his home, his saddle horses and also his appearance.

Once when Dr. Erich Salomon was in his office, about to take a series of photographs for *Fortune Magazine,* Eugene suddenly held up his hand.

"Wait," he said.

Going to the other end of the long room he pulled aside a green curtain, sat down before a concealed mirror and toilette set and carefully brushed his hair.

"Go ahead," he said, coming back to the camera.

More particularly, Eugene has been proud of his job. He has been content to perform mediocre jobs and be proud of the fact that he performed them with distinction. But to be left high and dry with no job at all was a distressing blow to his pride. He could not go back to a private business which long before had begun to bore him. So he sat in Washington and Mt. Kisco and played dominoes while his friends said, "Poor Eugene," and called Herbert Hoover all sorts of names.

Only once before in his service under two administrations had Eugene Meyer ever been without a job. That was in 1920, when David F. Houston, Secretary of the Treasury under Wilson, too mindful of big business demand to "take the Government out of business," had abruptly terminated the War Finance Corporation of which Meyer was managing director. For one year Eugene led a life of aimless idleness until Warren G. Harding came to his rescue by reviving the Corporation.

It was Bernard Baruch who was Eugene's godfather in first securing his appointment in government service, just as it was Bernard Baruch who has waved the magic wand in a good many other successes Meyer has achieved. Baruch took Meyer in under his financial wing when the latter was just starting out, and some of the tips he received from the all-knowing "Barney" helped materially in sending the Meyer fortunes up the success ladder.

Eugene did not need a great deal of coaching, however. He is an expert at reading balance sheets, has an uncanny aptitude for predicting the future, plays his cards close up and makes up for a woeful lack of imagination by doing a great deal of reading. And Eugene's assortment of literature would make some of his banking friends, most of whom never open anything heavier than a murder mystery, brand him as a dangerous radical.

When Baruch came to Washington to head the War Industries Board during the War, he brought his young friend down as adviser on non-ferrous metals. Meyer's first purchase of a non-ferrous metal—45,000,000 pounds of copper—saved the government around $7,000,000. Copper at that time was selling for as high as 37 cents a pound, but Meyer and Baruch called in their friend Daniel Guggenheim and suggested that an appeal be made to the copper men to set an example to other business executives by filling the government's initial needs at a lower price. After some dickering the copper men agreed to sell at the average price during the past ten years, and at this figure—16.6739 cents a pound—they delivered 20,000,000 pounds to the army and 25,000,000 pounds to the navy.

With big business making tremendous war-time profits in every other field of industry, Meyer could not keep the copper men in line after that purchase, but he continued to make what economies possible as adviser with the War Industries Board until 1918, when he was made managing director of the War Finance Corporation. In this job and later as head of the Federal Farm Loan Board, Meyer incurred the unremitting enmity of certain congressional leaders who have done their best to block his senatorial confirmation every time he is appointed to a new office—which is often.

One factor which got him into trouble was his belief that money loaned by the government should be returned. Another was the contention that in buying and selling bonds for the War Finance Corporation, he used his own brokerage office in New York, collected a brokerage free of $2.00 for every thousand dollars' worth of bonds handled, and when a congressional committee got wind of this, had auditors work at night changing the accounts.

The charge was a serious one and a Select Committee to Investigate Destruction of Government Bonds reported to the House of Representatives March 2, 1925, as follows:

"During the period of these transactions and up until a quite recent date the managing director of the War Finance Corporation, Mr. Eugene Meyer, in his private capacity maintained an office at No. 14 Wall Street, New York City, and through the War Finance Corporation sold about $70,000,000 in bonds to the Government and also bought through the War Finance Corporation about $10,000,000 in bonds and approved the bills for most if not all of these bonds in his official capacity as managing director of the War Finance Corporation.

"When these transactions just referred to were disclosed to the committee in open hearing the managing director appeared before the committee and stated that while the books of the War Finance Corporation disclosed the fact that commissions were paid on these transactions, they were in turn paid over to the brokers, selected by the managing director, who executed the orders issued by his brokerage house; and immediately after this disclosure to the committee the managing director employed Ernst & Ernst, certified public accountants, to audit the books of the War Finance Corporation, who did, upon the completion of their examination of these books, report to the committee that all moneys received by the brokerage house of the managing director had been accounted for.

"While simultaneously with the examination being made by the committee, the certified public accountants, heretofore referred to, were nightly carrying on their examination, it was discovered by your committee that alterations and changes were being made in the books of record covering these transactions, and when the same was called to the attention of the treasurer of the War Finance Corporation he admitted to the committee that changes were being made. To what extent these books have been altered during this process the committee has not been able to determine.

"Notwithstanding the fact that there was no authority for the purchase of bonds above par, such purchases were made. The dates of purchase of bonds as given by the Secretary of the Treasury, which would have shown that about \$24,000,000 had been paid by the Government for bonds in excess of the highest market rate for the various days on which it was alleged that the purchases were made were found to be incorrect. It was also found that the dates given by the War Finance Corporation and the Federal Reserve Bank of New York City, N. Y., did not agree and that the records of the former also vary as to dates of purchase. For example, the dates furnished by the Federal Reserve Bank statements were sometimes given as the date of delivery of the bonds, sometimes the date of the transaction, and sometimes the date on which the transaction was reported. The dates given by the records of the War Finance Corporation were equally confusing. One transaction in the books of the War Finance Corporation has journal entry as of November 15, 1918, a sub-entry in the journal as of November 12, the detail sheet is dated November 11, and the dates of purchase given as November 8 and 9. The market prices varied each day. Only a complete audit will disclose how nearly correct is the loss of $24,000,000 which the dates given by the Secretary of the Treasury show."

As to Meyer's guilt in this transaction, opinions in the House of Representatives differ. Representative Strong of Kansas, staunch Administration supporter and a member of the special investigating committee, claims that "Mr. Eugene Meyer came before that committee and proved to them absolutely that every dollar of that $2.00 per thousand was paid to brokers for the purpose of buying bonds, and he did not receive a red cent of it."

Representative Steagall, Democrat, now chairman of the Banking and Currency Committee, believes that Meyer "was not guilty of misappropriating any funds that came into his hands or violation of the law except the technical provisions of the statutory regulations under which he acted."

Representative La Guardia, fighting Republican independent, who made an issue of the report when Mr. Meyer's name came up as a member of the Reconstruction Finance Corporation, declared: "I will not say Mr. Eugene Meyer was dishonest in this thing, but he did what the law said he could not do. What necessity was there to employ a broker to buy those bonds? The mere call on the member banks of the Federal Reserve system would have brought in all the bonds they wanted."

La Guardia also charged that while the Special Investigating Committee was examining the altered reports; "Along came the end of the session, and when they asked to be continued it was denied, and the committee died, and this hearing ... with the exception of Volume I has never been printed."

Representative McFadden, chairman of the investigating committee, said that "at the most interesting phase" of the inquiry certain "influences" had been brought to bear on the leaders of the House to throttle the probe.

"We were compelled to stop right in the midst of the examination," McFadden said.

McFadden, however, is doubtless prejudiced, having long been bitter against Meyer for the part he claims Eugene played in withholding credit from some of McFadden's banks in Northern Pennsylvania—following which McFadden was indicted by a grand jury.

Unquestionably Meyer made no money out of the transactions in government bonds. Unquestionably also his brokerage friends did, which is the natural penalty paid by a country which puts wealth in control of its destinies. For wealth plays ball with wealth, and big business, once seated round the council table of government, instinctively calls the cards that those who know its game shall profit most.

Illustrative of the paradoxes of public life, the other charge against Eugene Meyer—that of making borrowers repay what they were lent by the government—has caused him much more difficulty than the one just referred to. Meyer, shortly after the War, had become a financial trouble man for the Harding and Coolidge Administrations and was shifted from one bad financial mess after another. And what aroused the Mid-Western opposition against him was the fact that in all of these financial activities he insisted upon hard-boiled business methods. He was willing to let the brokers in Wall Street make a commission of $2.00 per thousand on handling government bonds, but he was not willing to let the farmers, or the politicians who claimed they represented the farmers, keep any part of the money they received. The War Finance Corporation, when Meyer wound up its affairs, turned back to the Treasury all but $10,000 of the $500,000,000 original principal it had borrowed, together with a profit of $64,352,768. Later Meyer subjected the Federal Farm banks to a thorough house-cleaning. He had some officers indicted. He got some convicted and sentenced to the penitentiary. Some avoided exposure of incompetency by resignation. Stricter accounting systems, and a uniform method of bookkeeping were established and misleading advertising was eliminated.

Meyer was high-handed, autocratic and beyond the pale of

political pressure. Nothing moved him except economic soundness and business efficiency. In the end he had put the Federal Farm Loan Banks on a sound basis, but he had also aroused the opposition of small but vociferous groups in the Middle West.

"A Judas Iscariot," "a decoy duck and trader sent in by the Wall Street crowd," were some of the epithets which Senator Brookhart hurled at him.

"An ordinary tin-pot bucket-shop operator up in Wall Street.... Not even a legitimate banker," Huey Long of Louisiana took up the cry.

Sweeping aside the superficiality of the Brookharts and the Longs, there are two outstanding points in Eugene Meyer's pre-depression service which have direct bearing upon his present efforts to succor the nation. The first of these is the fact that he was one of the few who predicted a slump immediately after the War and urged the Wilson Administration to take steps to prepare for it. The second is the fact that all of the depression remedies which Meyer has put forward run along the same identical channel of loaning more and more money, regardless of where the money eventually must come from.

When, in May 1920, Houston suspended the activities of the War Finance Corporation, Eugene Meyer, its managing director, was the only one who objected. His own objection was not the fact that he had divorced himself from a private investment business and had just settled down to a comfortable career of perpetual office holding at the munificent salary of one dollar per annum. He argued that after every war must come a period of deflation and falling prices and that instead of taking the government out of business, the period immediately after the War was exactly the time to keep the War Finance Corporation functioning in order to ease the fall. And there were many other people, who, without working it out in black and white, arrived at the same general conclusion.

So the summer of 1920 saw Meyer touring the country as a

private citizen lecturing agricultural communities on the importance of reviving his Corporation, and receiving genuine support. By the next winter, what Meyer had prophesied, began to take place: the first wave of post-war deflation struck, and shortly after Warren G. Harding took the oath of office, he revived the War Finance Corporation.

Meyer immediately began pumping credit into agriculture. His idea was that if you convinced the country that there was enough credit behind agriculture, confidence would be restored, and food would not be dumped on the market at rock-bottom prices. The plan seemed to work. Later President Coolidge called upon him to head an emergency cotton committee to prevent the record 1926 crop of 17,977,374 bales from being dumped on the market. Meyer packed his bag, visited Raleigh, Atlanta, New Orleans, Dallas—the great cotton centers of the South—and organized the bankers and business men into corporations to hold 4,000,000 bales of cotton off the market.

Again the plan worked—at least it gave every appearance of working. Of course it was a fact that the carry-over from cotton bulged the warehouses of the South more than ever before and that the basic problem of crop diversification in the South was not solved, but these points escaped attention in the general inflation of Mr. Coolidge's much vaunted prosperity, and Mr. Meyer was hailed as a great man.

So it was not unnatural that when Herbert Hoover finally realized prosperity was not just around the corner and that the passive policy of the Federal Reserve Board under Governor Roy Young would have to be replaced with something more positive, he called on the man who had acquired the greatest kudos in pulling people out of previous depressions.

Thus it was that Eugene Meyer who had been twiddling his thumbs with increasing impatience on the side-lines, suddenly found himself leading the prosperity revivers as governor of the Federal Reserve Board.

*

THE PICTURE of Ogden Mills, become the chief financial trump of the Hoover Administration, is painted against a long, vivid and most unusual background. In 1840, the three Mills brothers from Oswego, New York, started for California and gold. Two of the boys went overland, but Darius Ogden, the grandfather of the present Secretary of the Treasury, took his $6,000 savings from the local bank where he worked, invested them in tents, picks, shovels and frying pans, and carried them around Cape Horn to the West Coast where he proceeded by diligence, fair play and good economics to amass a small fortune in attending the wants of the Forty-Niners. From these small beginnings grew the Mills Bank of San Francisco, the Comstock Lode, the Santa Fe Railroad and half a dozen other noteworthy undertakings in railroad stock and timberland, the sum of which netted Grandfather Darius several million dollars and the ability, after thirty years of pioneering, to retire to New York and buy up everything but the Statue of Liberty and the Brooklyn Bridge, including a safe and irreproachable perch near the top of New York's social ladder.

From this well-chosen pinnacle the Mills were destined, like the Vanderbilts, the Whitneys and the Astors, to make an effective sortie into the world of affairs. A daughter strengthened and enriched the family crest, as well as the family coffers, by marriage to Whitelaw Reid and, as Mrs. Reid, cut a memorable figure on two continents, while a son, Ogden, brought into the family a new pipe line of blue blood by taking unto himself as wife Ruth Livingston, thrice greatgranddaughter of New York's illustrious Robert Livingston. Neither of these branches of the family had any difficulty in financing any adventures they might undertake—social, political or industrial—out of the $41,000,000 fortune left them by Darius Ogden Mills, one time Oswego bank clerk.

Into this golden circle on August 23, 1884, was born at Newport, Rhode Island, at the height of the social season, a sturdy boy with a large nose and a pair of unusually bright blue eyes. After the usual tutoring, young Ogden, like nearly every other rich man's son went to Harvard, but, somewhat unlike many of them, actually took degrees in both arts and the law. Thereafter he shocked the entire family out of about ten years' growth by rushing into politics by way of the ward-heeler route—then very much in vogue, but then, as now, regarded as distinctly vulgar. Somehow it seemed a startling innovation for a product of the Mills and Livingston families, with one sister married to Banker Henry Carnegie Phipps and another to the Earl of Grannard, to be running around New York ringing door bells and standing at polling places as a solicitor and poll watcher.

But Ogden had his unusually bright eyes fixed on a goal and he persisted. In 1912, much to the secret amusement of the family, he was badly beaten for Congress by his Democratic opponent, John C. Carew. Two years later, with better luck, he got himself elected to the New York State Senate, and afterwards went to France where he served as a captain throgout the war.

Somebody must have kept the home fires burning for Ogden, because he returned from overseas to be elected the first New York State Commander of the American Legion and to slide gracefully into Washington in the year 1920 along with Mr. Harding and the Boys from Ohio, as the representative of the High-Hat Seventeenth New York District. In the succeeding six years, he served what must have been for him a painful apprenticeship among the House rabble, and, for all his flair for statistics and facts, found himself the poor little rich boy of the party, cordially envied where he was not actually disliked, good-naturedly tolerated where he was not acrimoniously repulsed.

Of course he could have joined the relatively silent and unquestionably correct stuffed shirts, along with such scions of wealth and respectability as Piatt Andrew, Dick Wigglesworth, Bob Bacon and Dick Aldrich. His silk-stocking district, which required only a dignified speech on rare occasions and a conservative vote at all times, would not have objected.

Instead he seldom missed an opportunity in committee room or on the floor to sound off in a high-pitched booming voice in which disdain for the social and intellectual inferiority of his colleagues was all too evident. If there was a more unpopular member of the House of Representatives at that time none of his former associates remembers his name.

Gradually, however, he did make an impression, if not for affability and warmth, for his ability, integrity and independence, and in 1926, he was chosen by his fellow New York Republicans, in convention assembled, to lead another forlorn hope against Alfred E. Smith.

The hope might not have been so forlorn had not all the hereditary encumbrances of a multimillionaire snob been pitted against all the popular appeal of an astute and able East Side politician. Sixteen years before, the Republicans had ventured the wealthy and aristocratic Henry Lewis Stimson against the experienced Tammany candidate, John A. Dix —and they should have learned their lesson. "Little Oggie," as Mills was promptly dubbed, provided not even a good opening round for the incomparable Al. He straddled on prohibition, and although as wet as the Atlantic Ocean, declared "milk was more important than whisky." He raised a milk-scandal issue against New York City and not only offended the dairy interests in upper New York State but failed to prove his case when his laboratory tests were repudiated by the authorities quoted. And finally he put both feet in a mess from which he never was to extricate himself, when, in the course of an argument with Al over some figures, he declared, "There is no truth in this man Smith either in private or in public life."

The always expensive, and in this case annihilating, game of personalities was about the most stupid and dangerous thing Mills could have indulged in—especially in view of a recent divorce and a pretty gay record for nocturnal escapades. There were some who had not yet forgotten the time Ogden Livingston Mills had wandered out of a New York-

Washington Pullman at Baltimore, clad in white tie and tails, been picked up by police walking down the tracks near the Bolton Street Freight Station and was thrown into a cell for a brief period, despite the fact that he gave his identity as a Congressman from New York.

Anyway, this was the opening Smith wanted, and Alfred Emmanuel waded in with his "Great White Throne" speech which literally ripped the hide off "Little Oggie" and left him panting for breath until the last vote was counted on Election Day.

Four months later, President Coolidge picked up the shattered bits from under a 250,000 adverse majority and put them together as Under-Secretary of the Treasury.

*

ONE HEARD a lot around Washington, after the New York political deluge, about "the new Mills." Ex-enemies around Capitol Hill said he was a chastened man. They said he had come out of his shell, had become ingratiating, tolerant, affable, democratic. Newspapermen covering the Treasury rated him as able, candid, honest and approachable.

While Under-Secretary of the Treasury, much of this undoubtedly was true. Mills always has had many admirable qualities. For one thing, he has worked hard, very hard, where he could just as easily have loafed on the job. For another thing, he has had a passion for facts and statistics, spending many a night with Treasury actuaries poring over them as an old book-worm would gloat over precious tomes. He has had courage and independence. He opposed the soldiers' bonus and had the temerity to come out unmistakably for Herbert Hoover when that appeared an unhealthy thing to do politically in New York. He also kept the conduct of such business as came before him as Under-Secretary of the Treasury singularly free from partisan politics and special favors. In one case he refused even a small favor of a clerk's transfer to a life-long friend. He is said to have made it a rule when he entered the Treasury to attend to the public business and to keep his fingers out of patronage and prohibition, and to have done a fairly clean job in the way of living up to it.

And as Under-Secretary he had been a very human person and a good sport against the almost invincible handicaps of tremendous wealth, the necessarily stilted environment that goes with it and a naturally retiring disposition. He is deeply sentimental, preserving with pride and loving care the old desk, clock and pipe of his pioneer grandfather, and carrying to this day the leather brief-case he used during the World War, marked "Captain Mills." He is generous with his money, as he can well afford to be, but he keeps his acts of generosity well concealed. He likes any good sporting proposition, whether it is a race horse, a yacht or a snappy game of poker. He owns a fine racing stable, can fall from a horse as gracefully as the Prince of Wales and recently purchased the contract of Hank Mills, celebrated Colorado jockey for $10.000. He has a perfectly equipped yacht, the *Avalon,* on which he delights to gather a company of friends and some books and some good Burgundy and explore the azure green islands of the Adriatic. And to the reports that he "plays a card game in which the essential arts are an instantaneous insight into your adversaries' mind and an equally instantaneous mobilization of your own intellectual powers," he says: "I must admit I'm keen about poker." One of the most prominent things on his mantelpiece is a large, personally inscribed picture of the man to whom he has probably lost the largest amount of money—Jack Garner, old friend, political adversary and champion poker player of the House.

Mills' sense of humor is not anything startling, but it is generally adequate. Once when criticized for going to France on a French boat, he said he went on a boat where he could be "accommodated"—and recommended that the prohibitionists "dry up the land before they started on the ocean."

His home life, for many years frustrated as a result of his divorce from the haughty Margaret Rutherford, later Lady Dukes and still later Princess Charles Michael Joachim Napoleon Murat, has become healthy and happy since he married Mrs. Dorothy Randolph Fell of Philadelphia in 1924, and has the companionship not only of a charming woman but of three equally charming step-children, Dorothy, a recent débutante, John, 21, who is starting an industrial career in Brooklyn, and Philip or "Tiny," aged eleven. The Millses have, of course, a dignified New York mansion at Fifth Avenue and 69th Street as well as a Newport villa, but in Washington they are the tenants of the American Ambassador to France, Walter E. Edge. Here they entertain on a scale commensurate with the Mills' millions, although Mrs. Mills did make the depression an excuse for reducing servants, until her husband, just before one dinner party remarked: "Dorothy there are only ten servants in the house; never before in my life have we had fewer than fifteen."

Every morning to this house in 18th Street a physical trainer goes to give Mills a rigorous round of boxing and setting-up exercises before he has his orange juice, toast and coffee and leaves for the office at 9:15. And on very rare occasions when he isn't sitting late at his desk planning new moves for Herbert Hoover, Mills slips out to a nearby golf course for a round of golf in not more than ninety. In spite of this, he continues to take on weight and doesn't like it.

Long before the actual date on which he took the oath of office as Secretary of the Treasury, Ogden L. Mills had taken over the reins from the old gentleman under whom it has been said that three Presidents have served, and was driving the wild horses of Bond Issues and Tax Increases down Pennsylvania Avenue. The gradual eclipse of Mr. Mellon and the rise of Mr. Mills has been one of the outstanding features of the depression. The suave and unimpassioned former Secretary of the Treasury took none too kindly to the thinly veiled suggestions that he was approaching dotage and had to have his mental hat and overcoat held for him every day by his young and more vigorous understudy.

But between the two men, despite this fact, there existed a father-and-son relationship. "The Old Man," as Mills called him—although not to his face—had every confidence in the younger man's loyalty, and from the time the silk-stocking Congressman from Park Avenue stepped into the sacred temple of the nation's fiscal affairs he grew steadily in the esteem of his boss, so that eventually it was Mr. Mills who took the underground passage to the White House with important memoranda; it was Mr. Mills who conferred with leaders from the Hill; it was Mr. Mills who covered up as quickly as possible Mr. Mellon's garrulous slip about the sales tax; it was Mr. Mills who explained away as best he could Mr. Mellon's error of $723,000,000 in his 1932 budget estimates; it was Mr. Mills who got credit for the Department's new policy of short term bonds; and it was Mr. Mills who, with a hero worship rarely equaled since the days of Joe Tumulty, defended the Treasury Department and the Hoover Administration against any and all comers, high and low, big and little, no matter the day, hour or policy involved. For to this young scion of gold, silver and precious stones, the Republican Party is money—and money is king—and the king can do no wrong.

But while he was sustaining Mr. Mellon's waning reputation as the greatest Secretary of the Treasury since Alexander Hamilton, Little Oggie also was carving out a place for himself in the turbulent political and economic life of Herbert Hoover, and the latter was beginning to find him indispensable. This place was deepened when Mr. Mellon was out of the country for part of a year and when, to the amazement of all good Republicans and the discomfiture of the Mellon myth, the country did not go to the bow-wows—at least any faster than it had been going. Instead, Mr. Mills stepped in—or rather jumped in—threw his marvelous array of statistics and his indefatigable energy into the breach, and almost overnight came to be a most—if not indeed the most—important figure in the Administration's attempt to turn the tide of the depression. He had a wonderful opportunity—and opportunity didn't have to knock twice on Little Oggie's door. It was Little Oggie, who, together with the State Department and the late Dwight W. Morrow, persuaded the President to declare the now famous and futile Hoover Moratorium, a declaration which precipitated a month of wrangling with the French over the details of the debt holiday. During this period, Secretary Mellon was ordered up to Paris from his pleasant villa in the South of France, and Secretary Stimson was en route to Europe. Hoover, however, had no illusions about either of them. He pinned his confidence on the young man whom he had come to rely on most, and during those days, Little Oggie went back and forth between the Treasury basement and the east wing of the White House like an animated shuttle installed in the dark little tunnel under East Executive Avenue.

The President sweated, fumed and raged. He became even more violently anti-French than during the London naval negotiations. Mills, on the other hand, was never more urbane and happy. His voice boomed over the trans-Atlantic telephone giving orders to his chief in London. The big Benson and Hedges cigars, made especially for him, were tilted at even a cockier angle. The close-fitting linen suits, the monogramed silk shirts were more limp than usual at the end of the day. But in spirit Mills was perpetually fresh and more effervescent than ever.

And having done more than any other one man to bring Mr. Hoover around to the moratorium idea—although a year too late—Mills now proceeded to convert the White House to the idea of its extension. The pilgrimage of M. Laval, Premier of France, was a step in this direction. Inspiration for the trip did not originate with Ogden, but in the end he took it over completely. It was Mills who drafted the Hoover-Laval communique, carried it personally to the French Premier for his approval, and served as chief interpreter during the conversations in a voice so loud that it could be heard outside the conference room.

Subsequently he inspired a meeting in the White House of the big chiefs and little braves of both the political parties for the purpose of sounding Congress out on an extension of the moratorium—and nothing else. As a piece of camouflage to make the moratorium extension less conspicuous, an extremely vague plan for a national credit corporation also was put forward; but Hoover knew, as did every one else that it was not necessary for him to consult Congress for that. And so when the moratorium extension idea fell out of the bag quite as if by accident and landed on the big toe of Senator William Edgar Borah, Mr. Mills, the originator of it all, was left to take care of the explosion which followed. The Old Man, Mr. Mellon, never opened his lips. Mr. Hoover, himself, had precious little to say. It was Little Oggie's party and he was left to pick up all the pieces.

And since Mr. Hoover had got into the habit of seldom tying his tie or shifting his feet without calling upon his Under-Secretary of the Treasury, it surprised no one when the President announced shortly after this that the third richest man in the United States would abandon his twelve-year reign over the Treasury and take up "important" duties at the Court of St. James. Ogden Livingston Mills, born with a silver spoon in his mouth, cradled in the lap of luxury, pampered in the boudoir of snobbery and fine conceit, finally had arrived at the Treasury of the United States, full panoplied from the brow of that tremendous Jove who rules the world—Money.

*

THERE are many who believe that Ogden Mills has passed through two distinct metamorphoses and is now in his third. The first was his period of blatant unpopularity in the House of Representatives. The second was his period of straightforward efficiency as Under-Secretary of the Treasury. The third is the present period of political deviousness which has been eminently unsuccessful.

Mills has now reverted to his ward-heeler days and gone political in a big way. In the inner circles of the party his efforts are hailed as the acme of finesse. He has come to be the innermost political adviser of the White House. But whenever the President acts on his advice he puts his foot in it.

This was especially true during the congressional debates on the 1932 tax bill. Mills devoutly believes that the wealthy are born to rule, the poor are born to serve and that taxes should not be imposed in such a way as to lessen the gap between them. In this he sees eye to eye with his chief in the White House, who once was given the suggestion by his young Secretary of War, Patrick J. Hurley, that eventually big incomes would have to be scaled down and small incomes up.

"Not if I can help it," remarked the President dryly.

Although Mills is sincere about this philosophy, he realizes that it is bad politics to be branded too publicly as a taxer of the working people, and therefore he dodged all over the political lot last winter trying to get the highly unpopular sales tax written into the tax bill without the White House getting the blame.

Even before the congressional bout began, however, Mills inadvertently had shown all the trumps—or rather lack of trumps—in his hand.

Andrew W. Mellon, still Secretary of the Treasury and sometimes addicted to moments of extreme candor, once discussed the sales tax with newspaper men, giving them all the arguments conceivable for the measure. A day or two later the same correspondents saw Mills and told him what his venerable chief had said.

"Did the Old Man say that?" observed Mills. "I'll have to keep an eye on him."

So Mills kept his eye on Mellon, his mouth shut about the sales tax, and at the same time adopted the strategy of sending new estimates to the House Ways and Means Committee and the Senate Finance Committee, engaged in writing the tax bill. These constantly revised estimates, interpreted even by Mills' kindliest critics, meant one of only two things:

Either the Secretary of the Treasury was such a bungler that he was not able to furnish Congress with correct estimates of the amount necessary to raise in taxes;

Or the Secretary of the Treasury was deliberately endeavoring to snare Congress into passing the sales tax by sending last minute estimates for additional funds which could be met in no other way than by a sales tax.

Whichever of these was correct, it was the second which Mills got credit for as far as a majority of Congress was concerned. The facts which led up to this conclusion were these:

At the start of the congressional session, the Treasury followed usual precedent by sending to Congress an estimate of the amount of money needed to run the government during the coming fiscal year—1933; and the House Ways and Means Committee, acting on these figures, proceeded to search for ways and means of raising this amount of money by taxing the people of the United States. Twice, however, after sending up the original estimates, Mills rushed to the capitol and told the committee that additional funds would be needed, thus playing into the hands of William Randolph Hearst and his hoop jumpers, John Nance Garner and Judge Charles R. Crisp, who were leading the fight for the sales tax. Even more upsetting were the revisions Mills repeatedly made of Treasury estimates of the yield which might be expected from different taxes.

Whenever a tax was proposed and seriously considered which Mills did not like, word was pretty sure to come from the Treasury that this tax would not result in as much revenue as the Department had first supposed. Time after time the committee thought it had gathered up enough revenue from a tax of a few cents here and a few cents there and some more some place else in order to balance the budget, only to have the Treasury re-check its estimates and decide that these taxes couldn't possibly fill the bill. There was very little the committee could do to disprove the complex calculations of the financial experts, and it finally wrote the sales tax into the bill and was assured by Mills that it had done right by the budget. However, the House itself was more concerned about doing right by the average citizen. It voted the sales tax down in no uncertain terms, amid sly suggestions from Administration spokesmen that the House had gone wild, had revolted, had imperiled the budget's earnestly sought state of balance.

The tax bill then went to the Senate, where it was sent to the Senate Finance Committee for study and revision. The first meeting of the committee was held on April 6th, and the first witness to be heard was the young and vigorous Secretary of the Treasury who gesticulated with pudgy fists and submitted new estimates of the amount needed in taxes to balance the budget. Following this, the committee began a new preparation of a tax bill to raise the money Mills said was needed.

Days of confusion followed in the committee room and on the floor of the Senate. The sales tax was not included in the tax bill. On May 8th, Mills again revised his estimates of the amounts certain taxes under consideration would yield.

By May 28th, the bill was virtually ready for passage in the Senate. According to the latest Treasury estimates at hand, it carried enough revenues to balance the budget. The bill was not passed on that day, however, because a few small details remained to be debated; so final action went over until Monday, the 30th.

Monday came and with it a dolorous announcement from Senator David Aiken Reed, spokesman for the White House and Treasury. The tax bill, he said, still fell short of balancing the budget by an amount somewhere between $250,000,000 and $300,000,000. Congress was considerably baffled, and put over passage of the bill once more.

That night Democratic members of the Finance Committee

were called to the White House for a conference with the President and his Secretary of the Treasury. The Democrats assured the President that they were just as anxious to balance the budget as he, if he would only tell them, once and for all, the exact amount of money needed. Mills said he couldn't furnish the figures just then but would have them ready early the next morning.

This he did at ten o'clock, when he announced that an additional $285,000,000 must be added to the tax bill if the budget was to be balanced; and finally, for the first time, he urged the committee to adopt the general sales tax on manufactured articles already vetoed by the House. His gesture came too late. Sales tax opponents, fearing just such a move had quietly circulated a written pledge among members of the Senate, and fifty-five—a safe majority—had signed it.

So, instead, the Senate Finance Committee agreed within an hour and a half to support the Connally amendment which provided for a tax on the sale of gasoline and another on electricity which would produce the necessary amounts. It was 11:20 when the committee reached this agreement and decided immediately to put the new taxes up to the Senate and pass the tax bill.

However, it then developed that Mr. Hoover and Mr. Mills were not in such a hurry to balance the budget, after all. Word leaked out that the estimates submitted by Mills that morning had been ready for several days but had been withheld to give Hoover time to prepare a special plea to Congress to do what it was then just about to do—balance the budget. Little Oggie had reverted to his ward-heeler days, and was trying to arrange a master-stroke for the President to deliver. The country had been clamoring for a balanced budget, and he figured that the President rather than Congress would get the credit for its final accomplishment if passage of the tax bill seemed to come only after a scourging, publicly administered, to a recalcitrant Senate by a righteously indignant executive.

Mills and Hoover had not believed that the Senate Finance

Committee would act so rapidly. So at 11:20, when the Finance Committee made its report of new taxes to raise $285,000,000 and balance the budget, Senator Hiram Bingham, staunch Administration supporter, scheduled to ask for an immediate vote on his motion to impose gasoline and electricity taxes, withdrew it until later. The reason soon became apparent. It was noised around the floor that President Hoover would appear in person at twelve noon, to urge the Senate to balance the budget. Obviously, therefore, no good Republican could move to balance the budget before the President arrived.

So Mr. Hoover delivered a speech which had all the earmarks of having been written by his financial right bower, and a few minutes later the Senate went ahead with the business it had already planned—adoption of the Connally amendment for gasoline, electricity and gas taxes, thereby balancing the budget.

The only result of Little Oggie's strategy was to arouse the antagonism of the Senate to such an extent that even such staunch Administration supporters as Reed Smoot of Utah thought it necessary to praise the fairness and nonpartisan coöperation of the Democrats who helped write the tax bill.

"I have been in the Senate nearly thirty years," said Smoot, "and I have never witnessed such unity of purpose as there has been in the passage of the revenue bill."

*

BEFORE the ill feeling aroused by Ogden and his chief over their vacillation on tax estimates had a chance to die away, the two plunged into another quarrel with Congress over methods of making that Frankenstein monster, the Reconstruction Finance Corporation, salve the woes of some one besides bankers, railroads and insurance men.

Early in May, President Hoover, who had for two years turned a deaf ear to all suggestions that the Federal Government must aid in reducing want and unemployment, underwent a sudden change of heart. His own friend, Colonel Arthur Woods, had tried to tell him, in 1930, that this must be done. Again, in 1932, two Democrats, Bernard Baruch and Owen D. Young came to Washington to urge the same policy. The President, however, continued to be uninterested. But Joseph T. Robinson, Democratic floor leader of the Senate, was. He promised action at once. So on May 11th Robinson announced that the Democrats proposed to support a vast relief bill containing funds which the States might borrow to relieve their needy, and more funds which the Reconstruction Finance Corporation might loan to make possible construction of various public enterprises and employment of many workmen. On May 12th, the President called Robinson to the White House and later in the day issued a statement in which, in effect, he put forward as his own the Robinson plan—the same one which had not interested him earlier. But he went a little farther. He proposed that loans be made to private firms contemplating construction work as well as to public agencies.

Around this additional clause there was to be a bitter controversy.

The proposal for loans to finance private building projects was one of Ogden Mills' ideas, and he at once became its chief champion on Capitol Hill, telling the Senate Banking and Currency Committee that it would provide much more employment than construction of public works. The President also championed it before Republican members of that committee whom he called to the White House to discuss the matter. And when Senator Couzens, millionaire ex-partner of Henry Ford, wanted to know just how these loans to private industry were to function, Mr. Hoover cited the case of John N. Willys, American Ambassador to Poland and head of the Willys-Overland Corporation. Mr. Willys had resigned his ambassadorship and was now willing to undertake a large construction project giving employment to many persons if he could obtain a loan from the Reconstruction Finance Corporation, President Hoover explained. But private industrial firms were not eligible for such loans. In the new bill, therefore, Mr. Hoover proposed to make them eligible.

Whereupon Senator Couzens hit the ceiling. He said that this kind of a dole to big business—helping one company with public funds while their competitors got none—was going entirely too far. Senators Reed and Watson, both strong Administration supporters, agreed with him. However, Ogden Mills did not, and he drew up a model bill, embodying the private construction loan provision, and sent it to the Senate Banking and Currency Committee.

And it took all the persuasive powers of Eugene Meyer, left financial bower of the Administration, to convince the President that the idea of Oggie Mills, right bower, was impracticable. Finally, under Meyer's firm insistence, the President dropped the plan for private loans.

Speaker Garner, however, did not. He, meanwhile, had introduced a relief bill of his own, and in it he had not only incorporated the President's idea of loans for private construction but had gone farther and provided for government loans to any company or individual for any purpose serving the general ends of agriculture, commerce, industry or reduction of unemployment.

The bill was before the House of Representatives while Hoover was still clutching at the Mills idea of private construction loans, and while Administration supporters in the House found plenty of other things to criticize about the Garner bill, they were very quiet on this loan provision.

Garner succeeded in getting his bill passed and later kept this provision in the compromise bill which was worked out between House and Senate. And it was this provision for loans to private corporations and individuals—only a step more advanced than the proposal Mr. Hoover himself had made—which called forth fireworks of righteous indignation from the White House in the Hoover statement of July 6th.

This one provision, so close to the one he himself had favored, Mr. Hoover gave as his principal reason for vetoing the $2,300,000,000 relief bill first sent him by Congress.

"Any attempt to carry out such a law must mean the squandering of hundreds of millions of dollars of public funds," Hoover announced. "...Huge losses and great scandals must inevitably result....It would undermine Federal credit and bring a vast increase in unemployment....The proposal violates every sound principle of public finance and of government."

Mr. Hoover was more nearly right in his second position than in his first. But, apparently, without the persuasive eloquence of Mr. Meyer, he might never have discovered the point of view he so glowingly upheld toward the close of the controversy. At the very end he signed a relief bill giving Meyer's Federal Reserve Board almost exactly the same power in regard to aiding private industry that had been proposed in the first bill for Mills' Reconstruction Finance Corporation, a power which the Board promptly began to exercise.

*

THE Reconstruction Finance Corporation, which Ogden Mills and Eugene Meyer helped bring into the world and over which the former unobtrusively reigns supreme, is not the most happy and homogeneous body in the world. That fact, perhaps, is understandable from its make-up. At its head during the first six months of its existence sat Eugene Meyer, smoking a Corona-Corona, conservative, slow-moving, enjoying the confidence of New York bankers and appointed chiefly for that reason. At his right sat Ogden Mills, loud voiced, positive, willing to take chances, smoking especially made Benson and Hedges cigars, appointed as ex-officio member through the fact that he is Secretary of the Treasury. At the left sat Charles G. Dawes, nervous, squeaky-voiced, puffing an underslung pipe, appointed because of the public enthusiasm he inspired—until his financial troubles.

In addition, there is Jesse H. Jones, Democrat, richest man in Texas, who began life in a lumber yard, who put up $200,000 to bring the 1928 Democratic convention to Houston, and who has decorated the plains of Texas with skyscrapers, among them the home of the Houston *Chronicle* which he publishes. Another newspaper reconstructer is Gardner Cowles, Republican, publisher of the Des Moines *Register,* director of Iowa banks and a power in President Hoover's native State. Also there is Harvey C. Couch, head of the Arkansas Power and Light Company, biggest group of utilities on the Lower Mississippi, close friend, client and controller of Senator Joseph T. Robinson and the man Hoover appeals to when he wants to win the Senate Democratic leader to the Republican cause. Beside Couch on the Democratic side sits Wilson McCarthy of Utah, whose father was a pony-express rider, later big cattle man, and who has worked himself up through law to banking, who does not look his forty-eight years and who still blushes when he talks. Finally on the Republican side there is Charles Addison Miller, Utica bank president, head of the New York State Bar Association, appointed to take the place of the retired Dawes.

To this, the greatest banking institution in the world, is entrusted the placing of $3,800,000,000 in such a way as to bring back the prosperity of the United States. Over the railroads, the insurance companies, the banks, this board has the power of life and death; yet among its members there has been no unity of thought, but constant friction. Friction was first apparent between the chairman of the board whom Hoover had appointed to win the support of the bankers and the president of the board whom Hoover had appointed to win the acclaim of the country. Between Dawes and Meyer there was no open break nor any noticeable straining of relations, but an over-present difference of opinion. Meyer leaned back and Dawes leaned forward, until finally the latter resigned.

Dawes' departure caused Jim Watson to remark: "Charley always jumps ship when the water gets above the second deck."

But the reverse was true. Dawes had gone to the rescue of his bank; and a very brief interval after he left Washington, the R. F. C. got a phone call from Chicago saying that he would need $80,000,000 or the bank's door would not open Monday morning. This was on a Saturday night. Dawes already had told Melvin Traylor, foremost Chicago banker, that he would have to have $95,000,000 by Monday morning, and Traylor, try as hard as he could, was able to raise only $10,000,000 in Chicago and $5,000,000 in New York. The Dawes threat of closing his doors meant the collapse of the entire banking structure of Chicago, with probably serious reverberations in New York, so the R. F. C. sent him $30,000,-000 immediately and promised $50,000,000 later.

One of those most aroused over this transaction was Senator Dickinson of Iowa, Republican keynoter in the convention which had just renominated Hoover, and in whose State two large banks went to the wall in the same week because the R. F. C. refused help. Dickinson was not appeased until Hoover threw him a bone in the form of Gardner Cowles' appointment to the board. Senator Couzens, one of the busiest watchdogs of the Treasury, might have been expected to feel indignant. Earlier he had become aroused over a loan of $12,800,000 to the Missouri Pacific Railway, granted after all kinds of pressure had been brought upon the R. F. C. to offset the Interstate Commerce Commission's finding: "We are not convinced that the Reconstruction Finance Corporation should be expected to take up bank loans of this character."

Couzens' antagonism was particularly worrying to Mr. Hoover because the Missouri Pacific is a part of the Van Sweringen lines in which Joseph R. Nutt, treasurer of the

Republican National Committee, is interested through his Union Trust Company of Cleveland. So Harvey Couch, the conciliator, was sent down to see Couzens, and Harvey Couch keeps on seeing Couzens and asking his advice regarding every loan liable to cause trouble. So when the Dawes loan claimed attention, Couzens contented himself with having a senatorial committee named to investigate the whole matter of loans, and with announcing, thereafter, that apparently all was well behind the locked doors of the great "Romance Corporation."

Not only had the R. F. C. granted loans tinged with past or expected loyalties to the G. O. P., but Mr. Hoover had begun to realize that every street-car conductor and taxi driver from Miami to Seattle branded it as a gigantic handout scheme for big business; and he was afraid of the reaction.

So the President resorted to unusual lengths to steady the foundering financial course of the Republican ship of State. He decided to abandon Republican responsibility for the Reconstruction Finance Corporation, of which he had once been so proud and which he had announced to the world as the harbinger of prosperity. To this end he asked Congress to change the law constituting the R. F. C., so that he could appoint four members from each party instead of three from one and four from the other.

Ordinarily this would have won for Mr. Hoover much praise as an impartial, fair, and far-sighted statesman. But the Republican majority on the R. F. C. already had loaned more than a billion dollars to banks, railways and insurance companies, and the Democrats smelled a rat. For them to come into full membership of this gigantic machine meant whitewashing all the past mistakes, all the politically prejudiced loans placed by it during the past six months. So they refused. They blocked the change Mr. Hoover had asked Congress to make.

But the mistakes of the Reconstruction Finance Committee during those first six months must have been greater than any one, except those on the inside, knew. For Eugene Meyer, cautious, conservative, nursing a fondness for public office second only to that for his family, decided to step out. Also the President persisted in his determination to get the Democrats to share responsibility. Failing to get an equal division of responsibility he went to the extreme and unprecedented length of putting the Democrats in control. To this end he offered the chairmanship to Owen D. Young, head of the General Electric Company, and one of the outstanding Democrats in the ranks of big business. Mr. Young refused. Next he offered it .to Alfred E. Smith, then at odds with Mr Hoover's Democratic rival, Franklin D. Roosevelt. To have Smith acting as head of the gigantic finance corporation, Hoover argued, would increase the enmity between the two former contenders for the Democratic nomination. Mr. Smith, however, also refused. Next Mr. Hoover offered the job to Barney Baruch and Newton D. Baker. By this time the President's strategy had become noised around Democratic circles and it was a foregone conclusion that Baruch and Baker would refuse. They did.

Then the President, desperate to find a Democrat upon whom he could saddle the responsibilities of Republican errors, selected, as Chairman of the Reconstruction Finance Corporation, Atlee W. Pomerene.

Mr. Pomerene is a thoroughly honest, well-meaning, conscientious gentleman, and as well fitted to be a wizard of reconstruction as any man who has spent most of his life in politics with no experience as a banker or business executive and no groundwork in economics. After leaving college, he had served as city solicitor for Cincinnati. He had then headed the Democratic Committee for Ohio. He had been Lieutenant-Governor of the State and he had served for twelve years as United States Senator, being defeated in 1922 by Simeon D. Fess, who put up a bone-dry ticket against Pomerene's wringing wet platform. After that Pomerene practiced law and lent feeble but willing assistance to Owen D. Roberts in the prosecution of Harry Sinclair, Albert B. Fall and Edward L. Doheny in the oil scandals.

And this nice old man, at the age of seventy, was appointed by Herbert Hoover as chairman of the corporation charged with spending nearly four billions of dollars and upon which the country had placed its hopes for economic recovery—merely because he happened to have a definite Democratic label to his name.

It later developed that the man who had evolved the President's strategy was none other than Little Oggie Mills. With the chairmanship filled by Atlee Pomerene, comparative babe-in-the-woods when it comes to high finance, Mills figured that as ex-officio member of the board, he could dominate its policies and at the same time place all the responsibility on the Democrats.

It also developed that the President had no right to appoint Pomerene or any other man as chairman of the Reconstruction Finance Corporation. The law creating the corporation is specific on this point. It reads: "... and the powers granted it by law may be exercised and enjoyed, including the selection of its chairman and vice chairman." But Mr. Hoover appointed him just the same.

Moreover, it developed that the President had no right to appoint Charles G. Dawes as president of the R. F. C., nor Charles Addison Miller as his successor. This point was threshed out on the floor of the Senate when Senator Robinson of Arkansas threatened to hold up the appointment of Gardner Cowles. In order to get Cowles confirmed, Senator Watson, Republican floor-leader, on June 28th, gave the Democrats this assurance:

"I have direct authorization to make the statement that the President does not assume the authority to name the president of this corporation, nor does he intend to try to do so; that he believes the members of the board have the right to select their own president."

Senator Robinson accepted the assurance and let the appointment go through.

But on July 26th, Congress having adjourned, President Hoover announced Atlee W. Pomerene as chairman of the board, and on July 28th, he announced the appointment of Miller as president. The statute creating the R. F. C. makes no provision for a president. It does not even mention any such officer.

*

THESE latter days of the Romance Corporation were not happy ones for Eugene Meyer, and he is glad to be out of it. The President's maneuvering to shift responsibility on the Democrats had been opposed by him, but urged by Hoover's other financial bower as a political master-stroke. Instead it was received as a piece of small-town political chicanery at a time when the country needed outstanding statesmanship.

These latter days brought out for the first time a long-smoldering conflict between Ogden Mills and Eugene Meyer —the reason Mr. Hoover cannot play his two financial trumps in the same game. This was not so much a conflict of personalities as of policies. True, the two men did not harmonize personally as well as they might. As Governor of the Federal Reserve Board while Mills was an underling in the Treasury Department, Meyer had listened sympathetically to Mills' views but always had been in a position to overrule them. But when Mills became Secretary of the Treasury, Eugene not merely had to listen to Little Oggie's loud, positive and sometimes arrogant pronouncements, but frequently had to accept them. Also he had to watch Little Oggie become closer and more necessary to his chief in the White House until he dominated the political panorama. Every statement to the press, every message to Congress, every move the President made—even to the eviction of the bonus army—was advised or dictated by Little Oggie.

This importance to the White House became all the greater

after the Republican National Committee discovered Mills had a voice. Prior to his advent, the committee had been sorely in need of another Hughes or Borah. It even had to fall back on such oratorical lightweights as Dolly Curtis Gann and Patrick J. Hurley. Then suddenly Mills produced a radio voice with personality and appeal, plus a rare gift for taking credit for everything and admitting nothing. Little Oggie's oratory even induced the usually bitterly critical *Nation* to brand his speeches as "straightforward, full of meat, clear and presented in excellent form."

Therefore, when Mills and Meyer came into a head-on collision as members of the Reconstruction Finance Corporation, there was no doubt at all as to who would remain.

The issue on which they collided was security for loans advanced by the R. F. C. Meyer, hard-boiled and conservative in his banking methods, believed that the corporation should be conducted along such strict lines that the loans advanced should be returned to the Treasury and eventually to the taxpayers of the country. He proposed to show the same record of loans returned that he had made with the War Finance Corporation. Particularly he was opposed to loans to institutions made under political pressure to boost the patronage for Herbert Hoover. Part of the time he had his way in this, but a lot of the time he didn't.

Mills, on the other hand, believed in action. Never having been a banker, he was less concerned with whether loans were repaid and gave even less attention to security. Having spent all his life in politics, Mills did not look askance at loans which might promote the chances of Herbert Hoover at the polls. His chief idea was to get the money out into industry and set it to work. Like his chief in the White House, Mills is a promoter.

Up to a certain basic point, both Mills and Meyer are motivated by the same economic and political theories. They believe that the destiny of the United States must remain in the hands of those who already are operating the big banks, the big factories, the big business of the country. They believe that the road to prosperity is in loaning money to the big operators. And having several million dollars in their pockets and a long history of social pretension and culture behind them, both believe that the great fortunes of the Mellons, the Millses and the Meyers should be placed around the council table of government and be permitted to gather momentum and power like a snowball rolling downhill.

Mills once gave a trenchant example of this during the sterile but prosperous days of Calvin Coolidge, when he proposed to Congress a bill to have the American taxpayer pay alien property claimants and let the government try to collect from a semi-bankrupt Germany. Great care was taken in the preparation of the measure and the stage-setting was superb. Mills was making excellent progress in getting the bill through the House when his friend Jack Garner arose and pointed out that Little Oggie himself was a large shareholder in some of the concerns which would profit enormously by the passage of the bill.

Mills claimed he was completely ignorant of having any money invested in these companies and that he had to call up his investment manager in New York to learn the facts. Perhaps now he is also ignorant of the fact that some of the loans which he passes upon as a powerful member of the Reconstruction Finance Corporation give indirect aid to companies in which he is interested. Even more important, perhaps he is ignorant of the fact that some of these firms will have extreme difficulty in paying back the money borrowed, and that the Federal Government will be faced with the problem either of taking over banks, railroads and industry as a socialistic enterprise or else of allowing these companies to keep their loans as outright gifts from the taxpayers.

No matter how impervious Ogden Mills may be, or may pretend to be, regarding these facts, Eugene Meyer is not. Underneath his exterior of cold-blooded and calculating conservatism, Meyer has a faintly perceptible streak of social thinking which has crept in from the days when his family faced persecution in Europe. And, compared with most bankers, Eugene thinks. So gradually the fact has begun to percolate to his hard-boiled brain that when his credit saved the cotton crop in 1926, he only tided one bad market over to certain subsequent price falls in future years; that when loans from his War Finance Corporation eased the depression of immediate post-war days, he only postponed the break which was to come in 1929; that the cheap money which the R. F. C. has been handing out cannot turn the wheels of industry until the manufacturer can find a market for his goods; that there can be no buying of goods until the man in the street has the wherewithal to buy; and finally that he cannot get that wherewithal until, by taxation or some other distribution, big incomes are scaled down and little incomes are scaled up, and eighty-eight per cent of the wealth of the country is taken out of the hands of two per cent of the people.

So Eugene, by some canny instinct always able to feel the future, decided to retire from the firing line of the Reconstruction Corporation to the relative peace and security of his old job on the Federal Reserve Board, leaving Ogden Livingston Mills, prodigy of wealth, ability, arrogance, insensibility and disdain, one of the greatest hopes of conservative vested interests and one of the greatest menaces to democratic governments, sitting in the lap of the god of big business—a lap which has cuddled Little Oggie always.

*

CHAPTER FOUR

THE COTILLION LEADER

ON New Year's Day 1932, President and Mrs. Hoover gave their annual White House reception for official Washton and, afterwards, any one else who cared to come. The nation's capital was going through its ritual of gold braid and tinsel, unmindful of the woes of the country, and many people had stood in line since early morning to shake the hand of the President. For them it was a big day. It was, however, a bigger day for Peggy Ann and Herbert Hoover III. Most White House receptions began long after their bedtime, but on this occasion—it being only noon—they were allowed to see Grandpa and Grandma hold their big party.

So when the trumpeters sounded the signal of the President's approach, they were stationed with their nurse in a room at the immediate right of the base of the grand stairway. Guests in the main reception room, just around the corner, could not see them, and yet they could see almost everything.

Their grandfather and grandmother, first to descend, could not help seeing them, however, and the former twisted his plump face into what is for him a rare triumph—a really genuine smile.

And coming just behind, Mrs. Edward Everett Gann and Vice-President Curtis also saw them. In fact, Charley blew them a kiss, which started a whole volley of much more audible kisses floating back in his direction. The Secretary of State and Mrs. Stimson, who have no children, came next and ran right into the kisses. Even they seemed to appreciate them and waved in return. Secretary of the Treasury Mellon followed, alone. He gave the children one of his wan smiles.

Then, according to strict protocol, came the Secretary of War Patrick J. Hurley and his wife, Ruth. Youngest and handsomest couple in the Cabinet, the Hurleys are accustomed to a burst of under-the-breath "Ahs" and "Ohs" whenever they make their entrance. But it was not quite time for these "Ohs" and "Ahs." The waiting guests were just around the corner. Only two small curlyheads delightedly blowing kisses could see them as the Secretary of War puffed out his immaculate shirt front, gave a final touch to his white tie, and, chin up, eyes riveted over the heads of Peggy Ann and Herbert III, strode past the two children to the ovation which awaited him just around the corner.

*

PATRICK J. HURLEY has spent a lifetime pulling himself up by his own boot straps and, in his own opinion at least, has succeeded. So also in the opinion of a great many other people who point out that there is a long and difficult road between the eleven-year-old youngster in blue denim overalls driving a mule in an Oklahoma coal mine and the suave and self-conscious Cabinet member who puts the finishing touches to his white tie just before the grand entrance at a White House reception. It is a long and difficult road, but in traveling it, Hurley has achieved most of the material things in life that any man could want to achieve, and a great many more than most people ever would dream of achieving.

He is, for instance, Secretary of War, a job which, it is true, usually is awarded to a good party wheel-horse who must be taken care of; but nevertheless it is a Cabinet post, and there are only ten of them in the country.

Not only is he Secretary of War, but next to the Secretary of the Interior, Ray Lyman Wilbur, he is that Cabinet member closest to the President. Of course there are many people these days who turn up their noses at the idea of being close to the President and insinuate that such intimacy is more of a liability than an asset; although usually they relegate this idea to the back of their minds when they want an appointment from the White House, and promptly come to Hurley— the boy who can put things across.

It goes without saying that being a member of the Hoover Cabinet, Hurley has the money that goes with that environment. It does not go without saying, however, that on the less material side of life, Hurley is blessed with a wife whose beauty is over-rated by every society editor in the capital but who, nevertheless, is a charming hostess, an excellent mother and has consistently and faithfully played the game of pushing her husband forward.

Finally, but not least important—in his own eyes at least— Hurley is blessed with a face and figure that have made him the secret passion of a score of Washington society matrons and which he preserves with all the diligence of a dieting débutante.

Taking it all in all, a cursory appraisal of Patrick J. Hurley would indicate that there was little he lacked either in character or in accomplishment.

And yet Hurley misses it by a hair's breath. He is the most energetic member of the Cabinet. He is the most talked-of member of the Cabinet. He has more ambition, more personal charm, more future ahead of him than any other member. And yet he never quite clicks.

The tragedy in Hurley's life is that he takes himself seriously, but nobody else does. And yet if he had not taken himself seriously, he never would have got anywhere. All through life Hurley has studied his exits and his entrances.

If he had not done this, probably he would still be leading a mule in an Oklahoma coal mine, or at best would have been a hick lawyer in Tulsa. But the fact that his big moments are studied instead of spontaneous spoils his climaxes.

Coupled with this, Patrick J. Hurley never has grown up. Therein lies one of his chief handicaps and also one of his chief charms. As a youngster, he got ahead fast in the world. He cut corners. He made progress in the boom days when young men went West and the wide open spaces of the Oklahoma oil fields were awaiting exploitation. Now progress is more painstaking, and corners are more difficult to cut.

Like most youngsters, Hurley lacks a sense of humor—especially about himself. To Patrick J. Hurley life is a very serious thing. This is not surprising. Life has all the seriousness now that it had when he was a small boy of eleven and went to work in an Oklahoma coal mine. His mother was dead then, his father crippled for life, and Hurley had to take things seriously. His father, Pierce Hurley, a poor Irish immigrant, had married Mary Kelly in Texas. She brought six children into the world before the work and worry of supporting them, together with a crippled husband, contributed to her early death.

Young Patrick went to work immediately afterward, tending a trap door at Shaft Number 6 of the Atoka Coal and Mining Company. His wages were seventy-five cents a day. His first promotion came early and as unexpectedly as his later promotion from Assistant Secretary of War to Secretary of War. A famous character in the mine was "Kicking Pete" a mule of obstreperous capabilities. Hurley's first contact with the mule was sudden and from the rear, following which, the young miner, according to Oklahoma legend, won Kicking Pete's confidence and became his driver.

The biographers of Patrick J. Hurley have failed to establish whether it was this early persuasiveness with animals or the haphazard luck which has shaped much of their hero's career that caused him to jump from an Oklahoma coal mine to an

Oklahoma cattle ranch. At any rate, he did so, and at the age of fourteen became a cowpuncher with the Lazy S outfit. Nor have his biographers established the reason why Hurley should have been different from any other young cowpuncher and should not have been contented to spend his days lolling on the range and his nights shooting craps in the bunkhouse or swapping yarns over the bar. The fact is, however, that he did none of these things. He was taking life very seriously. Hurley, in his mature years and speaking for publication, attributes this to his mother.

"Mother's death hit me terribly," he said. "I was dazed for weeks. What I have made of myself has been due in no small measure to her, to my sisters and, in later years, to my wife. I've been mighty fortunate with my womenfolk."

While still a cowpuncher, Hurley enrolled in a night school started in his home town by a Scotsman named Tom Golightly. About the same time a Catholic missionary named Ketchum established a mission school among the Choctaw Indians and took an interest in Hurley. It was he and Tom Golightly who persuaded the young cowboy to enter the Baptist Indian University—later Bacone College—when it was established at Muskogee.

At this point Hurley who had been brought up a devout Catholic, two of his sisters becoming nuns, abandoned his faith for that of his Alma Mater. Hurley's scholastic rise was rapid. He first earned his tuition by driving a delivery wagon for a Muskogee grocer, and Oklahoma legend has it that the college authorities were particularly impressed by the fact that Patrick carried a book with him while he drove from house to house. At any rate, he became, in his sophomore year, an instructor of American history, and before his graduation a full-fledged professor in the same institution where he studied.

By this time Father Ketchum had gone to Washington to become director of the Catholic Indian Mission Bureau, and he urged Hurley to come to Washington and live with him.

Hurley accepted the invitation and studied law at the National University, later at George Washington, and with the prestige of a law degree from the nation's capital, went back to Oklahoma, where he hung up his shingle in Tulsa.

That was in 1908, and Hurley was twenty-five years old. Tulsa was then a mere collection of wooden shacks on the prairie and just on the verge of its oil-boom days. Hurley was a raw youngster with a little law training and a rough-and-tumble education in human nature. As Tulsa developed, Hurley developed. He was in on the ground floor. As oil boomed, Hurley boomed. As Tulsa became a thriving metropolis of skyscrapers, Hurley came to own some of those skyscrapers, until gradually he became the city's leading citizen and his home, overlooking the banks of the Arkansas, was one of the show places of the town.

This meteoric and material rise, however, was not accomplished in one night; nor was it accomplished without serious and studied application on Hurley's part, plus a very considerable contribution from that guiding star which has faithfully lighted his footsteps—luck.

Hurley had a good friend in Victor Locke, part Indian and an energetic Oklahoma politician. One day while fishing together, Hurley asked Locke what his life's ambition was.

"To be appointed Chief of the Choctaw Nation," Locke replied. "What is yours?"

"To be attorney for the Choctaw Nation," Hurley shot back, thinking rapidly.

Those were the days when the rights of Indian tribes, only recently moved to Oklahoma from east of the Mississippi River, were still unadjusted, and when millions of dollars worth of claims were outstanding between the Federal Government and the Indians. The claims of the Choctaw Nation alone totaled $35,000,000, so that the job of being their attorney carried considerable political influence in Oklahoma.

Hurley served as attorney for the Choctaw Nation from 1912 to 1917, even persuading Woodrow Wilson to reappoint him, over the head of an Interior Department which opposed his reappointment. Hurley's legal duties required that he spend much of his time in Washington, which he was not averse to doing, for it gave him added prestige in Tulsa and a start in Washington real estate, which was just beginning to feel the effects of the war-boom days.

Locke fulfilled his life's ambition, and so did Hurley. The only difference was that Locke subsequently murdered a man, while Hurley's ambition did not stop at immediate fulfillment. Probably it never will be fulfilled. Hurley's present ambition is to be Vice-President of the United States. After that he wants the Presidency. And after that—perhaps there will be a Federation of American Republics, so that Patrick J. Hurley can go on forever.

*

HURLEY should be an excellent Secretary of War, and gauged by Hoover standards he is. What Washington generally has come to expect of a Secretary of War is that he let his generals run the army while he devotes most of his time to receiving Congressmen who want the channels of backwater creeks deepened to accommodate ocean-going vessels, and to making barnstorming trips over the country keeping the party's political fences repaired.

Hurley does all of this and does it well. In addition, he has some other accomplishments. He is the best showman in the Cabinet, and also he has a genuine love of anything smacking of the military. Both qualities dovetail beautifully. There is nothing Hurley would rather do than strut before an admiring audience, unless it is to strut on horseback as Secretary of War reviewing a regiment of carefully drilled troops. The pomp and ceremony, the fanfare and trumpet-blowing of all things martial send a tremendous thrill up and down the spine of Patrick J. Hurley.

Hurley's love of all things military even made him desert

the Lazy S ranch during the Spanish-American War and go down to Fort Sam Houston, where he tried to join the Rough Riders. He had been accepted before it was discovered he was only sixteen; so he was sent back to Oklahoma. Four years later, Hurley joined the Indian Territory volunteer militia, eventually became a captain in the Oklahoma National Guard and saw a little service in a desultory campaign against an Indian chief named Crazy Snake.

So when the World War broke out, Hurley's martial instincts caused him to be among the first to enlist. Like almost everything else in his life, his military enthusiasm was carefully studied. He was one of the few soldiers who fought in France and at the same time profited by the War at home. At the very outbreak of the War, Hurley saw that the Federal Government would have to undergo a tremendous expansion, and that office buildings would be at a premium. Accordingly, he took time, before he went to France, to get in on the ground floor of supplying buildings to the government—a bit of business foresight which netted him a handsome profit but was looked upon as a serious indiscretion later when he became Secretary of War.

Hurley's war service was meritorious, but it followed a carefully charted course. He had got a commission as major, and, because of his legal qualities, was placed in the Judge Advocate General's office. This put him well behind the lines. No matter what his enemies may say about him, Hurley is no coward, but what irked him most about his war service was his inability to get his name in the papers back in Oklahoma. Months passed, and Hurley remained behind the lines. Many of his old comrades went to the front and covered themselves with blood and glory. There was talk of an armistice, and still Major Patrick J. Hurley remained unnoticed, his breast unadorned. Finally, on the morning of November 11, just two hours before the armistice, Hurley somehow or other arranged that he should be at the front with the 76th Field Artillery near Louppy and should carry a message between two commanders.

For this he received a silver star citation for "voluntarily making a reconnaissance under heavy fire." No one has ever discovered just how a lawyer in the Judge Advocate General's office arranged to be at the front two hours before the armistice, why fire should have been heavy just as the War was ending, or how he arranged to carry a message for a field artillery outfit; but the fact remains that Hurley got his silver star citation and is proud of it.

After the armistice, Hurley was promoted to the rank of lieutenant-colonel and received the Distinguished Service Medal in a manner much more in keeping with his natural abilities. The citation for this medal states:

"As Judge Advocate of the 6th Army Corps he ably conducted the negotiations arising between the American Expeditionary Forces and the Grand Duchy of Luxemburg, wherein he displayed sound judgment, marked zeal and keen perception of existing conditions. He has rendered services of material worth to the American Expeditionary Forces."

To put it in demilitarized language, what actually happened was that the American Expeditionary Force, in order to occupy certain German territory after the armistice, had to cross through Luxemburg, the territory of which, although extremely tiny, was, after all, neutral, and therefore could not be violated without permission. It fell to Patrick J. Hurley to get that permission.

"The existing conditions" which Colonel Hurley found in Luxemburg were a flaxen-haired Grand Duchess, aged nineteen, and an aging minister of foreign affairs. "The keen perception" which Hurley displayed was to feed the minister American slang, for which he discovered the diplomat had a great fascination and of which Hurley in his cowboy youth had acquired a bountiful supply. "The marked zeal" was the military term for the energy which Hurley displayed in teaching the young Duchess Oklahoma horsemanship and the latest American fox trots, during the course of which he managed to work out an agreement for the legalized invasion of Luxemburg by the American army.

With this insatiable love of all things military it was not surprising that Patrick J. Hurley, when asked by President-elect Hoover whether he would like to become Assistant Secretary of War, a member of the Shipping Board or Assistant Secretary of Commerce, replied:

"Mr. President, I'd crawl on my hands and knees to be Assistant Secretary of War."

How he happened to be offered the job of Assistant Secretary of War is a story of typical Hurley opportunism, energy and showmanship. Hurley had become something of a factor in Oklahoma politics ever since his days as attorney for the Choctaw Nation. His power increased as he amassed millions and became Tulsa's most respected citizen. He wanted to do something in a big way politically, but did not know exactly how to go about it. There was some talk of putting him up as Republican candidate for Governor and of nominating him for the Senate, neither of which materialized. By 1928, however, it was quite apparent to Hurley as well as to a great many other people that one Herbert Hoover had far better chances of landing the nomination as Calvin Coolidge's successor than any other man in the United States. Hurley, accordingly, decided to climb on the Hoover bandwagon. His opportunity came when John S. McGuire, Republican congressman from Oklahoma, launched a vitriolic attack against Hurley's new hero. Hurley's friends point proudly to the fact that he "spent all day Sunday in his dressing-gown writing a response" to McGuire, though why it should have required a day to write the statement, or why his purple dressing-gown should have been conducive of inspiration, always has remained a mystery.

Oklahoma, at the time Hurley became the State's chief Hoover booster, was expected to vote solidly at the Kansas City convention for Charley Curtis, through whose veins coursed Indian blood, and Hurley started out to swing the State for Hoover. He did his stuff well. Flying in his own plane, he hit every important town in the State, zoomed over the main streets, landed in vacant lots and using the fuselage of his plane as a platform, harangued the quickly gathered crowds on the prosperity promises of Herbert Hoover.

Oklahoma loves a good piece of showmanship almost better than it loves corn likker, and Hurley's barnstorming trip went over big. At the Kansas City convention, half of Oklahoma's delegates lined up for Hoover.

At Kansas City, Hurley won another political triumph. He was taken into the innermost councils of the Republican Party and allowed to sit with the high moguls who really run things. For a political newcomer this was not to be sneezed at. What the boys who really run things wanted of Hurley was to have him act as go-between in patching up the row between Hoover and Charley Curtis and to persuade the latter to run for the Vice-Presidency. Charley had announced that the Republican Party should not nominate a man it "would be ashamed of"—meaning Hoover—and Republican chieftains figured that Hurley's direct and breezy personality plus his experience in handling Indians were the qualifications needed to put Curtis in a more amenable mood.

As a matter of fact, Charley was as docile as the reformed "Kicking Pete" of Hurley's boyhood. He accepted the proposal almost before Hurley had a chance to put it up to him.

From that time on, the boys who handled the big campaign contributions had their eyes on Patrick J. Hurley. Politically, he had arrived.

One of these big boys was James W. Good, manager of Hoover's Mid-Western campaign, with headquarters in Chicago. Jim turned Oklahoma over to Hurley, and Hurley delivered it with some 175,000 votes to spare. Later, when Hoover gave Good the job of Secretary of War, despite a previous promise to William J. Donovan, Good was only too glad to have Hurley appointed his first assistant.

Hurley went to work at his new job with as much enthusiasm and energy as if it were the most important post in the Cabinet, and simultaneously he started giving the same enthusiasm and energy to President Hoover's morning medicine-ball meetings. The result was that when Jim Good passed away from a severe attack of appendicitis one year later, Hurley already had made something of a reputation as Assistant Secretary, and in addition had won the President's personal favor. Shortly after Good's death, therefore, Hurley was appointed his successor.

There are only two ways of handling the post of Secretary of War. One is to give the generals all the rope they want; the other is to hold a whip hand over them, and rub their gold braid rough and ragged. Hurley tried the latter system first, but with dire consequences. The War Department was rent with friction. General Charles P. Summerall, Chief of Staff, and Major General Preston Brown, Deputy Chief, had got into the habit of ruling the army under the easy-going Jim Good, and they resented intrusion—especially from one who took his job seriously. This is exactly what Hurley did. He liked to sit in on War Councils. He had his own ideas to express regarding appointments and promotions. He worked later hours than almost any one else, and also he never hesitated to keep staid old generals who had been given specific appointments waiting in his anteroom while he chatted interminably with any one who had come in from the old home town and who wanted to talk politics, personalities or persiflage with Oklahoma's most distinguished citizen.

After a year of this, however, Hurley settled down to the routine into which most Secretaries of War eventually ease themselves. He developed the junketing habit and spent much of his time on tours of the Mississippi flood area, Panama, Porto Rico and the Philippines—all of them a part of the War Department's far-flung domain. Also he got in a new Chief of Staff, who strangely enough was not of his own choosing, but with whom he has developed a strong personal friendship. Douglas MacArthur was the youngest major general in the army when it came time to select Summerall's successor, but he had probably the most brilliant record. Furthermore, he had been a great friend of the President, and Hoover wanted his appointment. Hurley at first opposed. MacArthur had gone through an unfortunate divorce experience with the daughter of the wealthy Philadelphia Stotesburys—who later became Mrs. Lionel Atwill —and this had left a trail of stories behind him in the Philippines. Hurley, a good old-fashioned moralist, who had always been "mighty fortunate with his womenfolks," held that a man who couldn't hold his women shouldn't be Chief of Staff. But when the President held otherwise, Hurley decided that expediency was the better part of valor, and the decision proved a real gain both for him and for the War Department. From that time on, the Secretary of War left virtually all army administration in the hands of his Chief of Staff, who, being about the same age, had much of Hurley's energy and enthusiasm, plus a similar breezy, ostentatious way of going about things.

Thereafter, Hurley's major function, as far as the army is concerned, has been to act as go-between for the high-ranking generals of his department and the White House in trying to smooth out the President's desire for budget reduction and the army's desire for budget boosts. In this fight, Hurley has been pressed between his desire to please Hoover and the insistent and constant clamor of his generals that they could not run the army on less money. In this dilemma, the generals invariably have won. Hoover has announced publicly on more than one occasion that War Department expenditures were all out of proportion to those of other departments and to the pre-war strength of the army, but each time when it came to the final showdown, the generals backed both Hurley and Hoover into a corner. The result has been that while the budgets of every other government department, except the navy, suffered drastic reductions, the War Department remained blissfully unscathed. And it was not until Ross Collins, a Mississippi Democrat who refused to be awed by gold braid and high-sounding titles, came into power on the House Appropriations Committee that the army really had to fight for its budget.

*

SECRETARY HURLEY has been accused by his critics of "conducting cotillions while hard-boiled, hard-riding generals run the army." This is especially true if the cotillions are described as political, for with the ascension of Douglas MacArthur as Chief of Staff, Hurley has definitely gone political and in a big way. The reason was not because he had MacArthur on hand to run the army; on the contrary it was chiefly because he wanted to go political that he let MacArthur take over the army. Hurley had spent two years playing with the detail of running the War Department. He knew all he wanted to know about it. And stirred by the ambitious energy which had taken him from the Lazy S ranch to the Indian Baptist University and from there to Washington, Hurley felt that there were bigger and better things ahead. At first it looked as if the next stepping stone was the Vice-Presidency. Charley Curtis, the man Hurley had approached at Kansas City to take that job, had worn out his welcome with Herbert Hoover. His fight over the social rank of his half-sister, Dolly Curtis Gann, had not helped the party, and on the whole he was considered more of a liability than an asset. Also the White House figured that if Curtis got back into the Kansas senatorial race he might win back the seat lost to the Democrats by Henry J. Allen in 1930.

But Charley proved an unwilling victim. In the first place he likes the Vice-presidency. The right to go in first at official dinners has a real appeal for him. And, furthermore, he was not at all sure that if he went back to Kansas and re-entered the senatorial contest, he would not be snowed under by the anticipated anti-Hoover landslide. So Charley remained obdurate and Hurley, always the acme of discretion, came out with the statement that he was "for Curtis for Vice-President."

Hurley then turned toward the chairmanship of the Republican National Committee which had needed a real pilot ever since the unsavory Claudius Huston was dumped out and the pious senior Senator from Ohio, Simeon D. Fess, given the helm. To this end, Hurley was told to go out, do a little promiscuous mud-slinging and see what he could do about bolstering up a few of the weak spots in the political armor of Herbert Hoover.

Hurley took his instructions seriously. He went to work with all the old energy he had put into the 1928 pre-convention campaign which had won over half of Oklahoma's delegation. Also he applied all of his natural qualities for showmanship. In the first place he made his trips by a special airplane set aside for his use by the Air Corps; and in the second place he transferred to the Military Intelligence a fast-thinking young captain who had just finished a course at the University of Missouri School of Journalism and was well qualified to write his speeches.

Ever since he had entered the War Department, Hurley had used government planes for his junkets over the country. Part of these had been on legitimate government business; part on political barnstorming tours, but the latter were so mixed up with inspections of various army corps areas that Hurley had no trouble getting away with it.

However, when he swept aside all camouflage of troop inspection and started in on a series of air tours purely in defense of the Hoover Administration, the Secretary of War began to attract attention. And when during a trip to address a conference of newspaper editors at Indianapolis he was forced down and later crashed, economy-minded Democrats in Congress let loose a barrage. It was not so much that they minded the loss of a Republican Secretary of War, but they did begrudge the loss of a $70,000 airplane.

Later Drew Pearson pointed out in the Baltimore *Sun* that one of Hurley's jaunts to the Oklahoma and Michigan Republican conventions had cost the government about $3,400 for the operation of the airplane alone, and that it was the constant complaint of the Assistant Secretary of War for Aviation and of the Chief of Air Corps that the flight training of reserve officers was woefully neglected because they could not get funds to operate planes. Hurley is as sensitive as a small boy about his successes and his failures, and this last criticism got under his skin. He made a tabulation of the favorable and unfavorable editorials regarding his air-speeches and was partially reassured when a majority proved laudatory. All this was upset, however, when the *Sun* came out the next day with the following editorial attack:

> "As the playboy of the Hoover Cabinet—and what a help a playboy is to a Cabinet in this fix!—Secretary of War Hurley ought to be allowed a certain number of 'flying hours' in government planes. But whether his aerial expeditions are worth $3,400 to a harassed country depends largely on the kind of material he hands out. The country does not question the necessity of junkets by plane for such state business as the gathering of portraits of George Washington, Nellie Custis, Lafayette and Light-horse Harry Lee, but it does demand, above and beyond these staples of a Cabinet member's program, something rather better than the ordinary in speeches and public appearances. With excellent after-dinner orators looking for work, the taxpayer does not see why flying secretaries should not give at least a dollar's worth of speech for ten dollars' worth of gas and oil.

> "For this reason it is rather difficult to withhold criticism from Mr. Hurley's comings and goings.... Mr. Hurley's speech was not worth more than the bare mileage.

> "... This great nation is still rich in material resources and it still enjoys the sight of debonair War Secretaries zooming

across the country in airplanes. It still has $3,400 in the Treasury. But at the same time it does feel that, after this great drop in the prices of raw materials, finished products, and semi-manufactured goods, there should be better speeches by Cabinet members who travel by plane. Mr. Hurley cannot escape censure if he insists on rushing about in expensive flying machines to give addresses that are worth no more than a ride in the caboose."

The editorial appeared at a time when the Secretary of War was having tough oratorical sledding anyway, and shortly after he had been held up to ridicule by the wielder of one of the capital's most subtly sarcastic pens—Carlisle Bargeron.

Bargeron had written a column in the Washington *Herald* relating how Hurley's speeches had won him great kudos with the Republican National Committee and how the boys at committee headquarters had chuckled to themselves that the speeches were "just Pat all over—just a reflection of his happy Irish nature," not knowing that his St. Patrick's Day address with all its Irish wisecracks was written by none other than Captain Abraham Robert Ginsburgh, born in Russia.

A day or two later, Bargeron received a call from two strangers who introduced themselves as Captain Ginsburgh and Horace Thompson, secretary to the Secretary of War.

"Have you ever met me before?" Captain Ginsburgh asked.

"You can see for yourself that I haven't," Bargeron replied.

"Had you ever communicated with Captain Ginsburgh in any way whatsoever?" demanded the secretary of the Secretary of War.

"I don't know what you all are gettin' at," drawled Bargeron, whose Methodist family has lived in Georgia for generations. "I have never had that pleasure."

At which point it developed that the Secretary of War,

irate at being exposed as not the author of his own speeches, had threatened to demote Captain Ginsburgh, despite the latter's plea that he had never seen Bargeron in his life.

In order to absolve Ginsburgh, Bargeron sent Hurley a letter, stating that he had never met the War Secretary's ghost writer, and never had communicated with him directly or indirectly. Bargeron sent the further suggestion that if Hurley really wanted to advertise the fact that his speeches were not his own, the best way to do it was to "break" Ginsburgh, in which case every paper in the United States would feature the story on the front page.

The next day, the brusque Mr. Thompson called on Bargeron again.

"The Secretary of War regrets that he cannot receive your communication," he announced, and handed back the letter.

No explanation was given, but one of Hurley's friends who called on him regarding the Ginsburgh incident furnished the reason. The friend found the Secretary of War extremely wroth and still determined to demote his Jewish ghost writer.

"He must have spilled the story to Bargeron," Hurley declared. "They're co-religionists."

Hurley did not know then and probably does not know now that Baron Ginsburgh, uncle of his ghost writer, had financed the building of the Trans-Siberian Railway for the Czar. In the end it required the Chief of Staff and some of Hurley's closest friends to persuade him that any transfer or demotion of Ginsburgh would make Hurley's future speeches the laughing stock of the political world.

After it was all over and Captain Ginsburgh had gone back to the job of grinding out Patrick J. Hurley's St. Patrick's Day polemics, the real story of how Ginsburgh's ghost authorship came to Bargeron's attention leaked out. Hurley had delivered an address before the Republican National Committee which had won him more than the usual acclaim. It was among the first in the series which the Committee planned for him to make, and the big boys crowded around to pat Hurley on the back and tell him that he was a sure-fire William Jennings Bryan.

Captain Ginsburgh was there to witness the maiden effort, and Hurley, in a spontaneous moment of genuine generosity, put his arm around his ghost writer's shoulder and said:

"Here's the man who really wrote the speech."

*

About the time Patrick J. Hurley got definite ideas about using the War Department as a stepping stone to bigger and better things, he began to take upon himself the job of acting as Presidential spokesman. He did this especially on the question of prohibition. As a Cabinet member, Hurley never has been known to take a drink, but politically he not only is wet but believes that the chief hope of the Republican Party lies in adopting a moist platform. To this end he spent hours with the President all to no avail. Failing to make headway, Hurley deliberately put forward the idea that Mr. Hoover's sympathies at heart really were wet. He did this rather disastrously when, after the Wickersham Report was released by the White House, Hurley gave out an inside tip that the wording of the President's introductory statement had been garbled, and that instead of opposing the revision of the Prohibition Act, Mr. Hoover had meant to come out for it. Hurley made the mistake of explaining this at a dinner table one night in the presence of Senator Hiram Bingham, who promptly passed around all the details of how Hurley had become the President's prohibition spokesman.

The next day William Hard called at the White House to check personally with the President on this idea that he was really wet and had been misrepresented to the great American public.

"Mr. President," asked the journalist, "I have been told you are a revisionist, but I cannot find out what form of revision you favor."

The President said nothing.

"Do you, for instance, favor light wines and beer?"

"No."

"Do you favor State enforcement?"

"No."

"Do you favor repeal of the Eighteenth Amendment altogether?"

"No."

"Then, Mr. President, is there any plan of revision which you do favor?"

"I am a revisionist in so far that I would be in favor of some form of revision if one came along that suited me. But so far none has come along that is any better than what we have now," the President replied.

"In other words, Mr. President," Hard suggested, "your position on prohibition is identical with my position toward my wife. I am in love with my wife. I want her to stay with me and I want to go on living with her. I love her more than any other woman in the world. However, being broadminded I cannot forget that it is barely conceivable that some other woman should come along whom I might like better."

Mr. Hoover smiled.

"That's about it," he said.

*

By this time Hurley's political gyrations were beginning to get just a little on people's nerves, especially on Capitol Hill, which long before had branded the Secretary of War as playboy, gladhander and showman. So, when he tried to pull some of his circus stunts with the Senate Insular Affairs

Committee, engaged in drafting a bill on Philippine Independence, its members gave him the razzberry.

Hurley had spent most of the summer in the Orient, where he had taken off his shoes to enter a Japanese geisha house, tried to manipulate chopsticks, reviewed the United States Marines during a soaking rain at Shanghai, watched some 100,000 Filipinos file past Malacanan Palace in a parade of welcome to him, and had made a special pilgrimage to interview the Sultan of Sulu. Hurley had had the time of his life, and incidentally come back with the definite opinion that he knew something about the Philippines and that it would mean nothing short of revolution to give them their immediate independence.

Summoned before the Senate Insular Affairs Committee, Hurley expected to be the star witness—and was, although not in exactly the way he had anticipated. He had come up to the capitol with a copy of a statement in his pocket given the day previous before the House Insular Affairs Committee. The Senate Committee members, however, said they were already familiar with those views and immediately launched into a cross-examination. During its course, Hurley became more and more aroused at the questions of the committee, and finally, his voice raised to a shout, described the independence bill introduced by Senators Cutting and Hawes as "cowardly."

Senator Hawes, leaning forward, attempted to stop him.

"I am making this speech. You wait until I finish," Hurley shouted in reply.

"Do you mean to say," insisted Hawes, "that Senator Cutting and I are cowardly?"

"The bill has not one bit of courage in it," Hurley replied. "It attempts to tear down all that has been built up in the Philippines over a period of years."

"Then you don't withdraw the word cowardly?" Senator Hawes asked.

"No, I don't," Hurley shot back. "I know that Senator

Cutting and you will understand that I mean no personal offense."

At this point, Senator King of Utah entered the fray with this remark:

"I should be very sorry if you remained Secretary of War for an indefinite period and the Philippines should be under you."

"I believe I'm the best friend the Philippines have," the Secretary of War retorted.

The next day, however, Hurley and King had a much more serious altercation. Senator Cutting had taken the Secretary of War over the jumps at the start of the hearing and put him in a thoroughly belligerent mood. Cutting asked him if the United States had not promised Philippine independence under the Jones Act, to which Hurley replied at some length.

"Pardon me, Mr. Secretary," Cutting suggested, "I asked a simple question. I did not expect a stump speech."

"Insomuch as you think anything I say in disagreement with you is a stump speech, I will go direct to the record," Hurley retorted.

"Haven't you been projecting the economic factor into the question, to the subordination of questions of political independence?" Senator King asked.

"Your question to me is not a direct statement of my position; it is a distortion of it," Hurley replied heatedly.

"I resent that statement as untrue as many of your statements have been untrue," Senator King shot back.

"You cannot call me a liar," Hurley shouted angrily and got up.

"You can run your star chamber session without me," he snapped, picking up his brief case. "I have taken all I can stand."

Hurley flounced out of the room.

Subsequently both men apologized and the Secretary of War came up two days later to continue his hearing before the committee. He entered the room with an imposing pile of books and documents, sat down at the hearing table, assisted by an aide, and looked about the room as though ready to proceed.

Nothing happened. The committee stared at him in cold silence. No one said "we are glad to have the Secretary of War with us." No one even said "Proceed Mr. Secretary." They merely gave him the silent treatment.

Hurley fidgeted with his papers, opened a book or two and finally announced that he was ready to tell them anything he could about the Philippines.

Still stony silence.

Finally the Secretary of War picked up his papers, stacked his books and walked out.

His appearances before Senate committees since then have been rare. But despite his lessons on Capitol Hill, Hurley has not yet seemed to realize that the stuff that will bring pæans of applause on a Mid-West aërial barnstorming trip does not go down at all with the political rough-necks who dominate Congress. And as a result, to Hurley more than any other single individual has been given credit for the move by the House of Representatives to cut 2,000 officers from the army's roster.

The War Department's extremely efficient lobby had fought this move so fiercely that there appeared to be a fair chance of blocking the cut on the floor of the House. To aid the fight, the Secretary of War slipped a story to the Associated Press that if there was to be a cut in the War Department it should come out of non-military activities, such as rivers and harbors.

Every Congressman immediately was on his toes. Many had not cared whether 2,000 officers were fired out of the army or not. But when the Secretary of War proposed cuts in the pork barrel appropriations by which each Congressman justifies his existence to his constituents back home, they immediately pricked up their ears. And when the roll was called, the "ayes" had it.

General Douglas MacArthur, sitting at the other end of a telephone, received the doleful news. "If Hurley only hadn't given out that story," he mourned.

*

HURLEY's political activities have not all been confined to the spectacular. He has tried to be helpful whenever and wherever he could, and some of his helpfulness took the form of undercover work. It was in such a capacity that Hurley brought the Washington *Post,* frequently critical of the Administration, under the wing of the Republican National Committee. After the Secretary of War had completed his work, it was the proud boast of Ira Elbert Bennett, editor of the *Post,* that the paper was being run as if President Hoover himself passed on every piece of copy.

How this came about is a long story and one which no newspaper ever published, either then or later. The papers even failed to publish an insignificant part of the charge which Mrs. Evalyn Walsh McLean, of Gaston-B.-Means-Lindbergh-baby fame, made before court in seeking the removal of her husband, Edward Beale McLean, as trustee of his father's estate, which includes the Washington *Post.* This insignificant portion of the charge read as follows:

> "The petitioner further avers that on or about the 10th day of July, 1931, the defendant, Edward B. McLean, received the sum of more than $100,000 in money upon his agreement to devote the same to the needs of the Washington *Post,* a daily newspaper conducted by a corporation of which said defendant is President, all of the stock of which is owned by the estate of John R. McLean, deceased; that as ostensible security for said money the defendant McLean caused to be executed a mortgage on farm property owned by him in the name of a 'dummy' near Leesburg in the State of Virginia; that instead of devoting said money, or any part thereof, to the needs of the

Washington *Post,* or applying it or any part of it to the maintenance of his children, the defendant McLean, almost immediately after getting said money in his possession, left the
United States for Europe, where he squandered much of the
aforesaid sum in extravagant living with the said Rose Davies."

The man who arranged to put up the "sum of more than
$100,000" was Patrick J. Hurley. How it all happened was
like this:

Ned McLean was having hard sledding from both a financial and matrimonial point of view. Receipts from his various
properties, including the Washington *Post,* had dropped to
infinitesimal proportions. He was being sued by the Ritz-
Carlton hotel of Atlantic City for a suite of rooms he occupied
there—according to his wife—with Rose Davies. He also was
being pressed by his wife who demanded a more regular allowance and at the same time refused to divorce him.

The combination of all these finally determined Ned to
sell the *Post,* which was making no money and from which
he could realize at least $1,000,000 in cash. However, the will
of his father, John R. McLean, provided that the *Post* could
not be sold and must be passed on to Ned's children. On June
15, therefore, McLean asked permission of Justice Jesse C.
Adkins of the District Supreme Court to accept an offer made
by David Lawrence, publisher of the *United States Daily.*
Two days later, William Randolph Hearst, always anxious to
obtain a monopoly on the morning newspaper field in the
nation's capital, stepped in with another offer. Justice Adkins
took both under advisement until June 26.

Meanwhile another factor had entered the situation. This
factor took the form of Ira E. Bennett, longtime editor of the
Post, whose servile and dreary editorials had contributed
largely to the paper's steady decline. Bennett realized that,
with either Hearst or Lawrence in control, he would be out
on the street. He also realized that while this would be a
serious inconvenience to him, it would equally inconvenience
the Hoover Administration to have such a critic as Hearst

completely in control of the Washington morning newspaper
field. Accordingly, Bennett approached Patrick J. Hurley and
other nerve centers of the Republican National Committee
who had been thinking along exactly the same lines.

Bennett got a welcome reception, and he and Hurley started
on a series of conferences with McLean at his suburban home,
"Friendship." Hurley went out to "Friendship" half a dozen
times, usually with Bennett, and usually late at night. Once
he did not depart until after midnight, leaving Bennett to
stay all night.

Meanwhile, Mrs. McLean, who always had opposed the
sale of the *Post,* made a counter-proposal, and on the night
of June 25, just before Justice Adkins' decision was to be
announced, her attorney, Frank J. Hogan, remained at
"Friendship" until 3 A.M., trying to persuade McLean to sell.
By that time the magic of Hurley and the Republican National Committee was working well, and McLean refused.

The next morning he walked into Justice Adkins' court
and calmly announced that on further consideration he had
decided not to sell the *Post.*

The final details of the Administration's political mortgage
on the *Post* had not all been ironed out, however, and negotiations between Hurley, Bennett and McLean continued. At
1:30 one morning, Frank Scott, treasurer of the *Post,* was
called out to "Friendship" to witness the signing of the papers.

Finally, on the afternoon of July 7, McLean surprised the
staff of the *Post* almost out of the newsroom by coming down
to his old office, where he awaited final word from Bennett
that the deal had gone through. Having received the money,
McLean announced salary cuts for every member of the staff,
fired Norman Baxter, his managing editor who refused to
accept a pro-Hoover policy, loaded his $20,000 Duesinberg
on the *Ile de France,* together with Rose Davies, and was off
to Paris, from which point of vantage he issued the following
statement:

"I want you to quote me when I say I have married Rose

Davies Van Cleve and will do anything to have that marriage legally recognized in America."

The money with which he financed the trip, according to the court charge by Mrs. McLean, was the "sum of more than $100,000" received for the Washington *Post*.

How the passage of this money was covered up is a piece of extremely clever maneuvering. Sometime before the Bennett-Hurley-McLean negotiations, the McLean horse-racing estate, Belmont, near Leesburg, Virginia, had been auctioned off for $95,000 to one Arthur L. Mittelle. Mittelle was none other than an employee in the office of McLean's attorney, Julius Peyser, who had bought the farm in for McLean. Immediately afterward, a $50,000 mortgage was placed on the estate by David N. Rust, who had trouble raising even that much money on the place, and finally had to use cash of his own.

What Hurley did, therefore, was to give the "sum of more than $100,000" to McLean for his Leesburg estate. But the peculiar thing was that this money was paid out on top of the $50,000 mortgage, and Rust, who held the mortgage, was never notified about it. Furthermore, the deed of purchase was not registered in the Leesburg court house.

In fact, Hurley had nothing to prove that he had title to Belmont until December 1, just five months after the deal had gone through in early July. And apparently the only reason Hurley registered his title even then was because on November 30, Leo Sack of the Scripps-Howard newspapers had cross-questioned him regarding the rumored purchase. The next day registration of the purchase of Belmont suddenly was filed in the Leesburg County court house.

But it was filed in a most peculiar manner. Although Hurley admitted that he had bought the place, as he described it, "to get the kids in off the pavements," yet the title vested ownership in the firm of Indian Plantations, Inc. This mysterious organization, bearing the earmarks of Oklahoma influence, had been born only one month before—November

4—in Richmond and had the following dummy directors: Wirt P. Marx, Jr., President, Edmund M. Preston, and Eppa Huntom, secretary. These happen to be members of the firm of Huntom, Williams, Anderson and Gale, and the key to this engaging puzzle is that the most influential member of this firm, Colonel Henry Watkins Anderson, is one of the highest ranking members of the Republican organization which carried the State of Virginia for Herbert Hoover in 1928.

Hurley had drafted Anderson to cover up his tracks so that the unsuspecting public would not know that the money paid for the Belmont estate really had been to buy the political support of the Washington *Post,* lock, stock and barrel, for Herbert Hoover, and actually had gone to finance Ned McLean's second honeymoon to Paris.

It has never been shown that Hurley actually bought the *Post* as a business proposition, but merely got a lease on its political policy until the end of the Presidential campaign, November 1932. Since the deal, McLean has continued to send his horses to Belmont as if the farm was still his. He also has used the place himself, and in such a manner that if allegations by Mrs. McLean are true, Hurley could be charged with assisting in a violation of the Mann Act.

For, according to Mrs. McLean's court allegations, her husband when informed on October 7, 1931, of a summons to appear in court "hastily left Washington and proceeded to his farm at Leesburg. Later Rose Davies left Washington and joined McLean, where she lived with McLean for the next forty-eight hours."

*

ONE of Hurley's greatest handicaps is that all his life he has traveled fast. He has cut corners. He has taken things by storm. He went through the Indian Baptist University so quickly that before he was graduated he was a full-fledged professor. He made money in the boom days of Oklahoma with such rapidity that before he was forty he was a millionaire. He toured Oklahoma with such speed that he won half the State for Hoover at the Kansas City convention. He saw Ruth Wilson, daughter of Rear Admiral Henry B. Wilson, at a horse show and announced: "Some day that girl is going to be Mrs. Hurley." The third time he met her he proposed.

And having been successful in all of these rush attacks, it is not surprising that Hurley should continue them and perhaps be a little bewildered now that they do not always succeed.

Washington probably is more accustomed to lithe young Lochinvars who ride out of the West than any other city in the world. Also it has become very hard-boiled about them and would much rather laugh at them than take them seriously.

Therefore, when Hurley attempted to crash the gates of the capital's social and political sanctuaries, he was bucking up against a much stiffer proposition than he ever had before. At first the capital was pleasantly amused and somewhat impressed by the handsome young Cabinet member who got his start in an Oklahoma coal mine. The fact that he had a hobby collecting hats, that his secret hero was Jesse James, that he was born, graduated, married, made Assistant Secretary of War and Secretary of War—all on Friday—was rather intriguing.

Soon, however, people began to get wise to the fact that a lot of this byplay was more studied than spontaneous. It became noised around that prior to their big dinners, the Hurleys practiced their exits and entrances before full-length mirrors. A special carload of guests came up from Oklahoma for the Hurleys' first dinner to the President. They spent a whole day at beauty parlors and in resting up for the big event. Washington takes its Presidential dinners more as a bore than an occasion, and the trek from Tulsa furnished universal amusement.

Then too Hurley has tried to take short cuts in other di-

rections. He arranged a business deal by which he was to
trade the Hurley-Wright building, built during the war-time
expansion of the Federal Government and rented to the government ever since, for the new Shoreham building. The
negotiation was arranged by the McKeever Brothers, but after
it had been put across they quarreled between themselves as
to who should receive the $100,000 commission. The dispute
was taken before an arbiter, and Hurley, appearing before
him, testified that Joe McKeever had brought the business to
him, but did not put it through, while Bob McKeever had
come in later and completed the deal.

The completion of the deal, however, was the interesting
thing as far as Hurley was concerned. Swartzell, Rheem and
Hensey, owners of the Shoreham building, had said that they
could not take the Hurley-Wright building in part payment,
unless they knew that the government was going to continue
to rent it. Hurley thereupon called in Lieutenant-Colonel
Ulysses S. Grant III, director of Public Buildings and Parks.
Colonel Grant is a member of the army engineers and a
subordinate of the Secretary of War. Also he has charge of
all government rentals of buildings. Informed of the situation
confronting his chief, Colonel Grant told Swartzell, Rheem
and Hensey that the Hurley-Wright building would be kept
fully rented by the government for the next five years.

The deal went through. Bob McKeever got his commission.
Hurley got his new building. Colonel Grant was faced with
the job of keeping an old building rented.

In the Cabinet, Hurley is treated as the youngest and most
irrepressible member and sometimes is definitely put in his
place. Mellon, the oldest member, once took it upon himself
to do this when Hurley brought up the question of limiting
oil production in Oklahoma in order to increase prices and
relieve the effect of the depression.

"Foolish idea," announced the venerable Secretary of the
Treasury. "The depression has got to run its course. I have
been through nine of them and they are all the same. The

quicker the drop, the higher the rebound, and if you prepare a cushion to break the fall, you delay the recovery."

Other members of the Cabinet laughed. Most of them rather enjoyed seeing their youngest and most energetic colleague reproved. But a few months later, Secretary Mellon, because of his *laissez faire* views, had been eased out of the Treasury and the Hoover Cabinet was experimenting desperately with almost everything any one suggested in an effort to cushion the depression.

Patrick J. Hurley has many real qualities. His critics are fond of saying that personality—not ability—put him ahead in the world. But no man could come as far as he without real ability.

Having come so far, it is unfortunate that Hurley muffs the ball on the one-yard line.

While the entire country is suffering, his greatest contribution to its relief is a series of airplane speeches on the benefits of the Hoover Administration, or denying War Department tents to an army of veterans sleeping in the open on the banks of the Potomac.

Hurley is the cotillion leader of Washington's Dance of the Depression.

While Congress was struggling to balance the budget, while thousands of bonus marchers were converging on the capital, it delighted Hurley to attend a newspapermen's barbecue of beef steers from Amarillo, Texas, where he went around with a toy, which, when turned upside-down, gave forth a noise like a yearning bull.

"I like my beef raw," quoth the Secretary of War, as he held his toy up to be listened to. Slapping his man on the back, he went on to repeat the performance.

If Hurley could grow up a little more and still not lose his charm; if he could unbend in a less obvious way; if he could forget about the cut of his waistcoat and the angle of his tie; if he could get over the idea that the eyes of an entire ball room are focused upon him when he enters; if he would be content to go a little more slowly—to make a record as Secretary of War instead of jumping into politics; if he could realize that the praise and salutes of fawning generals do not represent public opinion, Patrick J. Hurley might go even further.

Perhaps now, however, it is too late.

CHAPTER FIVE

GOLD BRAID AND EPAULETS

*T*HE chief function of the Department of War is to insure its own self-perpetuation.

It has other functions, to be sure. In fact, few government departments reach their tentacles so widely and deeply into the structure of the United States and of foreign nations. The idea that this vast organization, which annually eats up more of the taxpayers' money than any other department, exists solely for the purpose of maintaining a corps of generals and their riding horses to parade for the public and plot for the next war is at least partially exaggerated.

The War Department, among its other duties, is charged with lighting the Statue of Liberty. It supplies a collector of customs to the sovereign Dominican Republic and makes sure that a large portion of that country's revenues goes to American bondholders. It maintains a series of retail stores in Panama which sell Paris perfumes, South African diamonds, Chinese silks and Fifth Avenue suspenders—all more cheaply than you can get them in the U. S. A. It conducts child health centers in Porto Rico, organizes sugar centrales in the Philippines, leases brothels in Colon, maintains 800 infantrymen in Tientsin, operates a system of barges on the Mississippi, and takes care of the dredging of every river, creek and bay worth a name on the map.

All these and many other things the War Department does with some pride, considerable enthusiasm and a varying degree of efficiency. But none of them does it perform with such wholehearted enthusiasm and such unswerving devotion as it goes about the work of its own self-perpetuation.

Under the law, the War Department is charged with the national defense.

Apparently the war chiefs figure that constant practice in defense of themselves will skill the army in defense of the nation. At any rate, out of the 12,133 officers in the army, only 5,031 actually are concentrating on the art of warfare by serving with troops. The remaining 7,102 are occupied in more gentlemanly and pleasant pastimes. A large number of them are attached to colleges, universities and even preparatory schools where they can plant early in the minds of the impressionable young the idea that the army is the backbone of the nation. Some 466 more are attached to National Guard units where they can germinate the same idea throughout the States. One group has as its sole job contact with reserve officers and the missionary work of making sure they have not forgotten the aims and ideals of the army. Another group of officers keeps its eye on big industry and hands out commissions in the reserve corps to factory managers and the barons of big business. Still another group keeps relatively busy grinding out magazine articles and speeches for the war secretaries—all calculated to convince the American people that the War Department is the most efficiently run and worth-while bureau of the government and that not one penny of its appropriations should be eliminated. Finally one group is located in Hollywood to study the latest devices of the movie game. And in addition to all these, there is a very large number of officers stationed in Washington who have almost nothing to do, and who, unable to wait for the regular four-thirty closing time of government bureaus, invariably beat the clock by ten to fifteen minutes and scurry off to their golf clubs at four-fifteen every afternoon.

Probably without exception the War Department is the most overstaffed and inefficient organization in the vast machinery of government—none of it too overburdened with efficiency. This is due to two reasons. The first is the War Department's theory that a large number of idle officers must be maintained in peace as a skeleton for quick use in the emergency of war; the second is the army's promotion system.

Ever since the World War the army has shied like one of its own balky mules from putting into effect a system of promotion by selection, similar to that used in the navy. Instead of appointing a board, as does the navy, requiring officers to take examinations, and selecting the most meritorious for advancement, the army still limps along on the old system of promotion by seniority.

Every so often some of the younger officers, whose promotions are blocked far down the line, rise in rebellion and advocate a change. But always there are too many majors and colonels up above who got their rank by the happy coincidence of the World War and who know all too well that any system of promotion by merit would see them sidetracked for life—and so nothing happens.

The effect of this on army morale is devastating. There is no premium on efficiency. There is no impetus for outstanding ability. Every officer knows that if he keeps reasonably sober, is not absent without leave, keeps his company accounts straight and lives long enough, a certain number of years will see him automatically promoted to higher rank. If he works harder he will not be promoted any faster. All he needs to do is be patient and wait.

But his patience must be that of Job and the waiting almost eternal. For the congestion of officers in the army marking time for promotion is almost beyond belief—a long and dreary list of several thousand lieutenants and captains who have been waiting years, their promotions all converging at the same time in a sort of funnel. In the army this funnel is called "the Hump." The Hump is the goal toward which every lower-ranking officer looks. Once he is beyond the Hump the problem of promotions is relatively easy. But before he gets there he may wait a lifetime. That is why there are lieutenants in the army over sixty. That is why there are 274 captains in the army as old or older than the 52-year-old Chief of Staff, General Douglas MacArthur. MacArthur got ahead during the War, when promotions were being made on the basis of selection. He was jumped from major to brigadier general. The 274 captains have had to wait.

The convergence of officers at the rank of captain and major which is called the Hump accrues from the fact that in the rush of winning the World War, most of the National Guard units of the individual States were "federalized" and taken into the national army on a single day. This day happened to have been August 5, 1917. Another important date in the army is August 15, 1917, on which the first officers from the training camps were graduated. Some men were commissioned before that day and some after. But a tremendous number were commissioned on that specific day, and of that number some 1,200 officers still remain in the army. This is what constitutes the Hump.

A man who was commissioned on August 16, 1917—one day later—is out of luck. He has to wait for 1,200 men to be promoted ahead of him. The man who was commissioned on August 14, 1917, or still better on August 4th, is in luck. He is at least 1,200 jumps ahead of the others. The officer who belonged to the Nebraska National Guard is in luck. It was commissioned in March and he is now a major. The officer who belonged to the Kansas National Guard is out of luck. It was commissioned late in August and he is now a captain. The class which was graduated from West Point in 1916 is in luck. It got in ahead of the Hump and its members now are all majors. The class which was graduated from West Point in 1917 is out of luck. It got in during the middle of the Hump and its members until the summer of 1932 were all captains. The class which was graduated from West Point in the last year of the War—1918—are even more out of luck. Fourteen years later they are still first lieutenants, most of them 34 years old and, under the proposed congressional economy cut, faced retirement from the army.

It makes no difference how efficient any of these officers are. It makes no difference, within reason, how inefficient they are. If they got in early they get ahead. If they got in late, they don't. That's the way they do things in the army.

The efficiency of the army not only is sapped by its promotion system, but also by the part which personal prejudice and favoritism play, especially in the higher ranks.

After an officer has been promoted through the grades and reaches that relatively exalted position where he can wear the eagle of a colonel, he is eligible for any office or any rank. At that stage the antiquated system of promotion by seniority is junked and theoretically at least the best colonels are selected to become brigadier generals. Theoretically also when the Secretary of War wants the best man as Chief of Infantry or Chief of Cavalry or chief of any branch, he picks the best man for the job whether he be a colonel, brigadier general or major general.

But theory is as far as this ever goes. Actually political pull and personal prejudice play the biggest part in bringing down these prize War Department plums. For months before a Chief of Infantry or Adjutant General is about to retire after his customary four-year tour of duty, a dozen ambitious colonels swarm vulture-like around his expiring carcass, pulling every possible wire to get his place. And the man who gets the job is the man with a friend at the top.

Colonel Stephen O. Fuqua, now a major general, was one of these. His friend was General Charles P. Summerall, for many years chief of staff. In addition to this friend he had an ambitious helpmate in Mrs. Stephen O. Fuqua, slender, dark, wistful-eyed. She also was a friend of General Charles P. Summerall. All three got to know each other back in 1911,

when Summerall and Fuqua served a four-year tour of duty
with the National Guard. From that time on, wherever Summerall went, the Fuquas went also. In 1918 Summerall became commander of the First Division in France, and shortly
thereafter Fuqua became Chief of Staff of the First Division.
After the armistice, General Summerall went back to Camp
Dix. The Fuquas went with him. Later he went to Camp
Zachary Taylor. The Fuquas went too.

In August, 1921, General Summerall was transferred to
Honolulu where he took command of the Hawaiian De-
partment. The next month—September, 1921—General
Summerall got Fuqua transferred to Hawaii as his Chief of
Staff. Summerall remained there until August 12, 1924,
Fuqua until July, 1924. Summerall then took command of
the Eighth Corps Area with headquarters at San Antonio,
Texas. The Fuquas were there also. They remained until
January, 1925, at which time General Summerall took com-
mand of the Second Corps Area with headquarters at Gov-
ernors Island. The transfer of the Fuquas was simultaneous.

Governors Island at that time was one of the show places
of the army. It had been made so chiefly by Colonel Edward
Croft, commanding the Sixteenth Infantry. Summerall could
not replace Croft with Fuqua immediately, because the latter was only a lieutenant colonel. But the minute Fuqua attained the full rank of colonel, Summerall shipped Croft off
and put Fuqua in command. Summerall became Chief of
Staff November 21, 1926, and moved to Washington. Colonel
Fuqua stayed on at Governors Island, waiting for Major
General Robert H. Allen to retire as Chief of Infantry.
Finally Allen stepped out in 1929, whereupon General Summerall promptly promoted Fuqua to fill that post with the
rank of major general.

Fuqua at that time was one of the lowest ranking colonels
in the army, and his selection by the Chief of Staff, supposedly the ablest and broadest gauged man in the army,
took all the starch out of any officer who had labored under

the delusion that among the higher ranks, at least, promotions were made on the basis of merit.

The Fuqua-Summerall case is by no means isolated. Men are made or broken repeatedly in the army because of prejudice or pull.

One of the most notorious but most mysterious cases in the army was that of Colonel Dan T. Moore. Colonel Moore is still rated as the officer who did more for the Field Artillery than any other man in the United States. It was he who taught the American army the system of indirect fire. During the Russo-Japanese War, the Japanese suddenly came forward with the completely novel system of firing at an unseen target. The Germans perfected the idea and Moore went to Germany to study it. When he came back he became virtually dictator of the Fort Sill School of Fire. High ranking generals and colonels came to study under him, and Moore, then only a captain, ordered them around as if they were privates. He was not popular, but revolutionized the artillery, and was given universal credit for it.

Later Moore, then a colonel, was ordered to Washington and when the War came along, was expected to do big things overseas. While stationed in Washington, however, a frequent caller at Colonel Moore's house was General Peyton C. March, then chief of staff. General March was being attentive to a cousin of Mrs. Moore—although how attentive, Colonel Moore did not guess. One night, however, Moore returned home to find the chief of the army and his wife's cousin in an affectionate embrace, whereupon he showed the Chief of the Army to the door and helped him through it with a kick in the seat of the pants.

A little later Colonel Moore was put in command of a Negro regiment. After the war he resigned.

Even the present Chief of Staff, admitted by his severest critics to be one of the outstanding soldiers of the army, has not hesitated to pull wires to bring him promotions. Son of Lieutenant General Arthur MacArthur, one of the mili-

tary leaders of the last century, young Douglas MacArthur
accumulated a considerable amount of drag even without
lifting a finger. At the start of the War he was jumped from
the rank of major to brigadier general. Stationed in the
Philippines after the War, MacArthur thought he was not
being promoted fast enough. Other brigadier generals were
being made major generals—although none of them as
young as he or from his class at West Point. He chafed at
the bit and complained to his wife, the former Louise Cromwell and now Mrs. Lionel Atwill. His wife's stepfather was
Edward T. Stotesbury, wealthy Philadelphia financier, and
MacArthur demanded that something be done. So a cable
was sent to the elder Stotesbury, and the latter, being a most
obliging father and a heavy contributor to the Republican
campaign chest, came down to Washington and hammered
on the desk of the late John W. Weeks, then Secretary of
War. Thanks to his father-in-law, Douglas MacArthur got
his promotion. At 45 he was the youngest major general in
the army. No other member of his West Point class has yet
attained the rank even of brigadier general.

*

Taken man for man, the army is not composed of the individual bigots so many people think it is. The great majority
of officers have charm, ability and a devotion to the cause
deserving of a saint and just as impracticable.

Taken en masse, however, the army is dominated by
bigotry, race prejudice and narrow-minded patriotism. This
is not particularly the army officer's fault—especially the
younger officer. Army policy is dominated by an older group
of men whose minds have grown rigid through thinking
along one fixed groove, and who are ten or fifteen years behind the times even in military practice.

But even the younger officers under them suffer extreme
handicaps. Take any group of men, no matter what their

background, and make them mark time twelve to fifteen years waiting for promotions, and the resultant inertia is not conducive to breadth of vision. But if, in addition to this, the men are isolated in distant corners of the world during this period of stagnation and able to mingle only with themselves, and if, furthermore, their entire training is calculated to make them think along one single line, the fact that there is any liberalism in the army at all is nothing short of a miracle.

Although there are one hundred more swivel chair officers in Washington than efficiency requires, the great rank and file are stationed in such out-of-the-way and God-awful posts as Marfa, Texas, Fort Robinson, Nebraska, Fort Meade, South Dakota or in the even more isolated but somewhat more interesting posts at Hawaii, Tientsin, the Philippines and the Panama Canal Zone. In all of these, post life is a never-ending routine of drill, inspection, tennis, cocktails, dinner and bridge, varied occasionally by drill, inspection, golf, cocktails, dinner and bridge, during all of which the intellectual level seldom gets much higher than bridge scores, the high cost of living and who Colonel So-And-So's wife is sleeping with now.

The Mecca of most officers is Washington, especially if they are blessed with socially ambitious wives and independent incomes. Life in the nation's capital is much more alluring but not much more broadening. There the army and navy travel in their own set groove, see each other at the same cocktail parties, golf at the same clubs and hash over the same gossip. In Washington, however, the military circle is much larger, for that city is the military boneyard to which retired officers from all over the country come to spend the rest of their lives, ruminating over wars of the past and helping prepare for wars of the future. In such an atmosphere free thinking is stifled.

But regardless of the place or post, the great minds of the General Staff have taken pains that no officer shall be given opportunity to broaden his vision if they can possibly help it. Text-books and manuals have been prepared to do his thinking for him on almost every possible subject. A reading course of books requiring twenty-four years for completion is recommended to every officer, and these books are carefully arranged so that in his early and more impressionable years he shall be exposed only to the military masterpieces of the last century. For the first seventeen years he is carefully nourished only on such martial classics as Creasy's *Fifteen Decisive Battles of the World;* Maurice's *Robert E. Lee, the Soldier; Stonewall Jackson and the American Civil War* by Henderson; *Frederick the Great* by Young; *Hannibal, Gustavus Adolphus* and *Cæsar,* all by Theodore A. Dodge; *Napoleon the First* by Fournier; and *From Private to Field Marshal* by Sir William Robertson. Only after he has built up a resistance to pacifism and other "dangerous thoughts" is it considered "safe" for him to read such thought-provoking books as *The History of American Foreign Policy* by John Latane, the *Armies of Labor* by Samuel P. Orth, *America Comes of Age* by André Siegfried, and *The Destiny of a Continent* by that caustic Argentine critic of the United States, Manuel Ugarte.

No officer is supposed to form his own views even on an A B C subject such as citizenship or government, peace or war. On these points ready-made principles are ladled out to him by the General Staff.

"War," according to the teachings of General Summerall, "is a normal incident in the life of a nation."

"Democracy," according to the General Staff's Training Manual No. 2000-25 on "Citizenship," "is the direct rule of the people and has been repeatedly tried without success."

"Democracy," the manual continues, "results in mobocracy, demogogism, license, agitation, discontent, anarchy."

With this background it is not surprising that an officer takes with deadly seriousness all the vast array of detailed plans for the next war which the General Staff constantly is putting before him. These include machine-gun emplacements on the roofs of skyscrapers, the strengthening of railroad bridges for the transportation of Big Berthas, the transformation of public parks into parade grounds and the billeting of troops in hotels. All this and much more is being worked out by the General Staff, not only against the external enemy but against the enemy "within the gates," with the result that the average army officer comes to regard with suspicion anything that faintly challenges the established order.

Thus it was that when German-owned factories in Elizabethtown, Tennessee, paid "two dollars a day and all they can eat" to members of the Tennessee National Guard to break up demonstrations of union labor, the War Department saw no really good reason why these National Guardsmen should not wear the insignia and uniforms loaned by the United States Army and carry U. S. A. rifles.

Thus it was that when the Illinois National Guard issued instructions for dealing with riots by placing sharpshooters on the roofs of houses to "pick off rioters in the rear of the mob," and pointed out that "officers and men should not fear reprisal in case one or more people are killed," the War Department smiled benignly that its teachings were sinking home.

Thus it was that when Major General George Van Horn Moseley, Deputy Chief of Staff, concocted a mobile field gun placed on a specially constructed motor truck at a cost of $15,000 and then didn't know what to do with it, he decided to use it against rioters, despite the fact that the gun shoots four miles, would make mince-meat of a street full of people and is so powerful that the rush of air from the projectile invariably knocks out the glass in the truck's windshield.

In view of all of which, it is not surprising that the average army officer is featured by a blunt honesty which adds to his charm, plus a highly specialized and almost complete inability to do any free and independent thinking.

This would be all right if the army did not attempt to

think, or if at least it confined its thinking entirely to war plans and gun charts. But instead, the army has taken upon itself the task of doing a great deal of thinking for the legislative and educational forces of the country on everything from university training to disarmament. In fact, the army has established a gigantic machine for influencing legislation which Representative Joe Byrns of Tennessee correctly branded the most powerful lobby in the country.

Its ramifications are many. Its tentacles run into almost every stratum of society. It operates through the Daughters of the American Revolution, through the American Legion, the Veterans of Foreign Wars and various other "patriotic" organizations. It influences members of the Cabinet and Congress through their appointments to West Point and by passing out reserve officers' commissions to a whole battalion of them, ranging all the way from Henry L. Stimson, Secretary of State, brigadier general in the reserve corps, to Hamilton Fish, Jr., red-baiting Congressman from New York, a reserve corps colonel, and even the pink-whiskered J. Ham Lewis, ancient Senator from Illinois who is so old he keeps his age secret. It reaches into industry by the doling out of several thousand reserve officers' commissions to men whose factories presumably may need to be nationalized in war time and who, following the receipt of the commissions become ardent devotees of everything martial. Finally, through the Reserve Officers' Training Corps and the Citizens Military Training Camps it gets at the youth of the country at their most impressionable age.

Actually the R. O. T. C. and C. M. T. C. are the most extravagant and inefficient means of training officers the army has. War Department studies show that, because so few men attend the C. M. T. C. for more than one summer, to put one man through the four-year course necessary for a reserve commission means a wastage of $40,000 and that it would be much cheaper for him to attend West Point instead. The R. O. T. C. is equally inefficient. Most of the courses are made compulsory by the universities in order to save them the expense of organized exercise. The result is that most of the men who take the course drop out of it as soon as they can. Thus at Penn State, where the course is compulsory, only 107 cadets out of the 2,011 required to take the drill during the first two years advanced to the third year. Of these only 46 men were graduated as reserve officers. Similarly at Lehigh, where 743 were forced to take the course for two years, only 93 took advanced work and 33 were commissioned at the end of the four-year term.

Despite this inefficiency, however, the army considers these university units extremely valuable as a means of getting an early hold on the youth of the nation, and it fought to the last ditch to keep them in the army appropriation bill during the economy fight of 1932. Letters in envelopes bearing the War Department's frank were sent to students all over the country warning them: "The communistic elements argue that if we have no C. M. T. C., no R. O. T. C., no Reserve Officers Corps, National Guard or Regular Army, they can by secretly arming themselves at the zero hour, the more easily overthrow our Government and control it hereafter by an armed majority."

But of all these agencies of self-perpetuation, probably the Reserve Officers Association is the most active, though the most inept propagandizer the War Department has. During the economy fight Colonel Orvel Johnson, head of the Association, broadcast an appeal against the dropping of 2,000 officers which created much amusement when read on the floor of Congress. It said:

"The Speaker of the House, Mr. John N. Garner of Texas, it is confidentially believed by the friends of the service in Washington, can cause the War Department appropriations to be made in accordance with the budget estimates if he so desires. His control over the affairs of the House is absolute, or more nearly so than that of any other Speaker for many years. Mr. Garner has been proposed as a Presidential candidate by William Randolph Hearst, who has more influence with him than any other person, it is believed. The home address of Mr. Hearst is San Simeon, California."

Colonel Johnson's bungling strategy plus all the carefully organized propaganda of the War Department, however, could not prevent the House of Representatives from doing its best to drop 2,000 officers during the 1932 economy drive. The army's *bête noire* in this campaign was Ross Collins—a Mississippi Democrat who, as chairman of the military subcommittee of the House Appropriations Committee, stood as watchdog of the Treasury scrutinizing every item of the War Department's program.

Single-handed he succeeded in doing what President Hoover had endeavored to do for two years, but which in the face of the barrage from the army's gigantic propaganda machine, he had surrendered. Four months after Mr. Hoover entered the White House he announced that army expenditures were out of all proportion to the other branches of the government and would have to be cut. He said he would appoint a special commission to cut them.

The army retaliated with brazen effrontery. Five days after the White House announcement, there was issued a joint army-navy plea for more money for almost every one in the armed service of the United States. Major generals were to get their salaries boosted from $8,000 to $14,000. Brigadier generals were to have their salaries doubled. Colonels now getting $5,000 were to get $10,200. And so it went. Not a rank in the army or navy was left unrewarded in the proposed Treasury raid except the buck private.

The President swallowed the militarist's retaliation without a murmur. He even let the great minds of the General Staff persuade him that the cuts he wanted should be worked out, not by a special commission but by the General Staff itself. From that moment Mr. Hoover might just as well have kissed a fond farewell to all idea of army economies. General Summerall shortly thereafter brought in a report showing that Germany with 60,000,000 people had an army of 100,000, considered by the Allies the minimum for the preservation of internal order, and that the United States, therefore, with 120,000,000 people could not reduce its army below the present figure of 118,750, especially since most of these are stationed in Pacific possessions or in swivel-chair administrative posts, leaving only 53,954 men as a mobile force to defend the continental United States. General Summerall reviewed with gusto the major wars fought by the United States in the past and maintained that this country could not possibly cut its military expenditures by more than a few pennies without inviting the rest of the world to land conquering armies on our shores and destroy our unprecedented prosperity.

The President pigeon-holed the report and said nothing. The army's appropriation went unscathed. Due chiefly to the persuasive influence of Patrick J. Hurley, Mr. Hoover even let the army get away with a cut of only $14,000,000 in its estimates for the 1933 budget, whereas he issued some of the most vitriolic statements of his administration demanding that the navy cut $20,000,000.

When the War Department's 1933 budget recommendation finally got to Congress, however, it encountered a more forceful opponent. The cherubic-faced, soft-spoken Mr. Collins had become chairman of the army appropriations subcommittee. For several years he had been sitting on the side-lines as a minority member, watching the Republicans give the army everything it wanted. He had clashed repeatedly with Secretary Hurley and most of the high-ranking generals, but had remained powerless to do much more than clash. The generals all disliked Collins, but respected him for being the only member of the committee who had the nerve to stand up face to face and tell the army what he thought of it.

So when a Democratic majority in the House placed Ross Collins in the strategic position of chairman of the War Department's appropriation committee, the Gentleman from Mississippi had his day. From the cost of lighting the Statue of Liberty to the use of polo hobby horses, and from the cost of Secretary Hurley's political air trips to the army's reported intention to pay for the new Purple Heart wound decorations by skimping on uniforms, Mr. Collins pried into every conceivable activity the army carries on.

"I suppose you take your bands up in the air—an instrument in every plane—to play heavenly music to the angels?" he asked Major General Benjamin D. Foulois, chief of the Air Corps, when probing into the reasons why the army aviators needed bands.

Of Major General C. H. Bridges, the Adjutant General, Mr. Collins asked:

"These army hostesses are to wet nurse these youngsters into military life whom you are constantly grabbing while they are too young?"

"I think it is necessary for the sake of national defense to do that," replied General Bridges solemnly.

"The post commanders all speak very highly of the hostesses, and they all try to get them," Major J. J. Teter came to his chief's aid.

"I know they want the ladies around the post," shot back the Gentleman from Mississippi. "These schools have a way of putting uniforms on the best-looking girls and making honorary colonels out of them. It is a part of the plan to play up sex appeal. You are putting women into the army every chance you get."

"Just wind officers—and propagandists," was the way Collins described the 1,760 civilian industrialists given reserve officers commissions in 1931 without previous military training.

After several weeks of cross-examination of this kind Representative Collins and his Committee reported out an appropriation bill which cut $24,569,000 out of the War Department's budget estimates. But most sacrilegious of all, the Congressman from Mississippi dared to slash a total of 2,000 officers off the army's 12,000 officers muster roll. Howls of anguish came from the army's far-flung battalion of propagandists. They were pitiful and penetrating. Let other branches of the War Department be cut if necessary; let anything be cut, they wailed; but at all costs spare the army's muster roll. Capitol Hill was deluged with letters. Political wires were pulled to the breaking point. Secretary Hurley rushed to the Hill with a belligerent appeal to the House Military Affairs Committee. General MacArthur broke out with a thousand-word moan in which he warned that the cut would leave the army "prostrate" and meant the "difference between victory and defeat."

And for MacArthur's pride and prestige as Chief of Staff there was no doubt that it did. But for several thousand officers whose promotions had been side-tracked for years by a group of decrepit colonels and inefficient majors blocking their path above, the cut of 2,000 officers meant the difference between rejuvenation and permanent stagnation.

It was one of these who wrote Representative Collins the following letter:

"I am a Regular Army captain and also, I believe, a loyal and patriotic citizen. What is more, I am a taxpayer.

"I like the army; I believe in it, and yet I am not blinded to the fact that 2,000 officers can be removed from it without decreasing our national defense one iota. In fact, it is evident to me that, if it were possible to remove 4,000 of the most ineffective officers, the present work of handling regular troops and instructing the civilian components could be handled just as effectively and, of course, more efficiently by the remaining 8,000.

"I am prompted to write by the barrage of such talk as 'hamstringing national defense,' 'wrecking the army' and the like. We who are engaged in the workaday jobs of the army know what nonsense this is. Whether the high army officials and others who shape our policies know this is problematical. When they inspect us everything is rehearsed ahead of time; they see only what they are supposed to see and are told what they want to be told; they deal with the army in theory more than in fact.

"Will it wreck the army if 100 'gilded aides' (private secretaries) have to be put to military work; if 100 post-exchange officers (small-town storekeepers) on posts now adequately served by civilian stores and markets are put back into military productivity; if several hundred property officers now counting socks and ash cans (the work of an $1,800 bonded stock clerk) go back to the work of military training; if 100 broken-down colonels puttering around corps area headquarters while juniors do their work are put on the retired list, where they should have gone years ago; if several hundred officers sitting around offices in Federal buildings of every large city, sending out mimeographed pep bulletins and getting up smokers for reserve officers are put to constructive military work?

"No more will we see a colonel commanding a second lieutenant and 20 men on a caretaking job, or twenty-odd officers on a post with but 150 men, or 25 officers of field grade on a post of 2,500 men, or two companies fully officered, but with so few men that they are combined as one for drill each day, while on alternate days one batch of officers twiddle their thumbs. We spend so much time checking property, sitting on boards and courts, running post exchanges and movie shows, policing up the post, acting as office manager and private secretary, acting as adjutant or executive for some 'done-with-detail' superior, that we are lucky if we are able to spend on technical advancement the one night per week usually spent by the guard officer.

"I am conscious of the courage and good sense of the backers of this bill, in spite of the cries of 'pacifist' and 'politics.' May all government departments be snapped out of their lethargy by the same drastic methods."

There were other letters like this—400 of them. Probably fifty per cent of the officers in the army, although not all feeling as strongly, believed that the retirement of 2,000 officers would help army morale and efficiency. Even the jingo-militarist Chicago *Tribune* came out editorially in support of the appropriation bill, with the result that Ross Collins of Mississippi came out victorious in the House vote.

By the time the bill got to the Senate, however, the powerful propaganda machine of the army had rallied even greater strength. Also it had the support of its chief tool, David Aiken Reed, most brazen Muscle Man in the Senate. Operating in secret committee sessions Reed put the 2,000 officers back on the army's rolls, railroaded the bill through the Senate and then took it into conference with the House. Here he encountered the unrelenting opposition of Ross Collins. Collins refused to yield. Reed also refused to yield. Weeks dragged by. The new fiscal year began and the army was without funds. The War Department finance officer had to arrange to make expenditures without authority from Congress. Clerks were delayed in getting their pay.

Finally it was agreed to send the question of the 2,000 officers back to the House and Senate. By this time the Generals had brought forward all their biggest guns and used their cleverest strategy. They had even approached Tammany, and persuaded John F. Curry, Tammany leader, to save the army. Curry obliged. The twenty-one Tammany members of Congress got instructions. They obeyed. When the bill came up again they voted as a unit to restore the 2,000 officers to the army.

Afterward the Generals wrote letters to the gentlemen, whom, when Herbert Hoover was running against Tammany's candidate, Alfred E. Smith, they had so bitterly denounced. "The Tammany Society was founded on patriotism," they said. John F. Curry they described as "that brilliant leader."

The army was saved.

*

SINCE Patrick J. Hurley began to take himself seriously as a politician, commandeered a ghost writer and started touring the country as a Hoover ballyhoo artist, two men—aside from the permanent clerks—have pretty well run the War Department. They are Frederick Huff Payne, assistant Secretary of War, and Douglas MacArthur, Chief of Staff. Both are men who love their jobs, work at them almost every minute of the time and, compared with other executives in the army, are highly efficient.

Between them the work of the War Department, with the exception of the Air Corps, is pretty well divided. Payne, although superior to MacArthur, lets him have a fairly free hand with all things military, while Payne, himself, who was an ordnance officer during the World War, specializes on all problems of materièl, river and harbor improvements, bridges and the civil branches of the War Department such as the Philippines, Porto Rico, the Canal Zone, army transports and the army engineers.

Payne is a successful small-town New England business-man who is ambitious for bigger and better things. As a youngster, ambition first lured him from Greenfield, Massachusetts, to the Boston financial world, where he ran one bank and held important offices in two others. Then ambition lured him back again to the town where he was born and the presidency of the Greenfield Tap and Die Corporation. From that comparative obscurity and a few years of dignified dabbling in Massachusetts politics, a job in Hoover's "Little Cabinet" looked like big-time stuff, and Payne moved to the War Department.

There he has become surprisingly popular. He gives quick decisions—something hitherto unheard of in the War Department—and usually good ones. He has a real sense of fairness and is a good business man. An atrocious glad-hander, Payne labors under the impression that this is one of his great assets, and from the rather shy New Englander, who when he first arrived almost trembled at the idea of making a speech, Payne has now followed in his superior's footsteps by getting a ghost writer and never missing an opportunity to address an audience.

Douglas MacArthur owes much of what he now is to his mother. Wife of General Arthur MacArthur, famous for his cleaning up of the Philippines immediately after the Spanish-American War, she lived in an atmosphere of military rivalry between the two outstanding military families of the country —that of the MacArthurs and the Grants. Each family had a boy, one year apart in age. Both of the boys embarked on military careers in the footsteps of their illustrious fathers. They entered the United States Military Academy in the same year, and simultaneously Mrs. MacArthur, realizing the competition her boy Douglas would have from the grandson of President Ulysses S. Grant, moved to West Point. Mrs. Frederick D. Grant, daughter-in-law of the Civil War hero and the wife of a major general, also moved to West Point to look out for her boy, Ulysses III.

For four years off and on, the two ladies stayed there, mingled with the officers in command and spurred their boys on against each other. When they were graduated in 1903, Douglas stood first in the class. Ulysses III stood second. Since that time the gap has widened. MacArthur in 1932 is Chief of Staff with the rank of full general. Grant is a Lieutenant Colonel in charge of buildings and public parks in the District of Columbia, where he makes such a fetish of a Washington Memorial Highway along the Potomac that he suppressed the report of his superior officer, the late Lieutenant General Edgar Jadwin, Chief of Engineers, taking issue with him.

The reason for the gap is the dashing, swagger tactics of Douglas MacArthur plus a lot of good luck and a tremendous amount of wire-pulling. Also MacArthur, who first entered the Engineers, was yanked out by his father and made the latter's personal aide. Grant entered the Engineers and is still there. While with the Engineers during the Mexican border raids in 1917 he was detached from duty by General Lytle Brown, now Chief of Engineers, who wrote on his record: "Suave, polite, courteous, indifferent to his duties as an officer, utterly worthless."

MacArthur is a real soldier and is loved by the army. During the World War he was one of the army's bravest and most picturesque higher officers. Always unarmed, always carrying a swagger stick and always wearing an officer's slouch cap with the stiffening wire pulled out, MacArthur lolled continually in the front-line trenches. His appearance made him readily distinguishable from the enemy lines as an officer, and his carelessness in exposing himself seriously detracted from his value as a general staff officer, causing him to be reprimanded.

MacArthur's bravery was foolhardy but colorful. On one occasion when he wanted some information about the enemy which no one had supplied him, he went over the top himself, took a German dugout by surprise and came back with a prisoner under his arm.

MacArthur had advanced from major to brigadier general during the War, and he was the only brigadier general below the grade of colonel to keep his temporary rank afterward. To do it he had to resort to all kinds of wire pulling, and afterwards Congress passed legislation requiring that future promotions to brigadier general come only from the rank of colonel. The act was aimed expressly at Douglas MacArthur, but it carried a provision that its terms did not apply to lieutenants colonels having twenty-two years' service. Lieutenant colonels George Van Horn Moseley and Hugh A. Drum were the only officers in this category. They had got some one on Capitol Hill to slip their exemption into the bill and now they rank high among the generals of the army.

Ulysses Grant III married the daughter of Elihu Root, and MacArthur married a daughter of the Philadelphia Stotesburys. The former has given Grant three charming children. The latter gave MacArthur his promotion to the rank of major general, a lot of juicy gossip in the Philippines, and a divorce.

It was while MacArthur was serving his most recent tour of the Islands as commander of the Philippine Department that news of his divorce reached Manila. A group of Filipino newspaper men came out to MacArthur's headquarters, asking whether he would object to publication of the story. They promised to hold it up if he did.

"No," replied MacArthur, "put it on the front page if you want to."

This increased his popularity with the Filipinos, already at a high pitch. All during the governorship of Henry L. Stimson, the Filipinos ran to MacArthur with their troubles, until, when Dwight F. Davis came over as Governor General, they had come to look upon MacArthur almost as the real ruler of the islands. Davis was slow and could not come to decisions without days of deliberation, and MacArthur became more and more disgusted with him. Toward the end he was admitting, more or less publicly, that he didn't like Davis and didn't care if Davis knew it.

MacArthur is as good a glad-hander as the Assistant Secretary of War is a bad one. He is tall, youngish looking, bald and nervous. He uses a small Japanese fan, and an assortment of long ivory cigarette holders are always on his desk. Either through nervousness or affectation he uses a fresh holder with each cigarette. When he is concentrating on any major problem he invariably gets up and paces the floor, with the invariable result that those who are conferring with him get up and pace by his side until they wake up to the fact that they are making themselves look ridiculous.

Now that Douglas MacArthur has become Chief of Staff he takes as good care of his mother as she once took of him. She makes her home with him at Fort Myer, Virginia, just across the river from Washington, where the army supplies the Chief of Staff with a red brick house and wide verandas.

In recent years the office of Chief of Staff has come to be that of virtual dictator of the army. The development of its importance is chiefly due to General Summerall, whose forty-four years of vigorous army life left an indelible stamp on the service. Summerall was the strictest disciplinarian, the most high-handed autocrat the army has seen in years. He was as unpopular as he was strict.

Summerall it was who suffered such acute agony when his battery at Governors Island failed to roar a salute to the President of Haiti, Louis Borno. It turned out that Lieutenant William W. O'Connor, son of a New York policeman and with a certain aversion to gentlemen of color, was in charge of the battery supposed to fire the salute, and, for some unexplained but strongly suspected reason, fired none at all.

Since the Marine Corps band had played "Bye-bye Blackbird" just as President Borno was getting on his ship in Port au Prince, the State Department was rather cut up about the army's omission at Governors Island, and General Summerall, who then was in command of the Second Corps Area but making a strong bid to be Chief of Staff, was even more so. Summerall demanded O'Connor's resignation, but Colonel James T. Watson, in command of the battery, protected him. He informed Summerall that the responsibility was his own, and at the court martial which Summerall insisted upon, Watson was acquitted.

When President Borno was ready to sail back to Haiti, however, all of Governors Island was ready for him. Flashes and blinkers had been arranged on the Statue of Liberty to show when the boat passed the imaginary line between the Statue and Governors Island, which is the signal for firing the salute. General Summerall himself was out to see that all went right. As the vessel crossed this line, the lieutenant gave the order to fire. The gun missed—a faulty shell. The second gun was ordered to fire. It missed also. Then before they could be unloaded, both guns went off simultaneously. General Summerall grew red in the face, fumed, sputtered and ordered the ordnance officer investigated for giving him poor shells.

Despite the saluting fiasco, General Summerall got his coveted post of Chief of Staff about a year later. One of his first acts was to bring about the retirement of Colonel Watson for "disability in line of duty."

General Summerall was a gauche and backward cadet when he was graduated from West Point. He got his first real start in life when he married the daughter of General Noah Mordecai, an ordnance officer.

Mrs. Summerall took her young husband under a motherly wing, and her father's influence sent him ahead fast. Perhaps realizing the aid the opposite sex can be in a man's life,

Summerall always has been a great ladies' man. It is true that he has not been altogether impartial, and has distributed his favors much more among the wives of young lieutenants than among ladies of more advanced years. But on one occasion, at least, he was impartial. Summerall was invited to speak before the Gold Star Mothers and did so. The old general has cultivated a forceful style of oratory, and in this particular speech he carried the old ladies almost up on the platform with him. They wept and applauded and then wept some more. And then, not knowing what else to do, they made him, by a rising vote, a Mother.

Summerall was Cromwellian in his devotion to Christ and the army. He felt that a soldier was a worker for God and always linked the two together.

He was a man who never hesitated a moment where his own physical safety was concerned. He did not know what fear meant. During the Boxer Rebellion, Summerall was a young lieutenant and led his troops against the walls of Peking. His men could not get the range against the gigantic gates which defended the city, so Summerall ran out in front of the enemy's guns, climbed the gate and marked a white cross on them with chalk.

"Fire there," he commanded.

A man of this caliber could not but leave his stamp on the army, and even though he has retired, the influence of his potent personality still persists.

Son of a Confederate Army officer, Summerall and his family long will play a part in the United States army. On the day he retired, Lieutenant Charles P. Summerall, Jr., fired the battery which gave his father a seventeen-gun salute, while at Fort Myer the Chief of Staff left behind him twin grandchildren, nicknamed "Punch and Judy," one of whom at least probably will carry the Summerall army tradition even further.

The dynamic old soldier now has become head of the Citadel, South Carolina's prize military school, and is busy turning out more candidates for West Point and cannon fodder. But he has taken with him his old ghost writer and confidential aide, Lieutenant Colonel John W. Lang. It was Colonel Lang whom Summerall placed in the War Department's press relations section when he was Chief of Staff to boost him for the vice-presidential nomination, and it is Colonel Lang who still is working on Summerall's perennial and persistent hope that the vice-presidency yet may come his way.

*

ANOTHER man who has left an indelible stamp on the army is John Joseph Pershing, although perhaps not so heavy a one as Summerall. Pershing still retains the rank of "General of the Armies" and with it a corps of aides, a salary of $22,000 and the most spacious and ornate office in the War Department. Next to the President of the United States, Pershing remains the highest paid servant of the public. Since attaining his present rank he has drawn more than half a million dollars in salary and allowances.

Pershing's present job is that of raising money for the National Cathedral, which the Episcopalians are erecting on one of the capital's hills, supervising the erection of war monuments in France, and writing his memoirs. For the latter he leans heavily on his aides, especially one young lieutenant, Reginald W. Hubbell, who whipped into shape his Pulitzer prize volume on the World War.

It requires much of the time of one aide to keep track of all the medals, decorations and swords which General Perishing has acquired. Among these is an $18,000 sword studded with rubies and diamonds which was presented him by the people of Missouri, his native State, and also a sword presented by President Gomez of Venezuela, which Venezuelans claim belonged to their famous revolutionary leader, General Paez, and was stolen by Gomez from the National Museum. Much has been written about this in the Latin-

American press, and the matter at one time was referred to the State Department. Pershing gave Gomez a pistol in return.

Pershing's only other occupation is nursing the pet hates which most of those who led the A. E. F. to victory seem to have acquired for each other as they wait to see which of them will first drop by the wayside.

Perhaps because of the circumstances under which Pershing was made commander of the A. E. F., his pet hates are many. The late Theodore Roosevelt was Pershing's first and greatest friend, having jumped him from the rank of captain to brigadier general. Pershing was then forty-six years old, had been in the army twenty years, and at the same speed of promotion would have retired no higher than a major. Pershing's subsequent best friend was his father-in-law, the late Francis E. Warren, ranking member of the Senate Military Affairs Committee.

When the United States entered the World War, Roosevelt immediately proposed leading a division to France, as he had once led the Rough Riders to Cuba, and a resolution calling upon President Wilson to accept Roosevelt's services passed the House of Representatives with a whoop. Much to the consternation of Wilson, there was also every indication that it would pass the Senate. So he called to the White House Senator Warren, one of the most powerful Republican influences on the Hill. That afternoon, before the Senate voted on the Roosevelt resolution, Wilson announced that a Division of the United States Army would be sent to France immediately. General J. J. Pershing, son-in-law of Senator Warren, would be in command. The Senate then defeated the Roosevelt resolution and Pershing's first benefactor was forced to stay at home.

One of Pershing's colleagues in France was General Tasker H. Bliss, then a member of the Allied Conference. Although numerous stories have been written about the feud between Pershing and Leonard Wood, it is not generally known that when Wood wanted to come to France, Pershing immediately

consulted Bliss. In his hand he had a cable from Secretary
of War Baker which read:

"Wood wants to come to France. Tremendous pressure from
newspapers and all sides to send him."

Pershing looked worried.

"What shall I do?" he asked Bliss.

"I am not commander of the A. E. F.," Bliss replied.

"I am asking your advice."

"All right," returned Bliss, "I've campaigned with Wood. I
know him. I know he's a trouble-maker but that he always
comes out on top. If I was commander of the A. E. F. and
wanted to remain so, I would keep Wood in the United
States."

Pershing cabled Baker accordingly.

Twelve years later, Tasker Bliss lay on his death-bed. The
end was expected momentarily. A group of newspaper men
visited General Pershing and told him that his old colleague
was about to die and asked Pershing to tell them about some
of the achievements of Bliss' career for inclusion in his
obituary.

"I am extremely busy now and can't talk," Pershing replied.

"We can come back later, General."

"No, I'll be busy then too."

"We can come back any time at all."

"No I shall be busy all day. I have nothing to say."

When General Bliss finally passed on, one of Pershing's
aides issued a cryptic four-line statement of regret.

Another of Pershing's pet hates was the late Major General
Clarence R. Edwards who organized the Twenty-sixth Division from New England and had led it, with considerable acclaim, overseas. At the height of his most successful
campaign, Edwards suddenly was ordered home as incompetent and although many believed his removal was inspired by
Pershing's jealousy, this blot on his record never was cleared
up. Therefore, after Calvin Coolidge was elected Vice-President of the United States he was asked by various Boston

friends to have General Edwards reinstated to high position. Coolidge went to see Pershing about it. The Generalissimo was distinctly cool.

"Don't you know, Mr. Coolidge, that this is an improper thing for you to do. Your job is to preside over the United States Senate—not tell me how to run the army. The office should seek the man, not the man the office."

And he virtually showed the Vice-President to the door.

Pershing at that time was Chief of Staff by virtue of an Act of Congress which permitted him to continue, regardless of age, but did not make it mandatory upon the President to reappoint him.

Sometime after this incident, Warren G. Harding died and Calvin Coolidge became President of the United States. Sometime after this incident also, Pershing's tour of duty as Chief of Staff approached its expiration, but it was taken for granted that President Coolidge would re-appoint him. However, as the date of expiration drew nearer and no appointment was announced, Pershing began to get distinctly uneasy and finally went to ask the President about it.

"General," replied Coolidge dryly, "don't you know that it is highly improper for you to tell me whom to appoint. The office should seek the man, not the man the office."

The next day Coolidge announced the appointment of General Summerall as Chief of Staff.

*

THE Army Air Corps is an entity, almost separate from the rest of the War Department. In fact, most Air Corps officers, because of the slowness of promotions in the army have been campaigning to make the Air Corps a new and distinct department of the government.

It is under the direction of its own Assistant Secretary of War, F. Trubee Davison, and its own chief, General Foulois. The latter rose from the ranks of enlisted men and is one of the first men in the army ever to have flown an airplane. The former rose through having inherited the fortune of his father, Henry P. Davison, and is the first man to be appointed Assistant Secretary of War in charge of aviation.

Davison is an enthusiastic, hard-working executive and loves his job almost as much as he does his family. If ever a Democratic administration forces him out of office, Davison probably will feel that there is very little in life worth living for. As a result he contributes heavily from the Morgan-made family fortune to Republican campaign chests.

Although personally wet, Davison officially is a strict dry and once hesitated about buying a summer estate at Turkey Point, Maryland, on Chesapeake Bay, because it was reputed to contain a large supply of pre-war liquor. Being a convivial person, however, Davison has discovered an effective means of entertaining his guests and still remaining officially dry. Next door to him lives Representative Lewis W. Douglas, a young Democrat from Arizona, who is dry neither officially nor personally. Davison's guests foregather at Douglas's house, enjoy their cocktails, and then file over to the Davison house, each carrying with him a generous fortification against the possibility of a boring evening.

Although constantly putting up a wail against budget cuts with such anguish that the man in the street would believe most army planes had to fly on one wing, the Air Corps actually has suffered less than any other branch of the service. Furthermore, it has built up a force which now makes it the foremost air army of the world. This is chiefly because the late Dwight W. Morrow and the aviation planning board appointed by Calvin Coolidge carefully worked out a Five-Year Plan which Congress has seen fit to follow, plus the incessant propaganda pounding on the public by Trubee Davison and his assistants to the effect that the Air Corps is the backbone of national defense.

This propaganda came to a climax in May, 1931, when Davison staged the greatest air circus held at any time or at

any place in the world—and pulled it off, much to the astonishment of his critics, without a fatality and with no serious
smashes. It had more value as ballyhoo than tactical experience,
however, and for a time threatened to split the army and its
chiefs into two hostile camps.

Davison and his privately employed publicity man—Hans
Adamson—flooded the country with advance notices of the
great armada of the air. A total of 672 planes from all parts
of the United States were to converge in an attack on Boston,
New York and other cities of the Atlantic seaboard.

"The planes will fly down the Hudson River along River-
side Drive and deliver a series of attacks upon the financial
district at Battery Park," Davison announced. "As the Battery
is approached, the lower tier of planes will gradually lose altitude until they are flush with the skyline. With roaring
engines and air whistling through the rigging the pursuit
planes will pounce on the bombers at a speed of more than
250 miles an hour."

"The bombardment group will be timed to hit Times
Square just after 11 P.M. during the after-theater rush hour,"
chimed in General Foulois. "Million candlepower parachute
flares will light up the outlines of Broadway with the clearness of day. The planes will circle the park, and turning south,
roar down Broadway from Columbus Circle to Times
Square."

"If you plan to go to bed on the night of the twenty-fourth
you will be just wasting your time," Mr. Davison gleefully
told a Boston audience.

He told them a lot more besides. He and his publicity agent
were busy turning out advance ballyhoo at the rate of one
mimeographed statement every three days during March and
April.

But all of this did not go down so well with some of the
people involved. Sober-minded citizens of Boston wrote to
Secretary Hurley that they did not propose to be kept awake
all night. Prospective theatergoers in New York wrote that

they did not want to have airplanes cavorting over their heads. But worse than this, many pilots in the Air Corps objected. They pointed out that flying in close formation is extremely dangerous and should only be done by pilots who know each other. This would be impossible, they said, where 672 pilots were gathered together from all parts of the country.

Officers from other branches of the army also objected— probably because the Air Corps always has been the spoiled child of the army and they felt it was getting too much publicity. Finally, General MacArthur took a hand in the dispute. He announced that the night maneuvers over the Times Square theatrical district would be abandoned.

"I am sick of this circus ballyhoo about flying over cities," he said.

Trubee Davison, who was in Cleveland at the time, returned that night to find a fast one had been put over in his absence. Hurley came out with an emphatic statement that there was no dissension within the army, but there was no doubt that there was. Davison, however, went ahead with everything except the night demonstration over New York. Beyond doubt he accomplished one of the most remarkable feats any air army ever has achieved.

*

PROBABLY the most efficient branch of the War Department is that of the army engineers. Their work in peace time is almost altogether civil and consists largely of surveying, dredging and maintaining the vast network of rivers and harbors of the United States. Under the constitution, all navigable streams come under the jurisdiction of the Federal Government rather than the States, and since the Supreme Court has construed this to mean any stream whose upper reaches affect navigation in the waters below, the War Department has jurisdiction over almost every stream of any importance in the entire United States.

This brings the army engineers, under the efficient command of Major General Lytle Brown, into close contact with the great pork-barrel bills which Congress votes annually, to dredge creeks and harbors throughout the nation. Regarding the political phases of this, the engineers scrupulously maintain a hands-off attitude. Their study of the practical phases, however, is thorough and to the point. They report whether the project is practical from an economic point of view, and then state whether it can be accomplished from the point of view of engineering. Congress does the rest. After Congress makes the decision, however, the army engineers carry through the operations with far greater savings to the Treasury than could be attained through the use of civilians.

It is chiefly the army engineers who have been responsible for disproving one of Herbert Hoover's most emphasized theories: that government in business is unsound and a menace to the country. The army engineers have disproved this in two important instances, the Inland Waterways Corporation and the Panama Canal.

The government of the Panama Canal Zone is one of the most remarkable demonstrations of practical socialism on record. In the narrow strip of American soil which extends from Atlantic to Pacific along the canal, the United States operates under Governor Harry Burgess one of the most prosperous industries and successful governments in the world. It maintains not merely docks, warehouses, coaling stations, oil tanks and cold storage plants to supply ships passing through the canal, but it runs its own printing presses, buys and sells cattle, and operates a railroad and a steamship line to New York. It maintains a dairy herd of 634 pure-bred Holsteins. It owns and operates the Tivoli and Washington Hotels. It even rents electric clocks to private individuals, the profit from this and the canal telephone and electric printer telegraph machines amounting to $46,194.71 in 1931.

So intent is the United States upon carrying out a profitable experiment in socialism in Panama that it even rents two breweries to Panaman citizens, together with some 300 saloons and two or three blocks of brothels. Its operation of commissaries, which sell goods from all parts of the world, has been a bone of contention between the United States and the Panaman Government for years, partly because the United States is in business competing with Panaman merchants. Panama has refused to sign a new treaty with the State Department, giving the War Department radio and aviation control of the Republic, together with a great many other concessions.

The result is that the Panama Railroad Company, which carries on these socialistic enterprises, and whose stock is owned entirely by the United States, pays regular dividends and is a highly profitable organization. The profits from these government-owned activities, exclusive of tolls from the canal itself, have averaged a million and a half dollars annually during the last five years.

The Inland Waterways Corporation, under the efficient direction of Major General T. Q. Ashburn, also of the army engineers, is another rebuke to President Hoover's plea that the government stay out of business. Operating a fleet of river barges between New Orleans and St. Louis, from St. Louis to Minneapolis, and also on the Warrior and Illinois Rivers, the Inland Waterways Corporation brought in a profit in 1931 of $298,756.51. This was earned despite the business depression, despite the lowest water level on record, which added to costs, and does not include a depreciation charge of $563,287.85 which was deducted from revenues. In addition the corporation had a reserve of $3,000,000 on deposit with the Treasury, and $2,000,000 with various banks throughout the country.

In fact, the efficiency of the Inland Waterways Corporation has brought back a revival of some of the old Mississippi River traffic of pre-Civil War days, encouraging private companies to inaugurate the Memphis Packet Line and Union

Barge Line on the Mississippi, with smaller carriers of cotton and oil on the Warrior River.

According to War Department ballyhoo, one of the most efficient projects of the army is that of mechanization, which means the substitution of trucks, armored cars and tanks for cavalry and horse-drawn artillery. Miles of mimeographed statements have been issued to the press on mechanization. General MacArthur, himself, using his best and most vigorous language, delineated a special policy for mechanization and decreed that hereafter the army was to be on wheels or caterpillars. Furthermore, mechanization is one of the few things the army and Ross Collins see eye to eye, the latter being a great advocate of the machine. Over his desk hangs a picture of Captain Liddell Hart, famous mechanization expert of the British army, while the books of the British officer fill his library.

Despite this, the horse still holds his own in the American army. Virtually all of its tanks and armored cars are those acquired during the War, now as out of date as a 1917 Ford.

There are three reasons for this: politics, lack of money and inertia.

Some time ago the General Staff decided to bring the First Cavalry from Fort D. A. Russell up to Camp Taylor, Kentucky, where it was to be completely mechanized. For the first time the equipment was either on hand or the funds appropriated, and it was decided to abolish the horse from that one regiment entirely.

Politics, however, interfered. Fort D. A. Russell happens to be in the little border town of Marfa, Texas, one of the hottest holes in the civilized world. But hot or not, it happens also to be in the political domain of Senators Connally and Sheppard, both Democrats, but both, for some unknown reason, powerful with the War Department. Probably it was not so much power on the part of Messrs. Sheppard and Connally as it was timidity on the part of the War Department; but at any rate, their objection kept the troops at Marfa and the First Cavalry remains unmechanized.

Major General Harry Bishop, chief of Field Artillery, was more energetic. He worked out a system of eliminating the horse by mounting French seventy-fives on rubber-tired wheels and hitching them behind Ford trucks. The trucks carried the ammunition, ordinarily hauled in the limber, and the whole process eliminated six horses, two men and about fifty dollars of expense per day. A battery of these mechanized guns were sent from the Holabird Ordnance Depot in Baltimore to Fort Bragg, N. C., in thirteen hours at a cost of less than $100 per gun. Horses would have required twenty days and cost $2,000 per gun.

After the battery was completely mechanized, however, and the trucks bought and paid for, J. H. McCarl, Comptroller General, ruled that they were illegally purchased and would have to be paid for personally by the officers of the Field Artillery. He claimed that Chevrolet had made a lower bid than Ford. The Field Artillery replied that a certain type of transmission had been specified which Chevrolet had not supplied and that Ford had produced a much better car. The Comptroller General, however, remained adamant.

Probably it had nothing to do with the case, but later the army claimed that Mr. McCarl had received from General Motors—manufacturers of Chevrolet—a courtesy card for the use of any General Motors car in any city at any time.

Despite the drive for mechanization, the army horse and mule, like the political forts which the War Department cannot get rid of, still remain. The forts, however, have their powerful proponents. There is Senator Reed Smoot who will not let the army abandon Fort Logan, Utah, despite the fact that it long ago lost its value as a stockade against Indian attacks. There was Senator Francis E. Warren, who never would permit the abandonment of the Wyoming fortress named after him, despite the fact that it is one of the most barren and useless posts in the army. Then there was Senator

Proctor of Vermont who forced the establishment of Fort Ethan Allen, despite the fact that it is so cold that the army has been wanting to abandon it ever since.

The horse and mule, however, have no political friends. Their only champions are a few cavalry and field artillery officers who claim that the army cannot be completely mechanized. Among these is Major General Guy V. Henry, who as a cavalry captain back in 1912 rode the American army team to victory in the Olympic Games at Stockholm, thereby getting a start for his present job as Chief of Cavalry. There is also Lieutenant Colonel "Toddy" George, son-in-law of Vice-President Curtis who headed the American army team at the Amsterdam Olympics. Great hopes were pinned on George, and under his leadership the team made a remarkable showing. When the riders had raced to the tape, however, it was disclosed that George had forgotten to take one jump, and the remainder of the team, necessarily following him, had failed to take it also.

As a result of the efforts of these few enthusiasts, fifty of the finest horses in the army were culled out one year in advance of the Los Angeles Olympics and shipped to Fort Rosecrans, San Diego, where fifteen crack cavalrymen did nothing except train their mounts for the great event.

General Henry, however, fights a losing battle. Against him is pitted Representative Ross Collins of Mississippi, the enemy of the horse. No opportunity does Collins miss to bring up the question of army horses.

"Have you investigated the number of horses in the Air Corps?" he asked Major General John F. Preston, Inspector General of the army, at the 1933 appropriation hearings.

"No, sir," General Preston replied. "I know at San Antonio they did have some for polo and for exercise."

"For the officers or for the womenfolk?" Mr. Collins asked.

"No, sir; for officers."

"For airplane duty?" Mr. Collins persisted.

"For airplane duty," General Preston replied.

"They must be flying steeds," Mr. Collins grunted.

During the same hearings, Collins got into a heated debate with General Henry on the value of polo at the cavalry school at Fort Riley, Kansas. Their repartee follows:

Mr. Collins: If you got rid of polo, would you have to abolish the school?

General Henry: No, we would not have to do that, but any good, hardy game is a fine thing for officers.

Mr. Collins: Some general testified the other day that polo was still the rich man's game.

General Henry: No, it does not cost the government a cent.

Mr. Collins: General, in playing polo, you have to have a horse?

General Henry: Yes, sir.

Mr. Collins: You not only have to have one horse but you ride a horse for about fifteen minutes and then you change horses, so you have to have a string of horses.

General Henry: Yes, sir.

Mr. Collins: Then you have to have a place to house the animals, do you not?

General Henry: Yes, sir, but they are all included in the regular strength.

Mr. Collins: I expect we would have gotten rid of the horses a long time ago if it had not been for the polo feature of it. Now you have to feed the horses, you have to shoe them about eight times a year; then you have to house them, and all those things cost money.

General Henry: It costs money, Mr. Collins, but all those things are included with the rest.

Mr. Collins: But if horses are kept in the army largely because of the fact that you play polo with them, then the game would cost something, wouldn't it?

General Henry: Yes, but the horses are kept in the army because they are needed.

Mr. Collins: I do not know about that. I think they are kept in many branches solely because of the fact that horseback riding is a popular sport. I am beginning to think you should call the cavalry the polo branch of the army.

General Henry: But it is not, Mr. Collins. It is a thoroughly and absolutely efficient branch of the army.

Mr. Collins: I think we ought to re-name it and call it the polo branch of the army.

General Henry: Well, it is not. It is a good, hard-fighting branch of the army.

Mr. Collins: It looks like polo rapidly is becoming the major function of this particular branch.

General Henry: The cavalry is an important branch of the service.

*

LIKE all other sprawling and heterogeneous government organizations, the army has its fits and its misfits, its wastes and its efficiencies, its popular officers and those who are hated.

It has, for instance, a finger-print system so efficient that it was able to distinguish from 5,000,000 others the thumb print of a dazed veteran who didn't know his name but who had served in the army fourteen years before, and to tell him that he was Ben Islip of Norfolk, Virginia, write his name for him on a piece of paper and send him back home.

It has, for instance, developed an army plane which once flew from Dayton, Ohio, to Washington with no human hand balancing its wings, governing its altitude or keeping it headed in the right direction.

It has also, for instance, developed, despite the treaties of the State Department prohibiting the use of poison gas, a death spray which can be released from the air on thousands of civilians, and is so powerful that it has been known to remain potent in swampy areas for two years.

Then the army also has an interesting habit of conferring the rank of colonel on beautiful ladies; Marion Davies having been made colonel in the Twenty-sixth Infantry, at the instance of William Randolph Hearst, Mary Pickford a colonel in the 143rd Field Artillery, and an unknown number of Ziegfeld Follies girls commissioned in miscellaneous outfits in a come-on movement for recruits.

There are all sorts and sizes in the War Department—a strange conglomeration of people and personalities.

There is old General Bridges, the adjutant general, who knows the pedigrees of every stallion in the country and who seldom is to be seen without a racing chart occupying the central position on his desk.

Then there is Colonel Osmun Latrobe, whose wealth of amusing stories when he met Coolidge out in the Black Hills won him the post of Presidential aide, but who now sits at a desk in the Chief of Cavalry's office, poring over hunting and fishing journals and yearning for the great open spaces from which he came.

Then there is Captain John E. Adamson, who enlisted as a private and being both a faithful sergeant and from Missouri—Pershing's home State—won his way to Pershing's heart and was commissioned. Now, still faithful to the man he served, he sits outside the ornate office of the "General of the Armies" and studies stock-market reports.

Then there is General Harry Bishop, chief of field artillery, who never misses the circus when it is in town, and refuses to ride in a Pullman when he can ride in a smoker. Bishop's wife left him when he was a young lieutenant and ran away with the chauffeur. For years he remained a bachelor and did not re-marry until the wife of General Foulois, chief of the Air Corps divorced him and took a chance with Bishop, then a colonel. Now she is a general's wife again, and just as keen a circus fan as her husband, although she refuses to feed peanuts to the elephants.

Then there is General Moseley, who as Deputy Chief of Staff is one of the fast-thinking supports of Douglas MacArthur; but who, when stationed on the Texas border during the Mexican revolution of 1929, thought he would do his bit by ordering field pieces placed on flat cars hauled up to protect El Paso, and received as a reward one of the quickest spankings from Frank B. Kellogg that the army has ever got from a Secretary of State. One of his chief interests is rushing out of the War Department at noon to see whether George Abell has mentioned him in his Washington *News* column. If he is taken for a ride, the General is sore; if he is omitted he is even sorer.

Then there is Major General Preston Brown, one of the hardest-boiled corps area commanders in the army who, as Deputy Chief of Staff, was constantly fighting with Hurley and who in a war council once carried in a Bible, opened it to Daniel V, 8 and read: "Then came in all the king's wise men; but they could not read the writing, nor make known to the king the interpretation thereof." "That," remarked General Brown, closing his Bible, "is a description of the General Staff."

Then there is Lieutenant Alfred M. Gruenther who made himself famous as umpire of the Lenz-Culbertson bridge contest, and whose wife fixed up a bed for him in the rumble seat of their car so that he could sleep each night while she drove him back to West Point, where he taught chemistry.

Then there was Colonel Harrison Hall, who started to emulate Gruenther, and who, at his first match on December 13, reached over the table to pick up a card, was stricken with a heart attack and died shortly afterwards—the army's first contract bridge casualty.

Then there are Major General Blanton Winship, fashionable former aide to the White House and now Judge Advocate General, who once appeared at a dinner with a rosy ring of rouge in the very center of his white mustache; Colonel Gordon Johnston, the most decorated man in the army, who has received every medal it is possible for an American officer to receive; and Colonel Alfred T. Smith, who all his life cherished the ambition to become a brigadier general, whose name at last was sent to the Senate, but was returned because the appointment came in a year too early. The candidate now is known in War Department circles as General Hard-Luck Smith.

Then there are, of course, a corps of old and patient clerks who actually are the backbone of the War Department, who remain on with each change of administration, and tell their new chiefs how to sign on the dotted line. They have a canny way of sizing up the new Secretaries of War who come and go, and their estimate for the last fifteen years runs like this:

Newton D. Baker—the most human Secretary of War.

John W. Weeks—the most efficient.

Dwight F. Davis—the most gentlemanly.

James M. Good—the most ignorant.

Patrick J. Hurley—the best looking.

All of these personalities and people are heaped together in one vast uncoagulated bureau. There is no unity about the War Department. The West Pointers are for the West Pointers and the officers who rose from the ranks are made keenly and constantly aware of that fact. The infantry knocks the cavalry, the field artillery has little love for the coast artillery and nearly all branches are jealous of the Air Corps. The Army War College is a little nucleus which leads a cloistered existence on the banks of the lower Potomac, but is not as exclusive as the Intelligence Division, commonly branded the snobs of the army. Made up for the most part of ex-military attachés or those who aspire to that honor, the snobs have a club of their own on the upper Potomac—an estate loaned them by the late Joseph Leiter, once Chicago's grain magnate. There they foregather on summer Sundays and from these meetings come some of the army's best strategy for its own self-preservation. For it is only when the army is under fire that its clashing forces come together in any degree of unity.

CHAPTER SIX

ADAMS AND HIS ADMIRALS

*C*HARLES FRANCIS ADAMS is God's answer to the admiral's prayer. He is the navy's proof that all things come to him who waits.

It is true that the admirals had to wait sixteen years for Charles Francis, but when he finally arrived they had their man. For Charles Francis advocates as big a navy as any admiral, can sail a ship better than most of them, and has repeatedly risked his Cabinet job for them—which is more than the admirals are willing to do in turn for their U.S.N.

The admirals are convinced that this heaven-sent Secretary of the Navy is due restitution for all the trials and tribulations of the past. And there is no doubt that, from their own point of view at least, they have suffered.

For sixteen years prior to the advent of Charles Francis Adams, the navy was run by secretaries it either loathed or did not respect; for sixteen years the admirals have felt it necessary to thwart, circumnavigate and ridicule their civilian chiefs.

Josephus Daniels, the man who built up the navy to its greatest strength, and whom history will record as the most genuine idealist in Woodrow Wilson's Cabinet, was despised by the admirals. He eliminated wine from their mess and was called a Sunday-school teacher. He provided schools by which enlisted men could become officers and was called a Bolshevik.

Edwin Denby, who followed him, was too phlegmatic and too deeply interested in the political grab-bag which featured the Harding Administration to arouse any great bitterness in the navy. The admirals found him an easy mark and turned their eyes the other way when he permitted the steal of the navy's oil reserve by Albert B. Fall and Harry Sinclair.

Curtis Dwight Wilbur was ridiculed by the admirals. Tall, gawky, a slow-thinking but scrupulously fair California Judge, Wilbur knew nothing about the navy but felt that he ought to. As a result, he wanted at least to be consulted on main policy, just to prove that he was Secretary of the Navy. Under him the admirals alternately chafed and chortled.

But Charles Francis Adams makes up for all of them. His union with the navy has been one long and blissful honeymoon. They harmonize perfectly. This is because Adams lets the admirals have their own way. There is never any argument. The admirals simply run the show.

There are three reasons for this:

First, Adams is a consistent and ardent champion of a big fleet. The admirals need not fan the fires of his enthusiasm.

Second, Adams, although he can sail a boat more skillfully than any navy man, knows little about the technique of a Navy Department, and is a wise enough executive to turn all his administration over to one man.

Third, the navy is such a far-flung, heterogeneous and unyielding body that it could have defeated Adams just as it has defeated every other recent Secretary except Josephus Daniels, had he not yielded first.

The Navy Department is probably the most technical and widely scattered bureaucracy of the Federal Government. Its hold reaches out to the Philippines, where several thousand sailors whirl nightly with Filipino maidens at Santa Anna, largest dance hall in the world; up the Yangtze where specially built river patrol boats protect American shipping from Chinese pirates a thousand miles upstream; to Chefoo where the Asiatic Fleet summers every year, and which port consumes more chewing gum than all the rest of China combined; to Guam and Samoa, pin-points on the map of the Pacific which the navy rules with an iron but benevolent hand; to Hawaii which it would like to rule in the same manner; to Haiti and Nicaragua where it manages, with the Marine Corps, and through no fault of either, to keep Latin America constantly reminded of the political ineptitude of the Colossus of the North.

In addition to these foreign tentacles, the navy's yards and dry-docks, all the way from Seattle to San Diego and from Portsmouth to Pensacola, are inextricably bound up with the economic and political structure of the nation.

The nerve center of this sprawling conglomeration is a top-heavy organization in Washington, over which Charles Francis Adams reigns supreme. It is housed in a white concrete structure, the direct antithesis of the ornate and ponderous place in which live the idolators of gold-braid who run the War Department. A temporary structure, rushed to completion during the War, the Navy Building is to a certain extent symbolical of the navy itself, which owes its present power and prestige to, what was for it, the fortuitous fact that German submarines were churning the waters of the Atlantic over which 4,000,000 Americans had to be transported to France. Lacking the massive columns, the frescoes, the gilded ceilings of the War Department, the Navy Building is stripped for action like the decks of one of its own battleships. It has plain concrete floors; its white plaster walls are adorned with nothing superfluous, save a few ships' clocks and an imitation colonial mantel-piece in the office of Secretary Adams.

Not so stripped, however, are the desks of the admirals or the departmental machinery which directs the far-flung activities of the fleet. Differing from the efficiency of the individual battleship, the Navy Department is cluttered up with a maze of red tape and unnecessary overhead which sometimes drives to distraction the officer afloat. One of the chief difficulties with the navy is that most admirals yearn for desks ashore and especially the socially soft berths in the nation's capital, with the result that Washington is constipated with admirals.

Every so often, it is true, one of them rebels and bursts forth with the real truth about naval efficiency—as did Rear Admiral Thomas Pickett Magruder—and gets properly punished for his pains. Magruder, who described the inefficiencies of the navy in the *Saturday Evening Post,* was detached from active service; but a year and a half afterward the European fleet, which he had ridiculed, was abolished.

Despite its inefficiencies, the Navy Department can properly make one boast—although whether or not it should be proud to make it is another matter. It can correctly say that it is more efficient than the antiquated system by which the crusted generals of the army run their department. This is true all down the line. The average naval officer, compared man for man with the army, is of higher caliber, and taken in the aggregate the navy accomplishes far more with fewer men.

There are several reasons for this, among the most important of which is the difference in promotion system. The navy fires an officer out of the service without blinking an eye if he fails to be promoted, while the army puts a premium on quantity rather than quality and will retain an officer *ad infinitum,* regardless of promotions. In the navy, space is limited. No man can be taken aboard a warship unless he is worth his cubic displacement. In the army, however, battlefields and parade grounds stretch out to the horizon, and the more men on the battlefield, regardless of brains, the better the chances of dividing bullets.

This is a crude and indelicate way of putting it, but the fact is that a naval officer requires more brains than an army officer. For instance, only a few in the army are engineers. But in the navy every officer must be an engineer, qualified to handle the technical intricacies of boilers, turbines and engine room. In addition, he must also know navigation, which in itself requires a highly technical training. Finally, the conditions of combat and gunfire are more technical than prevail in the army. Instead of firing from a stationary position, a naval gunner must figure the speed of his own ship, the speed of the enemy vessel, and the strength of the sea and wind which is causing his own ship to roll, pitch, or bob up and down like a cork.

Except in athletics, the superiority of the navy over the army extends all along the line. The navy even has a slight edge on the army when it comes to that function in which they are both super-perfect—lobbying for self-aggrandizement. In this, both departments rate higher than any others in the government, although the navy has developed one or two extra flourishes which the army has not yet achieved. It has, for instance, dressed up Ramon Novarro, Mexican movie star, as a midshipman in order to promote the glories of Annapolis. It has, also, developed the scheme of loaning the fleet for the purpose of booming real estate on the tip of Long Island in return for assistance with congressional appropriations. Finally it has fallen for the idea of coöperating with steel manufacturers who are attempting to sabotage naval disarmament conferences. In fact, recent history shows that there is no depth to which the navy will not dive for its own self-promotion.

*

Over this powerful propaganda agency, Charles Francis Adams rules with a tight-lipped smile, a biting sense of humor and the appearance of really enjoying himself.

How Herbert Hoover happened to select him as Secretary of the Navy no one knows. Perhaps it was because he needed a New Englander in his Cabinet. Perhaps it was because Charles Francis was a great yachtsman, and Mr. Hoover therefore pictured him as a great naval expert. Or perhaps it was because there had been so many Adamses around Washington from the days of John Adams down, that the President-elect felt it would be a humane thing to help perpetuate that tradition. Certainly there was no burning political reason for the appointment, because until 1924, when he voted for Calvin Coolidge, Adams had classed himself as a Democrat.

But at any rate Mr. Hoover did appoint him, and probably has regretted it ever since, for his Secretary of the Navy is the one man in his Cabinet who has stood up and fought him so consistently that at one time it seemed inevitable Adams would resign.

When Adams' appointment was made, but not yet announced, the fact leaked out to a Boston sports writer who was in Miami with the Boston Braves, where Hoover was occupying himself with deep-sea fishing while waiting for March 4 to come around. Calling up his editor, the sports writer said:

"Hoover's appointed a guy named Charley Adams as Secretary of the Navy. It's not *the* Charley Adams (meaning the baseball star) but some other fellow from Boston by that name."

Probably the oblivion which Charles Francis enjoyed at that time, as far as the sports writer was concerned, was universal for all those outside a limited circle of Boston blue-bloods.

Great-great-grandson of the second President of the United States, great-grandson of the sixth, grandson of the American Minister to England during the trying days of the Civil War, and nephew of two great historians, Charles Francis Adams had done relatively nothing to distinguish him in the mind of a sports writer or any one else. Until the time Mr. Hoover singled him out for naval fame he had been content to bask in the sunshine of family fame and do relatively nothing. His uncles had struggled diligently, at times even desperately, to add new luster to the family tradition. The uncle for whom he was named was a pioneer in railroad regulation and planted the seeds from which grew the Interstate Commerce Commission of to-day. His uncle Henry was the leading historical writer of his day, and once wrote an exposé of Jay Gould and his railroad machinations so radical that the *Edinburgh Review* refused to print it.

Adam's father, John Quincy II, was the most independent and active member of the generation. Disgusted with the scandals of Republican administrations immediately after the Civil War, John Quincy bolted the party which his forefathers had founded and became a Democrat. Not only that, but he added to his heresy by leading the Democratic Party in the Commonwealth of Massachusetts and by twice running for Governor. Although never elected, Grover Cleveland offered him, as a reward, the same Cabinet post which his son later accepted.

But the senior Adams' health had begun to fail, and instead of becoming Secretary of the Navy, he was forced to go abroad. When he died about a year later, he left an estate of more than $1,000,000, the care of which fell into the hands of Charles Francis.

Between that time and 1929, when President Hoover offered him the navy portfolio in a Republican Cabinet, Charles Francis followed phlegmatically in his father's footsteps. He continued to be a Democrat, although by no means carrying out the fiery and energetic tradition of his father. And he continued to administer and increase his father's estate. In fact, Adams attained some little reputation as a financial administrator, and even became Treasurer of Harvard University. Under his shrewd New England management, that institution's endowment increased from $12,000,000 to $100,000,000, on which Charles Francis obtained a return of 5½ per cent, in contrast to the 4½ per cent received by other colleges.

Having more or less unlimited funds at his disposal, young Adams had tried out three racing sloops of his own by the time he was twenty-one, and since then has owned the *Gossoon, Harpoon, Baboon, Rooster* and *Crooner,* all of the names, for superstitious reasons which he can best explain, containing the double "o".

Whether because of this or not, Adams' yachting luck has not been bad. In 1892, he sailed the *Harpoon* to victory for the Goelet Cup off Newport and with his hand on the helm of the *Resolute* won the right to defend the America's Cup for which Sir Thomas Lipton had challenged in 1914.

"Who is this man Adams?" Lipton asked, when he heard the name of his adversary.

It took him six years to find out. Because of the World War, the race was not held until 1920, when the *Shamrock IV* won the first two heats, and the *Resolute,* with Adams at the helm, the second two. In the deciding race, the *Shamrock* gained the coveted weather position, blanketed the *Resolute* and held the lead for mile after mile. On the home stretch with his ship under so much sail she was half under water, Adams brought the *Resolute* in, just ahead of the challenger.

Aside from his yachting and investment achievements, however, the life of Charles Francis Adams, prior to the time Herbert Hoover rescued him from oblivion, had been much like that of any other rich man's son. True, he had been a member of the Municipal Council at Quincy, village of his forefathers, from 1892 to 1895, but that was expected of the Adams family. Also he had even been mayor of Quincy for one year.

Other than this, Adams never had held public office. He had been a typical Boston blue-blood—studious, unostentatious, sedentary. He was graduated from Harvard, where he had been president of his class for four years, was elected life president, and later coached the varsity crews, together with Senator Henry W. Keyes, of New Hampshire, famous as the husband of Mrs. Frances Parkinson Keyes.

That was his sum total of accomplishment for a family which has served the nation since its founding and which in recent years has been anxiously eager—futilely eager—to serve.

"The Adamses," once said his uncle Henry, "are on sale cheap."

So when Herbert Hoover proffered the post of Secretary of the Navy, Charles Francis Adams III jumped at the chance.

*

THE new Secretary did not know the location of the Navy Building in Washington, a rear admiral from a vice admiral, or whether the Marine Corps was a part of the War or the Navy Department. He knew the rigging of a sailing vessel as he knew the assets of the companies in which Harvard University had invested, but he knew nothing of turbines, guns, nor the intricate organization of his Department.

Realizing all this, Adams settled down to his new job with the quiet simplicity characteristic of his family. In his Boston office, destitute of rugs or easy-chairs, Adams kept no office boy and greeted visitors himself. At the Navy Department he is much the same. The navy almost held its breath one day when their chief executive walked into the navy cafeteria, picked up a tray, and proceeded to stand in line with the stenographers, clerks, enlisted men and admirals who helped themselves to desserts, salads, hash and navy beans. Nor was this a mere play to the galleries. Every day from that time on, Adams has stood in line, tray in hand, at the navy cafeteria.

In spite of his aristocratic lineage, Adams has been consistently democratic throughout his career as Secretary. Arriving at Mare Island, California, to review the Marines stationed there, the commandant trotted out the usual folderol and formality of a review, to which Adams remarked:

"Cut out the gold braid; I see enough of that in Washington."

Although a democrat around the Navy Department, Adams is an autocrat aboard his own sailing ship. Even his son, Charles, who crossed the Atlantic with him in the King of Spain's yachting race in 1928, calls him "Mister" when afloat.

Adams has a face which lends itself to autocracy. In fact, it was his face which, during his undergraduate days at Harvard, won him the nickname of "Deacon." Usually he wears a high stand-up collar which gives an even more solemn appearance to a narrow and severe mouth, a high forehead and the over-size nose typical of the Adams family. It is an ensemble which carries dignity, even when all that can be seen is a large nose and a semi-bald head bobbing up and down over the waves of the swimming pool of the *Leviathan,* on which Adams and other members of the American Delegation to the London Naval Conference returned in 1930. Adams, who loves to swim almost as much as he loves to sail, was in the pool almost every day, where he paddled as placidly as is possible around a mixed mob of youngsters more concerned with throwing a rubber polo ball at one another than with showing proper respect to the Secretary of the Navy.

Adams' stern face, however, is not all that it indicates. With the possible exception of Ray Lyman Wilbur, Secretary of the Interior, he has the keenest sense of humor in the Cabinet, and partly because of this is in great demand at the dinner parties which have featured the capital's Dance of the Depression. Mrs. Adams, daughter of Congressman Lovering of Massachusetts, had known Washington before and is an expert hostess. Their house is one of the most popular and exclusive in the capital, although neither as popular nor as exclusive as Charles Francis' Uncle Henry's.

In coöperation with John Hay, who later became Secretary of State, Henry Adams had built a red brick mansion facing the White House, and to it streamed all the intellectuals in Washington. The house, according to Cecil Spring-Rice, later British Ambassador, was "full of strange trophies from Japan and a precious idol given him by the Japanese Minister." The home of his nephew, in contrast, is featured by a rose-colored drawing-room, on the walls of which hang the portraits of John Adams and his wife Abigail, together with those of John Quincy Adams and his wife Louisa Catherine. They look down a little grimly upon the élite assemblages of their great-great-grandson as if they did not quite approve of such be-jeweled ladies and their smug escorts at times like these; but the net effect appears to add rather than to detract from the popularity of the Adams' parties.

Adams' sense of humor has been one of the great delights of his admirals, not too well endowed with this characteristic themselves, and certainly not accustomed to it in previous Secretaries of the Navy. They got an inkling of what their new Secretary was like on the day he took the oath of office. A battery of photographers was busy firing flares and shouting commands.

"Look this way, Mr. Secretary."

"Hold the Bible a little higher."

"Now just repeat that oath again."

"Make your lips move, anyway."

The new Secretary of the Navy obeyed dutifully. Finally they put him at his desk with a pad of paper in front.

"Now write something."

He did so.

After it was all over, one of the photographers happened to look at the pad of paper on which the new Secretary of the Navy had scribbled. It read:

"This is hell."

Adams' sense of humor has sometimes run away with things and on one celebrated occasion indirectly led to additional complications during the famous dispute with Major General Smedley D. Butler, U.S.M.C. retired, who had told a Philadelphia audience how Premier Mussolini had refused to stop his automobile after running over a child.

During the summer of 1930, Butler was in line for promotion to become commandant of the Marine Corps, and in order to impress upon the Secretary of the Navy his efficiency as an officer, invited Adams to Quantico, on the banks of the Potomac just below Washington, to visit Marine headquarters there. The admirals who surrounded Adams, all of them prejudiced against Butler, had tipped off their chief that the aspiring candidate to be Marine Corps commandant would stage a pretentious show, and they gave him facts and figures regarding some of the alleged inefficiencies of Quantico. Adams therefore arrived all primed for the occasion.

General Butler, meanwhile, also was primed. He and his men had been working for days in preparation for the inspection, and as Butler and Adams rode into the town they passed a large and ornate sign along the Virginia highway which read:

"Welcome to Secretary Adams."

"Hmph," snorted the guest of honor, "why waste money on that?"

Undismayed, General Butler took Adams over his model establishment, pointing with pride to his modern parade grounds and barracks.

"Hmph," snorted the Secretary of the Navy again. "Most expensive place for training men in the United States."

The unquenchable Butler then brought out his crack regiments for parade and inspection. They had been drilled for days in preparation for the event and they did their stuff well.

"Don't carry themselves as well as the midshipmen at Annapolis," Adams remarked dryly.

By this time Butler was beginning to be a little irked and Adams highly amused. But the Marine Corps general continued with his program. The next inspection was the airplane hangar, of which all Quantico is proud.

"What is the Marine Corps doing with airplanes?" Secretary Adams remarked. "They ought to leave flying to the navy."

This was a little too much for Smedley Butler, and while entertaining his chief at luncheon a little later, he told the assembled table the story of a Southern hostess who had invited to dinner a Methodist preacher whom she was especially anxious to please. The hostess brought forth her choicest dishes, among them some young fried chicken, but was informed that her guest did not relish chicken.

"Then have some of my fresh lima beans just picked from the garden," the hostess suggested.

Her guest declined.

"Well, here are some lovely damson plums that I put up myself. Won't you try them?"

Her guest turned up his nose.

Finally after several other suggestions, all of them spurned, the hostess turned to her guest and asked:

"Well, what do you eat? Do you suck eggs?"

The story went down much better with Adams himself than it did with the admirals who surrounded him. That a mere Marine Corps general should exhibit such levity in the presence of his chief shocked them profoundly and the next day they summoned Butler to Washington for an explanation. He had none to give. Shortly after that the admirals sent to Adams their recommendations for the new commandant of the Marine Corps. The name of Smedley Darlington Butler was not on the list.

*

LATER the story helped to intensify the consternation of the admirals and the merriment of the public during one of the silently waged but highly embarrassing feuds between the Secretary of the Navy and his chief in the White House.

These feuds have been the outstanding feature of the Adams' administration of the Navy Department. They are the chief reason why the admirals all love Charles Francis. This is the first time a Secretary of the Navy has stood up for them against the President of the United States at the risk of losing his own job—and they appreciate it.

Theodore G. Joslin, before becoming a White House secretary, wrote of Adams in *World's Work:* "He represents President Hoover as loyally as the earlier Adams expressed the sentiment of the electorate that honored him."

Probably Joslin has had occasion since then to regret that statement. For sometimes he, himself, has been in the thick of the Hoover-Adams controversies. Once when the President and Adams were at odds over the size of the navy's appropriation, the latter indicated to newspapermen that Joslin, not he, was now running the navy.

"If you want information on that," was Adams' daily reply to inquiries in press conferences, "you will have to ask Mr. Joslin."

At one time, also, relations between Hoover and Adams became so strained that White House instructions to the Navy Department were sent, not to the Secretary of the Navy, but to Ernest Lee Jahncke, Assistant Secretary and intimate friend of the President.

The underlying factor in this strained relationship is the navy's powerful propaganda machine.

There was a day when the navy did not need propaganda. There was a day when the navy could get all it wanted, regardless of the Senate. Those were the glorious days when Admiral Meade, cruising the South Seas, could discover the Islands of Samoa, which he considered a strategic naval base, and persuade a native chief to sign a treaty ceding the islands to the United States. And when the Senate refused to approve the treaty, the navy was strong enough in those days to prevail upon President Grant to send an agent to Samoa who made himself prime minister and placed the islands under American protection. When the Senate again refused its approval, the navy was strong enough to induce a local chieftain to come to Washington and cede the islands anyway.

That the navy is able so deftly to defy the welfare and wishes of the nation is because the admirals have decreed that the chief function of the navy is not to fight but to mesmerize the American public regarding the value of a big navy to the country.

This it does by various and devious formulas, some subtle, some blatant, but all based upon the thesis that the taxpayer pays the cost of propagandizing the taxpayer.

One of the more open and aboveboard of these formulas

is Navy Day, which would appear to be an innocuous sort of thing, were it not for the fact that instead of being a spontaneous move of the people, it is given months of artificial respiration at a large cost to the taxpayer. Long before Navy Day comes around a special unit of Naval Intelligence is busy flooding the press with photographs and propaganda.

"The small town and farm papers are fairly easy," according to one of the lieutenants in charge of this work. "We just send them the stuff and they play it up big. The higher class magazines are a little more difficult. For them we have to get an admiral to write a signed article and they usually are tickled to death to be able to use his name. Of course, we write the articles ourselves and put the stuff in it we want to get across, but we give the check to the admiral and it works out very nicely all around."

A little more invidious, but even more effective, is the navy's liaison with Congress. Through either an act of God or deliberate wire-pulling—probably the latter—the navy always has been blessed with having some of the most moronic members of the House and Senate appointed on the Naval Affairs committees. The roll-call of the Senate Committee, for instance, sounds like a roll-call of that body's famous Mutes. They include:

Freddie "Rowboat" Hale, Chairman, Republican of Maine, whose father once set a tradition by heading the Naval Affairs Committee, whom Freddie ever since has been struggling valiantly to emulate.

"Semaphore Sam" Shortridge, Republican of California, who doesn't know the difference between a cruiser and a tug.

Tasker L. Oddie, Republican of Nevada, a State which has never seen a ship larger than a mud scow.

"Trained Seal" Hamilton F. Kean, Republican of New Jersey, who "sugared" his way into the Senate.

Phillips Lee Goldsborough, Republican, the "Gentleman from Maryland."

"Puddler Jim" Davis, Republican of Pennsylvania, the lightest featherweight ever representing that State in the august upper chamber.

Park Trammell, Democrat, ex-traveling salesman of Florida, who still sleeps in hotels and on office couches.

Edwin Sidney Broussard, of Louisiana, a Democrat in name, but actually a Republican.

David Ignatius Walsh, Democrat, the bellowing bull from Massachusetts.

All of these cherish a reverence for the gold braid of the navy second only to that of the Deity, and a statement made to them by an admiral carries more weight than the gospel. With a committee like this, all the admirals have to do during a row with the White House is to slip quietly up to Capitol Hill and unfold the wrongs and injustices of the President to their patron saints on the Naval Affairs Committee who fix things for them every time.

Devout as is the obeisance of the Senate committee, however, none of them, with the exception of Freddie Hale, is as prostrate in his abasement as are Representatives Fred Britten and Carl Vinson, the first an Illinois Republican and former chairman of the House Naval Affairs Committee, the latter a Georgia Democrat, and the committee's present presiding officer.

To Fred Britten as much as to any one goes the credit for the navy's new big building program. Britten is not merely a worshiper of all things naval. He is also a blatant, belligerent fighter. An ex-pugilist from Chicago, Britten has now transferred his fistic prowess from the ring to the House of Representatives, where he fights for everything and anything the navy wants.

And the navy, knowing on which side its bread is buttered, has responded.

It even sent the entire Atlantic fleet to maneuver off one of Mr. Britten's real estate projects, thereby boosting property values.

The project was located at Montauk at the tip end of Long Island, where Promoters Clinton L. Bardo and Laurence R. Wilder, of the New York Shipbuilding and the American

Brown-Boveri companies, had invested heavily with the idea of establishing a terminal for a four-day express service across the Atlantic. Their venture depended upon raiding the United States Treasury through either Congress or the Shipping Board, and to aid them in this they brought in the Honorable Fred A. Britten, as a heavy stockholder, and paid $25,000 to William Baldwin Shearer for disrupting the Geneva Naval Conference and for other lobbying services.

When their raid on the Treasury failed, however, and they found themselves with a lot of worthless Long Island real estate on their hands, the shipbuilders decided to boost Montauk as a summer resort. To promote the plan Britten conceived the idea of having the Scouting Fleet hold its annual maneuvers off Montauk instead of Newport. He put the proposition up to the admirals and the admirals obliged.

The only hitch was that the men and officers didn't like Montauk. Prices were too high. Pretty women were too few. There was no place to go—not even a good movie house. After Newport, Montauk was a wash-out. So the younger officers, not realizing the delicate responsibilities which the admirals carried on their shoulders, spilled the beans.

When the New York papers splashed the incident over their front pages, Britten admitted he was a stock-holder in the real estate project, but countered with the claim that the navy was needed here to counteract pacifist propaganda. The admirals countered with the plea that they always tried to please congressmen.

In this they told the truth. Where congressmen are concerned the navy struggles to please. Whether it be free trips to Panama, the Far East, or the sending of a cruiser to a Senator's home city for a civic festival, the navy is there with the goods. The admirals know that it pays.

The most devious and probably the most effective propaganda work of the navy, however, is carried on through such patriotic organizations as the Daughters of the American Revolution, the Daughters of 1812, the Gold Star Mothers, the

National Defense Council and a half dozen others. These usually work hand in glove with retired naval officers, or in many cases direct with the admirals of the General Board. During the negotiations prior to the London Naval Conference, the latter was the case, the General Board doing its best to sabotage the negotiations every step of the way.

The State Department at that time was trying to work out the basis for a naval treaty with Great Britain, following which it planned to call a general naval conference. A conference was considered futile until the American and British navies had an understanding over their major difficulties, and to this end the State Department was in consultation with the admirals all during the summer of 1929.

The issue at stake was the number of eight-inch gun cruisers to be built by the United States in comparison with the number in the British fleet. The admirals threw up every conceivable objection, and, when all of these failed, began to feed out subterranean information through their pipe lines to patriotic organizations. Their most effective organ was *The Woman Patriot,* edited by Mary Kilbreth, sister of Brigadier General John W. Kilbreth, Jr., and close to the members of the General Board. The attack was based not on the issue involved— the size of the American and British fleets—but was launched against the character and personality of the admirals' chief enemies, Secretary Stimson and his Under Secretary, Joseph P. Cotton.

"He is a perfect pacifist," *The Woman Patriot* said of Stimson, "Secretary of Statements extraordinary and minister plenipotentiary of surrender—whose record could only be improved by his resignation!"

And finally after describing Stimson's chief characteristics as "ignorance, pacifism and the spirit of surrender," *The Woman Patriot* dug into his war record.

"Why," it asked, "did he come back from France just at the time when officers fitted to command American troops in combat were most sorely needed? Why was Colonel Stimson sent home? He knows, of course, and the high army officers who ordered him home know—but the general public does not, because his war record on this point is secret."

Of all the patriotic propagandizers in favor of a big navy, however, the most powerful, unscrupulous and consistently irrepressible is the Navy League. There is good reason why it should be. It pays. Those who have stepped forward from the ranks of American taxpayers to save the country by placing armor-plate orders with the steel companies are not actuated entirely by patriotic motives. The names of the founders of the Navy League read like a meeting of metallurgical magnates. They include:

Charles M. Schwab, Bethlehem Steel Corporation.

J. Pierpont Morgan, United States Steel Corporation and owner of a controlling interest in the Carnegie Steel Company.

Colonel R. M. Thompson, International Nickel Company.

B. F. Tracy, attorney for the Carnegie Steel and Harvey Steel Companies, and director of the Tennessee Coal and Iron Company.

George Westinghouse, of the Westinghouse Electric Company.

Clement A. Griscom, director of the Cramp Ship and Engine Company, the Electric Boat Company and the United States Steel Corporation.

S. S. Palmer, director of the Lackawanna Steel Company.

Eighteen members of the Midvale Steel Company.

These men have been working quietly and effectively behind the scenes to promote the cause of bigger and better battleships ever since 1904, and few people realized the ramifications of the League until Herbert Hoover gave it a million dollars' worth of free publicity in 1931 by answering its charge that he was "abysmally ignorant."

The uncomplimentary epithets exchanged at that time between the White House and William Howard Gardiner, president of the Navy League, got nowhere and settled nothing. The Navy League board, packed with big-navy advocates, upheld Gardiner, while the board of Navy League judges, packed with friends of the President, decreed that he was not "abysmally ignorant."

Every writer on naval affairs has long known that the officers of the Navy League repeatedly have resorted to the "distortion of facts" and figures of which they were accused by President Hoover. Members of the League also have been active, and have admitted their activity, in sabotaging attempts at naval reduction through international conferences. It was Schwab and his associates with the Bethlehem Steel Company who paid $25,000 to "Big Bass Drum" Shearer, one of the most effective naval propagandists in the country, to frustrate the Geneva Conference of 1927.

Shearer's efforts at that conference contributed toward its disastrous failure, but his contribution would have been infinitesmal had he not secured the all-too-eager coöperation of several naval officers attached to the American delegation— supposedly sent to Geneva to aid the cause of disarmament.

Entertaining in his own spacious apartment over Lake Leman or seated in the saloon of La Residence Hotel after dinner, Shearer spent most of his evenings in the company of Admiral Frank H. Schofield, now commander of the fleet, Rear Admiral Joseph M. Reeves, Commander Harold C. Train and Lieutenant Commander H. H. Frost.

Although the assistance which Admiral Reeves gave Shearer toward wrecking the Conference subsequently was brought out before a Senate investigating committee, the part which he played in attempting to sabotage another naval project and the displeasure which he incurred from Secretary Adams have not hitherto been revealed.

The incident occurred during deliberations to decide upon the location of a dirigible mooring mast for the navy's airships, the *Los Angeles* and the *Akron,* on the Pacific Coast. Admiral Reeves was appointed a member of a committee to decide upon this location, the other members being Rear Admiral William A. Moffatt, chief of naval aëronautics, Chairman; Commander Garland Fulton; Lieutenant Commander

Charles E. Rosendahl; and Lieutenant Commander E. L. Marshall. All of these were aviation officers except Reeves, who was the only member representing the General Board.

The committee decided to locate the dirigible base at Sunnyvale, California, near San Francisco, the decision being unanimous except for Reeves, who favored Camp Kearney at San Diego. When the report went to the General Board, however, Reeves, being a member of that august body, used his influence, with the result that the General Board, having the navy's last say in the matter, recommended San Diego.

When Secretary Adams sent this to the Naval Affairs Committee of the House, which had the final choice in selecting the site, the committee in turn asked Adams for a copy of the General Board's report. Adams refused. Later Representative William E. Evans, Republican, who comes from Southern California, and therefore favored San Diego, turned up in the committee with a copy of the General Board's report favoring that city for the dirigible base.

Representative Arthur M. Free, of San José, California, charged that Reeves had given the report to Evans, despite the refusal of the Secretary of the Navy to give it to the whole committee. Reeves never denied this charge, and Secretary Adams wrote a letter apologizing for the incident in which he said that it "reflected no credit on this Department."

What Admiral Reeves carefully withheld from Representative Evans, however, was that part of the General Board's report, disclosing that Admiral Schofield, then in charge of naval war plans, had found San Diego could not be used as a dirigible base in time of war and that it was essential, for considerations of strategy, to locate the base at San Francisco.

Representative Free, commenting upon Reeves' subterranean disclosures, said:

"The navy has been leaking like a sieve and it is time something was done about it."

Perhaps it was because Free had not enjoyed long association with the navy that he was so naïve as not to realize that "leaks" are among the admirals' most effective means of propagandizing. When a White House decision has gone against them, when the State Department is carrying on a negotiation which the admirals oppose, when they fail to get their full appropriation, then the safest and best strategy is to leak. This they do to the press or to a discreet member of Congress. Both channels are effective. A furore is stirred up. The President or the State Department is pictured as stripping the country of its defense and baring its bosom to the enemy—and after all the furore has subsided, the admirals usually find themselves on top.

More recently the admirals have found a safe means of leaking by which they incur no risks. This is through the medium of Captain Dudley W. Knox. Captain Knox is retired. The admirals find him a useful servant, however, and keep him on the pay-roll at $6,000 a year as naval librarian. Captain Knox's chief duty, however, is that of admirals' copy boy to the press. Whenever the big-navy New York *Herald Tribune* or the Washington *Post* publishes a story upholding the admirals and attacking the administration, it is a safe bet that Knox has made the rounds of the press bureaus the night before.

It was through this channel that the row between Admiral William V. Pratt and Rear Admiral Hilary P. Jones, on the eve of the London Conference, first became known. This clash was the first in which Charles Francis Adams found himself differing with his chief in the White House. And the discord which it sowed still has its repercussions in the Navy Department.

Hilary Paul Jones is a white-haired and turbulent old gentleman. He inherited his militant patriotism from a father who commanded an artillery company in Lee's Army and from a mother who was a great-granddaughter of John Marshall, Chief Justice of the United States. Jones first went to sea in the days when marine guards had to be stationed over the hatches to prevent mutiny in the crews and when the sailors swam out to their vessels when they weighed anchor. As an ensign just out of Annapolis he got his first taste of salt water in the famous Samoa hurricane in 1889—an act of God which probably prevented war between the United States and Germany, but which blew Jones and the cruiser *Nepsic* high and dry on a Samoan atoll.

The United States had sent a small squadron, including the *Nespic* and the *Adams,* to Samoa to prevent the islands' annexation by Germany. That country claimed the natives had murdered German missionaries and blew up a couple of Samoan villages in retaliation. One morning while the Germans were about to bombard another village, the *Nepsic* with Jones aboard, slipped in between the German cruiser and the shore, defying her to fire over the *Nepsic's* decks. The German backed out and came in between the *Nepsic* and the shore, whereupon the *Adams* slipped in front of her guns. The German repeated the process, this time coming so close to the shore that neither American vessel could follow. Then a British gunboat took up the game and blocked off the German cruiser's guns.

The hurricane struck next day, preventing further strained relations. Two American vessels went down with all hands lost. The *Nepsic,* with three anchors dragging, engines going full speed ahead and Ensign Jones on watch, was gradually being forced by the wind back on the reef. Finally Jones gave the order to slip the anchor chains and headed the ship for the sand. It piled up just a yard from the reef. Later the *Nepsic* was patched together and started for New Zealand. but was forced back by storms. On a second attempt to make Honolulu, she ran out of coal and took refuge on a coral atoll called Fanning Island, from which she was finally rescued by a convoy.

With this background Hilary Jones labored under the conviction that he knew what the navy needed and was qualified to fight for it. His outstanding conviction in this respect was that a large number of cruisers carrying eight-inch guns was essential to the efficiency and combatant strength of the United States Navy. On this point he had been adamant during the Geneva Naval Conference of 1927, and on this point he was also adamant during the negotiations leading up to the London Naval Conference of 1930.

The State Department, however, held a somewhat reverse view. It pointed out that the United States Navy never had built an eight-inch gun cruiser, never had sailed one, never had fired one of its big guns, and therefore was not qualified to say whether they were or were not essential to the efficiency and combat strength of the fleet. It proposed, therefore, that the United States accept a sliding number of cruisers, building eighteen if it found them to be really efficient, and only fifteen, plus a greater number of six-inch gun cruisers, if they did not come up to expectations.

This point was argued back and forth during the entire summer of 1929, the admirals getting more and more irritated, and resorting to increasing retaliation against the State Department through such subterranean channels as *The Woman Patriot*. At one time Charles Francis Adams got his New England dander up and engaged in a heated debate with his Cabinet colleague, Mr. Stimson. Mr. Adams was sticking with his admirals.

There was only one outstanding admiral who differed with Jones. He was Admiral William V. Pratt, commander of the United States Fleet. Pratt came from a much more modern and realistic naval school than Jones, sometimes called the "Sims school," which was noted for its willingness to scrap old-fashioned methods of warfare. Pratt was one of the expert advisers at the Washington Conference who approved the Hughes reduction program for battleships, and certain die-hards in the navy have never forgiven him. Nor have they forgiven him for approving the State Department's position regarding eight-inch gun cruisers in 1929. Nevertheless, Pratt did approve, and perhaps partly because of that fact was ap-

pointed one of two chief naval advisers to the American Delegation at London. Admiral Jones was the other.

The appointment of the two men was officially announced
by President Hoover, himself. All the names of the civilian
members of the delegation had been made public. Everything
was set for the conference.

Then suddenly it leaked out through the Washington *Post,*
one of the big-navy organs through which the admirals operate, that Admiral Jones never had accepted the appointment
and did not intend to go.

Consternation immediately broke forth at the State Department. Secretary Stimson scoffed at the idea. He denied there
was any truth to the report. But Admiral Jones remained obdurate. He was polite but firm. And the admirals who had
put the whole thing up to him chortled up their sleeves and
egged him on further.

Adams at that time did not know very much about naval
reduction, but the admirals had pretty well sold him on the
value of the eight-inch gun and he stood up for them.

So, to save the embarrassment of having Admiral Jones
drop out of the London Conference at the last minute, the
White House yielded. Hoover appointed an additional delegate. Charles Francis Adams, Secretary of the Navy, already
regarded as its great protector, became a member of the already over-staffed American Delegation. The theory was that
Adams could see that Jones got a square deal for his eight-
inch gun cruisers; and under this compromise, the recalcitrant old sea-dog agreed to go to London.

It was Adams' first brush with the President and before he
left London he had completely reversed himself on the question of cruisers. This brush was settled more amicably than
any of the others.

The second started out by prodigiously amusing Adams'
sense of humor but ended without any one thinking there was
anything funny about the incident except General Smedley
D. Butler, whom it chiefly concerned.

Butler had told a Philadelphia audience how Benito Mussolini, driving his own high-powered car from Rome to the
Italian naval maneuvers had struck a child, and instead of
stopping, had put up his hand reassuringly on the knee of his
American companion and said: "What is one life in the affairs
of a state?"

Nothing could have so upset the State Department or so
pleased the austere members of the General Board. All of them
had repeatedly been the butt of Butler's caustic criticism; and
with the publication of his speech and the Italian Ambassador's request for an apology, the admirals went around con-
gratulating themselves.

They placed Butler under arrest and decided to court-mar-
tial him. Rear Admiral David F. Sellers, Judge Advocate, prepared drastically worded specifications, pyramiding two
charges on only one incident. The White House concurred
heartily in this, and the State Department, having apologized
abjectly to Italy, applauded. Adams, highly amused, gave his
admirals free reign.

Within a week, however, the entire Navy Department
changed its tune. The drastic charges against Butler, for which
if convicted, he could have been dismissed from the service
and given fifteen years' imprisonment, plus the unpopularity of Mussolini, aroused an avalanche of public opinion
supporting the Marine Corps officer. Several thousand letters
flooded his office at Quantico, many of them containing checks.
Editorials supported him, at the same time castigating the admirals, Hoover and Mussolini. A large section of the public
appeared to believe that Mussolini really was a hit-and-run
driver.

Whereupon the admirals went into a blue funk. Their broad
grins disappeared. They had started out to crucify Butler and
were beginning to find themselves on the cross instead. So
they launched a counter-campaign. They put out the idea that
they had never favored Butler's trial by court martial at all,
but that it had been insisted upon by Hoover. They were un-

wittingly aided in this counter-campaign by a story which Butler himself had unleashed.

When he was a young lieutenant in the Boxer Rebellion, he told some of his friends, he had been called out of his head-quarters at Tientsin by a messenger who said that an American civilian was in a go-down where a large number of women had been placed for their own safety. The man, he was told, refused to come out. Butler, according to his story, went up to investigate, found the man, and hauled him out by the scruff of the neck. The man, Butler said, was Herbert Hoover.

This was the reason, according to the report circulated by the admirals, why the President was so relentless in his determination to punish the critic of Mussolini.

Whether or not this was true, and whether or not the Butler-Hoover story in Tientsin was true, never has been established. Probably neither ever will be. It is a fact, however, that the entire incident increased the ill-will already existent between the White House and the Navy Department, and Charles Francis Adams, who had let his admirals and his sense of humor run away with him, came in for considerable Presidential displeasure. In the end, all sides were glad when Ambassador de Martino, realizing that his Premier rather than General Butler was going to be on trial, asked that the court martial be dropped.

As a fitting climax to the buffoonery, it took the navy and the State Department three days to negotiate a basis on which Butler would consent to drop the court martial, and finally he agreed only on one condition; that he write his own reprimand—which he did.

All of this paved the way for the latest clash between Charles Francis Adams and his chief in the White House— a clash which nearly brought about the resignation of the Secretary of the Navy. The dispute was made more bitter by the attack of the Navy League on the President, but the issues at stake, from the navy's point of view, were much more fundamental than the Navy League.

It happened that during the few remaining hours of debate in the Seventy-first Congress, an appropriation for $10,000,000 had been rushed through for the purpose of building eleven destroyers. The navy had put up a hard fight for this appropriation. It had wanted money for an airplane carrier, a mongrel cruiser with airplane deck, a six-inch gun cruiser, four submarines, some additional airplanes for the carrier *Ranger* and $3,000,000 with which to experiment on Diesel engines for submarines.

All it got was the eleven new destroyers, and in order to get them it had to enter into a last-minute dicker with Senator Smith, Democrat of South Carolina, who wanted the navy to construct new ways for building destroyers at the Charleston, South Carolina, Navy Yard. The navy had not built a ship of any kind at Charleston since 1923 and did not propose ever again to do so. But for Senator Smith, politics was politics, and he blocked the appropriation for new destroyers until the navy promised to spend $150,000 on the new ways in his State.

Having suffered all these birth pangs in delivering the appropriation, and having gone so far as to open bids on their construction, the navy received a hint from the White House that the ships should not be built after all. The admirals, to put it mildly, were miffed.

These were days of economy and naval reduction, President Hoover suggested, and the expenditure of $10,000,000 meant just that much more to be raised in taxes.

The White House cold sponge took the form of a hint rather than an outright prohibition, and Adams, just as anxious as his admirals to build the new ships, adopted cautious tactics. He decided to proceed as if the destroyers were to be built, until definitely notified to the contrary. Congress had appropriated the money, Adams and his admirals argued, and it was up to the navy to carry out its program unless ordered otherwise.

About this time, however, the admirals made an extremely unwise move. Despite the fact that it was a year of stringent economy, they requested an appropriation of $400,000,000 for 1933, which instead of being a decrease, was just $40,000,000 more than they had received for the year 1932. The White House, considerably irritated, sent back the budget with the demand that it be cut $20,000,000 under 1932, or down to a total of $340,000,000.

It was at this point that the Navy League muddied up the waters with the charge that President Hoover, commander-in-chief of the navy, exhibited "abysmal ignorance." The commander-in-chief in question immediately saw red. He has, on various occasions, shown an exceedingly nasty temper, and this time he lost it completely. That he should have issued a statement castigating the Navy League was amusing but unimportant. That he summoned his Secretary of the Navy to the White House, however, and demanded a statement exonerating him of "abysmal ignorance" and of meddling with the navy was much more serious.

Adams, at the time, was totally out of sympathy with the President. He had followed a straight course. He had been for a big navy—the bigger the better—and he had not equivocated. Unlike his Cabinet colleague in the War Department, he had no political ambitions and did not try to carry water on both shoulders. He had not tried to curry favor with the President. The latter was quite aware that he and his Secretary of the Navy were completely out of step. So out of step were they that Hoover's instructions to the Navy Department during that period were sent not to the Secretary of the Navy but to Ernest Lee Jahncke, the Assistant Secretary. The President did not trust Adams, and he made no bones about it.

Thus slapped in the face, most men would have resigned. That Adams did not was due to two traits of character. In the first place he has always been a follower. He followed in his father's footsteps. All through life he has shown little initiative. In the second place, he is a long-suffering and silent fighter. His tactics are to wait, concede and wear down an excitable adversary. There was also the subsidiary fact that Adams liked his job and did not particularly want to lose it.

So he wrote the statement Hoover demanded. It said all that Adams and the entire Navy Department knew to be false— in effect that the President had not meddled in naval affairs and was not "abysmally ignorant" regarding them. Not only did he write the statement, but sent it to the White House for approval, and, when it came back with the initials "O. K. H. H." on the margin, made it public despite the fact that "H. H." had re-phrased some of Adams' language, making it much more critical of the Navy League.

Probably never before has a member of the proud Adams family bowed his head so low.

From a practical point of view, however, Adams' strategy probably was wise. In the end he got five of his eleven destroyers, and even Rear Admiral Ridley McLean, budget officer, admitted that the navy's appropriation was not cut nearly as severely as those of other departments. Finally, Adams' patience has now brought him back into the confidence of his chief, and the two men are reasonably good friends.

*

ALTHOUGH the feud between the White House and the admirals has been inextricably interwoven with naval policy all during the Hoover Administration, the navy also has been vitally influenced by another feud—that between the eight-inch gun admirals and those who favor the six-inch gun.

That two inches in the size of a gun could rend a navy literally asunder is hard for the average layman to understand. Yet this happened.

Even before the London Conference started, these two inches had caused a wide schism between the Navy Department, on the one hand, and the State Department and White House, on the other; but at London and afterwards, the admirals themselves were split into two bitter camps over the size of guns for their new 10,000-ton cruisers.

Admiral Pratt informed the American delegation that while he believed the eight-inch gun best adapted for the majority of American cruisers, the six-inch gun could shoot faster and was much more effective at close range, at night or in foggy weather. He argued that at least some criusers should be armed with six-inch guns in order to balance the fleet. He put up so convincing an argument that he even won the Secretary of the Navy, who had come to London to guard the interests of Admiral Jones and the General Board.

Admiral Jones, on the other hand, maintained that the eight-inch gun was so far superior that it should be used on every cruiser. When he failed to convince even Adams, he packed his trunk and came home, broken-hearted.

But it was not until after the Conference adjourned and the Senate held hearings on the merits and demerits of the Naval Treaty that the real fighting began. By this time every admiral of any standing had lined up on one side or the other. They belonged either to the Jones group or the Pratt group—and only two inches of a gun's diameter separated them. But those two inches were to them wider than the distance between heaven and hell.

The battle raged passionately. In open hearings and with newspaper men cabling several thousand words of their testimony to London and Tokyo daily, the admirals forgot themselves and disclosed secrets of naval strategy hitherto regarded as strictly confidential—secrets which had serious after-effects on relations with Japan, and which Secretary Stimson still is trying to iron out.

Privately, the feud was even more heated. Behind his back, Admiral Pratt was accused of selling out the navy to curry favor with the administration. It was said that he had agreed to champion the six-inch gun in order to be made Chief of Naval Operations—which subsequently he was.

But the point which most of the admirals missed completely was that the eight-inch gun was untried and that none of them, from actual experience, knew anything about it.

How abysmal was their ignorance, Senator David Aiken Reed demonstrated in cross-questioning Rear Admiral Jehu Valentine Chase, then a member of the board and about to become commander of the United States Fleet.

"You said you wanted to talk about technicalities," Reed said by way of preparation. "Were you graduated from the Naval War College?"

"No, because when I served for two terms on the staff of the college, there was no graduation."

"Have you ever commanded the Fleet?"

Chase replied that he was about to do so.

"Have you ever been Chief of Naval Operations?"

"No."

"Have you ever been Chief of the Bureau of Navigation?"

"No."

"Have you ever been to sea on an eight-inch gun cruiser?"

"No."

"Have you ever seen one in target practice?"

"No."

"Do you know the thickness of armor on their turrets?"

"I do."

"How thick are they on the *Salt Lake City?*"

"I don't recall."

"They are not so thick that they cannot be easily penetrated by a six-inch projectile at a range of 20,000 yards," Reed informed him.

"I would say 15,000 yards," Admiral Chase corrected.

"Do you know the thickness of the armor on the barbettes?"

"Three and one-half inches."

"Have eight-inch gun cruisers any barbettes?"

"Not strictly."

"Without asking your aide, do you know the thickness of the armor over the machinery spaces?"

"Ninety pounds."

"What is that in inches?"

"Two and one-quarter."

"At what range will a six-inch gun penetrate that?"

Admiral Chase turned to his aide, who fumbled through his papers.

"I haven't my penetration figures with me, but I can have them looked up," the admiral finally replied.

"I have the information," Senator Reed told the future commander of the fleet. "I wondered if you had it. How fast can the eight-inch guns on the *Salt Lake City* be fired?"

"The ship is brand new. I don't know."

"How fast can six-inch guns be fired?"

"It depends on how they are mounted."

"Assume they are mounted on turrets."

"About four times as against three for the eight-inch gun."

"Would you be surprised to know that they can be fired once every five seconds?" Senator Reed shot back.

"Yes, when mounted in the open."

"With a limitation of 10,000 tons you cannot put eight-inch guns and armor on ships, can you?" Reed continued.

"You cannot to any extent; but I think we have in later designs put quite adequate armor on."

"Tell us the name of those."

"I say the latest designs that we are now working on."

"You mean the designs that are not even completed yet?"

"No, sir, but they will be undertaken under this treaty."

"Some designs that are under way?" Senator Reed repeated.

"Yes."

"Which are not yet completed and under which no ship has been built, which you think will give some protection to the eight-inch gun ship, is that it?"

"It will not only give some but a very fair protection. I will not say wholly adequate, because I do not believe you can give wholly adequate protection to a cruiser."

"You surprise me," the Senator shot back. "Do you say that in these eight-inch gun ships that we are going to build we are not going to keep the *Salt Lake City* class?"

"I most surely say we are not."

"Then the *Salt Lake Cities* are no good?"

"They are as good as we understood at the time we built them."

"They were built under specifications laid down by the General Board?"

"They were, but we profited by the experience in building them."

"And only three out of the eight have been finished according to the specifications of the General Board," Senator Reed reminded him, "five are still being built, and yet you now find they are so defective you are not going to build any more of them."

Admiral Chase nodded.

*

How serious were the defects in these new eight-inch gun cruisers the admirals did not then know. They found out shortly thereafter.

They found out first of all that the stern posts on five of them had cracked. The stern post of any vessel is one of the most important parts of the ship, for on it hangs the rudder.

A little later the admirals discovered that the new cruisers rolled so much, even in calm weather, that it interfered with gun fire. This applied not merely to the five cracked cruisers of the navy but to all of them.

The former were sent back to the shipbuilders for new posts at a cost of $30,000 each. And as an experiment to prevent rolling, one of the cruisers was fitted out with bilge keels— steel fins extending along the side of the ship near the bottom

—while another was equipped with rolling tanks, placed on either side of the ship and connected by a pipe which distributed the water equally when the shipped rolled too far to one side.

Unlike the case of the defective blowholes found in armor plate during the Cleveland Administration, which Charles M. Schwab, then superintendent of the Carnegie Steel Company, admitted the company had concealed, the navy had to pay most of the cost of remodeling its new cruisers.

Both defects were admitted to be faults of naval design, due to the fact that the navy had never before built an eight-inch gun cruiser, or as the State Department expressed it during the London Conference preliminaries "never had sailed one around or shot off one of its big guns to see if the ships really were all they were supposed to be."

And yet the navy's adamant stand in favor of building twenty-five of these vessels had helped to wreck the Geneva Naval Conference in 1927, had caused the contention that the London Naval Treaty providing only eighteen of these ships jeopardized the national defense, and had split the higher officers of the Navy Department into two bitterly hostile groups.

After it was over and the defects of the new cruisers had been announced, Charles Francis Adams, always a sportsman, admitted that perhaps after all the State Department had been right.

Adams was sporting enough also to admit that perhaps the begrudging way in which Congress had voted funds for new cruisers in the last ten years was a godsend after all.

What he referred to was the fact that, whereas Great Brittain and Japan had built all the cruisers permissible under the Treaty and had made mistakes in their construction, the United States still had a large number of vessels to build and in doing so could profit by its own mistakes as well as the others. Thus, the United States can place airplane landing decks on all its remaining cruisers, while other nations, having completed their quota, cannot. Thus also, the United States, not having built up to its ratio of airplane carriers, can go in for new types—the fashions in this vessel being about as temperamental as women's styles. Airplane carrier design has shifted from the ample girth of the 33,000-ton *Lexington* and *Saratoga* to the slim 13,000-ton *Ranger,* and back again to the medium-waisted 20,000-ton displacement. As each of these modes was evolved the Navy Department pronounced them absolutely essential to national safety until another style came along more modish than the first.

*

THE wounds inflicted by the six-inch-eight-inch gun controversy have never healed. They still have an influence on naval policies and upon the stations to which certain admirals are transferred.

Admiral Pratt, who won the controversy, now rules the navy as Chief of Operations with a benevolent but iron hand. Secretary Adams places complete confidence in him and gives him almost entire control. He is a broad-gauge individual, probably the strongest man in the navy and unquestionably deserves this trust.

Born on the Maine coast, whence so many other seafaring men have come, Pratt entered Annapolis at the age of sixteen and has spent his entire life in the navy. Despite surroundings which tend to narrow most men, Pratt has kept a reasonable perspective. He likes to think of himself as a diplomat as well as a naval officer, and to some extent he deserves such a rating.

During the Shanghai crisis in the winter of 1932, when Japanese troops over-ran the International Settlement, even encroaching upon areas policed by American marines, Pratt gave evidence of a much steadier head than the man at the helm of American foreign policy. Secretary of State Stimson was convinced that war with Japan was inevitable, and his military aide, Captain Eugene Regnier, passed the word to newspaper men that nothing could avert hostilities between the two countries. The State Department at that time was discussing with Great Britain the possibility of an economic boycott against Japan, which admittedly would not have stopped with a mere boycott. Realizing the dangerous drift, Pratt and Adams called at the White House and did some straight talking to the President. Pratt did most of it. The idea of being dragged into a war with Japan was absurd, he told Hoover. The American Fleet was in no shape to fight. The Japanese navy could take the Philippines overnight and it would require two years for the United States to take them back again. Certainly if the State Department declared an economic boycott against Japan, Pratt concluded, war was inevitable.

Secretary of War Hurley took the same stand and Hoover called the State Department off.

Simultaneously, Pratt made some other moves which materially eased the crisis at Shanghai. Vice Admiral Taichisaburo Nomuri, whom Pratt had known at the Washington Conference, was appointed commander-in-chief of the Japanese forces at Shanghai. Pratt seized the opportunity to calm the hostility between the beleaguered Japanese and American forces by sending a cable expressing his confidence in the new commander.

Again when a Chinese shell slightly damaged the Italian cruiser *Libia,* lying off the Shanghai Bund, and the Italian commander issued a warning that if there were any more firing he would bomb the native city, Pratt immediately made public the text of Admiral Montgomery M. Taylor's admonition that such action would be foolish. Its publication had a calming influence on all foreign naval commanders at Shanghai.

Although usually the most forthright and straightforward admiral in the navy, Pratt can be just as devious as the diplomats he emulates. When Stimson first suggested that he keep the Atlantic Fleet in the Pacific during the period of the Far Eastern crisis, Pratt made a hurried trip to the West Coast, and, after a careful investigation, came back to Washington to explain that it would cost more money to retain the Fleet in the Pacific, but that it could be done. He explained carefully that the reason for the extra costs was that the West Coast navy yards were not equipped to overhaul and repair so many vessels at one time.

Two weeks later, however, after Stimson had requested the retention of the Atlantic Fleet in the Pacific regardless of cost, Pratt, the would-be diplomat, announced that the plan would save money.

Reminded of his earlier statement, the admiral grew livid with rage and forbade newspaper men to question him further.

Pratt's diplomacy also took devious channels when the navy decided to make an air survey of the Aleutian Islands to gauge their value as an aviation base in a war against Japan. In order to camouflage the fact that the survey was being made, Pratt called in the Commerce Department, and had Secretary Lamont write Secretary Adams a letter stating that the Coast and Geodetic Survey was anxious to have a scientific survey of the Aleutian Islands west of Kodiak Bay and requesting the navy to do the work for the Commerce Department. Thus the project was camouflaged.

When Admiral Pratt was questioned about the survey he insisted it was purely scientific. Unfortunately, Commerce Department officials did not tell the same story.

*

THE man who has given the admirals their greatest victory during the Hoover Administration is Ernest Lee Jahncke, assistant secretary. Ernest, as he is affectionately called by Charles Francis Adams, came to scoff and stayed to worship. He now plays the admirals' game.

Their conquest, however, was a long and difficult one.

When Jahncke took the oath of office, he was the first assistant secretary in many years not a Roosevelt. It has become a tradition both in the navy and the Roosevelt family that one of them shall serve as assistant secretary, no matter whether the administration be Democratic or Republican. The late Theodore Roosevelt set this precedent, it being continued several years later by Franklin D. Roosevelt, then by Theodore Roosevelt, Jr., and finally by Theodore Douglas Robinson, nephew of "T. R."

Despite this handicap, Ernest Lee Jahncke felt that he knew something about navies—certainly as much as Charles Francis Adams. He was president of the Jahncke Dry Dock Company of New Orleans, a member of the Southern Yacht Club, the New York Yacht Club and had been Louisiana State Chairman for the celebration of Navy Day since 1925. In fact, Jahncke was considered such a naval expert in his own home town that every one called him "Commodore."

When he got up to the Navy Department, however, the admirals claimed that he knew as much about the navy as one of their Negro messengers. This was not so much because of Jahncke's actual ignorance, but because he took his job seriously. He took the view that he had been appointed Assistant Secretary of the Navy and that he should earn his salary. He wanted to be useful. Unfortunately, he did not know that an assistant secretary of the navy merely is required to be ornamental.

The last thing the admirals want is a civilian executive who is always poking his nose into things. So they resented Jahncke and made life difficult for him. He was always calling them in for explanations which they thought unnecessary. He did not like to sign papers unless he knew what they were all about. He wanted to know what was going on. Against this the admirals rebelled. They ignored him as much as they could, and put him through a severe hazing.

Jahncke is a great joiner and the admirals publicized this fact. He belongs to the Boston Club, the Pickwick Club, the Audubon Club, the Metarie Golf Club, the New Orleans Country Club, India House, the University Club, the International Olympic Committee, the American Society of Mechanical Engineers, the American Society of Naval Architects, the Louisiana Engineering Society, the National Foreign Trade Council, the Board of Trustees of Newcomb College for Women, the Board of Administrators of Tulane University, and, last but not least, he is the king of the Mardi Gras.

The admirals made the most of this.

The result was that in those early days Jahncke commented continually and caustically about the admirals, and sometimes Adams. Even now, although harmony prevails, there are times when Ernest forgets that he is a chastened man and unburdens himself about the gentlemen who really run the navy.

*

ONE of the problems on which Jahncke painfully stubbed his toe was the century-old and never-ending dispute between the army and the navy. That Jahncke tackled the dispute at all proves him an optimist. But that he began with that particular part of the dispute which he did proves him a super-optimist of the Rotary-Kiwanis variety. Army-navy rivalry runs all the way from pride in their service bands to duplication of radio networks and squabbling over the honor and privilege of protecting the nation's coasts. These are comparatively simple, however, compared with the deep-seated jealousies engendered by athletic relations between the United States Military Academy at West Point and the United States Naval Academy at Annapolis.

Not since 1927 have athletic teams from these institutions battled against each other in regularly scheduled games of football, baseball, basketball, lacrosse, track, water polo, tennis, or even chess. Regarding the first of these especially, super-human efforts have been made to bring the two teams together. No problem of naval parity, slashes in national defense budgets or low service pay has so ruffled army-navy circles as the moot question of whether or not eleven men from West

Point and eleven men from Annapolis should line up against one another on a muddy field every year to satisfy an ancient rivalry between the two branches of the service.

The navy has contended that West Point should adopt the three-year eligibility rule and limit her men to three years of intercollegiate athletics.

The army has replied that forty-four per cent of her cadets come from other colleges, in view of which fact it would be unfair to discriminate between men prepared at other colleges where they played intercollegiate athletics and those prepared at high schools where they did not.

The navy has countered that the army deliberately went out scouting for these college athletes and enticed such men as Red Cagle, Carl Piper, Buster Perry, Polly Humber, Laurie Hillberg, Bill Parham and a host of others to West Point, where it helped with their expenses.

The army has replied with an investigation by Major General Hugh A. Drum, Inspector General of the army who refuted some of the navy's charges but did find West Point guilty of "scouting," of "interesting friends from or through whom appointments could be secured," and of "securing special scholarships at West Point preparatory schools."

"I am of the opinion," reported General Drum, "that such methods do not accord with the recognized high ethical standards of the academy."

Into this mêlée of charge and counter-charge jumped Ernest Lee Jahncke, just as blithely as though he were stepping into his bathroom to take a shower. And after a brief interval of conversation with the army, he informed the Secretary of War just as blithely that the dispute had been settled. Word to this effect was promptly passed out.

But Jahncke had reckoned without his admirals. Apparently he had not even taken the trouble to consult them, for when the new athletic rapprochement was reported, they flatly and firmly denied the whole thing. Furthermore, they had their way. It did not matter that the Assistant Secretary of the Navy had informed the Secretary of War that athletic relations between the two institutions were to be resumed. Rear Admiral S. S. Robison, Superintendent of the Naval Academy, put his foot down and the other admirals supported him. So the Secretary of the Navy again swallowed the pride of the Adams family and walked up to the office of the Secretary of War, where they issued a joint statement that the agreement was off.

To save face, Jahncke got the admirals to consent to a charity football game for the unemployed, regardless of eligibility rules.

Almost as bitter is the dispute as to whether the army or the navy shall have the honor and responsibility of guarding the coasts of the United States.

The controversey began with the advent of aviation as a real military weapon after the World War. Prior to that, it was decreed the army was responsible for protecting the coasts, since the guns of its Coast Artillery could shoot several miles out to sea. Beyond that distance the navy had the responsibility.

The advent of the submarine caused this antediluvian arrangement to be challenged for a time by Major General Arthur Murray. General Murray was Chief of Artillery and proud of his outfit. He felt that it was quite capable of protecting the coasts of the United States without the interference of the navy, and yet he saw in the perfection of this new and diabolical weapon of the under-seas a challenge to his coastal guns. So he submitted a formal proposal that the army build and operate submarines, thus preserving its historic responsibility of coastal defense.

The question arose again when Brigadier General William Mitchell, stormy petrel of the Air Corps—later demoted for his storminess—endeavored to head off any aviation ambitions on the part of the navy by asking Congress to limit the navy's aviation duties entirely to the sea. Congress refused, but did decide, in the National Defense Act, that the navy should confine its aviation activities to scouting and patrolling.

All went well until the army woke up to find that Rear Admiral William A. Moffett, Chief of the Bureau of Aeronautics had quietly slipped one over. He had built what the navy called "Three-Purpose Planes," adapted not only to scouting, but also to torpedoing and bombing. Furthermore he had stationed forty-five of these planes at Pearl Harbor, Hawaii and at Coco Solo, Panama.

This, the army claimed, was a clear violation of the will of Congress. It infringed on the historic responsibility of the army. A terrible furore was raised. The Bureau of the Budget was asked to stop the navy's appropriation for more of these planes. The Bureau of Efficiency was brought in to see which branch could most efficiently handle air coast defense. Finally the question was referred to Attorney General Mitchell and to the President. They were asked to interpret the will of Congress as outlined in the National Defense Act.

Meanwhile the acrimonious debate continued. The navy informed the army that its aviators did not know how to shoot at warships. The army replied that the only warships that ever had been sunk by airplanes were sunk by General Mitchell's army planes off the Virginia Capes.

To the army's contention that it always has been charged with the responsibility of coast defense, the navy retorted that the army had seemed unable to prevent the British Fleet from burning the city of Washington in 1814. The army replied that it was not navy, but army guns at Fort McHenry, Baltimore, which hurled back the British fleet while Francis Scott Key was composing the "Star-Spangled Banner."

The army contended that while it hated to drive all the navy's admirals out to sea, and away from their cushy desks in Washington, yet the army was not asking for battleships or airplane carriers and therefore did not see why the navy should want to come ashore. The navy, in reply, pointed out that the planes on its carriers are not equipped with pontoons, but with wheels, so that they land better on aviation fields than on water.

Finally the navy told the army that it was highly impractical for its planes to confine their belligerent efforts to scouting, since by the time a naval scouting plane sighted the enemy and then took time to fly back and hunt up an army bombardment plane to come and fight the enemy, the enemy might have vanished entirely. There is no guarantee, the navy complained, that the enemy will stay put.

The unfortunate thing about the dispute, from the army's point of view, was the fact that during the height of the controversy it chose to illustrate its ability to defend the coasts of the United States by sending an air squadron seventy-five miles off the Virginia Capes to blow up the *Mount Shasta,* a discarded Shipping Board freighter set adrift without a living soul aboard.

The army made great preparations. Arrangements were made to take newspaper men in transport planes and in a mine sweeper to witness and photograph concrete and convincing evidence of the army's air prowess. A "blow-by-blow" account of the bombs as they struck the wallowing freighter was to be broadcast to the breathless public.

Alas, that "blow-by-blow" account never was broadcast. The blows never hit. On the first trip, the army squadron, led by one of its crack pilots, Major Herbert A. Dargue, got lost and did not sight the *Mount Shasta* at all. On a second trip, they sighted the vessel and dropped all their bombs without a single hit. Three trips they made to find and finish off the patient *Mount Shasta.* On the last of these, they finally scored a semi-hit in the water alongside, but the Coast Guard had to be called in afterward to blow the tired vessel to her final resting place.

The navy did not even try to conceal its laughter. To drop one-hundred and three-hundred-pound bombs on a decrepit and defenseless freighter without armor plate, without antiaircraft guns, without protecting airplanes, and so old the

Shipping Board considered it valueless, the navy remarked, was like shooting crippled ducks from a boat. But under these circumstances not even to be able to hit the derelict was ample proof that the army had forfeited its ancient responsibility of protecting the coasts of the United States.

After which, the astute Admiral Moffett wrote out an order transferring the command of his land air bases to an admiral supposedly at sea. It was merely a move on paper. The planes still remain on land. The admiral also remains on land most of the time. But technically the navy's planes are commanded from the sea and therefore part of a sea force. So the army has no grounds for complaint. Even if it had, it would not have the face to complain—not after the *Mount Shasta*.

Continual bickering between the army and navy has contributed materially to the drive on the part of Democrats in Congress to amalgamate the two services into one fighting force. This bickering is constant and extends all along the line. There is even great jealousy between the army and navy bands because the army band went to the Seville Exposition not long ago and played before the King of Spain. When it came back it boosted its charges for private concerts twenty-five per cent over that of the navy band. It had played before a king.

*

THE Honorable Fred A. Britten has fought many battles for the navy but the best thing he ever did for it was secure passage of the so-called Britten Bill which provides that there may be only a certain percentage of officers in each rank. Thus all promotions from the rank of lieutenant commander up are made by a selection board. An officer must either pass or get out of the navy. The plan is based on the thesis that no inferior officers are wanted. If an officer fails to be selected he is given one year in which to study for a second test, and then if he fails, he retires. One year sixty-three lieutenant commanders passed and forty were retired.

Very little personal politics enters into navy promotions. When it does, it is bitterly resented. Recently it was injected by President Hoover in the promotion of Dr. Joel T. Boone from lieutenant commander to commander. Dr. Boone is the President's personal physician and also a first-class naval officer. However, his name was not on the list of lieutenant commanders sent by Secretary Adams to the White House for promotion. But on the list was the name of Lieutenant Commander William B. Hetfield, hero of the Nicaraguan earthquake disaster. President Hoover sent the list back with the notation that the name of Commander Hetfield be stricken off and Boone's name substituted.

The reason was that Hetfield had forced his way into the house of Pesident Moncada of Nicaragua and insulted him.

The circumstances surrounding this event were somewhat unusual. An American Marine, Sergeant W. H. Pigg, had been shot by native Nicaraguan troops. The State Department later said he had become "demented." His body was carried into the home of President Moncada, and Dr. Hetfield, having been informed that a wounded Marine was inside, rushed to the house. He was stopped at the door by Nicaraguan officials, among them Flores Vegas, Minister of Public Works, who does not speak English. Hetfield demanded entrance and was refused. Thinking the Marine was wounded and needed his attention, he thereupon forced his way in. When he found Sergeant Pigg dead, Hetfield told the assembled Nicaraguans, among whom was President Moncada, what he thought of them. Moncada then told Hetfield that he, and no naval officer, was President of Nicaragua.

The State Department later explained that Dr. Hetfield had performed more than one hundred major operations during the past twenty-four hours and had had little sleep. However, he was recalled immediately.

The navy considered that Hetfield's work merited promotion. He ranked in seniority any other lieutenant commander whose name was sent to the White House. He outranked Dr.

Boone by fourteen numbers, the latter being almost the lowest on the list. But the navy carried out the President's orders. Boone was promoted. Hetfield was not.

*

THINGS change gradually in the navy, but they do change. Charles Francis never fails to get to his office at 8:30 every morning. The navy cafeteria never fails to offer beans at luncheon. The navy press room never fails periodically to announce the number of Marine Corps officers killed by General Augustino Sandino in Nicaragua.

Nevertheless, things change. The advent of steam once brought changes. Now it is naval treaties. They place a premium on weight—to build the vessel under treaty limits and yet not waste any tonnage. To this end, rivets are giving way to welding, ordinary paint is being replaced by aluminum paint, and officers' steel furniture is now aluminum—all for the sake of less weight and a treaty navy.

Gradually also the navy is losing the romantic figures of the hard-boiled days when Captain Alexander Slidell Mackenzie hanged the son of John C. Spencer, Secretary of War, "at the mainyard-arm of the brig *Somers* for insubordination and attempted mutiny."

Mutiny is still a factor in the navy, but it is of the variety which caused the fire in the control-room of the *Colorado*—and never gets discovered. The fire started when phonograph needles were mysteriously hammered into cables, short-circuiting dozens of small wires connecting the guns with the control-room. After $100,000 had been spent repairing the loss, the officers of the *Colorado* found the cables stuck full of phonograph needles again.

A few remnants of the old hard-boiled days linger on. There is Rear Admiral William A. Moffett, three times appointed chief of the Bureau of Aeronautics, who once got the cruiser *Chester* off a bar in the bombardment of Vera Cruz. And there is Rear Admiral Ridley McLean, who went around the world with Fighting Bob Evans in 1907 when Theodore Roosevelt determined to show Europe that the United States had a fleet. Both men remain among the most efficient officers in the service.

Depression has helped more than anything to dispel the old romantic easy-go-lucky days of the navy. No longer can an officer junk the service and be sure of picking up a good civilian berth at a higher salary. No longer does Annapolis plead for more midshipmen. Naval salaries look more generous now. And the Naval Academy, instead of bemoaning a total of seven hundred and eighteen vacancies as in 1929, has been petitioning the Coast Guard, the Bureau of Lighthouses and the Coast and Geodetic Survey to take the surplus of young ensigns off its hands ever since 1930.

A youngster has to watch his step these days if he wants to keep a good navy berth; and the result is that the depression and the competitive promotion system are bringing forward a younger generation which some day may dispel the pungent atmosphere of petty politics and stultification so nutritious to the admirals.

CHAPTER SEVEN

CHIEF COOK AND BOTTLE WASHER

*P*OSTMASTER General Walter F. Brown is the political hatchet man of the Hoover Administration.

Behind the carefully draped scenes he pulls the wires and wields the ax. His cool ruthlessness supplies the force and decisiveness in the President's devious political machinations.

Walter is splendidly equipped to fill the requirements of his gory rôle. He has brains, courage, an iron stomach, a nimble conscience and the silken manners and irreproachable appearance of an Episcopal rector.

This galaxy of talents Walter embellished with four years in the rarefied atmosphere of Harvard and twenty-five years in the sordid depths of Ohio politics. During the course of the latter he learned the importance of keeping his own counsel and always doing his political skullduggery behind a respectable front. At Harvard he was taught the value of the gentlemanly air—a lesson he has never forgotten.

Other Harvard alumni, notably Big Bill Thompson, the mayor who bankrupted Chicago, and the late Senator Boies Penrose, one-time dictator of Pennsylvania, deliberately discarded genteel bearing in their political operations. But not Walter. He carefully eschews anything savoring of the political in his manner, speech and appearance. No baby kissing, back-slapping or glad-handing for him. No bellowing and fulminating. He is soft spoken and reserved. His face is pleasantly round, his hair neatly trimmed and carefully parted in the middle. The cold, calculating glint in his eyes is screened behind octagon-shaped glasses. He dresses well and quietly.

Walter's silk-gloved suavity and his inscrutability and agility in under-cover intrigue have created a legend of Oriental wiliness about him. It is an illusion he is very fond of and craftily fosters.

As the Republican boss of Toledo for over a quarter of a century, Walter always kept himself in the background in inconspicuous rôles, such as County Republican Chairman, and used respectable but complaisant puppets to mask his political dealings. In the national arena he has done the same.

In 1928, when he was doing Hoover's political dirty work, Walter shrouded himself in the imposing robes of Assistant Secretary of Commerce. In 1931 and 1932, when he wielded the patronage hatchet to bludgeon Republican leaders and Federal office-holders into supporting Hoover's re-nomination, Walter did his work behind the sanctimonious skirts of Senator Simeon D. Fess, dummy Chairman of the Republican National Committee. In the 1932 election campaign, when Simeon's usefulness as a marionette had evaporated, Walter substituted Everett Sanders, another stuffed shirt.

In his suave but firm rejection of Mr. Hoover's repeated efforts to make him Republican National Chairman, Walter was not only following the dictates of his own subterranean nature but his sound judgment of the underlying character of the President. Walter is a realist. He serves his masters well, but he has no illusions about them.

Walter saw what happened to Mrs. Mabel Walker Willebrandt, Horace Mann, Claudius Huston and "Wild Bill" Donovan after they had done Hoover's political skullduggery in 1928. The President washed his hands of them with dispatch and finality. In fact, Hoover's cold-blooded dismissal of these erstwhile henchmen is one of the few decisive acts of his administration.

Walter is very fond of his Cabinet sinecure. He loves the high honors that go with it, the opportunity it provides for dashing about the country and being in the center of the political merry-go-round. So he takes no chances with Hoover. Walter is willing to do the President's hatchet work, but he is careful to keep his skirts clear; so that if public clamor arises and Hoover has to have a goat, he will not toss Walter to the wolves.

How successful Walter has been in this crafty business is evidenced by the fact that, while three Republican national chairmen and a number of other White House satellites have walked the plank, he is still a member of the Cabinet and in the good graces of the President.

As a political hatchet man, Walter is unquestionably the ablest man in the Cabinet. Secretary of the Treasury Ogden L. Mills is no less astute, decisive and expedient, but he hasn't the political touch. "Oggie" is too conscious of the blue blood that courses in his over-stuffed torso to suit the average politician. Ancestry may go well at exclusive poker tables and at snooty Virginia horse shows, but the Republican boss trying to hornswoggle a constituency of Negroes, hunkies or Swede farm hands has no use for such trappings.

Walter is not only able, but he is a master craftsman at the business of practical politics. It is significant of his character that he alone of the Cabinet has never laved Hoover with the soft-soap that the President loves so much. Nor has he ever indulged in any prosperity-just-around-the-corner outpourings.

It is not that Walter does not value and understand the use and need of blah and hokum. But they are not in his line, and he leaves them for others. When a job of political hatcheting comes up, he does it promptly, thoroughly and without hosannas.

When Hoover set him to getting the Southern delegates, Walter issued no pronunciamentos about reforming Southern Republican politics. He had a job and he went at it directly and realistically. The President early in his administration had spoken unctuously about cleaning up Southern Republican politics. But Walter said nothing. He went South, trafficked with the "boys," as they are accustomed to being dealt with, and returned to Washington. When he was asked about the Southern situation he laconically expressed the opinion that "everything was all right."

To the knowing, that meant a competent man had done a thoroughgoing job and that when the roll was called at the Chicago convention the Southern delegates would be found voting for Hoover. Which is exactly what happened.

Early in 1932, Representative Louis T. McFadden, Republican regular of Pennsylvania, and Representative Victor Christgau, Republican progressive of Minnesota, attacked Hoover. The President excitedly demanded they be exorcised from the party.

The fatuous and sycophantic White House clique, Simeon D. Fess, Dave Reed, Walter Newton, Ted Joslin, "Tanglefoot Bob" Lucas and other of the brethren, tore their hair at the impiety of McFadden, who had accused Hoover of being a tool of the international bankers. They raged at Christgau's insurgency.

Walter indulged in no antics. He moved with vigor and ruthlessness. To him the two representatives were enemies of his master and he used the hatchet on them without chanting any litanies. He would have expected them to handle him just as mercilessly if the position had been reversed, and despised them if they hadn't.

While mild-mannered and soft-spoken, Walter can be tough and hard-boiled, when the occasion demands. When he addressed the convention of the National Association of Postmasters in Los Angeles in 1931 and ordered them to disregard civil service obligations and get busy reëlecting Hoover, Walter talked bluntly and to the point. Hoover needed votes and Walter told the postmasters to go out and get them.

When a nation-wide uproar arose over this brazen

demand, Walter offered no apologies and indulged in no hypocritical alibis that he was "misquoted," as did Irving Glover, Assistant Postmaster General, when he was caught red-handed doing the same thing.

In his appearances before congressional committees, Walter is equally direct and decisive. He is the only member of the Hoover Cabinet who has the private respect of members of Congress, regardless of what they may think of his policies and methods. He indulges in no long-winded and dreary lectures before committees, as Secretary of State Stimson does. Neither does he stage such puerile exhibitions of temper and petulance as posturing Secretary of War Hurley did when asked some embarrassing questions about Philippine independence by members of the Senate Insular Affairs Committee.

If Walter is attacked he stays and fights it out, returning insult for insult. He doesn't run out as Hurley did, whining about his outraged dignity. Walter sticks to his guns and tosses a few choice aspersions in retaliation.

When Senator Blaine, insurgent of Wisconsin, hauled Walter before his post-office lease investigating committee Walter met Blaine's verbal vitriol with more vitriol. Blaine had assailed Walter on the Senate floor regarding his devious policy in a Minneapolis branch post-office lease. This lease was declared by Representative Melvin J. Maas Republican of Minnesota, to have been conceived in fraud and perpetuated in corruption. The lease had been signed by Walter's predecessor. Walter was in no way responsible for the unsavory deal, but when Maas attempted to end the outrageous plundering of government funds by terminating the lease, Walter did everything in his power to thwart him.

In the end Maas took the fight to the floor of Congress, where, with the aid of the Progressives, he struck from the Post Office Appropriation Bill the sum demanded for the continuation of the lease. Blaine, who led the fight in the Senate, demanded a thorough investigation of post-office leases, which was ordered. Walter has made no post-office leases and has advocated a policy of building government structures to replace those now rented. But his intrigues in defense of the indefensible Minneapolis lease outraged the Progressives.

When Walter appeared before Blaine's committee the room was charged with electricity. The two men disliked each other and made no bones about it. Walter was cool and deliberate. He repeatedly refused to give Blaine information he demanded concerning the location of sites on which Walter proposed the government erect post-office buildings. Walter maintained that to divulge such facts would be contrary to "public interest." When Blaine showed that much of the information was already public knowledge, Walter remained unmoved. When Blaine denounced him, Walter replied in kind.

BLAINE: I am going to ask you the same question with respect to every one of these sites.

BROWN: You may ask any question you please. However, I will do the answering.

BLAINE: Well, now, I don't know whether you will or not, Mr. Brown, except as the committee may direct you to answer. I don't want any personal disagreement with you, but when I ask you to state whether or not the location of the building, street and number is confidential, it is a very simple matter for you to say yes or no. If you say no, you may explain why. That ends it. If you say yes, you may explain why it is confidential. Now, let us proceed in a calm, orderly manner.

BROWN: I think that would be an excellent way to proceed.

BLAINE: ...there is no accusation made against you with respect to the manner in which you obtained this information. There is no need for you to make a defense.

BROWN: I am not making any.

BLAINE: Then let us proceed.

BROWN: There is no occasion for you to make a lecture, either.

BLAINE: I am just explaining to you, Mr. Brown. I understand your arrogance and your impertinence.

BROWN: And I yours.

BLAINE: I am not concerned with that.

BROWN: And I am not concerned with yours. . . . If you want

the question answered, I will answer. I don't care for your lectures.

BLAINE: Proceed. I indicated that we are not going—

BROWN: I am not sure whether you will or not.

BLAINE: I have no desire to stop your impertinence.

BROWN: I have no desire to stop yours. I know your limitations.

Walter has one serious weakness as an executive. He lacks the power for sustained concentrated effort. He abhors details. He likes to map out a program of action, lay down a line of strategy and let others do the work. But his intellect is keen, and if necessary he can quickly acquaint himself with detailed information. Criticism is one sure way of making him work. If he has to fight he applies himself. Because the Post Office Department has been under heavy fire the last few years, due to his brazen political operations, his curtailment of delivery service, his anti-labor policy, and his vicious ocean-mail subsidy and air-mail monopoly policies, Walter has fully informed himself about the affairs of the Department. He knows everything that goes on.

But when he is not under fire, his natural inclination is to float around the country and let others do the work. Walter loves to travel, and he is constantly on the go. No other member of the Cabinet travels as much as he. He demands speed and uses airplanes extensively. He is rarely in Washington between Friday and Tuesday—Cabinet meeting days. It is an adage in Washington that it is harder for a Senator to see Walter than it is for him to get an audience with the Pope. The Pope is always in the Vatican but no one can say when Walter will be in his office.

Walter's indifference to the details of the Post Office Department may or may not have been responsible for a blunder that some subordinate pulled there early in 1932, which outraged Indianians and caused a flurry in the White House. The Department decided to establish a branch post office in a ramshackle suburb of Terre Haute, Indiana. A name had to be chosen for the new branch and some Department underling decided upon "Offalaland."

When word of this was sent to Terre Haute, there was much bewilderment. No one had ever heard of the name. Local papers queried their Washington correspondents about the mystery and they went to the Department. No one there knew what the word meant and the file on the matter was examined.

Only then was it discovered that the Post Office Department had accepted the proposal of a practical joker who in an anonymous letter had suggested the name—which is a composite of the words offal, meaning garbage or refuse, and land.

*

WALTER comes naturally by his political aptitude and decisiveness. James M. Brown, his father, was for many years a Republican boss and postmaster of Toledo, Ohio. The elder Brown was noted for his violent, implacable temper and was involved in many feuds and controversies. Walter has all of his father's bulldog courage, but the gentle nature of his mother has tempered it with restraint and discretion.

In a fight, Walter is a bitter foe and will stop at nothing short of mayhem. But he does not carry on political vendettas. Once a contest is over, he is willing to deal with victor or loser. In his many battles in Ohio, Walter has been repeatedly beaten, but he has always managed to win the rebels over to his organization. Two of his former bitterest local opponents, Thomas C. Devine and Harry M. Curtis, one-time socialist leaders in Toledo, are now contented Republican office-holders, the former a deputy cigarette inspector and the latter clerk of the Board of Elections.

For many years Negley D. Cochran, fiery and liberal editor of the *News-Bee*, a Scripps-Howard paper, waged a furious campaign against Walter's reactionary political machine. The *News-Bee* accused Walter of almost every political infamy.

One day the Rossford post office, near Toledo, was robbed. Walter encountered one of Negley's reporters on the street just as the newsboys were shouting the extra about the robbery. Calling the reporter over to him, Walter said gravely:

"I just wanted to tell you before your noon edition goes to press that I can prove an alibi in that post-office robbery."

Walter got into politics early. Following his graduation from Harvard he returned to Toledo and became active in the local Republican machine, practicing law on the side. His first case was the prosecution of a ball team for playing on Sunday. Walter worked hard in preparation. In court he proved by numerous witnesses that the game actually had been played, and in a stirring speech called on the jury to uphold law and order. The jury filed out. It returned in fifteen minutes and announced that there had been no ball game. After that lesson, Walter has not practiced law seriously, although he is senior member of Brown and Sanger, a firm with a large and profitable legal business.

Walter began at the bottom of the political escalator, but he didn't stay there long. Within a few years he was an up-and-coming boss on his own account, challenging the control of George P. Waldorf. It did not take him long to dispose of Waldorf, who turned to Christian Science for consolation and lately has been a reader in that church.

Walter's hold on the Republican organization of Toledo has continued unshaken, but that has not prevented him from suffering a number of smashing defeats at the hands of the voters. Brand Whitlock, war-time Ambassador to Belgium, and a boyhood chum, defeated his machine four times as a mayoralty candidate. As a result, an independent, municipal reform movement, led by Cochran and the *News-Bee,* controlled the city's administration for more than ten years.

It was during this period that Walter turned his talents and attention to State politics. Within a few years he was State Republican Chairman, and continued in that position until 1912. In the turbulent political fighting of that year, Walter, the hard-boiled machine politician, turned Progressive and followed the bolting "Teddy." Resigning as State Chairman, Walter organized a Progressive machine which did a magnificent job, defeating the Old Guard and Taft, its candidate.

Walter's successor as Republican State Chairman was Harry M. Daugherty, appointed by Taft, also an Ohio man. Daugherty took his licking at the hands of Walter with ill grace and the two men were never friendly thereafter. Never a member of the so-called "Ohio gang," Walter bosses his own machine in and about Toledo, and while he coöperated with the Daugherty organization in State and national elections, they were separate and distinct groups.

When the Bull Moose movement proved abortive, Walter wasted no more time on it. He returned to the fold, and characteristically took most of his bolting organization with him. Walter continued his admiration for Roosevelt, however, and to this day is a close personal friend of Senator Hiram Johnson and Senator Robert B. Howell, Republican insurgents and bitter critics of Hoover, who were intimates of "T. R." At the 1920 Republican convention, Walter, as Harding's floor-manager, went to Johnson and offered him the Vice-Presidential nomination, which Johnson indignantly refused.

Walter has stood for public office only twice. He ran as a candidate for the Ohio State constitutional convention and was elected by a ballot count which, Toledo old-timers say, was a miracle of efficiency. In some precincts, they declare, not a vote was recorded against Walter.

Regardless of the means by which he obtained his election, Walter took his duty to the convention seriously. He made an extensive study of State governments, specializing on some of the popular reforms, such as the initiative, referendum and recall, which then were being widely agitated throughout the West. At the convention, to every one's surprise, Walter supported the liberals in writing these measures into Ohio's constitution.

Walter's second effort was for United States Senator, to fill the unexpired term of Harding. As Harding's convention floor-manager and the man who did more than any other to put him over, Walter had reason to expect that Harding would support him. But because Walter ran as a wet, Harding deserted him and supported "Chicken Gut" Willis. Harding was a heavy drinker, but he was running for the Presidency as a dry, with Anti-Saloon League backing, so he put aside personal obligations and preference.

If Walter could have controlled the ballot counting in the entire State, as he did in Lucas County, he would have realized his senatorial ambitions. Neither Willis' miraculous chicken-consuming capacity, the Anti-Saloon League's hostility, nor Harding's opposition would have mattered. The ballot counting in Walter's home district showed the same remarkable efficiency that had characterized it some years previous, but Lucas County, unfortunately, was not enough. Willis carried the rest of the State, and Walter, ordinarily an excellent loser, took his defeat hard. Yet he never held any personal animus against Harding for deserting him. He appreciated Harding's problem in the contest and did not allow his political disappointment to embitter their personal relations.

Walter's greatest ambition is to be a member of the Senate. He would rather be a Senator than a Cabinet member, and he still has hopes that a turn in Ohio's wheel of politics will open the way.

After being elected President, Harding set about squaring himself with Walter. He offered to make him Ambassador to Japan or Under-Secretary of State. Walter declined both. Harding then appointed him chairman of the Joint Congressional Committee on Reorganization with a salary of $10,000 a year. This committee was created for the purpose of recommending a reorganization of the government departments and bureaus, and was made up of members of Congress

and the Cabinet. The $10,000-a-year chairmanship was estab-
lished at the request of Harding, who wanted the job for
Walter. The committee made an extended survey and submitted a report, suggesting many consolidations. Nothing has
ever been done about them, however, except those affecting
the Department of Commerce, where Hoover, who as Secretary of Commerce, was the only Cabinet member to take any
interest in the work of the committee, used its report to
expand greatly his jurisdiction and functions.

It was as a result of this work that Hoover came to know
Walter. Walter made a distinct impression, and when the
committee disbanded, Hoover offered him a job as Assistant
Secretary. But Walter was not interested in "Little Cabinet"
jobs and returned to Toledo, where for four years he confined his interests to local and State politics.

But in the fall of 1927, following Coolidge's "I do not
choose to run" statement, when Hoover set his nomination
campaign in motion, he immediately sought out the man who
had made such a profound impression three years before.
Walter was put on the pay-roll as Assistant Secretary at $9,000
a year to aid in managing Hoover's Presidential race. It was
Walter's insistent counsel that put Hoover in the Ohio Presidential primary, the fortunate outcome of which was a powerful factor in winning Hoover the nomination. The Ohio
political situation was uncertain. Willis was a candidate for the
nomination and Hoover could only get the State by an open
fight, which he was afraid to tackle. His policy was to gum-
shoe.

Walter insisted that Hoover had to demonstrate his vote-
getting strength to secure the support of other important State
delegations. Hoover recognized the need, but feared a fight.
Walter literally forced him into the Ohio contest.

Walter's bold strategy won in an unexpected manner. In
the midst of the campaign, with the outcome uncertain, Willis
died. Whereupon Walter delivered the master stroke of the
contest. He sent public condolences to Willis' friends, whom

he privately despised. Shortly afterwards Hoover won the Ohio delegation by a large vote.

From the very start of the campaign, Walter set his cap for a Cabinet job. Hoover first offered him the chairmanship of the Republican National Committee, but Walter was taking no chances. The prospective President then asked Coolidge to appoint Walter to his place as Secretary of Commerce, and even made a special trip to the Brule River in Northern Wisconsin, where Coolidge was summering, to persuade him to name Walter. Cal scoffed at the idea:

"If you want him in your Cabinet, you can put him there when you are elected," he told Hoover. "I've got another man for the place."

Coolidge thereupon appointed William F. Whiting, wealthy Massachusetts paper manufacturer, whom he had wanted to put in Hoover's place as far back as 1924. Hoover's popularity with big business was the only thing that deterred Cal from dropping him from his Cabinet. Coolidge had also wanted to get rid of Dr. Julius Klein, a Hoover satellite in the Commerce Department and one of the trickiest jugglers of statistics in the government. Klein has outdone even Hoover in prosperity prognostications—no mean record for a little mouthpiece. Hoover kept Klein, despite Coolidge's dislike of him, and during Whiting's short tenure of office Hoover's pets in the Commerce Department carefully kept out of their new chief's way.

*

It is claimed by Walter's friends that when he was made Postmaster General he had every intention of eschewing politics and devoting his full time and attention to running the Department. They declare it was his ambition to make a record as a business administrator of the postal service. If he ever had such ideas, they were soon shelved.

They were abandoned about the time Hoover got into political hot water. This occurred early in his administration, after he had discarded the inept but well-meaning Dr. Hubert Work as Republican National Chairman, supplanting him with the even more blundering Huston. As a result, Republican leaders were in open revolt by the time the 1930 congressional election had rolled around and were demanding the removal of Huston and a reorganization of party affairs. Hoover again turned to Walter and asked him to take the National Chairmanship. But Walter was not to be lured from his safe Cabinet harborage. He suggested that a dummy chairman be installed, while he pulled the wires and pressed the button to run the merry-go-round.

Walter's administration of postal business is a matter of much controversy. His brazen political operations have provoked bitter criticism among friends of the civil service. His high-handed barring from the mails of *Haldeman-Julius' Weekly* and certain independent and radical publications has raised storms of protests. His cutting down of city delivery service, extending the routes of rural mail carriers, paring to the bone general postal employment and refusing to continue the system of maintaining a large standing reserve of substitute help that has been a feature of the postal service for decades, have aroused widespread antagonism. Particularly are the unionized postal employees hostile to him.

His policies in the awarding and administering of tens of millions of dollars of ocean and air-mail subsidies that the government pays out annually have also been fiercely assailed. He is charged by independent airline operators with seeking to build up an aviation monopoly through the use of government funds. Congressional critics of his ocean-mail contracts and policy cite his failure to force legal action against many contracts made by his predecessor which they hold are invalid, his discrimination against American lines in favor of foreign competitors in the handling of certain mails, and in one specific instance his making of an ocean-mail contract under the most extraordinary circumstances.

As an executive, the Post Office Department has not had a

more able man than Walter at its head in many years. Despite his political hatcheting and fondness for absenting himself from his desk, Walter knows what goes on in his great Department and keeps a close check on its affairs. Furthermore, no one in the Department has any doubts as to who is boss. His subordinates fear him and take no liberties as they did under the easy-going Harry New, his predecessor. Walter's annual reports on the Department are also the most intelligent and forthright in a long time.

As to his labor, mail delivery, ocean and air-mail policies, many factors enter. Postal employees and rural carriers assert that Walter is harsh and oppressive and has anti-labor views. In a time of widespread unemployment, they declare, instead of making every effort to maintain personnel he has slashed it drastically.

They cite the case of William C. Lang as an example of Walter's ruthlessness. Lang was a veteran postal employee with thirty-eight years' service. In 1921 he invented, and gave free to the government, a machine that has saved the government many millions of dollars in the manufacture of mail bags. Yet, following the enactment of the so-called economy bill by the 1932 Congress, Lang was retired on a $1,200-a-year pension without even an expression of appreciation for his long and loyal service. His notification of retirement consisted of a brief form statement.

Walter's reply to these charges is that the postal services are over-staffed and that the taxpayer demands that the postal business be put on a self-supporting basis. The extension of rural delivery routes he asserts is only fair under present-day conditions of hard-surfaced roads and motor transportation. Hundreds of rural mail carriers were working only a few hours a day and receiving $2,100 a year, plus a vehicle allowance of several hundred dollars. Good business practice required that they give more in return for this money, Walter contends.

As for the curtailment of city mail delivery, Walter's reply is that he has reduced such service, but only where he considered it a waste of money. With most businesses closing Saturday afternoon, there is no need for such a delivery, he states, and so he ordered it dropped in office buildings in the larger cities.

Congress had little time during the hectic 1932 session, overwhelmed as it was with the task of meeting the many urgent needs arising from the Hoover depression, to go thoroughly into Walter's air-mail policy. But the committees that did give some attention to it clearly manifested strong hostility to his course.

Addressing Walter at one of these hearings, Representative James M. Mead, of New York, chairman of the House Post Office Committee, declared: "We have been reliably told that it is your policy to destroy independent operators and build up a monopoly, and that the intent of Congress is being flouted. We have received testimony that the holders of air-mail certificates issued by the Post Office Department have been told to keep their hands off when new contracts were offered, which were intended for a certain company. Charges have been made that discrimination and favoritism are the policy of your Department. We have been informed that the Post Office Department in granting air-mail extensions, and in asking for bids on new lines, is doing so under such circumstances as to prevent open bidding."

Mead vigorously warned Walter that unless he acted to put an end to such complaints, Congress would force him to do so.

The monopolization of the air-mail business by means of granting "extensions" to favored air lines instead of throwing such contracts open to competitive bidding, as Congress intended in the McNary-Watres Act, is one of the most autocratic policies in recent bureaucratic history. It has resulted in the wiping out of many independent air lines and the paying over to a few large companies the millions of dollars that Congress appropriates annually for air subsidies.

The McNary-Watres Act provides that all air-mail contracts must be made on a competitive basis. Where air lines already exist, a special section gives the Postmaster General authority to grant "extension" contracts. Walter has not only ignored the specific intent of Congress and used the special provision to build up an air-mail monopoly but in many cases where bidding was thrown open, the Post Office Department has devised specifications, eliminating all but favored lines.

Scores of "extension" contracts have been granted favored companies in territory wholly out of their sphere, and in which other lines were operating. George E. Strong, attorney for the Western Air Service, which operated a successful passenger line for two years between Wichita and Sioux City, told the Mead committee that the Post Office Department put his company out of business by giving a competitor an air-mail "extension" contract paralleling his route. Colonel Paul Henderson, executive of the Boeing Line, which was given this contract, later told the committee his company had not sought the extension, did not want it and was making no money out of it.

Under this policy, favored air lines have had their routes doubled and tripled in length and revenue, while independent operators have been forced out of business. These latter, testifying before the Mead committee, declared that if air-mail contracts had been awarded on a competitive basis as Congress intended, the government would be getting from three to five times as much service. E. L. Cord, automobile manufacturer, who for a time was in the air-line business in the Middle West and unsuccessfully sought mail contracts, expressed a willingness to carry the entire air-mail of the country for approximately half of what the Post Office Department was paying.

Walter's answer to these charges is that he is trying to build up a commercial aviation system that "would best serve the American people." Instead of a net work of small weak operators, he favors a few strong lines covering extensive territory and easy to regulate. Holding this view he has gone ahead and put it in practice—Congress or no Congress.

The controversy over Walter's handling of the ocean-mail subsidies is again in the main a matter of conflict over policy. With the votes of Walter's most aggressive critics on this question, Senator McKellar and Representative Ewin L. Davis, Democrats from Tennessee, Congress in 1928 passed the ocean-mail subsidy act. This was a year before Walter became Postmaster General. New made practically all of the forty-four contracts which take $38,000,000 annually from the Treasury. Some of these contracts are unquestionably of dubious legal standing. McKellar charged on the floor of the Senate that as many as thirty-nine are "void in law."

Walter had nothing to do with the making of these contracts and he has reversed New's policy of viewing the subsidy as an instrumentality for assisting shipping line "cripples." Walter insists that the recipients of these largesses do their share by building new ships or modernizing old vessels. He has forced some of the lines to do construction work despite their violent protests and desperate lobbying in opposition.

Where Walter has fallen down is in his very grave failure to ask the Attorney General to investigate the standing of his predecessor's dubious contracts and in his paying to foreign shippers $1,450,000 a year for carrying mails that American lines could transport. Under the rules of the International Postal Union a country pays for the dispatch of mail from its shores to the main port of the country to which it is addressed. Practically all foreign countries make it a rule to use only ships flying their flags for the transportation of outgoing mail. But on the ground that the American business man demands fast delivery, Walter permits a large quantity of domestic mail to be carried on foreign-flag ships because an American vessel may not be sailing at the time the mail is ready for departure. He refuses to hold mail over twenty-four hours, with the result that American ships each year lose almost a million and a half dollars that their government pays to foreign competitors.

Walter has made only a few ocean-mail contracts of his own, but one of them, granted to the Seatrain Lines, Inc., was so discriminatory and made under such extraordinary circumstances that the House of Representatives at first specifically prohibited the use of Shipping Board or Post Office funds for its fulfillment.

The facts of the award in this amazing contract are these:

The Florida East Coast Car Ferry Company has been operating a train-ferry service from Florida to Habana for many years, but due to changed traffic conditions, decided to transfer two of its three vessels to a new New Orleans-Habana route. Pier facilities in the city of New Orleans were obtained.

In the middle of these preparations, the Florida East Coast Company happened across a press release announcing that the Post Office Department was advertising for bids for an ocean-mail contract over the New Orleans-Habana route. The Florida East Coast Company investigated. It prepared to submit bids. It discovered, however, that this was impossible. The specifications were so drawn up as to permit only one company in the world to bid. That company was Seatrain Lines, Inc.

The specifications provided that the vessel carrying United States mails between New Orleans and Habana would have to accommodate ninety cars. Only one vessel existed in the world of that size. This belonged to Seatrain Lines, Inc. Its ninety-car ferry, the *Seatrain,* was built in England, flew the British flag and was owned by the Over-Seas Steamship Company, a Canadian corporation. The operating company, the Over-Seas Railway, Inc., is a Delaware firm. The vessels of the Florida East Coast Company were built in the United States and fly the American flag. They carry only thirty cars and under the ruling of the Postmaster General could not submit a bid.

The Florida East Coast Company protested. Walter refused

to see its representatives. He even declined to await a ruling by the Comptroller General on the validity of his specifications. Instead he proceeded to grant the Seatrain company a ten-year contract at approximately $250,000 a year as compensation for carrying virtually non-existent mail between Habana and New Orleans. Then on the strength of this postal subsidy, the Shipping Board rushed through a $2,400,000 loan to the Seatrain company to finance the construction of two new ferries, thus making a total of $5,000,000 of government funds ladled out to one company.

At about this time, members of Congress began to get indignant. At the instance of Representative LaGuardia, fighting game-cock of the House, that body inserted an amendment in the Post Office Appropriation Bill denying the use of funds for fulfillment of the contract. The bill then went to the Senate, where Senator Oddie, servile henchman of the administration, in the secrecy of the sub-committee on Post Office appropriations, of which he is chairman, finally killed the item. Then administration pressure was brought to bear on the House conferees and they reversed themselves.

Aroused over Walter's discrimination and amazed that the Hoover Administration should dare openly to give such aid to one company, the House ordered a special investigation of the contract, and Congress prohibited the Shipping Board from making future loans to ship companies on the basis of Walter's mail contracts, unless such contracts had been formally approved by the Comptroller General. This action came after LaGuardia had read to the House a letter from Comptroller General J. R. McCarl to Walter, in which McCarl challenged the validity of the Seatrain contract and warned that as far as his bureau was concerned "no charges against appropriated funds will be approved in payment to Overseas Railway, Inc., under the contract you report as having been awarded, until there has been presented the facts requested in my letter of October 24, 1931, and such facts are shown to bring the contract within the terms of the statute."

Why Walter and the Republican henchmen on Capitol Hill fought so vigorously for the Seatrain contract has never been brought fully to light. However, when the House investigations gets under way it will reveal the significant fact that the trail leads direct to the door of the White House. James R. Nutt, Treasurer of the National Republican Committee and close friend of President Hoover, happens to operate a bank in Cleveland which, through the Van Sweringens and the Missouri Pacific Railroad, is interested in Seatrains, Inc. Another owner is reported to be Andrew W. Mellon's Gulf Oil Company; and it was Senator Reed, Mellon's attorney, on the floor of the Senate who fought hardest for the Seatrain dole when the bill came before the upper chamber.

*

WALTER's private life is as staid and mild as his external appearance. Before the depression he was known to his associates as a wealthy man. He is interested in several large banks in Toledo and has considerable real estate holdings there, but both have been hard hit by the Hoover panic. Walter once made money in Western oil lands, managed by his only brother, Ralph. Their sister, Amy, lives in Toledo and is most devoted to Walter.

Walter is philanthropic and gives generously to charity. His father, despite his turbulent and irascible temper, founded the Toledo Humane Society and was its mainstay during his life, a service which Walter has faithfully continued. Walter and Mrs. Brown have also given much of their means and time to the Lucas County children's home, another of the elder Brown's hobbies. Although devoted to children, the Browns have none of their own, which probably is the reason why Walter, since his father's death, has made the children's home one of the best institutions of its kind in Ohio.

In keeping, perhaps, with his propensity for political intrigue, is Walter's love for cooking. He likes nothing better than to spend a few hours with pots and pans, and his skill as an amateur cook is remarkable. His fricassee of chicken, spaghetti and salads have almost legendary reputations. When he became Postmaster General he equipped a small room in his office suite with modern kitchen devices, including a refrigerator. It was Walter's fond hope, so he told friends, to have time to regale them with samples of his culinary artistry.

Walter has done a lot of cooking since he has been in the Post Office Department. But not in his glistening little kitchen. The fricassees and sauces he has mixed were concocted in the smelly sties of Republican politics, and they were not for the delectation of friends but for the satisfaction of the privy political tastes of Herbert Hoover.

Whether cooking food or political skullduggery, it is results that count with Walter. If a sauce needs garlic, he has no squeamishness about using that noisome relish. And if principles interfere with political machinations, Walter always dispenses with principles.

Some years ago General Isaac R. Sherwood, a Civil War veteran and for many years a member of the House from Toledo, succinctly summed up Walter's personality and character. Speaking of him on the floor of the House, the picturesque old warrior said:

"Walter Brown reminds me of Lord Byron's ode to a leading pirate of the Mediterranean—

> *'He was the mildest-mannered man*
> *Who ever scuttled ship or cut a throat*
> *With such true bearing of a gentleman.'"*

CHAPTER EIGHT

THE CAPITAL UNDERWORLD

COMPARED with New York and Chicago, Washington is not a wicked city. It experiences brief flashes of gang warfare which the local press tries to play up as important. It revels in the murder mysteries of Mary Baker, Navy Department clerk, and of Virginia McPherson, daughter-in-law of the assistant to the Secretary of War. It is baffled by the robbery of the Salvadorean Legation, accomplished as a large consignment of Scotch whisky had arrived and was piled up in the rear garden. And it is horrified at the nocturnal operations of more than a hundred Negro degenerates who swooped down regularly upon the encamped Bonus Army as soon as it became dark.

Compared with the big-time racketeering of New York and Chicago all of this probably is puerile and petty, but it plays an important and influential part in the life of the nation's capital. Furthermore, Washington's underworld has two or three distinctions of which in a modest sort of way it can really boast. One of these is the ease of securing immunity. The capital may witness few crimes, but in few cases is the culprit ever brought to justice. Another distinction is the complete and unrestrained freedom of the neighboring counties of Maryland, where an amazing White Slave traffic, operating through a chain of tea houses, furnishes recreation to capital residents. Finally, Washington probably boasts more small, independent bootleggers per capita than any other city in the country and has established a unique and universal system of liquor distribution.

*

THE nation always has taken a genuine pride in the charm and beauty of its capital. This began back in the days when Washington was merely a muddy suburb of Georgetown, a dream in the mind of Major L'Enfant. To-day its stately White House, its Lincoln Memorial, its Corcoran Art Gallery, its extensive beautification program have made it the Mecca of sightseers from all over the country, comparable in beauty to Paris, Budapest and Rome.

Secreted among these historic landmarks are quiet unobtrusive places where, if the right word is spoken, one may enter a guarded door, place one's foot on a rail, and partake of Maryland rye, cut Scotch or beer, usually spiked, but sometimes the genuine article brought from Baltimore. Across the street from the Veterans' Bureau and within a stone's throw of the White House there was, until recently, one of the most sumptuous and prosperous of these. In an alley behind the Court of Claims, and just across the street from the State Department was another. Its old-fashioned bar and sawdust floors attracted an overflowing clientele until its proprietor became too ambitious. An act between a Follies girl and a derelict newspaper man brought bigger crowds—but also the police.

On the south side or front of the White House—for the Executive Mansion really turns its back on Pennsylvania Avenue and faces the Potomac—is a fence. It was designed by Major L'Enfant, and tradition has it that the aristocratic French architect felt that it should be a stout stone wall of respectable height and capable of giving privacy even to the Chief Executive of a democracy. However, the mansion which it surrounds was to house not a king or emperor, and so, no matter how far George Washington privately may have leaned toward the idea of royalty, the fence finally was built of the plain post-and-picket variety.

But had L'Enfant known the use to which his fence would be put, probably a stone wall would have prevailed. For the White House fence of to-day, rebuilt of steel pickets, has been reënforced by a thick privet hedge which gives to the Chief Executive all of the privacy he could desire. In addition it also gave profitable privacy for a considerable period to a clique of the bootleg brotherhood who cached in its thickness their supplies of corn and bath-tub gin.

No one ever thought of looking for contraband in so respectable a place, and the dapper gentlemen who used it as a base, became so prosperous that they began to complain about walking the distance from the hedge to the District of Columbia Building where they stood waiting for their customers.

But eventually a local reporter with a sense of humor and no taste for stimulants wrote a funny story about it for his paper. Though the article drew no official comment, it caused a small furore in Cabinet circles, and the cache in the hedge is no more.

The bootlegging fraternity then resorted to the shrubbery at the base of the Alexander Hamilton monument, quite unperturbed by the fact that the office of the prohibition enforcement chief in the south wing of the Treasury looked down upon the scene. However, morale had sunk so low that they began stealing each other's liquor, and the end came when the rival bootleggers—perhaps inflamed by reading of Al Capone's exploits—retired to the Highway Bridge to fight it out. A couple of penknives were drawn and in the mêlée, an intoxicated citizen, who had come along as spectator, was wounded. Terror-stricken at the sight of blood, the others jumped into their cars and "scrammed."

But the most successful site of operation for a long time was the corner of Fourteenth Street and Pennsylvania Ave-

nue, just a block from the Treasury and directly opposite
Detective Headquarters. Two or three unobtrusive trash cans
stood alongside the modest fruit stand of Nick the Greek.
Near by, as it became dark every evening, stood two or three
young men. As an automobile loaded with merrymakers drew
up to the curb, one of the young men stepped forward, his
eyebrows raised inquiringly.

"Two," was the laconic order from the car.

The young man stepped back. To have kept his supply in
his pockets was an invitation to be "frisked." So, like the
operations around the White House hedge, he went over to
his base. Negligently leaning against the trash cans for a
moment, he pulled out "two" and took the order noncha-
lantly back to the car.

For a long time this corner enjoyed a reputation among
the fraternity as a "good stand." Then a nosy cop developed
a penchant for sniffing around trash cans, and the police, with
a simple but tactful technique, bankrupted the business. Two
of them, "Monkey Face" Barnes and "Bad Sam" Davis were
assigned to stand on the corner for shifts of twelve hours
each. Their orders were merely to stand there. That did the
trick.

*

POLICE occasionally interrupt these too-obvious law-breakers,
but the great rank and file of bootleggers and petty criminals
who ply their trade in the nation's capital enjoy an immunity
almost unsurpassed even in New York and Chicago. This is
due to three factors. The first is the influence of Henry
Mencken's Free State of Maryland, which surrounds the District of Columbia on three sides. The second is the natural
laziness of the capital police. The third is the prestige and
pull exercised by so large a number of those enjoying official
status, a factor which makes convictions difficult and disrupts
police morale.

Probably the most lawless rural district in the United States is that strip of Southern Maryland which lies just south of Washington, between the Chesapeake and the Potomac. Here live the lineal descendants of those who came over with Lord Baltimore, settled in the inlets and creeks of the Chesapeake and Potomac and have been raising tobacco and minding their own business ever since. Cut off by water on all but one side, they have preserved traditions to be found in few other parts of the United States. In the court of Leonardtown, village metropolis of Southern Maryland, the judges still pay tribute to the first ladies of the land who sit with them as court convenes. But the courts and police of Southern Maryland are jealous of their rights, and one of the traditions they most carefully preserve is that of freedom from Federal interference and especially the right to drink where and when they please.

The result is that revenue agents seldom penetrate very far into St. Mary's, King George's, Prince George's and Charles' counties; and on occasion the local constables have given them a blunt warning to stay out. As a result, the peninsula is saturated. For most of the farmers there are two chief money crops—tobacco and rye whisky. And on Saturday afternoon they bring their newly distilled whisky, pure white in color, into town almost as if it were any other crop. That part of the crop which is not consumed by the farmers themselves, while en route, comes up to Baltimore and Washington, contributing materially to the gayety of life in the capital.

In addition to rye, Southern Maryland boasts a famous chain of gambling joints and houses of assignation, most of them closely adjacent to the District. In fact one of them— Jimmy Fontaine's Maryland Athletic Club—is so close to the boundary between the District of Columbia and Prince George's County that for a long time the authorities of each shifted responsibility to the other, with the result that Jimmy enjoyed immunity for years.

"Tea Rooms" is the cloak of respectability given to a chain of houses just a few miles from Washington which for years have been carrying on an organized traffic in Philadelphia and Baltimore girls. Two of the most notorious, Green Gables and the Old Colonial Tea Room, finally brought the wrath of an outraged citizenry about their heads after recent difficulties. The trouble at Green Gables started over "Hot Shot" Ruth Bradley and a dope transaction. Green Gables usually closes at three in the morning, but on this occasion some of the Philadelphia gang, who keep Southern Maryland's road-houses supplied with pretty women, were present and they started fighting over "Hot Shot." The shooting began at five. The lights went out. Neutral guests dove out of the windows. Some months later, Jens Christensen, a Coast Guardsman, and his brother Lauritz visited Green Gables, were recognized by rumrunners who had crossed their trail previously and a knock-down drag-out fight resulted. After that the more right-eous citizens of the county marched on Green Gables and pulled it to pieces.

The same Philadelphia gang caused trouble at the Old Colonial Tea Room just across the District line. Bursting into the place in the early morning, they lined up the "guests"— actually members of a rival gang—against the wall, killed one and wounded several others. The only penalties meted out were two years to Chester Renzulli of Philadelphia and one month to Anna Lutz of Baltimore for violation of the Mann Act. Several girls who appeared against them testified that they had been shifted around on a regular circuit of Maryland road-houses, the places being advertised by cards given to Washington taxi-drivers.

It is from these adjacent areas in Maryland and Virginia that Washington recruits most of its police. They come from poor white families who have lived on the land for years and never got anywhere. They are slow, not particularly intelligent, reasonably honest, and when they resort to graft it is of a small and petty type rather than the big deals put over by their confrères in New York and Chicago.

Even were they the most upright individuals, however,

their morale eventually would be sapped by the barriers which confront them in dealing with the privileged persons of official Washington. The most untouchable of these are the diplomats who enjoy complete immunity under international law. They cannot be arrested, and if an officer does so by mistake, he is subject to three years' imprisonment, while the State Department is in for a formal apology.

Diplomats, however, are relatively law-abiding people and it is the large and privileged class of Congressmen and high government officials who sap police morale. They are not entitled to immunity but get it through pull and influence.

Police were furious, for instance, over the case of Mrs. Bertha Huddleston, dashing young wife of Representative George Huddleston, Alabama Democrat. She was arrested on a charge of reckless driving while intoxicated after she had careened across West Virginia Avenue and crashed into another automobile. With her at the time was Mark Middleton Penn, a salesman. Mrs. Huddleston was brought into the Ninth Precinct station and the officer who arrested her testified that she "reeked with the fumes of liquor and talked foolishly."

It happens, however, that Mrs. Huddleston's husband is not only a member of Congress, but a bone dry representative from one of the dryest districts in the South. He is sixty-three. Mrs. Huddleston is forty. The story did not go down well in Alabama where Mr. Huddleston is up for reëlection. So at this point the Corporation Counsel for the District of Columbia came into action. Despite the testimony of the police, Mrs. Huddleston was allowed to plead guilty only of reckless driving. All she had to face after that was the threat of Mrs. Penn for a damage suit for the alienation of her husband's affections.

*

Washington's most select drinking is done in the diplomatic corps and by those who profit through friendships with diplomats. Every embassy and legation can order an unlimited amount of liquor, which comes by ocean freight to Baltimore and then must be hauled by truck to Washington under special diplomatic convoy. During the early days of Herbert Hoover, one truckload of rare wines and liquors assigned to the Siamese Legation was seized by the police, but the State Department intervened, and ever since then the diplomatic corps has enjoyed an uninterrupted flow of alcoholic beverage. This flow reaches its greatest volume around Christmas time. A month before, representatives of London's biggest wine merchants make the rounds, the most popular being Bernard L. V. Ellis, a dapper Englishman representing Saccone and Speed, wine merchants by appointment to His Majesty George V.

Hedges and Butler are the most popular importers of Scotch to Washington's diplomatic corps, and the Honorable R. Beecher Howell, Presbyterian Senator from Nebraska who prides himself on research into the capital's prohibition conditions, estimates that this firm "unlawfully delivered in Washington, by virtue of executive permits and protection, some 13,000 quarts of diplomatic whisky within a period of three months, the equivalent of twenty quarts for every diplomatic official and the members of his family, including also maids, cooks, laundresses, chauffeurs and janitors enjoying diplomatic status in the city."

Some diplomatic liquor unquestionably finds its way into illicit channels. But the percentage is small. One or two envoys have been known purveyors in days past.

The next most select drinking set is that which, five cases out of ten, drinks wet while at the same time voting for a stricter enforcement of the Prohibition Act. The congressional supply comes from a whole retinue of small bootleggers who operate on Capitol Hill, the most famous of them being the "Man in the Green Hat," who for two years was almost an official purveyor of liquor supplies to the solons on the Hill. Although in private life he bore the name of George B.

Cassiday, his distinctive headgear, like the white plume of Henry of Navarre, became a sort of symbol and the rallying point for thirsty law-makers.

Cassiday was caught as the result of a "buy" made by a Federal stool-pigeon, who worked for weeks as a clerk in the folding-room of the Senate Office Building before success crowned his efforts. With the arrest of Cassiday, the authorities got possession of the famous "little Black Book" in which the bootlegger kept the names and addresses of his customers. A shudder passed down the spine of official Washington when prohibition authorities threatened to make public its contents. This, however, they never did, and the "Man in the Green Hat" got off with a comparatively light sentence.

Lower down the rungs of the drinking ladder come a host of small-time government employees who resort to all sorts of liquid refreshments. It is a matter of official record that at one time the Smithsonian Institution found its reptile exhibit, pickled in glass jars containing alcohol, suddenly decaying because the alcohol had been drained off. Since then guards have been placed in the exhibit rooms. At one time also it was discovered that printers working in the Government Printing Office and the Bureau of Printing and Engraving were ordering twice as much alcohol for type cleaning as in pre-Volstead days. Their supply was cut down. But since then there have been cases where the alcohol, dirty from the cleansing of type, has been re-cooked and sold to an unsuspecting public.

It was to the Bureau of Printing and Engraving that Federal agents traced dope peddlers when they exposed a drug ring described as one of the largest ever caught operating in this part of the country. Seven members of the ring were arrested when Federal agents, after six weeks of mingling with the gang as alleged addicts, discovered an extensive dope doctoring plant near the Raleigh Hotel on Pennsylvania Avenue. Here narcotics were wrapped, packed and labeled, under a system whereby heroin purchased in New York for $25 an ounce was mixed with an ounce of sugar and sold to capital customers for $25 an ounce.

*

But the industry of which the Washington underworld is most proud is its quiet, steady, year-in-and-year-out bootleg business. Major Edwin B. Hesse, retired chief of police, once estimated there were 3,500 speakeasies and bootleggers operating in Washington. That was in 1929. Since then city officials have uncovered no evidence to indicate a decrease in the number. On the contrary, police maps of the District, ornamented with pins marking suspected locations of speakeasies and bootlegging establishments, indicate an increase.

Despite the huge volume of illicit liquor sold in the capital, the product is of fair quality. Health records show that Washington ranks far down the list of cities in the number of deaths resulting from poison liquor. Seven is said to be the maximum for a single year, and these for the most part resulted from drinking "canned heat" or other substitutes for "legitimate" liquor. In these figures local bootleggers take an honest professional pride. They are out to maintain, or even improve their record.

In another major respect, Washington differs from other cities of similar or greater size. Though bootlegging ranks as the District's second industry, being exceeded in importance only by politics, it is not dominated by the feudal or gang rule which controls the industry in New York, Chicago and many smaller cities.

Speakeasy proprietors are not under the thumb of lordly gang heads. The racket is open to any one who is financially able to establish himself in the business of dispensing liquor—whether by bottle or over the bar—and who is industrious enough to annex a clientele without resorting to the unfair practice of stealing his competitor's customers.

As a result of this open-shop policy, the city is swamped

with the small-time variety of bootlegger and speakeasy proprietor, whose net profits average as low as $50 a week and seldom as high as $150. These, for the most part, are gentlemen who have worked as "runners" or delivery men for more pretentious dealers, and being imbued with the old pioneer spirit, have saved enough to rent an apartment or a back room, and install a telephone. Usually they obtain their liquor from the same source as their former employer but in somewhat smaller quantities.

There are, of course, some dealers who have gone into the liquor business in a big way. They are few in number, but their profits are correspondingly high. There is, for example, the late "Alky Queen," who recently retired to a palatial home in Chevy Chase with her limousines, her blooded saddle horses and pedigreed dogs.

At one time virtually every bootlegger in Washington bought alcohol from the Queen at prices ranging from $6 to $11 a gallon, according to quantity purchased. She had scores of employees and many trucks and automobiles, one of them having been known to bring enough alcohol over from Baltimore in a single night "to keep all Washington tight over the week-end." Not long ago she retired, having made all the money she wanted—and with the unique record of never having been arrested for a liquor-law violation.

The most pretentious of Washington's speakeasies, operated on a club membership plan and frequented by the "big shots" of the business and professional world until recently, did a $100,000 business a stone's throw from the White House, when United States marshals closed it under a padlock injunction. Several others are operated on the same basis, but their intake is said to average less than $50,000 a year.

In the spring of 1931, Federal officials became exercised over the operation of a million-dollar liquor ring, with headquarters in Washington. The city was being flooded with alcohol, which sold for a price well under that ordinarily prevailing for the product.

A dozen Federal undercover agents were assigned to the case and the investigation continued for weeks. One Alfred Mendelson, who operated a malt, hops and bottle establishment in the capital, and one Milton J. Lerner were the reputed heads of the ring.

After weeks of patient effort, Herbert Johnson, an undercover agent, managed to ingratiate himself with the gang. Posing as an unemployed bootlegger from a distant city, he cultivated suspected members of the ring, drank with them, and eventually got a job at one of the two re-cooking plants maintained at Riverdale and Hyattsville, just outside of Washington.

Perfume and disinfectants, sent from a clearing house in Philadelphia, were hoarded at the two Maryland plants, passed through the re-cooking process, and distributed on the Washington bootleg market.

Approximately $300,000 had filtered into the coffers of the ring before government agents closed in. Twenty-two persons, including Mendelson, Lerner and two women, were indicted for conspiracy to violate the prohibition laws. The two ringleaders were given two-year sentences. Nine others were given shorter terms. With the ring smashed, Washington bootleggers have been forced to get their alcohol through the old channels, which lead principally to Baltimore.

Adopting the general policy of "live and let live," Washington bootleggers and speakeasy proprietors have effected a certain camaraderie which has kept the city relatively free from gang battles and other pranks of the underworld. Those who cut in on the other fellow's clientele, or consider it easier to replenish diminishing supplies by hijacking, usually wake up with aching heads, discolored eyes, cut lips and other painful but not very serious bodily injuries.

In most cases, a sound thrashing is sufficient to induce an erring bootlegger to mend his ways. But guns have belched their death-dealing slugs even in Washington's comparatively mild-mannered underworld. Squealers have been put on the spot, and "rats" have been given the works on occasion.

The most recent outburst cost the lives of two so-called big shots, and the serious injury of one of the small fry.

Jack Cunningham and Tally Day, the big shots, were buried within seventy-two hours of each other. Bert Smith, a lesser light of the bootlegging fraternity, "accidentally" shot himself in the leg a few hours before Day was put on the spot in a downtown speakeasy.

Tally Day, long an enigma to police because of his ability to wiggle out of trouble in the bootlegging and gambling rackets, got his, it is whispered, because of enmity created in trying to muscle in on a rival's business. One bullet in the head and another in the groin finished him.

Cunningham was cut down by a fusillade of shots fired from a green sedan which sped through a downtown alley in the rear of Cunningham's apartment home just as he was mounting the steel stairway to his door.

Cunningham had been a prizefighter, bootleg racketeer and chauffeur for Sam Beard, lord of Washington's gambling fraternity. He had just given the police information regarding the shooting of Tally Day, turned over to them the gun used in the shooting of Bert Smith, and fifteen minutes before he toppled over the steel stair rail in the rear of his apartment, he had complained to a police lieutenant that he was going to be put on the spot.

The bullets taken from Cunningham's body were fired from the same large caliber pistol used in hijacking the Salvadorean Legation, and in the brutal slugging of Don Carlos Leiva, then chargé d'affaires.

Unlike the big shot which Cunningham wanted to be known as, he failed to adhere to gangdom's code of dying with sealed lips. On his death-bed he gave police sufficient information concerning the fatal shooting to cause the arrest of former Policeman Wallace J. Middleton. Middleton was absolved of any connection with Cunningham's murder, but the investigation resulted in his indictment on a charge of hijacking a load of whisky from the midtown speakeasy of Milton "Shockey" Yudelevit.

Cunningham was implicated, police said, in the hijacking of Yudelevit, and owing to certain developments, was in favor of returning the purloined wet goods. Others who participated in the job, however, objected to his change of heart. Incidentally, Tally Day had been held by the police for questioning in connection with the hijacking of the Salvadorean Legation and was shot to death shortly after his release from custody.

The murders of Day and Cunningham and the slugging of Don Carlos Leiva, in which the latter suffered a fractured skull, remain unsolved mysteries.

*

LIKE most of their trade, Washington bootleggers take themselves seriously. They read of the exploits of such royal personages as Al Capone, Frankie Yale, Dion O'Bannion and Legs Diamond, and bask in the thought that they too belong to the gilded fraternity. This feeling of pride has been nurtured in some degree by the attitude of the local press, which at the time of the fatal shootings, generously referred to Cunningham as a "big shot" and Tally Day as a "well-known sportsman."

Convinced there was a reputation to be lived up to, the underworld decided upon a lavish funeral for Day, in the best Chicago style. It was announced the casket cost $10,000 and that other thousands were being contributed for flowers. Those on the inside, however, assert that while Day's casket was a good one, it could scarcely be called *de luxe;* that there were comparatively few flowers; and that the whole show cost less than $1,000.

Those in the know also cast a shadow on the achievements and professional standing of the two victims. In this they are corroborated by certain less romantically minded members of the bootlegging brotherhood, who assert that far from being the big shots they aspired to be, Cunningham was a police stool pigeon, and Tally Day a small-time gambler and bootlegger, who was accorded only in death the big-time publicity he had longed for all his life.

Despite these sporadic outbreaks, Washington's bootlegging gentry are not bad people with whom to do business. In general, they are out to make an honest dollar as quickly and inoffensively as possible. They may, in fact, be said to hold a unique position among lawbreakers. Because of their almost uniform gentleness of manner and willingness to accommodate, they have worked their way up the ladder of success. They have become a necessary adjunct of the family, like the corner druggist or the chain-store grocer. And like the latter, they have been stuck with many an unpaid bill.

With competition keen and government clerks paid on a semi-monthly salary basis, the liquor venders have found it practically impossible to get along without doing some business "on the cuff"—bootlegese for selling merchandise on credit. It is only the old and steady customer who is permitted to run an account. Thousands of dollars worth of business is transacted "on the cuff," however, and the gentlemen estimate that approximately eighty per cent of these accounts are settled in full.

But the fraternity has a wholesome fear of checks—especially third-party paper. It is axiomatic that a bootlegger would rather put an order "on the cuff" than have it paid for by check.

The speakeasies, with few exceptions, are foul joints. Those in the downtown districts are harassed in particular by the police vice squad. Nearly all are operated behind heavy oak doors with steel trappings. Close at hand is a waiting cesspool into which the liquor stocks are dumped in case of a raid.

It is the perhaps laudable ambition of every speakeasy proprietor to approximate as nearly as possible the appointments of the saloon of pre-Volstead days. He insists on a bar, if only a smooth pine board nailed across a couple of packing cases. An old-time bar, with a back-fixture, mirrors and an oil painting of Venus, is of course devoutly to be desired, but the *pièce de résistance* is a brass foot-rail. A few of the higher class speakeasies are fully equipped with orthodox furniture of the older and happier pre-war period, and one or two establishments also operate a really good restaurant.

Many of the raids staged by the police squad result in no liquor being found. This is due to two reasons:

First, it is difficult for the police to batter down the heavy barricades before the speakeasy proprietor and patrons can dispose of their contraband. Frequently there is time to rinse out the receptacles, so that not even "sniffing evidence" can be obtained.

Second, the proprietors sometimes are "tipped off" by friends. The police themselves often warn the intended victim. They have a habit, when on a raid, of racing through the city in high-powered automobiles, sirens shrieking. The clamor can be heard for blocks, and there is quick action on the part of every speakeasy proprietor within earshot. Of course, much liquor is dumped needlessly—and at considerable loss. But the proprietors figure that liquor down a cesspool is better than a term at Occoquan, and they soon recoup their losses.

*

LIQUOR-RUNNING into Washington, chiefly from Baltimore and Southern Maryland, has become a tame affair in recent months. In the old days, when the police motor corps patrolled the highways, it was a hazardous undertaking. The rum-runner had to have a car capable of carrying at least one hundred gallons, and fast enough to outstep the police. Good drivers—those who hit a seventy-mile clip, and with courage enough to run the gauntlet of waiting police—were at a premium in the early days of liquor running. The driver's pay for a night's work was usually $50, but he earned it. The police were quick on the trigger and, with Congress in one instance actually applauding the shooting of a rumrunner by a prohibition agent, the police saw to it that all their shots didn't go astray.

During the first few years after the city went dry, police and rumrunners figured in no fewer than fifteen running battles. Three of the smugglers were killed. Later, with the evolution of the smoke screen, the rumrunners had more than an even chance against the police. At the first warning from the pilot car, which usually preceded the liquor machine by a short distance, the bootlegger sitting beside the driver would get the "pump" ready. They called it the "pump" because the apparatus used to disseminate the eye-filling, nostril-biting smoke, resembled the old-time device for forcing air into a tire.

Two developments put a curb on the use of the smoke screen. First, Congress passed a law making it a felony even to have a smoke-screen apparatus in one's possession. Second, the need for smoke screens passed when the police liquor patrols were brought in from the near-by highways.

The business of running liquor into Washington thus has degenerated from a thrilling evening's job to one about as hazardous as carrying a half pint in the hip pocket. The bootleggers, however, have found it best to bring in smaller but more frequent loads.

Corn whisky had its brief inning during the first few months after Washington went dry. Everybody was drinking "cawn." Then the popular taste suddenly turned from that fiery beverage to Maryland rye and bath-tub gin. "Cawn" is still the staple stimulant of Southwest Washington, however, and thanks to this fact, numerous colored gentry find themselves possessed of limousines while their lady friends sport expensive fur coats. They regard Mr. Volstead as the greatest benefactor of their race since Abraham Lincoln.

The taste for gin has persisted. Probably more of this colorless fluid is sold by bootleggers than all the rest of the alcoholic concoctions put together. The reason is simple. It is more palatable than corn liquor, easier to handle, and the customer can see what he is getting. Gin as it is sold in Washington is a short fifty per cent alcohol, forty-nine per cent water and the rest essence of juniper berries, glycerine and orange-water compound.

Any impurities which gin might contain are easily detectable, which is more than can be said of the alleged rye and Scotch. Besides, the grade of alcohol used has been found to be fairly good. At least it does not poison immediately.

Most of the alcohol used by bootleggers in Washington finds its way over from Baltimore. Those wishing to save a few nickels, however, gather up perfumes and medicaments, re-cook them and use the product in their trade. It takes a little more time this way but those addicted to the practice say the saving is worth the extra effort.

Washington's real thirst is for beer—good beer. Real beer is obtainable in Pennsylvania and even in Baltimore, but beer is bulky and difficult to run in, so most of the capital's drinking population has been compelled to forgo this luxury.

Nevertheless, sales of alleged beer in the District rank next to those of gin in monetary volume. Home-brew, heavy with yeast and malt, and leaving a sluggish feeling the morning after, is sold throughout the city. The price is twenty-five cents a bottle. Needle beer, which has been "doctored" with alcohol to give it a kick, is much sought, chiefly because it is not as heavy as the average home-brew.

Shortly before he was retired November 1, for "physical disability," Major Henry G. Pratt, superintendent of police, urged "as a matter of real necessity" amendment of the National Prohibition Act to give members of the city police force the same authority as other officers of the government to enforce laws relating to the manufacture and sale of intoxicating beverages. In addition, Major Pratt recommended that the personnel of the police force be increased from its present strength of 1,400 men to 1,600.

As matters now stand only thirty-five members of the police department are vested with authority as special prohibition agents. Recently all members of the force assigned to enforcement of prohibition and gambling laws were consolidated into one squad consisting of twenty-two men, with an inspector in charge. This squad devotes its entire time and efforts to the enforcement of liquor and gambling laws, but lacking numbers, has been able to accomplish but little toward drying up a city of 485,000 population.

The District commissioners, who jointly hold the powers of a mayor and town council, have been endeavoring to get a special appropriation of $10,000 to be used by the police department solely for hiring "stool pigeons" and procuring evidence in liquor cases.

Stool pigeons have been employed in the past, but the experiment was not satisfactory. They were paid from $2 to $5 a case, provided convictions were obtained, but there were widespread charges of framing and scores of cases were thrown out of court by police judges, who apparently put little faith in the veracity of the stools. Also a good many of the informers came in for hard treatment at the hands of bootleggers. It has since been proposed, if the necessary funds are made available, to pay informers a fixed salary and endeavor to attract a better class of men.

To care for the record number of drunks, bootleggers and other violators of the probition laws, George S. Wilson, Director of the Board of Public Welfare, has urgently recommended an appropriation for a new jail.

Of the 14,437 prisoners received at the city jail during the fiscal year ended June 30, 1931, 7,205 were incarcerated for drunkenness and 1,031 for various violations of the prohibition laws. The present jail, more than fifty years old, is lacking in light, ventilation and modern sanitary conveniences, and, because of the great number of prisoners, does not permit segregation according to age, offenses or health.

As a result, many first offenders, a majority of whom are charged with prohibition law violations, are thrown with hardened criminals, many of them desperate characters. Conditions would be far worse, Director Wilson pointed out, were it not for the strenuous efforts by Lieutenant Colonel William L. Peake, jail superintendent, and court officials, to arrange for speedy trials of prisoners.

Meanwhile, business goes merrily forward in Washington's second largest industry. The thirst of the customers is alleviated and the bootleggers wax opulent. Nor is the industry without its lighter social side. Nearly a decade ago the bootleggers first decided to hold a ball. It was felt that in this way newcomers in the business would find opportunity to make the acquaintance of their older colleagues, exchange ideas, perfect technique and enjoy themselves in a congenial atmosphere.

The ball was held in a now defunct Bohemian club. It was a great success. Even the police admitted it. Since then the Bootleggers' Ball has come to be more or less an annual event.

The last one received considerable advertising in the local press and some one made arrangements to hold the ball in the city's largest auditorium, which seats close to six thousand persons. The newspapers carried announcements that even the police would be invited.

The evening of the celebration found more than two hundred policemen, most of them in plain clothes, waiting outside the auditorium for the celebrities to arrive. There had been a little dirty work in crime circles which the police couldn't fathom, and they were expecting to take some of the guests into custody for questioning. Here was a golden opportunity, the police reasoned, to pick up a few undesirables.

Eight o'clock came. The first of the merrymakers had not arrived. Eight-fifteen. Eight-thirty. Nine. Nine-thirty. Ten. Eleven, and midnight.

They couldn't be wrong. A thousand spectators were on hand. It must be the night. But the Washington police had been "stood up."

The bootleggers, not caring to have the cops on hand when they disported themselves, had circulated the report that the ball was to be held in the auditorium. Then they had quietly made arrangements to stage their festivities at a night club in near-by Maryland. The ball went off as per schedule.

A good time was had by all—except the police.

ever on the alert and ready to safeguard its hegemony. In times of plenty and in times of want they serve their masters. Political affiliations, sectional differences, all are mere trappings, scenic effects behind which they do their real work. Underneath the political hokum and palaver there is no more difference in fundamental economic philosophy between a Robinson and a Reed than there is between a British imperialist and a Japanese samurai.

The samurai, born an Englishman, would be a British imperialist, and the British Tory, born a Japanese, would be a samurai. Robinson, born in Pennsylvania, would have been a Tory Republican, and Reed, born in Arkansas, would have been a Tory Democrat. There would be no more difference in economic belief between them than there is today. Reed is a member of a great firm of corporation lawyers in Pennsylvania. Robinson is a member of a great firm of corporation lawyers in Arkansas. The Republican Party rules in Pennsylvania, and the Democratic in Arkansas. But in both the corporations rule.

When in 1927 a move was initiated for a Senate investigation of the power trust, Robinson, whose firm represents a number of the largest power corporations in the South, stood shoulder to shoulder with Watson, Smoot, Moses and Reed in defeating it. When in the past session of Congress the demand was made that the government strike at colossal concentrations of wealth by taxation, Robinson was as excitedly outraged about the matter as his Republican associates.

In this group of national political leaders is to be found the whole story of the failure and inadequacy of the political system in America to-day; why there is no such thing as an effective two-party system and why no "leader" of broad vision, courage and independence has arisen from either the Republican or Democratic ranks.

Between the Democratic and Republican parties there is not one jot or tittle of difference in basic economic thought. Both are owned and ruled by the economic masters of the country and the "elections" that occur at scheduled intervals are merely sham battles for place and preference at the public trough. The Ins wants to stay in and the Outs want to get back. No matter who wins, the public loses. The cards are always stacked.

Moses, Reed, Smoot, Watson and the others may be displaced, but always there will be other Muscle Men to take their places. Not as amusing, sly, blatant or pious perhaps, but still strong-arm men. As long as the system continues they will be on hand, regardless of whether they operate under the Democratic or the Republican mantle.

*

As the ranking member of the Quorum of the Twelve Apostles, the college of cardinals of the Mormon Church, Reed Smoot is a most devout and pious man.

He once gravely assured the Senate that if he "lost his virtue" he would leave the Mormon Church. But his piety and morality notwithstanding, the tall, gaunt Republican Senator from Utah is a firm believer in the doctrine that God helps him who helps himself.

Reed Smoot has been helping himself all his life. His father, a Mormon pioneer, crossed the plains with Brigham Young, settled at Provo, Utah, and became a man of wealth, property and great power in the church. Young Smoot got a head-on start and has made the most of his advantages ever since.

In Utah he is the possessor of much valuable real estate, a banker and merchant, the owner of woolen mill and sugar-beet refinery stocks, and next in line as head of the powerful and opulent Mormon Church.

In Washington, he owns choice property sites and is chairman of the Public Buildings Commission, which supervised the laying out of the $75,000,000 District of Columbia building program. As a member of the Senate Public Buildings and Grounds Committee, he is in position to work quietly for enhancement of his land values. He is chairman of the dominating Finance Committee, where he labors ceaselessly for high tariffs for his woolen and sugar mills, and for low income taxes for himself and the Mormon Church. Over a period of many years he has built up a dynasty of office-holders in the capital so extensive that it rivals that of the President.

All this he has done in his quiet, plodding, pious way during the thirty years he has represented his business interests, Church and State in Washington. To-day, only two clouds disturb his horizon: defeat at the hands of a depression-angered electorate when he comes up for reëlection in 1932, and apprehension of the death of Heber Grant, present head of the Mormon Church, which would put up to Smoot the problem of whether to continue in the Senate or resign to assume the high churchly office to which his seniority in the Quorum of Apostles entitles him.

Smoot's power and eminence were not always so great. When he came to the Senate in 1903, by appointment at the hands of an admiring Church, there was a fearful clatter. Feeling against the Mormon Church was still active and the usual busybody moral elements cried out in alarm. How little they knew the man! If they could have but foreseen the valiant battles he would one day wage in the Senate against such dangerous writings as the *Decameron* of Boccaccio, Rabelais' Works and *Lady Chatterley's Lover,* they would not have become so lathered over the discarded plural-wives doctrine of the Mormons.

But having no means of knowing he was so sturdy a puritan, the charge of polygamy was raised against him. Smoot, the stern, unbending moralist and monogamist, had to submit to humiliating examination about his private virtue and purity. He was a meek and humble suppliant in those days.

But all that has changed. He may, in his opinion, still walk humbly in the sight of God, but from his fellow-man he brooks no interference. He knows what he wants and how to get it, and he never lets piety or virtue stand in the way.

Several years ago, when the United States Tariff Commission was investigating the possibility of reducing the exorbitant and extortionate sugar tariff which Smoot himself had brought about, he summoned William S. Culbertson, a member of the Commission, to his private office, confronted him with a pack of tariff lobbyists, among them William V. Hodges, former treasurer of the Republican National Committee, and led them in a demand that Culbertson oppose reduction of the sugar rates.

Later, when the commission despite enormous political pressure and interference recommended to President Coolidge that the duty on sugar be lowered, Smoot headed the lobbyist drive on Coolidge to suppress the commission's report—a little favor which Cal accommodatingly granted.

In the 1932 session, Smoot pulled an even smoother job on behalf of the power trust. The Senate twice by roll call rejected Smoot's proposal that a tax be put on electricity consumers and voted it instead on the power producers. Despite this decisive action, Smoot, seconded by Senator Reed and Representative Charles R. Crisp, Democrat of Georgia, and acting in the secrecy of the conference committee on the billion-dollar tax bill, restored the tax on the consumer and forced its approval by both branches of Congress.

Other members of the conference committee stated that Smoot and Reed not only made no effort to uphold the Senate's action, but took the lead in persuading the House conferees to put the tax on the consumer. At least one member of the House group was prepared to support the Senate's position, had Smoot and Reed insisted on it.

It is characteristic of the Machiavellian personality and undercover methods of Smoot that he interests himself little in national politics. Such spectacular vanities and posturings are meat and drink to Reed, Watson, Moses and the others. But Smoot is indifferent to such false-front affairs. It is a matter of no concern to him who sits in the White House, as long as the incumbent is a stand-pat Republican and he, Smoot, is chairman of the Senate Finance Committee where he can put over high tariffs and low income taxes and can load up the government departments and bureaus with his henchmen.

The excitement and hubbub of the election campaign, the thrill of political intrigue, are distasteful to Smoot. A political speech is a great trial to him. His voice falters. His dry, restless hands grow clammy. He is terribly unhappy. He prefers the quiet security of the secret caucus where his skill and gall as a fixer can function freely.

That is why, although he is always in the midst of Republican scheming, it is never as a member of the little group of party bosses who sit in "smoke-filled rooms at 2 o'clock in the morning" and decide on the national nominee. Where Smoot does his work is on the Resolutions Committee. There, behind tightly locked and closely guarded doors, the platform is carefully woven. The roars of the crowd, the antics of the candidates hold no appeal for him. That is all right for those who care for such things, but the chief Apostle of the Mormon Church prefers to wield his power where it counts directly.

Nowhere is this characteristic more strikingly evidenced than in the tremendous personal machine Smoot has built up among the government services in Washington. No other Republican leader, excepting the President, has as many personal appointees in the departments and commissions as the senior Senator from the small and politically insignificant desert State of Utah. The thoroughness and extent of this patronage machine is one of the marvels of present-day national politics. Senator Norris recently told the Senate that Smoot has more constituents in Washington than he has in Utah. Smoot's concentration on building up his political fences in Washington to the exclusion of his organization in Utah almost cost him his seat in 1920. Only the great political power of the Mormon Church saved him. In the 1932 election he was confronted with the same problem, and again the Church had to rally to him.

How he built up this Washington dynasty and how he keeps it going is one of the most interesting untold stories in the capital. Smoot helped to create a government agency known as the United States Bureau of Efficiency. At its head he had appointed Herbert D. Brown, an insignificant and mediocre government clerk. The Bureau of Efficiency is largely a duplication of the Budget Bureau, without its extensive and vital fiscal responsibilities. The Budget Bureau could and does do the same work that Smoot's Efficiency Bureau does. There is no earthly reason for the existence and heavy cost of the Efficiency Bureau, except that it enables Smoot to maintain a strangle-hold on Federal patronage in Washington. Repeated efforts have been initiated to abolish this wholly unnecessary agency; but with Republican administrations in the saddle, Smoot so far has been able to ward them off.

Through Brown and the Efficiency Bureau, Smoot has what amounts to a personal secret service in the government offices. A constant flow of confidential information pours in to him, particularly about impending vacancies. He is thus in a position to plant appointees beholden to him in places of influence in every government bureau. So well and craftily has he maneuvered that to-day Washington's far-flung bureaucracy is saturated with his henchmen. The list of the leading figures of Smoot's private army of office-holders reads as follows:

Administrator of Veterans' Affairs—Brigadier General Frank T. Hines.

Disbursing Officer United States Shipping Board and Treasurer of Merchant Fleet Corporation—Heber M. Wells.

Member Federal Farm Board—Frank Evans.

Member United States Tariff Commission—Edgar B. Brossard.

Bureau of Home Economics—Mrs. Laura P. Brossard, wife of the tariff commissioner.

Chairman Board of Tax Appeals—Logan Morris.

Associate Justice of the United States Supreme Court—George Sutherland.

Member Federal Radio Commission—Harold A. LaFount.

Examiner Federal Radio Commission—Elmer W. Pratt.

Chief, Appraisal Division, Federal Farm Loan Bureau—Ariel F. Cardon, Smoot's son-in-law.

Senate page boy—John A. Cardon, Smoot's grandson.

Clerk, Senate Finance Committee—Isaac M. Stewart.

Commission of Customs—F. X. A. Eble.

Ambassador to Mexico—J. Reuben Clark.

Chief of Publications, Department of Agriculture—M. C. Merrill (a Civil Service appointment).

Member Reconstruction Finance Corporation—Wilson McCarthy (not suggested by Smoot, but approved by him before appointment was made).

Scores of others have been installed in minor positions by Smoot. No job is too small to escape his eagle eye and earnest attention. Each bit of patronage is another addition to his machine and puts another henchman on the public pay-roll.

Republican propagandists are fond of picturing the dour, humorless, gangling Smoot as a tireless and self-sacrificing public servant of great industry and deep knowledge of public affairs. Smoot himself is very fond of this fanciful myth, and coyly pushes it to the fore. Several years ago while making a speech to his home folks in Provo he slyly gave official approval to this fiction. It was evening and as usual he was reading his remarks. He had some difficulty in deciphering his manuscript. Finally, with a gesture of resignation, Smoot laid it down and with great deliberation, and amid the deep silence of his humble neighbors, brought out a pair of spectacles, wiped them carefully, picked up his paper and moved under a light.

"You will pardon me, my friends," he said sadly, "but my eyes are not as good as they once were. I have worn them out in your service in Washington."

Actually, Smoot works no harder or longer and knows no more about government affairs than any other ordinarily competent member of the Senate. The claptrap about his great industry and profound knowledge of fiscal matters is pure hokum. He spends hours on unnecessary office details. He personally insists on opening and reading every letter that comes to his office. It is also true that he puts in long hours on tax bills and tariff measures, but that is not due to patriotism or unusual devotion to duty. It is due solely to two reasons: first, because it takes him twice as long as the average member of the Finance Committee to grasp details, and secondly, because he needs a great deal of time to devise and put over his vicious, predatory schemes.

Smoot's actual knowledge of government finances is dependent chiefly on experts and clerks, whom he always has by his side when tax and tariff legislation is under consideration. He is always flanked by a corps of aides, whether he is in committee or on the Senate floor. Time and again he has been tripped up during the debates on fiscal measures and has extricated himself only because he had an expert by his side.

Smoot is a slow, ponderous thinker. On his feet he is impotent. He rarely talks above a whisper. He is easily flustered and often becomes hysterical under fire. During the Senate's consideration of the Smoot-Hawley tariff bill, when his beloved sugar duties were under attack, he broke down in anguish, buried his head in his arms and sobbed.

One of the screamingly funny spectacles of the Senate during the incumbency of Tom Heflin was the sight of the Alabama Pope-baiter heckling Smoot.

Smoot would wring his large bony hands agonizingly, a peculiar trait of his, and try to make a stinging rejoinder. But to no avail. The thundering Heflin was too much for him. Finally Smoot would lapse into outraged dignity and sit down.

Another spectacle of high humor was a debate between Smoot and the diminutive Furnifold M. Simmons, former Democratic Senator from North Carolina. Simmons, like the

towering Smoot, was also a whisperer. Facing each other
directly across the center aisle in the Senate, one more than
six feet tall and the other about five, they would wave their
arms and gesticulate excitedly as if in great uproar, with not
one word from either audible five feet away. It was hilarious
pantomime, but it was not so funny after the tax or tariff
bill was enacted. Invariably, the public was stung.

Smoot is completely humorless. He rarely smiles. When
the Smoot-Hawley tariff measure was under consideration he
repeatedly convulsed the Senate by his hysterical harangues
over "obscene" literature, but he could see nothing funny
about his ridiculous diatribes. Piled high on his desk, with
each alleged obscenity carefully marked by a strip of white
paper, were several score of classics. Smoot's prize example
was D. H. Lawrence's *Lady Chatterley's Lover*. He denounced
this book with great vehemence. As he fulminated, fellow-
Senators passed it and the other books round, smirking over
the marked passages. When Senator Bronson Cutting of New
Mexico, who led the fight against Smoot's censorship, teasingly
remarked that *Lady Chatterley's Lover* seemed to be Smoot's
"favorite book," the Apostle almost burst a blood vessel.
He denied he had ever read it. When asked how under such
circumstances he could say it was obscene, Smoot gravely
informed the laughing Senate he could "tell it was that kind
of a book by the way it began."

Except for his dull and strait-laced god, Smoot's most profound reverence is reserved for property and propertied men.
Nothing causes him to wring his hands in greater distress
than an intimation that a banker or an industrialist is not
exactly in the image of the Lord.

During the foreign bond investigation last winter he sat
in frozen silence during the weeks that the brilliant Senator
Hiram Johnson put the international bankers over the jumps
and revealed to a looted public the extent of their depredations. Smoot didn't dare interfere. The doughty Californian
had the facts and Smoot knew better than to attempt to stop

him. But when one of his own men joined in the attack on the bankers, Smoot, outraged, turned on him fiercely.

Johnson summoned Herbert D. Brown, head of the Efficiency Bureau, to testify concerning a visit he made to Panama with officials of the National City Bank of New York to inquire into the finances of the Isthmian Republic. Brown said he had advised against further loans to Panama, but that the National City Bank had suppressed his report. As he finished his story, Brown leaned back highly pleased with himself. Johnson complimented him on his testimony and Brown basked happily in this commendation.

But Smoot suddenly became loquacious. For one of his subordinates to cast aspersions on a bank was too much. He pounced upon Brown and gave him a savage going-over. Brown's smile faded from his face and when he finally left the witness stand he was a chastened man. His master had spoken and Brown knew only too well that his master would stand for no irreverence.

To Reed Smoot, property rights and business interests are holy and sacred. The god he worships is a well-heeled god, a man of substance and standing in the community.

*

JIM WATSON is the most scandal-smeared member of the United States Senate—and yet the most beloved.

He has taken part in more shady deals than any other member of Congress, and they have affected his political fortunes less than any other man in national affairs.

He can be more things to more men and get away with it better and oftener than any other man in public life.

And he can tell the best stories, wield the warmest, friendliest and heartiest glad hand, and is one of the most delightful and picturesque characters in all Washington.

Jim's whole philosophy—and the secret of his success—is summed up in two aphorisms that are great favorites of his:

"There is nothing like a majority" and "If you can't lick 'em, join 'em."

Jim has never allowed anything to stand in the way of his getting a majority, and he is without peer as a joiner.

The story of Jim's long and picturesque career is a Muscle-Man epic. It is a tale of endless demagoguery, repeated political scandal, the most sordid, petty and shameless alliances, deals and intrigues and, so far, unbroken political success. Only once did he go down to defeat at the hands of "the boys" out in Indiana. Amusingly enough, this defeat occurred while he was still pure and pristine and long before his record became splotched with the great smelly patches that are now to be found on it.

In the more than a quarter of a century that Jim has served in the House and the Senate there is not one single piece of constructive legislation that bears his name. Of tariff steals and tax grabs, pork, pension and patronage measures, there are many. Yet he has always fared well in politics and had his luck been just a little better he might to-day be sitting in the White House.

Jim began early in the business of politics. Graduated from law school in 1887, he entered his father's law office and devoted himself to getting in with the voters and the local party bosses. Tall, handsome, a ready and facile spieler, with a contagious laugh and imperturbable good humor, he was soon the idol of his neighborhood. He knew every one by his first name and there was a real genius in his handclasp. When he visited the farming communities to deliver a memorial address, everybody left the fields to hear him.

Jim is sixty-eight years old now, and age and Senate restraints have tempered considerably his flamboyant rhetoric. But in his day he put on a show that was matchless. He would work himself up to fever pitch, and then, one by one, shed his coat, vest, collar and tie, until he stood roaring and gesticulating before his entranced audience attired only in his pants, shoes and shirt. Then Jim really would cut loose. The Indiana folks just loved it.

Jim was thirty when he was elected to the House of Representatives. There he immediately became a favorite of "Uncle Joe" Cannon the Republican boss. Cannon, in his day one of the greatest Muscle Men that ever operated in Washington, found a willing and trusty henchman in the youthful and ingratiating Watson. He used Watson extensively in his under-cover dealings. Jim became known as "Cannon's messenger" and the man to see if business was to be transacted with the boss of the House.

Jim could have continued in the House indefinitely, but he was too ambitious. In 1908 he ran for the governership and was defeated by Tom Marshall, later Vice-President under Wilson. This is Jim's one and only defeat.

Jim retired from office-seeking after his defeat, but not from the political arena. His rare talent as a fixer was worth money and he soon found a good paying client. The National Manufacturers' Association employed him as a lobbyist and for the next seven years Jim took care of its many mercenary interests in Congress. Little or nothing would have been known of this chapter in Jim's career had it not been for the famous Mulhall lobby investigation of 1913. Michael M. Mulhall, chief lobbyist for the Manufacturers' Association, turned on his employers and told a startling story of lobbying operations. Among the revelations was the fact that Jim had an office in the capitol, given him by Cannon, and that from this point of vantage he conducted his far-reaching activities.

This was the scandal of the year, and the House investigating committee severely condemned Jim and his methods. Both Jim and his friends were convinced that he had no further political future. He ceased his visits to Indiana and practically took up a permanent residence in Washington, where he continued his lobbying.

But three years is a long, long time in politics. When, in

1916, one of Indiana's Senators suddenly died, Jim returned to the fray as unbowed as if the Mulhall exposures never had occurred. The nomination campaign was one of the bitterest in Indiana history. Opposing Jim was Harry S. New, later to be Postmaster General in the Harding and Coolidge Cabinets. The two men left little unsaid about each other.

When the votes were counted New had carried a majority of the counties, but Jim claimed the most populous. The State law required that a party convention confirm the nomination, which in this case both men claimed. The prospect at the convention was profoundly disturbing to party leaders. New secured one hundred and fifty affidavits charging fraud and corruption against Jim, and it was clear that if these were made public the nomination wouldn't be worth a nickel.

Feeling between the two factions was sky-high and it seemed certain the party would be irrevocably rent, when fate intervened and settled everything peacefully. Benjamin F. Shively, Democratic Senator from Indiana, suddenly died, thus creating another vacancy. Overnight Jim and New became reconciled. Everything was patched up, both were nominated and both elected. Thus, a little more than three years after the scandalous revelations of the Mulhall investigation and the official censure of the House, Jim was back in public office, a United States Senator from the sovereign State of Indiana.

Jim has been in the Senate ever since. For years he was a henchman of Senator Boies Penrose, Pennsylvania boss, and was known as his "errand boy." When Penrose and others of the Old Guard passed from the scene, Jim became a leader in his own right and has been Republican floor leader since 1928.

In 1926 he came within 11,000 votes of being defeated. Unquestionably he would have been thrown out if he had not made an alliance with the Ku Klux Klan, which then ruled Indiana. Jim is not a member of the Klan, but he entered into a political alliance with it to save his political hide, as in other years he had aligned himself with the Anti-Saloon League.

Jim has no real sympathy or liking for either organization. But a majority is a majority to Jim, and that is all that counts.

*

SENATOR GEORGE HIGGINS MOSES, of New Hampshire, is an all-around nimble man. He has a brilliant mind, a slashingly facile tongue, and a political conscience mounted on ball bearings in high-grade oil.

Moses can despise a Harding on the very prophetic ground that his election would "open the Presidency to a flood of mediocrities" and a few months later warmly support Harding and his pack of petty crooks in a Presidential election.

In 1920 Moses gravely pronounced against the "Hoover menace" and in 1928 he took the van in advocating Hoover's nomination, while privately wise-cracking that " 'erbert 'oover is my man."

Moses can heap ridicule and contempt on the Senate Progressives as a group with the stinging characterization "Sons of the Wild Jackass" and covertly seek to defeat Senator George W. Norris of Nebraska, one of the noblest and purest figures in American public life, while at the same time maintaining a warm personal friendship with Senator Robert M. LaFollette Jr. and Senator Henrik Shipstead.

He can discourse learnedly about the classics and speak modern Greek with ease, and desperately hang on to the presidency *pro tempore* of the Senate, through a technicality of the rules, despite the fact that a majority was opposed to him, because the empty honor gives him a certain precedence at Washington's fatuous society tables.

He is one of the greatest news leaks and gossips in Washington, yet he led an attempt to expel from the Senate a correspondent who revealed a secret roll call that Moses wanted suppressed.

And he can crudely and vulgarly castigate a political opponent, while his own record, hidden from public gaze, holds trafficking with a notorious lobbyist and heavy campaign contributions and other favors from big business men interested in vital legislation and government regulation.

Moses is Washington's slickest political manipulator, wise-cracker and Walter Winchell—all rolled into one. This explains why, despite all his striving and intriguing, he has never climbed higher than the Senate seat he has held since 1918, why he has never been able to realize his ambition to be Vice-President, and why he has had to hang on to the petty title of president *pro tempore* by a technicality in order to obtain some slight social precedence at dinner tables.

Moses is a tory of tories. He is shrewd and astute. There are few men in American public life his equal in personal charm, culture and genuine learning. He has many friends and admirers among the wealthiest and most powerful. His toryism coupled with his brilliant intellectual gifts should have taken him far. But his uncontrollable wise-cracking is too much for the politicians. He is a welcome and applauded dinner guest, but in the White House or in the Cabinet he might give the whole show away with one of his witty outbursts.

So the leaders take no chances. Moses has his Senate seat, his extensive and petty patronage, his tenuous social precedence and his nightly invitations to Washington's smartest and most fashionable dinner tables. With these he must be content.

Hoover was delighted to have Moses' early endorsement in 1928, even if he did wise-crack privately about Hoover's British career. The first was widely published and only Washington laughed over the latter. "'erbert" also readily assented to Moses as permanent chairman of the Kansas City convention. Hoover knew his steam-roller would be in safe hands.

But when the campaign got under way, Hoover took no chances. He put in Dr. Hubert Work as Republican National Chairman. Work is lumbering, blundering and stiflingly dull. But he is safe. Moses was shunted off into an imposing and innocuous office, well away from the machinations of the campaign.

Hoover shelved Moses not because he distrusted his loyalty or had any doubt about his political skill. Neither did Hoover worry about squeamishness on Moses' part in taking a hand in the devious bigotry of the 1928 campaign. Hoover knows only too well that Moses always is ready to go the limit. What Hoover feared was a wise-crack.

And with good reason, as Moses demonstrated at the very first interview he had with Work after the latter became National Chairman. Moses emerged from Work's office in a rage. The reporters crowded around him.

"Boys," snarled Moses, "at last we have found the man who can stop Hoover."

This sally reverberated throughout the campaign. It was the only effective *bon mot* made against the Republicans throughout the contest—and it came from Moses, the Republican leader.

Moses got his first political training as Secretary to Governor David H. Goodell, of New Hampshire. He left Dartmouth College to take the job. Then he entered the newspaper business, eventually becoming editor and owner of the daily Concord *Monitor* and the weekly *Independent Statesman*. In 1908 he took an active part in the Taft campaign, and in reward was appointed Minister to Greece.

Moses sought Athens because of his love of Greek classics. Hardly had he reached the city when the bloodless revolution of 1909 took place. Moses took an active part behind the scenes in the stirring events that followed, helping to return Venizelos as Prime Minister and to organize the Balkan League which defeated the Turks. The real story of his activities during that exciting period has never been told and

awaits his autobiography, which should be extremely illuminating—even if he tells only part of his story.

It was while he was Minister to Greece that Moses developed his strong antipathy to the socialite career diplomats
of the State Department. Because he was a political appointee,
these la-de-da statesmen looked down on Moses and snubbed
him. Moses has repaid them with compound interest.

In 1927 he had himself appointed chairman of a Senate
Foreign Relations sub-committee and proceeded to make a
quiet investigation of the operations of a clique of Harvard-
bred career diplomats. Taking advantage of "Nervous Nelly"
Kellogg, this small group had perverted the diplomatic services to its own end and was promoting its members and
their social friends with great speed. Able and experienced but
socially insignificant men, on the other hand, were being
shelved.

Having got all the facts he wanted, Moses prepared a bill
drastically reorganizing the entire diplomatic service which
is in effect to-day.

Moses came to the Senate in 1918, succeeding to the vacancy
made by the death of Senator Jacob H. Gallinger, Republican
boss of New Hampshire, who had secured Moses his appointment to Greece. When he came to the Senate, Moses sold
his two newspapers but kept his interest in the famous "Rum-
ford Press." This may explain why Moses has been the
Senate's most effective advocate of low mailing charges for
newspapers.

Moses is credited with giving Mary Baker Eddy, the founder of Christian Science, the idea of establishing the *Christian
Science Monitor*. He was never a member of the Christian
Science Church, but was interested in the doctrine for a time
and corresponded with Mrs. Eddy. Several years ago it was
reported that the Christian Science Church offered him a considerable sum of money for his letters from Mrs. Eddy.

Moses sprang into immediate prominence in the Senate by
joining the Jim Reed-LaFollette-Borah-Johnson "Bat-

talion of Death" against the League of Nations. His affilia-
tion with this bloc brought him the coveted prize of
membership on the Senate Foreign Relations Committee, and
with this start, Moses rapidly made himself one of the stand-
pat Republican leaders in Congress. He turned his attention
to the patronage committees, such as those on Post Office,
Printing, Privileges, Rules, and to the Republican Senatorial
Election Committee, and has kept a firm grip on them.

Moses' relations and dealings with the late John T. King,
National Committeeman from Connecticut, and super-fixer
and lobbyist, have long been a subject of conjecture in political
quarters. Several times it appeared as if they would be aired,
but Moses has been too adroit.

King, a notorious lobbyist, Thomas W. Miller, Harding's
Alien Property Custodian, and Harry M. Daugherty, former
Attorney-General, were indicted by a Federal grand jury in
New York on charges growing out of the administration of
the Alien Property Custodian's office. A jury disagreed as to
Daugherty's guilt. Miller was convicted and served a term
in prison. King died shortly after the indictment was re-
turned.

During the grand jury's investigation, Moses was summoned before it for questioning. What happened has never
been revealed, but it has long been related in political circles
that he was asked to explain various letters, telegrams and
checks for considerable sums, made out to him by King, that
were found in the latter's files. All these documents, including
many involving Senator Watson, were later subpoenaed by
the Senate Public Lands Committee during the Continental
Trading Company phase of the Teapot Dome investigation.
Senator Thomas J. Walsh, of Montana, examined the documents, but nothing was done about them. Members of the
committee later stated that it had been decided they were not
germane to the investigation they were making.

The second occasion when it appeared as if Moses' affairs
might be aired occurred during an altercation between Moses

and Senator Couzens of Michigan. Couzens had attacked Secretary of the Treasury Andrew W. Mellon and demanded his removal. Moses came to Mellon's defense with a sneering attack on Couzens whom he accused of personal animus.

Couzens was deeply wounded. He did not reply immediately, but he let it be known that he would take the floor in a few days and go into certain matters in which the New Hampshire Senator was involved. When Moses heard of Couzens' intention, he became greatly excited and sent mutual friends to Couzens, pleading with him to drop the matter. Moses promised to make a public apology and Couzens, one of the most tolerant and kindly men in the Senate, acquiesced. To the amazement of his colleagues, a few days later Moses took the floor and made an unconditional and abject apology. He ate humble pie in those few remarks, and there were many in Washington who vastly enjoyed the spectacle.

*

SENATOR JOSEPH TAYLOR ROBINSON, minority floor leader of the Senate, is a Democrat by birth, breeding and environment. But he would be much happier, far more properly placed, and unquestionably would have long since realized his ambition to be President or Vice-President if he had been a Republican.

By temperament, instinct and economic conviction Robinson belongs in the ranks of Bourbon Republicanism rather than in those of Jeffersonian Democracy. That he is a Democrat is due solely to the fact that he was born and reared in Arkansas, and only Democrats get elected in Arkansas.

But even as a Democrat, Joe has done well by himself. He has held public office almost continuously for thirty-eight years. Beginning at the early age of twenty-two as a member of the Arkansas Legislature, Robinson kept moving steadily ahead, until to-day he is, at one and the same time, senior member of a law firm that represents some of the greatest utility, banking and railroad interests in the country and floor-leader of his party in the Senate. The latter office he holds despite the fact that he is far from popular and despite the further fact that a considerable group of his colleagues would displace him if they did not fear his violent temper and his even more dangerous power of retaliation through a covert friendship with the Hoover Administration.

Robinson's sub-rosa understanding with President Hoover is indicative of his basic affinity with Bourbon Republicanism. That the President realizes this is manifested by the readiness with which he turns to Robinson when he is unable to control the Senate and the promptness with which Joe always comes to Hoover's rescue. No other Democratic leader in Congress, and few Republicans, is favored with such confidence by Hoover.

A striking instance of this intimacy occurred during the Senate's consideration of the Reconstruction Finance Corporation bill. The measure was under heavy attack, but the Republican floor-leaders were wholly uninformed as to the President's plans. Watson bitterly complained one day to a group of colleagues about his inability to get any information from the White House. As he was talking he noticed Robinson entering the Senate Chamber.

"There is Joe Robinson," he remarked. "Let's see him and find out what is going on. He's just come from the President."

Robinson did know what was going on. Later, when Hoover prepared to appoint the members of what is now sometimes called "the Romance Corporation" he consulted not with Watson and the other Republican leaders, but with Robinson the Democrat. Undoubtedly this was the reason Harvey Couch, Arkansas utility and railroad magnate, and close friend of Robinson, was named as an executive. It was Joe's reward for "coöperating."

An even more striking instance of Robinson's amenability to White House pressure occurred in 1931 when flood and drought relief legislation was under consideration. Arkansas had been tragically hit by the protracted drought. Farmers were starving. In the little town of England, Arkansas, a mob raided stores for food. Whole counties were deprived of credit and currency by wholesale bank failures. The entire economic structure of the State was prostrate.

Robinson demanded government relief in the form of loans to the farmers to enable them to purchase food for themselves and seed for planting. Hoover refused such aid. He was willing to permit loans to be made for seed and feed for cattle, but he grimly fought loans for human succor.

With the cries of distress and alarm from his State ringing in his ears, Robinson bitterly attacked the President and the Red Cross, which was cravenly supporting Hoover's inhuman policy. Robinson proposed a far-reaching program of Federal relief. He had the united support of the Democrats and the Progressives and was in complete control of the congressional situation.

At this point, and while Robinson was still assailing the President, the mysterious Harvey Couch suddenly appeared on the scene. Although nominally a Democrat, Couch, like Robinson, has strong Bourbon leanings. Long a close friend of the President, he has been called on repeatedly for counsel and assistance with obstreperous Democrats. So when Joe broke loose in favor of the farmers, and it seemed certain that he would put through his drastic program, Hoover hurriedly summoned Couch.

Up to that time Robinson was sitting pretty. His program was certain of passage and every one knew that Hoover on a show-down would not have the courage to veto it. But at that point in walked Couch. The next day Robinson junked his program and accepted a "compromise" from which the words "human food" were excluded. Hoover was willing to feed cattle and mules but was not then willing to feed human beings.

Robinson is not unaware of the suspicion in Democratic quarters over his amenability to White House pressure. To dispel this, he now and then loudly attacks the President and his policies. An instance of this was the speech he made suddenly in the Senate shortly after the Couch appointment to the "Romance Corporation." For no apparent reason at all, Joe took the floor and industriously belabored his friend in the White House.

It is significant, however, that these attacks are rarely answered by the President. Practically every other Democratic leader who fires a barrage at Hoover is certain of drawing a return fire, but Robinson seems to be immune from such reprisals. As an extremely sensitive man, it may be that Hoover is too deeply offended to answer Joe, but it is more likely that he considers Joe's remarks mere political persiflage, necessary now and then to keep the home folks quiet.

Hoover's appointment of Robinson to the London Naval Conference was highly appreciated by the Arkansan. The appointment should have gone to Senator Claude Swanson of Virginia, who is the ranking Democratic member on both the Foreign Relations Committee and the Naval Affairs Committee. Swanson resented the slight, but Hoover later made it up to him by giving him an extended European trip at government expense as a delegate to the innocuous Geneva Disarmament Conference in 1932.

Robinson, personally a backwoodsman, greatly enjoyed London and the British social atmosphere. Although Joe was eager to do his share of the negotiating, Stimson largely ignored him, and Robinson spent most of his time golfing with Lloyd George. Usually he left the hotel by a service elevator, so as not to be seen departing at midday.

Joe is an expert duck hunter, and would have liked some grouse hunting on the Scottish moors, but, unfortunately, the conference didn't last quite long enough to include the British shooting season.

Although ordinarily a staunch big-navy man, Joe warmly supported the London Treaty and joined with Reed in assailing the admirals and in securing Senate ratification of the pact.

Joe brought back from England noisy cream-colored spats, dark-blue shirts with collars to match and other youthful ideas. The spats and shirts attracted much amused attention and he finally discarded them for fear of reaction in Arkansas. But apparently Arkansas hill billies have no objection to what a man does about his hair. Joe's hair was originally brown. With the passing of time it gradually became almost gray. Then one day in the spring of 1932 it suddenly turned a brilliant patent-leather black—strikingly setting off the bald spot on the top of his head.

As a floor leader Robinson is noted for his roaring voice and hair-trigger temper. Working himself into a frenzy, he literally shakes the chamber. Of massive build, particularly about his chest, he shouts so loudly on the Senate floor that he can be heard in the corridors through closed doors.

His hair-trigger temper cost him membership in the fashionable Chevy Chase Club several years ago. He became angered at some golfers who were teeing off ahead of him and in the ensuing argument knocked one of them down. The victim, Dr. James Mitchell, a prominent surgeon, actually had no part in the dispute. The club struck Joe's name from its rolls.

SENATOR SIMEON D. FESS, known in irreverent circles as "Simian," is a congenital fundamentalist.

Born, reared and educated in a rural, fundamentalist and Republican backwash in Ohio, where he lived the larger part of his mature life, the little, bald-headed, bandy-legged, plaintive-voiced school teacher sincerely believes that Prohibition is a sacred institution, that no Republican can do wrong, that all Republican Presidents are divinely ordained and that no Democrat or Progressive is to be trusted. But, as is the case with so many fundamentalists, numerous contradictions and inconsistencies dog Simeon's unctuous footsteps.

Although he reverently revealed that the late Wayne B. Wheeler, master dry lobbyist, was his hero with whom he "aways liked to advise on all questions," Simeon warmly supported Postmaster General Walter F. Brown, a wet, when he ran for the Senate in 1920. Brown was opposed by the late Frank B. Willis, a dry zealot who had Wheeler's support, but Simeon lined up with Brown.

Fess was always envious of the hulking, bellowing Willis, known on the Ohio hustings as "Chicken-Gut Willis" for his awesome capacity to consume fried chicken innards. At one farmers' picnic, it is reliably reported, Willis disposed of an entire bucket of these delicacies. Willis had been one of Fess' pupils at Antioch College. The little history professor is said not to have thought much of the intellectual qualities of his burly student. So when Willis, notwithstanding, or perhaps because of such deficiency, achieved signal public honors, Fess was a bit miffed. Willis preceded him as a member of the House and had served several years in the Senate, despite Fess' opposition, before the latter was elected.

Fess' dry delinquencies have been of even more recent date. When the late Dwight Morrow was elected to the Senate in 1930, as an out-and-out wet over the hysterical opposition of the drys, Fess welcomed him with open arms. And in 1932, although for months he had publicly insisted that the Republican Party must remain dry, Fess accepted the hypocritical prohibition straddle that the President forced through the Chicago convention, and piously campaigned for Hoover's reëlection.

Fess' Republican fundamentalism, too, is not without its weak spots. He passionately assured the Senate that he "never doubted the integrity of Harry M. Daugherty," but when the roll was called on the Wheeler resolution to investigate that same doubtful integrity, Simeon voted for it. And, while in recent years Fess has lavishly greased Hoover as a noble and gifted leader, in 1921 he bitterly opposed Hoover's appointment as Secretary of Commerce on the ground that he was "temperamentally unfitted to coöperate." Even harsher things Simeon said about Hoover in the 1920 Presidential race.

If Fess could keep his mouth shut he would be one of the most popular men in the Senate, for personally, he is a mild, pleasant, kindly little man, with all the genuine friendliness of the Mid-Western small-town temperament. There is nothing snobbish about him. In his personal relations he is unfailingly courteous and considerate.

But on his feet in the Senate, there are few members so irritating and antagonizing as Fess. He never addresses his colleagues; he always lectures them. And no matter what he discusses, he always does so as a self-righteous partisan.

Fess is always the omniscient Republican doctrinaire laying down the holy law. No matter how idiotic and incoherent he is made to appear by interrogation and retorts, he is never dissuaded from his end. It is distressing to him that the Senate rules permit such interjections. He would much prefer the docile and respectful silence of an Antioch class, where for so many years he injected good Republicanism into American history.

The following, from a debate early in 1932 on the LaFollette-Costigan Federal Unemployment Relief measure, which Fess violently opposed, is a perfect example of his colossal obtuseness:

SENATOR BORAH: Mr. President, a few days ago the Legislature of the State of Illinois passed an act appropriating $20,000,000 to take care of the needy of the State of Illinois. The money for that purpose will be raised by general taxation, and the taxes will be levied upon all the people of the State of Illinois. The appropriation is made, and the individuals suffering get the benefit. The money is raised by taxation. The State is acting. The State is authorizing the action which it is necessary to put into effect in order to feed the people. What is the difference between that, so far as the effect upon the individual is concerned, and the case where the Federal government extends relief to the needy citizen?

Fess: The difference is as wide as the poles.

Borah: I must say that I cannot see it.

Fess: The Senator from Ohio is not responsible for the inability of the Senator from Idaho to see. Every city has its hospitals. In every hospital there is a provision for people who are not able to pay for an operation or treatment, the provision being made through gratuities of the people.

Borah: The Senator is dicussing something which I have not raised at all. If the Senator will discuss the proposition which I am submitting now, I think that, with my limited ability, I will still be able to follow him.

Fess: I doubt it very much.

Borah: It may be; I have had some difficulty in understanding the Senator from time to time, but I am earnestly and faithfully trying to understand him.

Fess: I appreciate that the Senator has tried.

Borah: I am speaking of a community which must have help in order to keep the people from starving.

Fess: The Senator is contending that there is no difference between a city taking care of its own and the Federal government taking care of the people in the city, that in one case it would have exactly the same demoralizing influence on a citizen that it would have in the other case. The Senator certainly does not think that.

Borah: The Senator is not willing to discuss the proposition which I am putting to him.

Fess: The Senator from Ohio is willing to discuss any proposition the Senator from Idaho wants to put to him.

Borah: The Senator is unwilling to discuss the proposition. When I say the State is levying a tax, the Senator runs off and talks about a city, a neighbor, a hospital which has a general provision for taking care of the needy. What I am asking is: what is the difference on the individual recipient between levying a tax upon the people of a State to take care of the hungry through the operation of the State Legislature and levying a tax through the operation of the Federal government to take care of them?

Fess: Just as much of a difference as the Federal government differs from the State government. Does the Senator understand that?

Borah: No; I do not.

FESS: Well, the Senator from Ohio is not responsible for the misunderstanding.

BORAH: The Senator—

FESS: I do not yield further.

BORAH: I know the Senator does not want to—

FESS: The Senator from Ohio does not yield any further.

BORAH: I know the Senator does not want to yield any further, because he has gotten to a place where he cannot yield; he is afraid to yield.

FESS: Mr. President, we will see whether the Senator from Ohio is afraid to yield.

BORAH: Very well. Now, tell me—

FESS: The Senator will please take his seat until I tell him.

BORAH: No; I will do nothing of the kind.

FESS: Very well; stand then. I am going to answer the Senator's question. The Senator wants to know what is the difference between the service of a State to an individual and the service of the Federal government to an individual.

BORAH: I did not ask any question of that kind at all. I asked what is the difference in effect upon the character of a citizen, how does it more demoralize or degrade a citizen to receive money from the Federal treasury than from the State treasury?

FESS: When the Senator is ready and takes his seat I will answer him.

BORAH: If my standing presence disturbs the Senator I will sit down.

FESS: The Senator's presence very seriously disturbs me, because he does not wait until I finish my answer. The Senator wants to know what is the difference in the influence upon the moral character of a citizen if he receives funds from State taxation or receives funds from Federal taxation. Is that the question?

BORAH: That is the question.

FESS: The difference is that the citizen receiving funds from the State taxation is nearer to the fountain where local administration is in the hands of the people of whom he is a part and who will understand his situation; and the man who receives funds from the Federal government is receiving from a bureau operating from Washington, with no contact locally with the individual, and it leads to this conclusion, that he is the subject of charity by the votes of the people who know him, live with him, know his wants, and know how much will satisfy him, as contrasted with a bureau located in the capital that knows nothing about him except as his situation is represented to it.

BORAH: I understand the Senator does not take the position that he would not feed the hungry if the necessity were shown upon the part of the Federal government.

FESS: What does the Senator mean by "the necessity upon the part of the Federal government"?

BORAH: Suppose the people were in actual hunger and the local authorities were unable to take care of them, does the Senator still say he would not appropriate money on the part of the Federal government?

FESS: If the local authorities are not able to do so; but if the local authorities refuse to do it, that is a different thing.

BORAH: Suppose, then, that the local authorities are not taking care of them, that they are actually suffering; would the Senator still refuse to appropriate Federal money?

FESS: I would. I would insist upon the local authorities doing their duty.

BORAH: Mr. President, we seem to have the philosophy of the Senator from Ohio in all its naked and hideous ugliness. He takes the position that the national government should not aid the suffering, the needy, the sick and the diseased, even though the local government is not taking care of them.

FESS: And able to do it.

BORAH: I say that the local government is not taking care of them. Of course, if the Senator says "able to do it," I suppose he would reduce the balance of the community to the same state of pauperization as the people who are in need. But the Senator takes the position that although there may be hunger, although there may be want and suffering, and though the people are not being taken care of by the local community, the Senator still would not help them.

Mr. President, what I am contending for is to place the individual human being upon the same level with the corporations and banks and railroads of the United States—nothing more.

FESS: Then the Senator would loan to every human being who wants money?

BORAH: I will venture to say that 90 per cent of the people who are out of employment to-day would be perfectly willing to give the United States Government a guaranty that they will pay back every cent loaned. They abhor charity.

Fess: And the Senator would make the loan?
Borah: I would. I would feed them in any way practical.
Fess: There is where the Senator and I differ.
Borah: I would save human life.

The Senate is not the only place where Fess's garrulity runs away with him. His weakness for posing as a Presidential spokesman repeatedly gets him into difficulties.

Fess adores going to the White House, having a little chat with the President, and then telling the "newspaper boys" all about everything. He always cautions the reporters that the President is not to be quoted, and he is only expressing his own views. But coming from an interview with the President it is assumed that he is giving vent to Presidential opinion and the stories never fail to convey that thought.

This Fessian vanity led to a distressing embarrassment during the Coolidge Administration. The incident occurred the winter following Coolidge's tricky "I do not choose to run" statement. Democrats and Progressives in the Senate were firmly convinced that the statement was meaningless and that Coolidge would accept another term if he could get it. To indicate how they felt about it, Senator LaFollette introduced a resolution putting the Senate on record against third terms. The Democrats and Progressives denied that the declaration was aimed at Coolidge, but no one doubted that it was.

Fess bitterly opposed the measure. When the Democrats twitted him for taking this position, pointing out that several months earlier following a White House visit, he had admitted to reporters that Coolidge had rebuked him for urging his renomination, Fess astounded the chamber by announcing that he had lied to the reporters and that Coolidge had not reproved him.

"When I got out to the newspaper boys," Fess said, after telling of his visit to Coolidge, "I said to the boys, 'make it perfectly clear that when I am talking about the President being drafted next year, I am talking on my own responsibility. I am not talking with his approval.'

"Then, I added, what was not true, but I wanted to get it across, 'I find the President seems to be greatly displeased with what I said.' "

For a time after he had been made Republican National Chairman, to fill the place vacated by the ill-fated Claudius Huston, Fess ran wild as a spokesman. Every few days he would burst forth with a weighty pronouncement. He made the mistake of taking his new job seriously, although every one knew that he was merely window dressing, installed to give the badly smelling office an odor of respectability and to act as a screen for his old friend Walter Brown, the Hoover political fixer.

The President had wanted Brown to take the chairmanship, but the latter objected to giving up the Postmaster Generalship, a position of social prestige which means a great deal to him and Mrs. Brown.

But as the man behind the screen, Brown had not sufficiently considered Simeon's weakness for posing as an echo of the great. He was no sooner made National Chairman than Simeon began a veritable flood of statements. As long as he confined himself to the Democrats and their iniquities, Brown and the President had no objection, but when Fess began to issue pronouncements about prohibition and the necessity of the Republican Party remaining loyal to the drys, they became alarmed. Wet Republicans raised a hue and cry and demanded that Fess be thrown out. Hoover and Brown finally told Fess to shut up, which he abruptly did.

Fess had no better luck among the Senate Republican leaders when he was so ill-advised as to attempt to exercise his authority on Senator McNary. Senator Vandenberg of Michigan, blatant and ambitious would-be leader of a group of first-term Republican mediocrities, known derisively as the "Young Turks," had come to Fess and persuaded him that they should call on McNary. Vandenberg proposed demanding of McNary that he join with them in opposing a flood-relief measure which the Democrats were pressing, and which the President was secretly opposing.

McNary is one of the ablest and most astute men in Washington. Universally liked and highly respected in the Senate, he is independent in his politics, despite the fact that he is assistant Republican floor leader. McNary is not affiliated with the Progressive group, but on some economic issues lines up with them. When Fess and Vandenberg called on him with the demand that he shelve the Democratic bill, McNary listened until they had finished. Then rising to his feet he shook his fist in their faces and said:

"You voted billions for the banks, for the railroads, for the insurance companies. And now when it is proposed to give the starving little fellow a few pennies you want the bill killed. You get the hell out of here."

The bejowled, bulging Vandenberg and the thin, bandy-legged little Fess scurried from his office.

*

As a Muscle Man, Senator Frederic Collin Walcott, of Connecticut, has a classification all of his own, in keeping with his peculiar tastes and talents.

He is President Hoover's personal strong-arm man.

He runs all the President's errands in the Senate, gratefully does all the little chores which the President cannot get the Republican leaders to do, and unquestioningly carries out under-cover legislative schemes for the President.

He is the President's most devoted Senate henchman. There are a few others in the chamber who would be willing to hold so intimate and honored a rôle in the President's confidence, but none quite come up to Walcott's capacity for worshipful complaisance.

In this regard Walcott is in a class all by himself. He comes by it honestly.

God made him a simple and trusting person. Life has

always been pleasant and comfortable. He was born in a family of means and educated in select and socially proper schools. He practiced as a broker when that business was respectable and profitable. He made considerable money.

During the World War his faith and confidence was further strengthened by becoming associated with Mr. Hoover in his Food Administration and receiving the Legion of Honor from France plus the Officers' Cross from Poland for such heroic service.

When he retired from business in 1922, fifty-three years old, wealthy, in perfect health, and in a modest way became interested in Connecticut politics, fortune continued to smile benignly on him. Generous, and obviously not endowed with too much "savvy," Walcott early won the approval of J. Henry Roraback, Connecticut Republican boss and water-power magnate.

Walcott particularly won Roraback's heart by his excellent work in reorganizing the Connecticut Fish and Game Commission and in stocking the State with fish and game. Roraback, an outdoor enthusiast, also found in Walcott a boon fishing and hunting companion and in appreciation sent him to the State Senate where he served two terms.

Walcott was popular in the Legislature and in his second term was made president *pro tempore* and Chairman of the important Finance Committee. Obviously he was an up-and-coming politician, destined for higher things. But at this point Fred was led astray from the safe and secure path of strict devotion to his political boss, and for a little time Hoover came very near losing his senatorial Fido.

Roraback has always maintained a strict "pay-as-you-go" fiscal policy in Connecticut. As a result, the State has little bonded indebtedness and its credit is one of the soundest in the country. The business men and real estate dealers would prefer the easier bonding method of financing State improvements, but Roraback thinks otherwise and the governors and and legislatures do his bidding.

In 1926 Roraback elected as governor John Trumbull, subsequently John Coolidge's father-in-law, and with everything apparently well organized, went off to Florida for some deepsea fishing. But Roraback took too much for granted. No sooner was he out of the State and his firm hand removed from the helm, than Trumbull, feeling his oats, summoned a big State convention and, with the support of Walcott, Chairman of the Finance Committee, proposed a ten-million-dollar good-roads bond issue.

Business interests and the newspapers warmly applauded the plan. Times were flush and they saw no reason why Connecticut should continue the tight "pay-as-you-go" policy that Roraback insisted on. They lauded Trumbull and Walcott as statesmen of vision and courage, urging them to rush through their program.

It appeared as if Roraback had been successfully flaunted at last. But Connecticut, Trumbull and Walcott quickly learned better. Informed of what was going on, Roraback rushed back to the State and got into action.

Overnight, Walcott changed his mind and humbly returned to the fold. He announced that he had discovered "many objections" to the bonding proposal. Trumbull, too, soon saw the light and dropped the scheme. Mr. Roraback's "pay-as-you-go" policy continued unchanged.

It was anticipated after this misstep that Walcott was through and that Roraback would discard him. But he succeeded in making his peace with the Republican boss and in 1928, when Senator George P. McLean retired, Roraback selected Walcott as his successor.

Walcott learned his lesson well. He has strayed no more. He is a contented one-hundred-per-cent yes-man, which suits his nature, and that of the President perfectly.

Early in the spring of 1932 the President, frantically searching for a goat on which to blame the depression, hit on the idea of laying it at the door of the stock market. He called in Walcott, who as a former broker should have known

better, but readily lent himself to the publicity scheme. At
the Presidential command he would rush to the White House,
hold a brief consultation with his chief and issue forth with
a hot statement denouncing bear raiders and their unpatriotic
designs upon prosperity. The idea was not a bad one and
had possibilities—if Hoover and Walcott had not overplayed
their hand.

After a particularly bad slump in the market, Walcott was
summoned to the White House and came out with the statement that the President had the names of wicked bear raiders
and would demand an investigation if they did not stop
their operations. This was extremely poor tactics. The Senate,
from long experience profoundly suspicious of such White
House outbursts, promptly ordered an investigation of every
phase of the stock market—bulls as well as bears.

Whereupon, the President and Walcott suddenly cooled off
and for weeks nothing happened. Numerous reports spread
through the capital that the administration had discovered
prominent Republican leaders, including a Cabinet member,
among the short sellers and did not dare press the investigation.

But, one Friday afternoon, after a week of continuous falling market prices which had greatly excited the President,
Walcott was called to the telephone and told by the President
that he had received a telegram from George Barr Baker
informing him that the following day the bears planned to
pull off a billion-dollar raid. He directed Walcott to get the
Senate Banking and Currency Committee to start the bear
investigation at once.

George Barr Baker is one of Hoover's numerous under-
cover publicity barnacles who acted as press censor during the
President's good-will trip to Latin America.

Walcott was greatly excited by the President's information
and in his agitation confused George Barr Baker with George
F. Baker, multi-millionaire New York banker. Baker had

been dead for some time, but in the excitement Walcott forgot this fact.

Senator Peter Norbeck, hard-headed banker from South Dakota, is chairman of the Banking and Currency Committee. From the first he had been cynical about the President's bear-raiding charges. But he was out of the city that day, so that Walcott rushed to Senator Brookhart, ranking Republican member of the committee, and imparted to him the harrowing news. Brookhart, always ready to believe anything about the denizens of Wall Street, immediately convened the committee, of which Walcott is also a member. Several members, among them the fiscal authority, Senator Glass, were not present. Glass charged later that he was voted in favor of immediate action despite his absence. Brookhart and Walcott stampeded those members who did attend and it was ordered that the investigation should begin the following Monday, with Richard Whitney, head of the New York Stock Exchange, as the first witness.

If the reported raid was actually planned it did not take place. When the investigation got under way and the source of the President's charges was uncovered, members of the committee branded the affair as a false alarm by the rumor-mongering Baker. After a few hearings on short-selling operations the committee turned its attention to price-rigging practices, and Norbeck permitted Representative LaGuardia to present a whole truck-load of documents showing how financial writers on leading New York newspapers had taken money from the publicity agent of large bull-market manipulators to puff stocks they were pushing.

The White House was deeply distressed by the trend the investigation took. The President had never intended to expose the bull operators and their transactions. He had wanted to hold up a few politically unimportant bears to public calumny and then drop the matter. But the committee took the bit in its teeth. It set up a steering committee to direct

the investigation and sent its own investigators to New York
to collect evidence on the bulls.

Walcott was pointedly excluded from membership on the
steering committee. But he made no protest. And throughout the sensational public hearings of the investigation he sat
with a blank stare on his placid face and with his eyes fixed
on the wall opposite him.

*

SENATOR DAVID AIKEN REED was born in the lap of the gods
of Plutocracy and Big Business and has unctuously served
them ever since.

The carefully nurtured son of a Mellon corporation lawyer,
Reed is a Muscle Man by birth and breeding. He makes no
pretense of being anything other than a plutocrat. To him
there are only two classes of people: "our kind" and the
"dunderheads." This latter should always elect the former to
public office, and David grieves greatly when they don't.

In his opinion, what the country really needs is a Mussolini,
as he told a startled Senate one day in the spring of 1932.
Then his kind of people could go about their kind of business
with comfort and security and would not have to put up with
all this pother and clatter about democracy.

Dave hastened to assure the Senate that he had no thought
of making President Hoover a dictator. When he said a
Mussolini, he meant a Mussolini.

The plutocratic little Senator from Pennsylvania is really
most unhappy in the American scene. He infinitely prefers
the English caste system, where a man of good birth, proper
breeding and wealth can hope for honors and titles from his
King without having to depend upon the wayward fancies
of "dunderheads."

England is Reed's spiritual motherland. He loves going
there and hobnobbing with the lords and ladies and recount-

ing the amusing things his "ghillie" said to him when he was shooting on the Scottish moors.

It is Reed's fond hope and ambition to round out his career as Ambassador to the Court of St. James. No greater happiness could come to him, and the British sovereign would have no more devoted and humble admirer in the whole of his realm.

When Reed came to the Senate in 1922, by appointment of a Mellon-controlled Governor, he was welcomed with open arms by the Republican bosses. In his early forties, with a "distinguished" record as an artillery officer in France, a director of the Mellon bank in Pittsburgh, and a member of a big law firm serving the Mellons, a place was immediately made where a man of his wealth and ability could best serve the vested interests.

Not merely one place, but many were found for him. Within a year Reed had smashed all Senate precedents. He was appointed to such powerful committees as Finance, Military Affairs, and Immigration, and, a little later, Foreign Relations, and Senate Rules. There were twenty-one other Republican Senators of much longer service than Reed when he was named to the great Finance Committee. But none of them was a Mellon lawyer. In those days the name of Mellon was revered throughout the land.

The circumstances surrounding Reed's appointment to the Senate furnish an amazing insight into the way politics are conducted in Pennsylvania. When Senator William E. Crow died, Mellon sent word to the Governor to appoint Reed. However, David, being a devoted son, wanted his father, Judge Reed, to have the seat. He was young and he could wait. Judge Reed was an officer and director of more than fifty great corporations and banks. He and his law partner, Philander C. Knox, Taft's Secretary of State and United States Senator from Pennsylvania, had served Mellon for many years. But the aged Judge had never held high public office.

It was a charming picture of filial love. It was also a profoundly illuminating spectacle of how much the "dunder-heads" of Pennsylvania have to say about who shall repre-sent them. For more than a week, father and son staged an Alphonse-and-Gaston act. Murmurs were beginning to arise from the "dunderheads" when Joseph R. Grundy, high priest of the tariff lobbyists, stepped in and called a halt. He got the two Reeds together and bluntly admonished them to cut out the comedy and get down to business. Congress was en-acting a tariff law and a man of youth and vigor was needed to carry on the high-tariff fight. Judge Reed agreed with Grundy and Dave accepted the appointment.

He has not disappointed his patrons and masters. He is to-day the ablest and most agile high-tariff and low-income-tax zealot in the Senate. In the last few years he has carried most of the brunt of the floor fighting on such legislation, relieving Smoot, who no longer has the endurance required for such battles and never did have the forensic skill.

Unlike Apostle Smoot, Dave revels in floor combat. He is a keen and nimble debater and an astute and shifty strategist. He has not hesitated to filibuster when it suited his purpose and to shed crocodile tears over similar tactics by others when delay brought him no gain.

When he came to the Senate, Reed's passionate earnestness and air of fairness made a most favorable impression. But as the years went by, the Senate came to learn that this was only a pose on David's part, designed to throw it off guard. To-day, when he solemnly assures the chamber that everything is hotsy-totsy and that there is no reason why the War Depart-ment appropriation bill should not be passed in an hour, Democrats and Progressives say "Oh yeah" and carefully ran-sack the measure to see what David is trying to slip over.

The Senate has come to feel that David's seeming forth-rightness is only unctuous glibness masking a sly, tricky na-ture. It saw him throw himself with zeal and passion into the campaign to reëlect the pious and well-born George Wharton Pepper and when he went down to defeat before the scandal-smeared and low-born William S. Vare, Philadelphia political boss, heard Reed bitterly denounce the entire Pennsylvania electorate as a pack of "dunderheads." Yet, a few months later it listened to the same Reed as, with equal fervor, he defended the fraudulent and corrupt election of Vare and struggled desperately to seat him in the Senate.

For many years also the Senate has seen Reed vigorously advocating a big navy and earnestly upholding the demands of the admirals. Yet, when he returned as a delegate from the London Naval Conference with a treaty placing certain restrictions on naval construction, the Senate watched him confound and bedevil these very same admirals he had once championed.

Being a man of wealth and social standing, David has gone in strongly for Washington society. He has a large house in S Street, a motor boat on the Potomac, a telephone with an unlisted number, motors, servants and an entry to rarefied social circles. His original Washington house was in R Street, but when Hoover, then Secretary of Commerce, William R. Castle, Jr., Under-Secretary of State, Adolph C. Miller, of the Federal Reserve Board, Frederic A. Delano, and others of the *haute monde,* built large mansions in S Street, David decided that he too must have a residence there. When the house was completed, he imported an American artist from Paris to decorate the rooms with murals. The painter was fond of absinthe and took his time. David was so eager to move that he made the transfer before the paint was dry, much to the anguish of the butler, who feared that everything would be ruined.

One of Reed's perennial worries has been his private telephone number. A Senator representing the populous State of Pennsylvania in the nearby city of Washington can easily degenerate into nothing less than an errand boy for his constituents. So Reed tries to protect himself from phone calls, at least at home. The trouble is that his private number is always leaking out. It used to be North 2417. When that was noised around among his constituents, Reed changed it to Decatur 1224. Eventually this also became public property and now Reed's number is North 2222—or at least it will be until the Senator reads this book.

Reed's work at the London Naval Conference and as administration floor-leader in securing Senate ratification of the Naval Treaty afterwards is his outstanding public service. He was Stimson's most effective negotiator. Stimson put Reed in charge of the Japanese phase of the deliberations and Reed was almost solely responsible for breaking down a serious impasse.

In the Senate committee hearings and the floor debate on the treaty, Reed conducted a brilliant fight against the admirals and other jingo opponents of the pact. Supported by a great mass of confidential naval documents, including numerous contradictory statements by the blustering admirals —all of which he bluntly refused to make public, despite the heated indignation of the opposition—Reed manhandled and routed the navy men with decisiveness and vigor. He kept the Senate in session despite the discomfort of an intensely hot July and forced approval of the treaty.

The months Reed spent in London at the Naval Conference were among the happiest of his public career. He worked hard, but not too hard to keep him from enjoying to the full the delights and associations of English society. He and Mrs. Reed, a charming, kindly woman, were made much of by Lord and Lady Astor and members of the British nobility. Particularly was Reed thrilled at the privilege of hearing and meeting the King. These were rare pleasures, and he cherishes their memory.

And when the King sent him, as he did all the delegates, a phonographic record of his speech of welcome to the Conference, Dave was deeply grateful. The record was encased in a beautiful morocco leather box lined with red velvet. On its top was the coat-of-arms of the British crown together with the gold-embossed letters: "To Senator David A. Reed from George V."

Dave was proud of the gift, and one day when Mrs. Reed was entertaining friends at tea, he brought out his royal treasure. But in carrying it across the room, the record somehow slipped to the floor and broke into many pieces.

"Oh, David," reproved Mrs. Reed.

And then she saw his face. It looked like that of a small boy who has just lost his dearest possession.

"Never mind, David," she said consolingly, "the King will send you another one."

CHAPTER TEN

THE MUTES

*A*RLINGTON has its Unknown Soldier and the United States Senate its Mutes.

Both rest peacefully in marbled grandeur on the banks of the historic Potomac—one in the beautiful National Cemetery on the Virginia side, and the other directly opposite in the domed national capitol on the District side.

Both are shrouded in impenetrable anonymity; the martyred warrior in the great stone tomb that holds his revered remains, and the Senate Mutes in the dense silence and intellectual vacuum that encompass them.

They are a unique band, this group of Senators, known to the galleries as The Mutes. They occupy cushioned seats in the Senate chamber, have beautifully appointed offices in the adjoining Senate Office Building, are duly inscribed on the Senate's rolls as members, and draw the pay and emoluments due them as such. With that they complete their rôle as statesmen.

For the rest they are mere scenery—figures that take on a fleeting existence during the moment in which their names are bellowed forth at roll-calls, after which they revert to the limbo of obscurity.

There are two species of Senate Mutes: those who never

talk, and those who, even when they do, rise and rend the air, still say nothing.

The latter slightly outnumber their silent colleagues, but there is no difference between them in intellectual vacuity. In this respect honors are equally low and uniformly dismal.

No section of the country has a monopoly on The Mutes. They come from all parts of the land, though it must be admitted that the Atlantic seaboard has the largest representation. But if that is true as regards numbers, the West and Pacific coast more than make up for that by the ultra-fatuousness of their representatives.

Senators Oddie, of Nevada, Robinson, of Indiana, and Shortridge, of California, stand out even among their dumber colleagues for the extent and variety of their vocal and intellectual inanity. Only in Hale of Maine, Kean of New Jersey, and Trammell of Florida, are their equals to be found.

It is perhaps unfair to the group as a whole, however, to set up invidious comparisons. Colorless, drab, innocuous, cockle-headed, silly and puerile though they may be, each, after his own fashion, has his own peculiar characteristics that set him apart from his fellow-Mutes. Each has his own special kind of incoherence. Little "Freddy" Hale of Maine, for example, approximates a water-logged rowboat, as a caustic colleague once bluntly described him. Then there is the elongated Shortridge of California, with a head shaped like an egg, and in full figure resembling nothing so much as Senator Pat Harrison's description of him, "a eucalyptus tree weaving and waving in the breeze."

On the other hand, the New Englander, Coolidge of Massachusetts, and the Southerner, Trammell of Florida, are intellectually alter egos. Both are in a complete daze as to what it is all about.

This characteristic is quite common among the entire group. The explanation of how these men find their way to seats in the august Senate is to be found in the vagaries of local politics. Several got by the golden gate through weight of money. Robinson secured his place through the patronage of a former Ku Klux Klan ruler of Indiana, who is now serving a life sentence for rape and murder. Some rode in on the crest of the Hoover landslide in 1928, and several others hold their places because they happen to bear the names of distinguished families in their States.

The effects of the election machinery in America are diverse and incalculable. It places a mining stock promoter, turned Great Engineer, in the White House, a half-breed Indian with social ambitions in the Vice-Presidency, makes a Texas cowboy Speaker of the House, a Lame Duck New Jersey politician Ambassador to France, and a motley crew of hacks sovereign United States Senators.

In their two classifications, the Senate Mutes consist of the following:

NON-TALKERS

Warren R. Austin, Republican, Vermont.

Marcus A. Coolidge, Democrat, Massachusetts.

Phillips Lee Goldsborough, Republican, Maryland.

Henry W. Keyes, Republican, New Hampshire.

Jesse H. Metcalf, Republican, Rhode Island.

John G. Townsend, Jr., Republican, Delaware.

THOSE WHO SOMETIMES OPEN THEIR MOUTHS, BUT SAY NOTHING

Edwin S. Broussard, Democrat, Louisiana.

Frederick Hale, Republican, Maine.

Daniel O. Hastings, Republican, Delaware.

Hamilton F. Kean, Republican, New Jersey.

Tasker L. Oddie, Republican, Nevada.

Arthur R. Robinson, Republican, Indiana.

Samuel M. Shortridge, Republican, California.

Park Trammell, Democrat, Florida.

Senator Austin is a young man as Vermont Senators go, but as a statesman he takes himself very seriously.

He dresses with meticulous formality and is one of the

two or three members who consider it necessary now and then to embellish senatorial deliberations with a frock coat.

For one seated in "rookie row," the last tier of seats in the Senate, this is a particularly statesmanlike act. For when he rises and turns to walk out of the chamber his smart coattails impart a touch of dignity and erudition to that part of the Senate that otherwise is totally lacking in either the intelligence, appearance or antics of its denizens.

Austin was bestowed on the Senate by the electorate of Vermont in 1931, as a result of two local disaffections which he astutely exploited to his own political profit. Vermont World War veterans wanted the bonus and another large section of the voters had become pained at the rule of what is known in the State as the "marble gang." This machine is made up of Republican politicians who are run by the wealthy and medieval local railroad and marble-quarry magnates.

For uncounted years the marble and railroad capitalists have run Vermont's politics. In 1931 they lost one of their Washington Senators, Frank L. Greene, who died of a bullet from the gun of a wild-shooting prohibition agent. In moving to replace Greene the "marble gang's" machinations were no worse than they had been previously, but the electorate was in a less docile mood.

The Hoover depression had penetrated even the rock-ribbed Republican fastnesses of Vermont, and there was a lot of hard feeling rampant among the faithful. So when the machine undertook to do what it had always done when a public office was open—nominate one of its tried and trusted henchmen—a murmur went up from the voters.

Austin set himself at the head of this disaffection and ran as an anti-machine candidate. As a further prop to his candidacy he declared himself a friend of the bonus-seeking veterans, who, also being harried by the depression, were clamoring for government pork. With these two more or less organized forces of public opinion behind him he defeated the machine and was catapulted out of comparative obscurity as a lawyer in Vermont to complete obscurity as a statesman in the Senate.

Insurgent as he may have been in his election campaign, Austin has been a regular of regulars in Washington. He is one of the most worshipful and reverent of the very small group of Hoover torch-bearers. The President does not even have to bestow on him the occasional beneficence of a hand-out at the White House table to keep him at the desired pitch of pious obeisance. Austin is a devotee for devotion's sake.

In fact, he is so worshipful of Hoover, that although he was the veterans' choice in Vermont he has not lifted a finger to further their bonus demands in Washington. Mr. Hoover does not go in for bonuses to veterans. Treasury largesses to panhandling banks, railroads and insurance companies are pleasing to the President, however, and Austin loyally upholds his hand. As his term runs until March, 1935, Austin doubtless figures that he has plenty of time in which to appease both the President and the veterans.

*

SENATOR MARCUS COOLIDGE is a Democrat and no relation to the somewhat better known former Republican President of the same name. But there are numerous marked similarities in fundamental traits and viewpoints between the two men.

Both are enormously pleased and satisfied with themselves and their little, comfortable, well-cushioned, bourgeois worlds. Both pinched themselves in ecstatic surprise when they found themselves in high office in Washington. Both are sublimely platitudinous and both are completely ignorant about world and domestic affairs.

Senator Coolidge's extensive preparations for obscurity as a statesman in the Senate consisted of the following: engaging in the manufacturing business of his father and, not unnaturally, rapidly rising to the top. This business he later moved from Massachusetts to New York because the former's labor code was too stringent and humanitarian. For a short time he was Mayor of the town of Fitchburg, Massachusetts, a delegate to the Democratic national convention in 1920, and a nominee for the Electoral College on the Smith ticket in 1928.

Senator Coolidge won his Senate seat because he had the rare good fortune to have William M. Butler as his opponent, and the further fact that in 1930 there was no other Democrat in Massachusetts who had the money or cared enough for the senatorship to spend the money to seek it. Butler had been in the Senate on a gubernatorial appointment for a few months during the Coolidge régime, but when the voters could get at him they threw him out with a resounding thwack.

Dour, dull, reactionary and unpopular, Butler was a set-up for any one, particularly in 1930 with the Hoover depression in full stride. Also, and this was particularly ironical in view of Butler's close friendship with Calvin Coolidge, the fact that his Democratic opponent's name was Coolidge helped the latter. Many a good Massachusetts voter in balloting for the Democratic Coolidge thought he was sending a kinsman of Cal to the Senate.

For platitudinous blatancy and inanity the Butler-Coolidge senatorial campaign was notable even in Massachusetts, where these two characteristics are the outstanding qualifications of most of the public men the State has produced in recent years. In this instance both candidates were unintelligible—publicly and privately—and the resulting dissonance was horrible.

The Democrats, however, craftily outsmarted the Republicans by keeping their candidate off the stump and out of sight as much as possible. Some unsung genius among the Democratic strategists conceived the plan and, without giving Coolidge an inkling of the real purpose, kept him safely in the background. The scheme worked perfectly.

The electorate, after hearing and seeing Butler, decided his unseen and unheard opponent couldn't conceivably be worse and they flocked to him on Election Day.

After a year in the Senate, Coolidge still does not know what it is all about. He takes his cue as to how he should vote from David I. Walsh, his Democratic colleague from Massachusetts, to such an extent that Walsh now has two votes in the Senate. Coolidge considers Walsh a great statesman and political leader, and painstakingly follows in his footsteps.

Walsh, one of the most raucous and demagogic stuffed shirts in the Senate, makes abundant use of Coolidge's slavish devotion, but privately speaks disparagingly of his well-meaning but naïve colleague. Coolidge's presence in the Senate is a double boon to Walsh. Not only does Coolidge follow him, but his negative quality is an asset. A colleague of any ability at all would quickly show Walsh up for the poseur and babbler he is. But with his facility for thunderous outpourings and his knack for tricky politics, Walsh easily outshines his associate and can publicly pose as the "able" Senator from Massachusetts.

As between the two men, Coolidge, despite his ignorance and complacency, actually is the more pleasant person. He doesn't strut; he is no demagogue; and in comparison with Walsh's insipid bellowings his silence is to be preferred.

Coolidge's naïveté was amusingly displayed shortly after he came to Washington. He found he needed a clerk; so he inserted an ad in a Washington newspaper. The next morning he was almost mobbed by several hundred unemployed women. It had never occurred to him that the demand for work was so tragically great.

Coolidge likes to extend gracious little favors to his friends and frequently places his large and luxurious automobile at their disposal. He does this with no thought of gaining favor, but merely because he enjoys making happy those whom he likes.

Newspaper correspondents are fond of him, but they don't

give him much time. This is not because he is secretive or close-mouthed. He tells them readily enough all he knows. But he doesn't know anything, and worse, when he gets hold of a reporter he catechizes him to find out what is going on.

*

ON one occasion, commenting editorially on his complete nullity as a public figure, the Baltimore *Sun* derisively referred to Senator Goldsborough as "the Maryland Gentleman."

Totally unconscious of the irony of the description as applied to him—a Republican politician in a State where only Democrats are gentlemen—Goldsborough promptly made the *Sun's* ridicule his proudest boast. A product of that section of Maryland known as the Eastern Shore, where the local preachers belligerently upheld a recent lynching and the rest of the populace boycotted those who dared denounce such barbarism, to be called a gentleman, even in mockery, was the height of glory to Goldsborough.

He made the characterization his campaign issue in the senatorial race and, aided by the wave of bigotry and moronacy that swept over the nation at the instigation of Mr. Hoover in 1928, was elected to the Senate. There he has sat for four years in the complete vacuity and obscurity from which he came and into which he will again retire, when in 1934 the Maryland electorate gets another crack at him.

Goldsborough has been a seeker after office all his life. He was out of law school but a few years when he got himself elected district attorney and from then on he has held elective or appointive office almost continuously. In 1912, as a result of a disordered condition in the Maryland Democratic Party, he was elected Governor, the second Republican to hold that office since the Civil War.

As a State executive he was as sterile as he has been as United States Senator. He devoted himself to patronage and local pork and rested content with such labors. When he retired from the governorship in 1915, some friends made him the head of a Baltimore bank on the promise that he would give up politics.

For the next thirteen years he held to his pledge and the State rejoiced. During the War he gained some slight derisive notoriety as a patriotic "sob sister," for his ready ability to produce a flood of crocodile tears on any and all occasions.

In 1928, however, his Eastern Shore background and training sensed the revival of bigotry and he decided to explore its promising possibilities. His instincts proved sound. He ran for the Senate, and the Hoover Ku Klux landslide swept him into office.

Goldsborough likes to affect a great show of elegant courtliness. He goes about the Senate with an air of deep secretiveness, giving off an impression that he is laden with secrets of state. The subterfuge has fooled no one but himself. Neither the Senate nor the press pays any attention to him.

*

SURPRISING as the news may be to the thousands of newspaper and magazine readers who follow the well-advertised and numerous literary and social peregrinations of Mrs. Frances Parkinson Keyes, there *really* is a Senator Keyes.

He is tall and bulky in appearance, has a smallish head with a pointed red face, eyes that are closely set together, wears pince-nez glasses, parts his hair meticulously in the middle, and although he has been in public life practically continuously since 1891 has never uttered a single word that attracted even passing comment. His record is as bare of legislative or administrative enactment as it was the day he took office.

Keyes is the most completely obscure and innocuous member in the Senate. In fact, he is so totally a blank that his very nullity has brought him a certain fame.

He is now pointed out to tourists in the Senate galleries as the man who has the longest record for total silence in the history of the chamber.

The only time Keyes ever rises to his feet is when he is compelled by sheer force of Senate rules to submit a report or a measure from the insignificant Committee on Public Buildings and Grounds, of which he is chairman. Senate rules require chairmen of committees to lay before the chamber reports of the work of their groups.

The rare instances when Keyes takes such action, not over a few times a session, always attract the attention of his colleagues and the galleries. He blushes a deep red and invariably stammers and falters as he goes through the routine formula.

There was one occasion, however, when the inarticulate Junior Senator from New Hampshire overcame his diffidence and acted with verve and dash. But it did not occur in the Senate.

One pleasant afternoon Keyes' very able secretary, Charley Wright, asked permission to leave early. Keyes does not intrude in the personal affairs of his staff, but on this occasion he was curious. He said he had no objection to Charley leaving before the usual quitting hour, but he wanted to know why he asked for the extra time. Charley smilingly told him he wanted to drive to a cock-fight that was going to be held on a farm in nearby Maryland that night.

Senator Keyes had never seen a cock-fight. Furthermore, he was a bit lonely. Mrs. Keyes was off on one of her literary junkets and it occurred to her husband that he would like to witness this legally prohibited spectacle. So he asked Charley if he could go with him. On the drive to the farm, Keyes made many inquiries about cock-fighting and by the time they arrived at the place where it was to be held he was as excited as young Captain Regnier, who raises Filipino game cocks.

His enthusiasm reached fever pitch during the course of the first fight. When the second pair of birds were thrown into the ring it boiled over. He became so excited that he leaped into the ring and began cheering the clashing cocks. They were making murderous leaps at each other, but upon Keyes' appearance they sprang apart. Then, as if by command, they jumped high into the air and hurled themselves on one of Keyes' bulky legs, which they promptly proceeded to lacerate with their spurs shod with razor-edged steel.

The Senator finally was rescued from the irate cocks, but not until his ankle was cut painfully.

*

SENATOR JESSE HOUGHTON METCALF of Rhode Island broke his seven-year silence in the Senate in the 1932 session of Congress with a speech favoring beer. Since 1924 he has sat in the Senate. Many great and far-reaching issues and controversies have been discussed and fought over in that time. But he has gone his mild, pleasant, little way undisturbed.

But one day this last session Metcalf startled his colleagues almost out of their wits. He stood up and read a prepared address advocating a liberalization of the prohibition laws. It was a friendly little speech, nothing violent or denunciatory. Just a gentle admonition that something really ought to be done about prohibition.

Surprising as was his vocal effort, both to the Senate and the correspondents, the little Rhode Island Senator nevertheless got only a passing press notice. But that did not distress him. In the Providence *Journal*, of which he is part owner, his remarks were carried at length. That was quite enough for him.

While totally unknown to the public, Metcalf enjoys a certain distinction in strictly Senate circles on two counts: the odd cut of his coat pockets and his ownership of a large, luxurious yacht, on which he lives during warm weather while in the capital. A few other Senators have yachts, but they do not use them as residences. Metcalf is very proud of his ship and likes to entertain friends on it.

His unique coat pockets are a design of his own. Instead of resting on the hips and being cut horizontally and fitted with flaps, his pockets are located slightly higher and are cut diagonally downward. They have no flaps, but are mere slits. When he walks about he thrusts his hands into them and saunters around with his hands folded comfortably out of sight across his stomach.

Metcalf is a wealthy textile manufacturer. He favors high tariffs for industry and opposes all progressive labor legislation. The past session he carefully ducked a vote on the Norris bill outlawing yellow-dog contracts. While hostile to labor measures he gives generously to charity. He is president of the Rhode Island Hospital and trustee of several schools, one of which, Brown University, conferred a doctor's degree on him several years ago in appreciation of his contributions.

In the last few years Metcalf and the State Republican organization in Rhode Island have not got along well together. He insists on keeping a firm hold on Federal patronage and the local boys want to have some say about these matters. They have repeatedly struck back at him, but he has maintained a firm hold on the pie counter.

When he was up for reëlection in 1930, Senator Moses, at the instigation of the local politicians, took the Chairmanship of the Republican Senatorial Campaign Committee away from Metcalf in a very rude manner. Being a candidate for reëlection, Metcalf had expected to give up the post. But without waiting for him to act, Moses ousted him and elected himself. Since then Moses has made Senator Felix Hebert, Metcalf's Rhode Island colleague, Vice Chairman of the Committee. Hebert stands in well with the State machine.

Metcalf was deeply offended by Moses' slight, but he said nothing. He was reëlected without trouble, and despite the covert opposition of the State machine. In 1932, as a further rebuke, the State leaders refused to make him a delegate to the Republican national convention, appointing Hebert instead. But, as the Senate remained in session throughout the convention, Metcalf had the laugh on them.

*

DELAWARE, the du Pont principality, has the distinction of being the only State with two senatorial members in good standing in the Order of The Mutes. Senator Townsend is a non-talker and Senator Hastings ranks as one of those who, even when he does speak, says nothing.

Townsend's deep obscurity as a Senator had a brief moment of respite in the spring of 1932 when it was disclosed that although he is a wealthy banker, real estate owner and contractor, he was carrying his son Paul, the vice-president of his large contracting firm, on the congressional pay-roll as a $3,900-a-year secretary. This revelation of Townsend's nepotism aroused considerable comment in political quarters, but he maintained a tight silence.

Whether he said nothing because he was at loss for an alibi, or whether he still vividly remembered his experience the last time he had expressed an opinion, is uncertain. This distressing incident occurred during the 1930 State election in Delaware. Townsend, in addition to his many business and banking interests, is also a large orchardist. During the State election a controversy arose between him and a political opponent over the auctioning of a crate of peaches. Townsend is known in Delaware as the State's most talented backslapper and glad-hander, but in the heat of the argument he forgot himself and expressed a forthright opinion. The unusualness of such courage was lost on his opponent, however, who took exception to his remarks and gave him a black eye.

The death of Senator Dwight Morrow stripped Senator Hastings of his once proud rôle as a Senate leader.

As long as Morrow was in the Senate it was Hastings' advice that he followed when the roll was called. The widely touted Morgan partner would confer at great length on important issues with such liberal Senators as Borah, Norris, Wheeler and La Follette, and while in their presence would agree with them. But when he returned to his seat, the little, squat, Buddha-like Hastings would lean over and hammer Morrow's desk with his pudgy hands, after which Morrow never failed to go down the line with the rest of the reactionary administration Republicans.

Morrow's docility was a great satisfaction to Hastings, one he now sorely misses as an aspiring Senate leader. For since Morrow's passing, the Senate has been cool to Hastings' leadership ambitions. When in the spring of 1932 he determinedly attempted to assert such a rôle, the chamber pushed him back into limbo in short order.

Hastings headed a sub-committee investigating the claim of former Senator Tom Heflin that he had been defrauded in the Alabama election when he was defeated in 1930. Hastings, one of the most rabid Republican partisans in the Senate, made a report charging all sorts of illegalities and frauds in the Southern State. Had the issue involved a Northern Republican State, Hastings, of course, would have found everything sweet and lovely. But Alabama being in the Solid South, the little Republican wheelhorse turned crusader and demanded a clean-up.

For several days Hastings bored the Senate with long, dull, inconsequential outpourings about the offenses he claimed had been committed against Heflin. The few Senators who stayed in the chamber listened to him in apathy. When the vote was taken the Senate expressed its opinion of Hastings' leadership by rejecting Heflin by the overwhelming vote of 63 to 19.

Hastings attempted a leadership rôle in the 1931 soldier bonus fight in the Senate, but with no better results than in the Heflin contest. Hoover was excitedly demanding that the bonus be rejected and Republican leaders as usual were using their own judgment, when Hastings decided that a champion was needed. He hurled his round little paunch into the breach in support of the President.

But try as he would, he could make no impression upon the Senate, until one day he launched a crude and slanderous attack upon the veterans. He expressed the solemn opinion that the desperately needy ex-service men, thousands of them unemployed for many months and with wives and children, would spend their bonus checks on fancy women. This cowardly accusation brought him plenty of attention, both in the Senate and country at large, but it was not the kind he had anticipated. A deluge of denunciation poured down on him and even those opposing the bonus avoided him.

Hastings was surprised at the widespread anger aroused by his remarks. Never having served in the military forces of his country, and not being in want himself, he insisted he knew what he was talking about.

*

For almost two decades there has been a Broussard from Louisiana in the Senate, but the year 1932 may see this long succession broken.

The current Senator Broussard is not highly regarded by Senator Huey P. Long, self-styled "Kingfish" of Louisiana, who has decided to elect a man of his own choosing. It is possible that the colorless and mediocre Broussard may escape the doom Long has marked out for him, but the chances are strongly against him. Long decapitated Broussard's veteran and equally innocuous colleague Joseph L. Ransdell in 1930 and all indications are that he will do the same to Broussard.

Louisiana and the Senate have nothing to lose by such an eventuality. Broussard's successor could not be less innocuous and colorless, or more reactionary.

Edwin S. Broussard has been in the Senate since 1920, when he succeeded his brother Robert. In the twelve years he has served, Edwin has hung up a high tariff record that is matched only by that of the extreme Republican high tariff janizaries. In other matters he is one of the most reactionary members on the Democratic side. In fact, he is a Democrat only in name. He votes nearly always with the reactionary Republican muscle men and unquestionably would be much more at home on their side of the chamber.

Broussard came to the Senate on the strength of his brother's name and reputation. The family is a prominent one in the wet, Catholic, southern part of Louisiana. It is of French-Arcadian extraction, known locally as "Cajuns." Broussard speaks French and is a wet, politically and socially. This combination of circumstances made him and has kept him a Senator for two terms. Broussard's rare speeches in the Senate are devoted to demanding and justifying high tariffs. Nobody pays any attention to them, the chamber emptying when he starts to speak.

Broussard's one "constructive" achievement in the Senate was his out-maneuvering some of his colleagues in getting a new street in Washington named after Louisiana. There was a scramble after this honor and Broussard outwitted his opponents by inserting an amendment naming the thoroughfare after his State in a bill authorizing another new street.

*

SENATOR "FREDDY" HALE is a big shot as a descendant. But as a statesman he is one of the total losses in Congress.

His mother was the daughter, the wife, and the mother of United States Senators. His father was Senator from Maine for thirty years, the second longest record for continuous service in the Senate. His grandfather, on his mother's side, was Zachariah Chandler, Senator from Michigan, who helped organize the Republican Party in 1854. He was also an intimate friend of Lincoln, and Secretary of Interior and Chairman of the Republican National Committee under Grant.

To this great family record, Freddy, after sixteen years in

the Senate, has added a little nose-tickling mustache, a Kodiak bear cub in the Washington zoo, and a reputation, as described by several colleagues restrained both by charity and parliamentary courtesy, of being "a mighty light cruiser."

The use of nautical terms in describing Freddy's general blundering obtuseness arises out of his big-navy activities. Through the operation of the rule of seniority, he is chairman of the Naval Affairs Committee. He is a zealous big-navy advocate, but it is a moot question whether he, or the clownish Representative Fred Britten, rabid jingoist of the House, is the greatest handicap to the admirals and the shipbuilding lobby.

The inanities and absurdities of the two Freddies unquestionably contribute more to the furtherance of the cause of peace than the combined efforts of all the professional pacifists.

Ever-increasing naval construction is Hale's preoccupation. In season and out of season he yammers about it. During the winter of 1932, when millions were out of work and in need, when the whole economic structure of the country was bogged in a mire of despondency and chaos, he had no other thought than to put through a big-navy program. That the Treasury was staggering under a three-billion-dollar deficit and that the highest peace-time taxes in the history of the country had to be imposed to meet the operating expenses of the government did not interest Freddy.

He demanded battleships and the maintenance of wasteful navy yards. He took up almost a week of the Senate's time trying to put through a huge naval construction authorization bill, and when, in conjunction with other Republican Senators, he was called to the White House to confer with the President on possible savings in government expenditures and was asked for his suggestions, all he had to contribute was the piteous plea, "You mustn't close any navy yards, you mustn't close any navy yards."

On the few occasions during a congressional session when Freddy takes the floor he always speaks on the navy. His addresses are dreadfully dull discourses, prepared for him by naval men, which he reads. They almost always begin with the profound observation, "The navy is the first line of defense"—which is probably Freddy's only contribution to the speech.

Freddy speaks in a squeaky voice that can hardly be heard. In debate he is easily discomfited. His usual practice, when he is about to deliver one of his harangues, is to ask that he not be interrupted.

As a floor leader on naval legislation, Freddy's blundering ineptness is the despair of his supporters and the joy of the opposition. When the fifteen-cruiser bill was before the Senate in 1928, a handful of opponents were able to prevent action on it for months, although an overwhelming majority of the Senators favored the measure and any kind of competent floor leadership could have forced a vote without delay. The supporters of the bill finally became so disgusted with Freddy's obfuscation that they took the matter out of his hands and quickly brought it before the Senate.

It was on this occasion that caustic Senator "Jim" Reed, of Missouri, observed "a rowboat was in charge of the United States navy."

Although an extreme reactionary and administration satellite on all other legislation, on the big-navy issue Freddy consistently differs with the President. When Hoover, as a preliminary to the London Naval Conference, proposed an investigation of the Shearer big-navy lobby, he asked Hale to handle it. Freddy and the admirals were alarmed at what might be revealed, and the former balked.

In distress, he went to see the late Joseph P. Cotton, Under-Secretary of State, one of the few really distinguished men appointed by Hoover. Hale and Cotton had been Harvard classmates and Hale appealed to Cotton for counsel.

"Freddy," said Cotton, "you have been here twelve years and you haven't done a thing. Maine hasn't had a statesman since James G. Blaine. Couldn't you try to be a statesman?"

This was asking too much. Freddy declined to investigate the big-navy crowd himself, but compromised by appointing a sub-committee at the head of which he placed Senator Shortridge, another big-navy zealot, who sabotaged the inquiry and has never made a report on it.

When the London Naval Treaty was finally placed before the Senate, Freddy led a revolt against it that was as funny as it was pathetic. The Senate Foreign Relations Committee, as was its province, conducted extended hearings on the pact. Freddy, at the instigation of the admirals and the big-navy lobby, convened his committee hurriedly and held a series of hearings that were burlesques.

Hale's petulant and puerile snobbishness and his preoccupation with big-navy agitation have aroused widespread resentment among his home folks in the last few years. Particularly has he antagonized the members of the Maine delegation in the House. He has insulted or snubbed every one of these men at one time or another.

Freddy dislikes bothering himself with State matters and is often rude and brusque with constituents seeking service. When they turn to other members of the Maine delegation and the latter get busy, Hale pouts and sulks like a spoiled child, and on occasion has even interfered to prevent them from getting results. He has repeatedly bawled out Maine representatives because they had undertaken projects which he had declined to bother about.

Until the last few years, Freddy was able to get away with this high-handed attitude because of the support of Guy P. Gannett, owner of a string of four Maine newspapers. In the Gannett papers Freddy is always pictured as a towering statesman, and no matter what any other Maine member in Congress may do, credit is always bestowed on Freddy's close-clipped brow.

But since Ernest Gruening established his independent Portland *Evening News* and through the realistic reporting of Miss Ruby Black, his Washington correspondent, has printed the real truth about Freddy, his star has begun to wane. It is generally agreed in Maine that if Hale were a candidate during the current depression, he would be soundly trounced. But his term lasts until 1935, by which time conditions may be more favorable for him.

Freddy is a bachelor and an active social light in Washington's depression dance. He lives in the Hale ancestral mansion, a huge brownstone house on Sixteenth Street, where his mother kept house for him until she died several years ago. He is a member of the very exclusive, but little known, Alibi Club, made up of wealthy men who are fond of cooking.

His great hobbies are athletics and hunting. He goes daily to a gymnasium to box or bowl, and golfs at the exclusive Burning Tree Club, where women are not allowed. During congressional recesses he goes big game hunting.

As a hunter he is more effective than as a campaigner, and during a hunting trip in Alaska in 1931 he bagged a giant Kodiak bear. His capacity as a campaigner was once summed up by an opponent who, commenting on a speech Freddy had made, remarked: "It was an excellent speech, indeed. It was no less a fine speech when his father first made it forty years ago."

*

SENATOR HAMILTON F. KEAN is known as "Ham" to his Senate colleagues, and his intellectual equipment and demeanor as a statesman do not belie this characterization.

Kean is proof of the axiom that *any* man, given sufficient millions and a willingness to contribute his money generously to "the boys" over a long period of years, ultimately can reach the Senate.

For almost half a century Kean has been active in New Jersey politics—as a large contributor. The senatorship is his only elective office, but as far back as 1884 the local Republican politicians spotted him as a budding—and well-heeled

—statesman and from then on they kept him "active" in State politics. Slowly they promoted him from one campaign committee to another, always seeing to it, of course, that he made a handsome contribution.

Kean proudly lists all these obscure little committees in his self-penned biography in the Congressional Directory. This laughable political background he really considers of great significance.

So, likewise, does he take himself seriously as a statesman. He loves to confer with Senate leaders on the "situation" and can't understand why neither they nor the President don't act on his advice. That he is so innocuous and insignificant that not even the President considers it necessary to patronize him has never dawned on Kean.

In the press gallery Kean is known as "the sea lion," a name inspired by his blank face, large scraggly mustache and docility. To his Senate colleagues, Kean is an inoffensive chair warmer who is always good for a couple of hours recess when he takes the floor with one of his stumbling speeches. When he begins to talk, the chamber empties, the members knowing that they will not miss a thing.

Kean's great wealth, reputed to be over fifty million dollars, was chiefly inherited. It took the form of a large banking business in New York, and considerable property in New Jersey. Some twenty-five years ago an elder, abler brother served a term in the Senate and "Ham" wanted to carry on this tradition. He achieved it by the contribution route.

When Kean first ran for the Senate in 1924, he preceded his election effort by several years of intense contributing. When he was defeated he did not become discouraged but increased his contributions. From 1924 to 1928 he spread his largess over the State. Its charm finally worked. Among those in the know in New Jersey politics it is said that his Senate seat cost him $1,000,000.

In addition to his weakness in considering himself a statesman, Kean likes to consider himself a farmer. He lists himself in his congressional biography as "banker and farmer." Just what kind of a farmer he is was revealed several years ago, when he besought the United States Board of Tax Appeals to allow him to deduct from his income taxes losses he claimed from the operation of "a farm," but which the government tax assessors declared was a country estate, approximating in its appointments a summer resort.

Arguing that it really was a farm, Kean in all seriousness cited as evidence that the place had no golf course, no tennis courts and that its extensive gardens were not formal.

*

THE great ambition of Senator Tasker Lowndes Oddie is to be taken seriously by the President and the Senate.

There are times when the realization of his insignificant rôle as a statesman during his twelve years in the Senate actually has caused Oddie to consider the desirability of bolting Republican traces now and then just to compel attention. But, although he has wistfully talked of such a possibility and for more than a decade given his utmost thought to ways and means of becoming politically potent, he is no nearer his cherished goal than when he first came to Washington.

Desperately determined to be taken seriously, Oddie of late has taken to making an occasional call at the White House for a chat with the President on the "situation." The results, however, have not been satisfactory.

During the protracted economy fight between Congress and the President, with the administration bitterly opposing the Senate's demand for a flat ten-per-cent slash of all departmental budgets, Oddie, with his weakness for regularity, was taken into tow by Postmaster General Brown, and used by him in his effort to prevent a reduction of the postal appropriation. As one of Brown's henchmen, Oddie in company with several other Senators was summoned one morning to the White House for a breakfast conference on plans to fight the Senate's economy program.

When the Senate convened at noon, Oddie, stimulated by his contact with the President and bulwarked by the White House breakfast food he had imbibed, launched an attack on the ten-per-cent cut. The Senate, having learned of his White House conference, leaped on him en masse.

SENATOR MCKELLAR: Will the Senator say whether or not the President is in favor of the Senator's motion to rescind the ten-per-cent cut in appropriations. Is the President in favor of the Senator's motion?

ODDIE: I have not the slightest idea what the President of the United States thinks about.

MCKELLAR: The President is giving out interviews every day in favor of economy and here is a motion of the Senator to do away with bringing about economy, at least to the extent of ten per cent. Is it possible that the Senator discussed the question with the President and did not get an idea from him as to whether or not the President is in favor of his motion or against it?

ODDIE: No, because very general things were discussed and I do not know how the President feels about the reduction.

SENATOR NORRIS: I should like to ask the Senator how in the world can we expect to follow the ideas of the President if we do not know what he thinks about this motion?

ODDIE: The Senate is an independent body. I feel that we have a right to our individual opinions and a license to do as we think best.

NORRIS: The Senator did not dare tell the President that, did he? (Laughter.)

MCKELLAR: Will the Senator from Nevada be good enough before he asks for a vote on his resolution to have a conference with the President and find out whether or not the President is in favor of the Senator's resolution?

ODDIE: No, I will not, because I consider myself an independent factor in this matter.

SENATOR TYDINGS: I appreciate the frankness of the Senator, but I am wondering if anybody on the Republican side of the aisle knows where the President stands on this resolution.

ODDIE: That is a very broad question. I do not want to get far afield in this matter. We are discussing one problem.

The barrage of derision finally became so severe and Oddie so confused that Senator McNary, Republican floor leader, curtly took him off the floor.

Oddie is a Nevadan by adoption. He was born and raised in New York. In 1898 he went to Nevada and engaged in mining. In his congressional biography he claims credit for being "one of the discoverers of the gold and silver camp at Tonopah in 1899," and "Goldfield, another famous camp which came into being largely as a result of this discovery." Oddie made a considerable fortune in mining and livestock operations and was Governor for two terms before coming to the Senate.

Personally, Oddie is a friendly and accommodating person, whose chief pride is his horsemanship. His equestrian skill, however, did not prevent him from experiencing a bad fall last winter which deprived the Senate of his eloquence for several months.

*

SENATOR ARTHUR R. ROBINSON is the Ku Klux Klan's gift to the American people.

The little, sly, ferret-faced, oily mannered Republican was sky-rocketed out of obscurity in the bigoted depths of Indiana backwoods politics into the national arena at the command of his one-time political boss and former Klan ruler of the State, D. C. Stephenson, now serving a life sentence for murder and rape.

Stephenson was already in jail, awaiting trial for his hideous crime, when he sent word to Governor Ed Jackson, another Klux henchman whom he had elevated to high office, to appoint Robinson to a Senate vacancy. Jackson, who later escaped charges of corruption by invoking the statute of limitations, already had offered the seat to George Ball, of Muncie, Indiana, a millionaire glass manufacturer, and Republican National Committeeman.

But at Stephenson's demand, coming from his murderer's cell, Jackson withdrew the appointment from Ball and named instead the little-known Robinson. In the wave of Republican-inspired bigotry that swept over the country in 1928, Robinson was elected for a full term which expires in March, 1935.

Robinson denies he is a Kluxer. That he was one of Stephenson's closest henchmen, however, and that it is a rule of the Klan that members deny any connection with it are incontrovertible facts. That he received his appointment at the instigation of Stephenson was publicly charged on the Senate floor. Senator Millard Tydings, of Maryland, also declared in a Senate speech in 1928 that Robinson's wife had accepted a pearl necklace as a Christmas gift from Stephenson when he was at the height of his political power.

Whether Robinson actually is a member of the Klan or not, everything he does in the Senate has the Klux imprint on it. When the Kluxer Heflin was waging his moronic bigotry campaign in the Senate, Robinson voted with him. In his self-penned biography in the Congressional Directory, Robinson significantly notes the fact that he is a thirty-third degree Mason. And he will never join with Senator Jim Watson, his Indiana colleague, in endorsing for Federal appointment a member of the Catholic faith, no matter how good or important a Republican the individual may be.

The six years that he has served in the Senate have brought Robinson no intimates there, even among reactionary Republicans. The camaraderie that exists, under the surface, among the members of the chamber is barred to him. The manner of his coming to the Senate, his relationship with the vicious Stephenson, his oily, pawing manner, and the astounding depths of innuendo and partisanship he displayed in the early days of his membership in the chamber have raised insurmountable barriers. He is disliked, distrusted and shunned by a large part of the Senate membership.

In the last few years Robinson has said little and kept in the background. But when he first came to the Senate he talked on everything. His manner was that of a police court attorney attempting to browbeat a witness, with the result that he irritated and disgusted most of the members to the point where they ignored him. So Robinson developed the tactics of waiting until one of the big Senate figures had spoken and then immediately following him while the chamber and press gallery were still filled.

Robinson hit his real stride when, at the sly instigation of such Republican leaders as Senator George Moses, he delivered a series of violent partisan attacks upon the Democrats and the character of Alfred E. Smith, then looming as a Presidential candidate. None of the responsible Republican leaders would publicly engage in such character defamation, but Robinson loved it.

Time and again, with covert innuendo he returned to the attack. When the Democrats finally turned on him he was in his glory. To him it meant that he had at last arrived. But his satisfaction was short-lived. The Democrats dug up his political record and unsavory political affiliations. They aired exhaustively the corruption and criminalities of the Klan-ridden Republican Party in Indiana from which he had sprung.

When, in one leering speech, he became so reckless as to refer sneeringly to Senator "Jim" Reed, as the "venerable Senator," that fiery warrior annihilated him with a devastating rejoinder that is one of the Senate's epics. Other Senators had indignantly resented Robinson's innuendoes, referring to him as the "callow," the "puerile" and the "juvenile" Senator. Reed waited until they had finished and then turned his scathing scorn loose on Robinson.

"The Senator referred to me several times as 'venerable,'" Reed said. "If I were venerable I would never expect to rise to such degree of dignity or respectability as to challenge the admiration or arouse a sense of decency in the Senator from Indiana.

"The Senator said that I had started an investigation, but it ended in the garbage wagon. Then he located the garbage wagon in Indiana. All I was putting in the garbage wagon was the testimony which was elicited from men who had been almost exclusively connected with the Republican organization of that State. If that be garbage I am quite willing to dump it in the Senator's front yard, where he will undoubtedly recognize a familiar odor."

Robinson's great ambition is to be another Albert J. Beveridge. Of all men, the late distinguished Indiana scholar, historian and courageously independent statesman is the Klan-minded Robinson's secret model. Robinson reads Beveridge's writings and speeches constantly, quotes him on all occasions and is even reported to be planning some historical writing of his own.

Because Senator Beveridge made a visit to the Philippine Islands and became an authority on insular affairs, Robinson, too, has gone to the Philippines and now talks with a show of great learning on the subject. As Beveridge was a Progressive and independent in his politics, Robinson also breaks with the administration occasionally and votes with the insurgents. But it is significant that he rarely bolts on important matters. And where a strictly partisan question is involved, he is always a regular of regulars.

Robinson's aping of Beveridge's genuine statesmanship is a joke among those who know him. That Robinson, intolerant Klan henchman and fanatical dry, petty, vain and secretive, should consider himself as walking in the footsteps of Beveridge, known for his broad tolerance, his sturdy political independence and his unimpeachable integrity, is a never-ending source of amusement to them.

While secretly aspiring to the political career of Beveridge,

Robinson molds his political manners after the delightful and incorrigible "Sunny Jim" Watson, prince of glad-handers.

Watson, tall and stately, has developed back slapping and hand pumping to a fine art. His height, his sunny nature, his picturesqueness and genuine friendliness make his hand whacking natural and a part of him. When he throws his arm around a caller and tells one of his rare stories, he is neither offensive nor ridiculous.

But when the short and churlish Robinson attempts the same thing, the effect is anything but pleasing. His glad handing is artificial and mechanical, consisting of a series of pawings and thumpings.

Robinson's startling insurgency on the famous Bingham censure resolution was far from the pristine deed which it appeared to be. For a long time Robinson had had it in for the tall, superior-looking Bingham.

Robinson was aggrieved at Bingham over a slighting remark. Bingham was making a speech and Robinson interrupted with a query. The erudite Bingham airily replied with a quotation from Virgil in the Latin. Robinson looked blank and said he could not understand. To which Bingham replied, "I can explain to the Senator, but I can't give him understanding."

Robinson flushed and sat down. He said nothing further but waited his chance for revenge. The opportunity came when Senator Norris exposed Bingham's secret employment on his official secretarial staff of a tariff lobbyist at a time when the Senate was considering the Smoot-Hawley tariff act. Norris introduced a resolution formally censuring Bingham. The Republican leaders fought this severe condemnation and it was assumed that Robinson would support them.

But, to their horror and Bingham's great distress, Robinson took the floor in his most leering and melodramatic manner. His opening remark was a blood-curdling cry: "So the Senator from Connecticut has been defrauding the United States Government."

Several Senators were so startled at the ferocity of Robinson's voice that they almost fell out of their chairs.

*

SENATOR PARK TRAMMELL was a traveling salesman at one time, and the habits he acquired then are still strongly with him.

He has a profound distaste for a fixed abode and, with no definite Washington residence, roves about, sleeping occasionally in hotels and the other times in his senatorial office. When his strange nocturnal habits came to light, the Florida yodeler had several explanations.

First, he declared he had some sick and needy relatives down home and by saving lodging costs he was better able to help them out. After thinking this over, he changed his explanation to read that he often worked far into the night and being too tired to go to a hotel made his bed on the big, soft couch that a thoughtful government had installed in his office.

Just why the Florida statesman should work late at night is a deep mystery in Washington. In sixteen years of continuous service in the Senate, Trammell has still to give any indication of knowing anything about anything. Big, heavy jowled and large bellied, his long hair curling up around his ears and the back of a bull-like neck, Trammell is one of the most vacuous men in Congress.

It is a standing rule in the Senate press gallery that when the Junior Senator from Florida gets up to talk, every one leaves for a recess. Either he was tipped off to this custom or he observed the exodus himself, for of late he has devised a pat little trick to circumvent the correspondents and a large number of Senators who feel the same way as the press does about him. Now he waits until just before a vote is to be taken, when the galleries and the chamber are filled. Then he heaves himself out of his seat and either offers an amendment or begins a declamation. Everybody groans and sinks back into lassitude until he stops.

Trammell executed this *coup* when the Norris anti-injunction bill was being acted on during the Seventy-second Congress, but it had unexpectedly disastrous results.

He produced a last-minute amendment which he insisted was extremely important. The amendment was read by the clerk and then Trammell spoke on it for some time, but even then no one could make head or tail of it. Finally he was asked to tell the Senate what the amendment proposed to do.

Trammell, after stammering around a few moments, admitted that he really didn't know. Some one had given it to him to introduce and he accommodatingly had done so.

*

THERE was a time a few years ago when Senator Shortridge decided to become a Senate leader. If he was a little late in getting under way toward that goal, he more than made up for his dalliance in bombast and rhetoric.

He spouted on all subjects. Nothing balked him. The less he knew the more he talked, for rare indeed are the occasions when the tall, Iowa-born Californian has anything other than a superficial knowledge of what he is talking about.

For a time the Senate was patient and amused. To watch Shortridge deliver one of his emanations was as good as a vaudeville show. For he never speaks; he always pontificates.

Tall and gangling, with a pate as bare and shiny as a door knob and shaped at the top like an egg, his face long and equine, and his attire of the most funereal formality, with starched cuffs, high stiff collar, morning or frock coat and patent-leather button shoes or loud spats, his appearance is enough to arrest attention.

But Shortridge does not stop with mere appearance. His manner and address are also Olympian. Words flow from him with sonorous redundancy. He may utter the sheerest balderdash—but words never fail him.

And neither do gestures, particularly, majestic gestures. Shortridge not only gestures with his hands—he throws his whole body into it. He bows and genuflects, all the time waving his long, carefully manicured index finger. It was from this unique system of wig-wagging that his colleagues drew the inspiration for the nickname "Semaphore Sam," as he is now known in the Senate.

For a time the Senate put up with Sam's long, dull, soporific exhortations. They had a certain usefulness, as members could go off and attend to correspondence and other duties and know that they were not missing anything. But after a time the novelty wore off; members caught up with their mail; and the Senate grew impatient.

Finally they began to heckle and badger Sam. When he still persisted in taking up the time of the chamber, the attacks on him became sharp and bitter. He was mocked and ridiculed and at last virtually driven to his seat. As a leader and administration spokesman he was a complete flop. Even Tom Heflin repeatedly took his measure in debate.

Since then Shortridge has confined himself to maintaining his sartorial preëminence. The arduous and dangerous rôle of floor leader he has left to younger and more accomplished colleagues. He now devotes himself to his coats and collars, his spats and his hats. Here he is on safe ground and in a class by himself.

In addition to being known as the Senate's most majestically attired member, Shortridge also has the unusual distinction of being the only chairman of an investigating committee who has never filed a report with the Senate. As far as Senate authorities recall there is no other case on record where a chairman did not make some kind of a report.

Shortridge was chairman of the Naval Affairs sub-committee that several years ago conducted the Shearer big-navy lobby investigation. The inquiry was making excellent progress, despite Shortridge's constant interference and bungling, but he suddenly broke it off just when it was really getting down to cases. Not another word has been heard from him since.

Why he abruptly halted the investigation and has never made a report on it to the Senate is still a mystery. Perhaps his attitude toward these matters is the same as that he expressed in a question once put to him by a little girl. He was addressing a group of women, some of whom had their children with them. One of these, a little girl, slipped away from her mother and wandered up the center aisle to the speaker's rostrum where she stood watching in great awe the tall wig-wagging orator.

Finally she broke into his remarks and, in a piping voice that could be heard all over the hall, inquired gravely, "Are you God?"

Sam never blinked. Looking down at the little girl, he solemnly replied, "No, my child. There is one greater than I."

CHAPTER ELEVEN

HEAD BOUNCER

*I*T is not every Virginia hill billy, beginning his career as a lowly laborer in the railroad yards of the Norfolk & Western at Bluefield, W. Va., who can rise to the puissant and glorious estate of Secretary of Labor in the Cabinet of a Great Engineer.

Such a trail is long and winding. Particularly, winding. To follow it successfully requires a peculiar fortitude and an acute sense of direction. It is exactly in these talents that one finds the key to the remarkable career of William Nuckles Doak.

To him the devious trail of politics holds neither terror nor revulsion. It may have its hazards, but to Doak they are not those of principle and consistency. Throughout his career his only worry has been to keep his feet planted squarely on the trail. He has no objection to winding and twisting as long as he can turn fast enough.

For a man of his many personal and intellectual limitations Doak has done remarkably well in this respect. Through a bewildering maze of labor and political intrigues over a long period of years, he always unfailingly found his way to the paying side. His associates, less adroit and facile in trail finding, lost their way.

Conscience, class interest, personal honor tripped them up

and undid them. But William Nuckles is not so careless. He permits nothing to distract him from the intricacies of the trail. He keeps his eye on it to the exclusion of all else.

His specialization has paid him well. Throughout his labor career he always had an easy, well-paying political berth. And in the realm of politics, although his elective efforts were rudely repulsed, he finally found his way to the Cabinet of a President who, like him, has a great aptitude for winding trails.

Other labor leaders might ponder well the lesson that Doak's career teaches. Many of them have been careless. They have permitted themselves to be swayed occasionally by interests other than their own welfare. By following Doak's example they could get much further. That is, of course, if the depression doesn't last too long, and labor leaders and politicians are done away with entirely.

William Nuckles comes of an old Virginia family—just how old and of what eminence is now, in his prideful days, a matter of serious preoccupation with him. Last summer, conveyed in a glistening limousine guided by a liveried chauffeur, Doak spent some time touring the by-ways of the Old Dominion, tracking down an ancestry worthy of the new family acres which adjoin the historic lands of the Lees and the Washingtons on the shores of the placid Potomac and worthy also of the big part Doak is playing in Washington's Dance of the Depression.

But despite his present social elevation, Doak began in humble circumstances—in the lowly rôle of a railroad yardman. Three years later, at the age of twenty-one, he joined the Brotherhood of Railway Trainmen, one of the Big Four railroad unions. Immediately he showed his skill as a political truckler and manipulator.

Within a few years Doak had gone through the various offices of the local union. By 1916 his repute among the trainmen had gone beyond the bounds of local fame and he was taken up by William G. Lee, then national president of the Trainmen Brotherhood.

Lee, hard-boiled and opportunistic, was one of the most reactionary leaders in the history of the American labor movement. He was finally forced out by a revolt led by A. F. Whitney, who succeeded him as president of the union. Under Lee's control the trainmen usually were at odds with the switchmen's union and the other three transportation brotherhoods, the engineers, firemen and conductors. Lee refused to house his union's national legislative offices in Washington in the same building with the others, and often fought them on legislative and political policies.

In 1912, when some of the railroad shopmen went on strike against a wage cut, the second within a year, members of some of the local unions of the trainmen refused to take out trains on the ground that the engines and cars were unrepaired and in a dangerous condition. Lee promptly expelled these members and announced that he would revoke the charter of any union aiding the strikers. As a result, the strike collapsed.

Doak rapidly became Lee's chief henchman and fixer. All through the years of Lee's vicious reactionary sway over the trainmen, Doak was his most trusted associate and accomplice. But this intimacy with Lee did not prevent Doak from keeping a sharp eye on the winding trail. When the trainmen finally rose in revolt and vented their rage on Lee, Doak unerringly saw where his duty lay. He deserted his one-time chieftain and flopped to the victorious rebels.

Doak's timely conversion to progress and liberalism proved profitable. He saved his national vice-presidency and its fat salary, as well as the editorship of the union's journal. Best of all, the job as legislative representative of the trainmen in Washington remained in his hands.

Doak coöperated as enthusiastically with the new régime as he had with Lee's. When it discarded the Lee policy of obstructing and fighting the other brotherhoods, Doak reversed himself without the loss of a step or the flicker of an eyelash.

But, although he adroitly managed to retain his standing among the trainmen, there was widespread hostility voiced against him among railroad men generally. Particularly indignant were they over his devious and reactionary course in the 1924 Presidential campaign.

That year the brotherhoods and the American Federation of Labor tossed the two old party candidates out of the window and announced for La Follette. This unseemly independence threw a cold chill of apprehension into the Republican Party and it envisioned another 1912 debacle. For a time, so serious did the situation appear, the Chicago *Tribune* began to raise the issue of Communism.

But, although the other labor leaders went "Red," Doak and Lee never wavered. They stood by the Grand Old Party and Calvin Coolidge. They fought the good fight to victory over the dark and evil forces of Progressivism.

In fact, Doak fought so good a fight that Whitney, then mobilizing his movement against Lee, publicly accused him of lying and double-crossing labor. These blunt charges Whitney made in an open letter that appeared in *Labor,* the weekly newspaper of the brotherhood. He declared that Doak had grossly misrepresented the labor records of the three Presidential candidates, suppressing a number of hostile and reactionary acts by Coolidge, while completely omitting from La Follette's record important labor legislation and the very pertinent fact that he had the endorsement of the three brotherhoods and the A. F. of L.

Finally, and more seriously, Whitney accused Doak of covertly opposing the Howell-Barkley Railroad Labor Conciliation Board bill, which the rail workers were then demanding of Congress against the determined opposition of Coolidge and the railroad owners. Whitney asserted that Doak had been "absent from Washington during all, or almost all, of the period when this fight was going on."

How serious an accusation this was to the railroad men may be grasped from the fact that the vote in Congress on the measure is one of the two tests for political endorsement that the brotherhoods apply to Congressmen seeking reëlection. Any one who opposed or voted against the Conciliation Board cannot hope to get their support. Their other test is the vote in the Senate on the nomination by Hoover of the Southern Republican politician, Parker, of North Carolina, to the United States Supreme Court. Parker, an anti-labor judge, was rejected by the margin of a few votes.

In the 1924 campaign, having declared for Coolidge, Doak was not content to let it go at that. He offered not only his heart, but his hand. The celebrated C. Bascom Slemp, of Virginia, Washington, and lately Paris—the last place at heavy government expense as Director of the United States display at the French Colonial Exposition—cordially welcomed him. Slemp, Republican boss of Virginia, champion garnerer of Southern Negro Republican delegates, and friend and confidant of Bishop James Cannon, Jr., decided that the most profitable thing that Doak could do was to run for the Senate.

Doak responded to the call, but Virginia stayed Democratic. In fact, there was considerable doubt in the State as to just who he was. It was known that a Republican was running against Senator Carter Glass, but neither Glass nor the electorate was quite certain who it was. Doak made a determined campaign, but this did nothing to remove the State's vagueness about his candidacy.

William Nuckles went down to an inglorious defeat, but expressed himself as satisfied. He had done his bit to save the country from La Follette and Moscow.

It was in this campaign that Doak disclosed again his finely attuned instinct for finding the trail that pays. Even in those far off days, his keen eye already had spotted the next conqueror, and he was busily courting him. As his opening campaign speech, he used almost verbatim an address made a short time before by Hoover, then Secretary of Commerce. In his remarks, Hoover attacked government ownership.

Doak, in plagiarizing the speech, ran in direct defiance of the railroad men's endorsement of the famous Plumb Plan of government ownership of the railroads. The subtle compliment to Hoover was lost on all but a few. But those few included Mr. Hoover. From then on the trails of the two men merged and they have continued to do so to this day.

Doak's desertion in the La Follette campaign definitely crystallized labor's hositility to him and ever since he has been unpopular with and distrusted by the workers. They opposed his selection as Secretary of Labor and for almost two years were able to keep Hoover scared enough to refrain from naming him. Ever since Doak's installation they have rebuffed all his attempts to woo them.

Many of the labor leaders lay at his door chief responsibility for the destruction of the United States Railroad Labor Board. The Board was established for the protection of the lower-paid rail workers. These are not organized in powerful unions, such as the brotherhoods, and so Congress set up the Board to safeguard their interests. The railroads, of course, bitterly fought the enactment of the measure and tried to cripple its operation. This they accomplished, some of the labor men assert, through Doak's direct connivance.

Two vacancies existed on the Board, and President Harding, against the recommendation and over the vehement protest of the brotherhoods, appointed two of Doak's henchmen, both unpopular among the railroad men. One of them, E. F. Grable, had been defeated for reëlection as president of his union, the Maintenance of Ways Employees. He was charged with many misdeeds and failings, among them, that of incompetence. The other, Walter McMenimen, legislative representative in the Massachusetts Legislature for the trainmen, was equally lacking in favor among the railroad men.

Railroad workers openly charged that the appointment of these two "labor skates," as they were called, would mean the sabotaging of the Board. They declared that Grable and McMenimen were put on the Board for the express purpose of preventing wage increases from being approved. Their fears were amply justified.

From the moment that these two henchmen of Doak went on the Board it ceased to function, as far as the workers were concerned. The brotherhoods, though they had fought for the Board's establishment, now repudiated it, and were glad to see it abolished by Congress.

Between 1924 and 1927, when Hoover came out in the open as a Presidential aspirant, the relations between him and Doak were most intimate. Doak was the Great Engineer's confidential agent and go-between in the labor field, managing and organizing his campaign in that quarter. When the campaign got into the open he was formally appointed Chairman of the Republican Labor Division. Whether Hoover was bound by a personal pledge to give him the labor post in the Cabinet, as union leaders now claim, is not known.

But the President was certainly heavily beholden to William Nuckles and would have been even more an ingrate than he was to some of his other friends—Colonel "Wild Bill" Donovan, Colonel Horace Mann, Mrs. Mabel Walker Willebrandt, and Slemp—if he had not finally rewarded him. But it took Hoover a long, long time to get around to doing so. And it was only because Doak is such a master of the winding trail that he finally trod his way to Presidential recognition.

When Hoover was elected and began working on his Cabinet, the A. F. of L. moguls believed the question of the Secretaryship of Labor was undecided. They assumed that Hoover would follow the custom of picking some one from their own ranks for the place, and they confidently laid before him a panel to choose from. On this list were the names of John L. Lewis, President of the United Mine Workers, and a friend of Hoover; William Hutchinson, President of the Brotherhood of Carpenters and Joiners; and John Frey, Secretary of the Metal Trades Department of the Federation.

President Green of the A. F. of L. was particularly active in Lewis' behalf, for it was to Lewis that he owed his election as head of the Federation. Lewis had thrown his support to Green after Gompers' death instead of to Matthew Woll, who was Gompers' Crown Prince and had been groomed by him as his successor.

Doak was not even on the A. F. of L. list submitted to Hoover, the organization being strongly opposed to the selection of any one as Secretary of Labor who was not one of its members. It is the Federation's contention that the Labor Department was established at its instigation for the protection of organized labor, and that it alone represents such labor. The railroad workers are under the jurisdiction of the Interstate Commerce Commission and the United States Board of Mediation. They have never made any claim to the office and did not do so in 1928.

The fight over the secretaryship quickly developed into a struggle between Doak and the A. F. of L. Hoover, it was apparent, was bent on appointing Doak, but was obviously hesitant about doing so without labor backing. The A. F. of L. men, realizing this, fiercely opposed the appointment. The three big brotherhoods, the engineers, firemen and conductors, also refused to endorse Doak, despite every effort made by him and Hoover to obtain their approval.

Officially, the brotherhoods explained their position on the ground that they were not interested in the question. The real reason for their refusal to act was their intense dislike and distrust of Doak. The only labor endorsement he was able to get was that of his own union, the trainmen, and even this came with manifest reluctance and distaste.

Hoover made repeated efforts to obtain Green's acquiescence. But Green insisted on Lewis, whom Hoover rejected on the ground that he was "unsafe." Failing to move Green, Hoover had Doak try his hand. Doak pleaded with Green to say he would not oppose his appointment, but Green refused.

Confronted with this unpleasant situation, Hoover was afraid to act.

Doak was speechless with fury at the brotherhoods and the A. F. of L. leaders, but Hoover, just beginning his administration, refused to name him against the united opposition of the labor men. So, much to the distress of the anguished Doak, Hoover turned to the surprised and overjoyed Puddler Jim Davis, who had come in with Harding and stayed on with Coolidge. Davis was asked to continue.

Davis had been mournfully packing up to leave when the unexpected tidings reached him. Exuberantly, he agreed to remain as long as his new chief, whom he secretly disliked very much and who on his part has a very low opinion of the Puddler, needed him. This turned out to be almost two years, during which time Hoover and Doak struggled to win A. F. of L. and brotherhood support. Finally, when both groups remained adamant in their opposition, Hoover called Green to the White House and informed him that he was going to appoint Doak anyway. Green departed in a huff and issued a statement demanding the appointment of an A. F. of L. man.

This was exactly the opening the Hoover board of strategy had been hoping for. The President immediately let out a cry about "coercion" and "undue pressure" by "class interests" and the Republican press responded with an editorial barrage along the same line. Under cover of the din, Hoover appointed Doak and the long travail seemed to be over.

But, even then, to the new Secretary's profane indignation, he had to wait a few days before he could actually occupy his high office. An hour before he was ready to take the oath he learned that Davis, ever the tight-fisted Welshman, insisted on delaying his departure until the hour before his name went on the payroll of the Senate, to which he had been elected from Pennsylvania. Only then was he willing to retire, and Doak, his eyes popping with fury, had to smile and wait.

He refused, however, to wait for the talkie-news-reel part

of his induction. William Nuckles went through that part of the performance on schedule. A zealous press association reporter, happening on the spectacle, thought it was the real thing, dashed to a telephone and informed his office that Doak was taking the oath. The story was flashed over the wires, much to the consternation of Davis, who spent a bad half hour trying to get hold of William Nuckles to find out if he had been double-crossed.

Doak was ready for action as soon as he was installed. Whether it was because he had plenty of time during the two years he waited to work out a scheme of ballyhoo, or because he was acting on orders from Hoover to stir up a clatter as an offset to labor's hostility, he was no sooner at his desk than he began a terrific uproar about the Foe Within Our Gates. The enemy alien suddenly became a national menace and had to be rooted out. There were, it appeared, 400,000 of them among the country's 120,000,000, and the issue could not wait. It was now or never, Doak roared, and the man-hunt was on.

He took up the trail with a display of patriotic frenzy worthy of a Grand Cyclops. His first attack upon the quarry is still talked about. Twenty Department of Labor agents, assisted by as many city police, swooped down on a dance given by the Finnish Workers' Educational Association of New York City, barricaded all entrances and exists, and amid the shrieks and hysterics of hundreds of women and children, lined up the crowd of a thousand people and required each to produce evidence of his or her right to be in the country. The illegality and brutality of the raid provoked a storm of denunciation. Even the New York *Times* ventured a mild protest.

But Doak was jubilant. Gloatingly, he told the newspaper men that sixteen men and two women had been netted.

"We found pay dirt," he explained. "What the hell do I care what the papers say. Let these foreigners go back where they belong."

From then on, no place suspected of harboring an alien was

safe from invasion. Homes, churches, missions, dance-halls, workshops, breadlines and picket lines were raided, with or without warrants. In one day in New York City one hundred and four victims were bagged. In one week over five hundred were rounded up. In August, 1931, Doak shipped out of the country, at government expense, a total of 1,584 immigrants, in September, 1,700, and in February, 1932, 1,505.

Until Doak came in, alien hunting was a routine procedure of the Labor Department, confined largely to foreigners who got tangled up with the law. It was carried out quietly and without ballyhoo. But under Doak it became a gladiatorial spectacle, with him as Head Bouncer.

No brutality or illegality stopped him in his attacks upon the helpless and hapless alien. For the year 1931 he achieved the unique record of running more people out of the country than had entered it.

Doak hit upon a number of ingenious tactics in pushing the harrying of aliens. It was his neat scheme that strikers, and particularly their leaders, should be grabbed by Federal agents and thrown into jail as illegal entrants. By this means he served both campaign contributors to the Republican Party and the patriotic requirements of the country. This innovation was started early in his administration and has grown into an established practice in every strike in which foreign-born workers are involved.

Another measure introduced by him is the scouring of breadlines and flop joints. Last winter Federal agents mingled with the hungry and homeless in the big cities, searching for aliens to devour. Still another tactic introduced by the resourceful William Nuckles is raiding places of business where foreigners are employed. In the Washington *News* of November 6, 1931, appeared an account of such a raid in the national capital. The speaker quoted in the story is Edwin W. Jones, Secretary-Treasurer of the tile plant that was attacked by Doak's sleuths:

"It was pay day, and I had just finished making up the pay-roll and had gone down the street for a few minutes when the Federal agents entered the shop. I returned to find the leader, a white-haired man of about sixty, sitting at my desk. He had pushed all my papers out of the way and appeared to be holding some kind of a court. I asked him what was his idea, and he replied, sharply: 'If you don't shut up, I'll have you arrested. We're from the Bureau of Immigration, and we'll do as we please.'

"My secretary, Miss Maud Richardson, the employés who had come after their money, and two salesmen from New York who were waiting to see me on business, were all locked in the shop, with a man guarding each entrance. The immigration agents began asking questions. They would get one of our men in a corner and then two or three of them would fire questions at him until he was so confused he didn't know what he was saying.

"This sort of thing began about 4 o'clock and continued until about 7. Then they took three of our men away. Two of them, Edward Talamini and Angelo Cappello, were released after they had gone to their homes and found citizenship papers that appeared to satisfy the agents. The third man, Luigi Rosa Valmarcon, they locked up at Third Precinct for the night. We were taking steps to get him out when he was turned loose about 11 the next morning. When Luigi attempted to tell the agents in broken English that his parents were American citizens, they stormed 'We don't want to know anything about your parents. We are asking about you.' They even got one of our colored employés in a corner and nearly succeeded in making him admit that he came from the Philippines, instead of from North Carolina, where he was born."

For a long time Doak was unmoved by the growing volume of protests. He could see no reason why homes, factories, churches and dance-halls should not be invaded.

"If we can't raid these places," he fumed, "where the hell do you expect us to get these fellows."

But if the clatter of newspaper publicity and the applause of the Daughters of the Revolution, the American Coalition, the Chamber of Commerce, and the Ku Klux Klan enthralled him, it didn't keep the White House and the Republican

State and local politicians from hearing the roars or protests booming up from the foreign-language groups and their newspapers. This outcry finally became so loud and ominous that Hoover became alarmed. Doak was called in and curtly ordered to stop his yapping.

The raids and attacks, however, still continue. But, instead of his accompanying them with gloating declamations and coarse grunts of satisfaction, William Nuckles now keeps silent, or what amounts to that for him. He still breaks out now and then in a patriotic address before some anti-Red society about the Alien Foe Within the Fold, but he no longer goes into the gory details of how many he has booted out of the country.

The Wickersham Report on deportations nearly caused him apoplexy. He received a copy of it within a few days after it had been submitted to the Commission, and months before it was made available to the press. Why this document, compiled confidentially, and severely criticizing his department should have been turned over to him before it went to Congress, for whose information it had been prepared, never has been explained. But it was secretly placed in his hands almost immediately upon its receipt by the Commission. Thus he had plenty of time to study its findings and prepare an answer to its serious charges.

Doak went wild when he read it. He characterized it as the work of Bolsheviks. In raging private comments he declared that law or no law he was going to continue his policy of wholesale deportations. Then he sat down and wrote a fifty-three page reply in which he violently denounced the report in detail and attacked the motives of Reuben Oppenheimer, its author, an able and respected Baltimore attorney. Doak even insinuated that Oppenheimer had been actuated by racial interests in his criticisms of the Department.

So frenzied was Doak's statement that his subordinates braved his fury and warned him against its publication. It was only after weeks of effort that they finally prevailed on him to tone down his remarks. When the Commission's report was finally published, it appeared without his broadside, as he had first demanded. He limited himself to a brief observation the following day, in which he set up the alibi that the abuses charged had not occurred during his term of office.

Whatever hope Hoover may have had that Doak eventually would placate the A. F. of L. moguls was destroyed by his desertion of them on the Wagner Unemployment Exchange bill. The entire organized labor movement, including his own union, was in favor of this measure and continues to be. While it was under consideration in committee in the last Congress, Doak, then still legislative representative for his organization, was a member of the labor delegation that appeared and urged its enactment. He personally presented his union's endorsement to the Senate committee.

But, by the time the measure had reached the stage of floor consideration, Doak had eased his way into the Cabinet. He promptly flopped on the Wagner bill. He completely repudiated his previous advocacy and lined up with the President who was opposing the measure. In thus reversing himself, Doak was following the example set by Hoover. The President, too, at one time had been for the Wagner bill. Three times, before he entered the White House, he specifically and categorically endorsed such a plan.

Hoover has never made an explanation of his flop. Doak, accused by the labor men of selling out for the Cabinet appointment, has announced that he personally was never really for the bill. His appearance before the Senate committee as a member of the labor delegation, he said, was only in his capacity as an agent for his union. Why he did not explain this at the time of his declaration for the measure has never been elucidated.

Unable to stop the bill in committee, Hoover had Doak offer a substitute measure. It was rejected indignantly by the labor leaders and by Senator Wagner, author of the original

bill. In an effort to force the former to accept it, Doak called
a conference in his office and told them that unless they
agreed to it there would be no legislation of any kind. If
any other bill was passed, he threatened, the President would
veto it. When the labor men refused to act without first hearing Wagner, Doak flew into a rage.

"Who the hell is Wagner?" he shouted. "I'm as good as
he is."

But the labor leaders insisted on Wagner's presence, and
Doak had to give in. Wagner appeared that afternoon and in
a half hour so thoroughly stamped the Doak bill as a
piece of political chicanery, designed mainly to create new
political jobs, that the labor leaders voted unanimously to
reject it and to stand by the original measure.

With their vigorous backing, and despite the maneuvers
and pressure of Hoover, both houses passed the Wagner bill.
The substitute, repeatedly offered as an amendment, was overwhelmingly defeated. In the House, when the hard-boiled
Republican chairman of the Rules Committee, Representative Bertrand Snell, of New York, tried to pigeon-hole the bill
in committee, Representative La Guardia, the fighting Progressive game-cock from Manhattan, shook his fist in the face
of the Republican machine and threatened a filibuster.

The House, in those days, was still feeling its oats over the
very thorough trouncing it had just given Hoover and Mellon
on the soldier bonus question, and boisterously followed La
Guardia's invitation to do the same to Hoover and Doak. It
passed the Wagner bill by an overwhelming majority. A few
weeks later Hoover killed it with a veto.

This crude piece of political shystering provoked widespread
criticism. Even some of the Republican journals sharply attacked Hoover's action. As unemployment continued to
mount, the denunciations increased in vigor and number, and
for a time Hoover and Doak issued statements in a vain and
hectic effort to justify themselves. When these proved unavail-
ing they hit upon the scheme of staging a fake "reorganiza-

tion" of the antiquated and ineffectual Federal employment bureau, which the Wagner bill would have replaced with an efficient and modern organization.

This fake "reorganization" consisted of creating from seventy-five to one hundred new political jobs, and filling them with labor "skates," local politicians and personal friends of Doak. Labor leaders charge that in at least one Southern State Doak's appointee was a Kluxer. This Doak vehemently denies. If the man is a member of the Klan, he declares, he knows nothing about it.

It is also charged by the labor men that Doak has political scouts and under-cover fixers on the payroll of the unemployment bureau. These men do no government work at all, labor leaders declare. Their operations are wholly political. No statement has ever been obtainable as to the actual number on the bureau's roll and what the agents are paid.

Shortly after the "reorganization" of the unemployment bureau Doak summoned the new officials to Washington for a pep meeting. The sessions were devoted mainly to swapping smoking-compartment stories. At the close of the first day's meetings, the agents were told to return the next morning at 9 A.M. They vigorously objected on the ground that the hour was too early. So it was set for 10 o'clock.

They were also advised to retire early that night and get a good rest so that they could return the next morning prepared to "ask some intelligent questions." After a few days of idling in the capital they were sent home with the only instruction given them about their duties consisting of the suggestion that they "coöperate with existing State and local unemployment agencies."

In the ensuing months so much ridicule was heaped on the organization that Hoover decided something had to be done. He therefore ordered Doak to prepare a report on the number of jobs that had been obtained by the new service. This report Hoover personally gave to the press at one of his semi-weekly conferences. It was a lengthy, closely typed statement, the first half of which was an effusive eulogy of the Federal bureau. Halfway down the second page, with no relation to anything that had preceded, was a two-line sentence, printed in capital letters, stating that the total job placements from April 1 to July 31 had been 636,689.

The hour was noon. The press association reporters, with early afternoon editions to catch, rushed to their telephones and flashed to their offices the capitalized figures as the number of jobs the government service had filled in the three-month period. It was only later, when the reporters had had time to read the entire report, that they discovered in the second last paragraph the information that instead of 636,689 jobs, the bureau had actually made only 200,000 placements.

The balance between the two figures were jobs obtained by State and local employment agencies. The first statement had been a deliberate misrepresentation, placed in the report where it was for the express purpose of misleading the hurried correspondents. When they discovered how they had been tricked they rushed corrections over the wires, but it was too late for the afternoon papers. Most of them carried the 636,689 figure.

The reporters made irate demands upon the White House press secretary for an explanation of the subterfuge. They were referred to Doak, who refused to answer questions. Even inquiries as to the nature and location of the 200,000 jobs that the Federal service claimed went unanswered. Subordinates in the Labor Department also declined to discuss the matter, saying they had been ordered to refer all inquiries to the Secretary.

Independent study of previous Federal employment reports for this period showed that the 200,000 jobs were below the figures of other years. These reports also disclosed the interesting fact that the jobs which Doak had claimed were mostly of the harvest-hand variety, where the problem is not finding jobs, but men to do this kind of work.

Doak's constant scheming to cover up the extent of depres-

sion unemployment came to light a year later when he forced
the retirement of Ethelbert Stewart, veteran Commissioner of
Labor Statistics. Stewart had served the government continuously for forty-five years, had achieved a national reputation,
and believed in telling the truth. Therefore when Doak enthusiastically told newspaper men in the spring of 1932 that
Labor Department reports indicated an upturn in employment, the reporters having had experience with Doak on this
subject checked the statement with Ethelbert Stewart. The
latter picked up his telephone and bluntly told Doak that the
Department's statistics warranted no such statement as he had
given the press.

Doak summoned both Stewart and the reporters to his office.
He asked the latter to disregard his previous statement, and
then in their presence, heatedly reprimanded Stewart.

A few months later, following the enactment of the government pay-cut bill, Stewart's name appeared on the list of
those forcibly retired.

The "reorganized" Federal Unemployment Service has
encountered repeated criticism from State officials. John
Hopkins Hall, Commissioner of Labor of Virginia, recently took the agency severely to task, charging that it
was a "political machine set up for the purpose of reëlecting
Hoover." Miss Frances Perkins, New York Industrial Commissioner, likewise arraigned it on the charge of ineffectual-
ness. She declared that in her State it was merely duplicating
the work already being done by State authorities and that
"It was a wicked waste of taxpayers' money when there is
very little money for public use."

But the most damning denunciation of all came from the
service itself. Some months after the "reorganization," Francis I. Jones, for many years chief of the bureau, resigned.
In leaving he issued a stinging attack. He declared that files
on record in the Department "showed that forty-six jobs have
actually been secured by the service." Seven of the new
officials appointed by Doak, with the title of "industrial super-

intendents" and receiving at least $3,500 a year, Jones asserted, were occupied chiefly in opening mail.

"They are performing tasks that should be done by $12-a-week clerks," Jones said. "A letter-opening machine had been in use, but it was discarded so as to give these men something to do."

One of the first things Doak did when he went into office was to imitate his master, Hoover, by enlarging the publicity bureau of the Labor Department. In taking this step he simultaneously clamped down an iron censorship on every employe. Under his predecessors, an inquirer could go to any office in the Department and obtain the information he sought. Doak put a stop to that. All inquiries now must be referred to his office, where his personal secretary passes on them. If they meet this functionary's approval, written or telephonic permission is given to answer them.

For a time Doak essayed the political spokesman rôle for the administration. But his success was so meager and he laid himself and his master open to so much ridicule and smarting repartee that Hoover ordered him off the platform. Doak was sent into New Jersey in 1930 to urge a winning Republican vote on the plea that such a ballot was needed to vindicate the Hoover Administration. Up and down the State he made his piteous request. When the votes were counted New Jersey was found to have gone overwhelmingly Democratic.

Shortly after this debacle Doak appeared before the American Association of Personal Finance Companies, and put the administration on record as favoring a three-and-one-half per cent a month interest charge on loans, a total of forty-two per cent a year. Doak waxed enthusiastic over the possibilities of doing a money-lending business at this modest rate of interest.

When a report of his remarks got into the press it was discovered that the day before he had talked to a gathering of social workers, during the course of which he had bitterly denounced the "piratical extortions of loan sharks." This adroitness of view aroused much comment and Doak thereafter was more or less permanently retired by the White House as an administration declaimer. He still orates occasionally, but his speeches are carefully scanned by the Presidential staff.

Doak is held in little esteem by Republican leaders and by his Cabinet colleagues. Particularly do leaders in Congress hold him in low regard. His ritzy Cabinet associates sneer at his social pretentions. He loves show and ostentation. The Nuckles in his name came into daily use after he entered the Cabinet. Before he had signed his name, William N. Doak. But even as a labor official he had a liveried chauffeur.

Despite his love of display he is frowzy in appearance. His clothes show spots and cigarette ashes. Last summer he wore white suits which invariably were dirty and bedraggled.

He is of a markedly nervous temperament, much given to explosive and obscene language. A favorite form of greeting of his is: "Well, you old ————— ———— —————, how the ———— ———— ———— are you."

Asked embarrassing questions, he assumes a hard-boiled attitude. "How would you like to put your tail in my chair?" is his stock reply.

When this is resented, he becomes argumentative and irrelevantly loquacious.

Since entering the Cabinet he has taken up residence on his Virginia estate, to which he has given the lyrical name of *"Notre Nid"* (Our Nest). Doak obtained the place at a bargain. The high bluff formerly was the site of a hotel owned by a woman living in Rhode Island. During her absence many years ago, one of the rivermen who live along the Potomac squatted on the place and refused to move.

Crandall Mackay, Arlington county attorney, fought for the squatter so successfully that it took the Rhode Island lady seven years to dispossess him. The case even went to the Virginia Supreme Court. By that time the hotel had burned down and the owner was thoroughly disgusted with the whole affair. Doak, looking for a home where he could live up to his alleged Virginia ancestry and play his part in the blind whirl of Washington society, bought the place at a bargain. Since then he has struggled valiantly to live up to the historic setting.

Situated on the Potomac, the estate has an excellent river view of the capital and is pretentious even for a Cabinet officer. Last summer, Doak went in for outdoor entertainment of the garden-party variety. Hardly a week went by without a tea, a picture, and a write-up in the society columns the next day.

One of the prize features of his estate last summer were two sheep that he said a friend had given him. One was black and one was white. The black sheep he called Senator Norris and the white Mr. Wickersham. The names, he explained, were true to the character of the two animals.

"Senator Norris, the black sheep, is true to life," Doak said. "He is always in mischief. But Mr. Wickersham, the white sheep, never gets into trouble. He is such a good sheep."

CHAPTER TWELVE

LAME DUCKS

*W*ASHINGTON is the greatest political game preserve in the world.

Per capita, there are more varieties and a greater proportion of Lame Ducks in Washington than in any other world capital.

Finding sanctuary for Lame Ducks has reached the proportions of a major industry in Washington. Every branch of the government has become infested with them. The White House, the Cabinet, the departments, the diplomatic service, the innumerable bureaus, boards and commissions, and above all the judiciary—all furnish green pastures for this unique species of animal life.

Whole agencies of the government have been turned into Lame Duck refuges. It has become almost unwritten law that high diplomatic posts and seats on such bodies as the International Joint Commission, the United States Board of Mediation, the United States Court of Customs and Patent Appeals and the Court of Claims of the United States, carrying salaries of $10,000 a year and over, are to be devoted to the comfort and solace of the casualties of public life.

Before his election, President Hoover spoke disparagingly of this practice. He declared his intention of abolishing the pernicious system. But that was while he was a candidate.

In the White House he quickly developed an entirely different view. He not only continued the established custom but created a special secretarial post on his staff to exploit it to its utmost political possibilities. And, on the theory that it takes a Lame Duck to handle a Lame Duck, he appointed one of them to the place.

Congress has kept abreast of the times in this profitable activity. It has developed a type of lame-ducking all its own. Through the instrumentality of the secretarial pay-roll, it has found snug places for wives, sons, daughters, fathers, mother-in-laws and other relatives at the public trough.

The highest members of the two branches of Congress have not been too proud to stoop to such nepotism. The list includes the Speaker and Democratic floor leader of the House, the Democratic floor leader of the Senate, Republican and Democratic chairmen of committees, and numerous other important congressional figures.

While the unemployed throughout the country increased by millions, Congress and the President took pains to keep their families and henchmen on the pay-roll.

Lame Ducks now fall into three categories. Originally, the term stood for an elective official who had been defeated. But in recent years, in keeping with the trend toward specialization, refinements have been introduced, so that there are now to be found three distinct types.

The first is the parent breed, the official who has experienced the vagaries of public sentiment and has been voted off the pay-roll. In Washington, this group descends largely from congressional ranks.

The second, an innovation that has been developed extensively during the Hoover Administration under the guiding hand of the White House Secretary of Lame Ducks, is a form of pre-lame-duck lame-duckery. This breed of Lame Duck does not actually suffer the indignity of being thrown out of office by his constituency, but the likelihood that he will be is so patent and insurmountable that in the hope of saving his place for the party he is "kicked upstairs" by being given an appointive job. With him thus out of the way, an effort is made to appease the irate electorate by putting up a more palatable candidate.

The third category might be termed a bastard form of lame-ducking. In the first two classes the lame-ducking is of a partisan character. Personal interest enters only indirectly. Nepotism is part of the spoils system and is used to build party machinery and to furnish sources of campaign funds. It is based on the theory that the party must take care of its own, in defeat as well as in victory.

But this third species is pure and simple private graft. Legal, of course, but still a form of personal enrichment at public expense.

Under the present law, each member of Congress is given a specified clerical allowance. For a Representative this amounts to a flat sum of $5,000 a year, which he can apportion among his clerks as he sees fit, with the restriction, however, that not more than $3,900 can be paid to any one person. Senators are allowed four clerks whose salaries are fixed by law; one, at $3,900, one, at $2,400, one, at $2,220, and one, at $1,800. Chairmen of committees are given extra clerks.

There was a time when the members were paid the money allowed them for clerks. They could pocket the money or not, as they saw fit. Criticism of the system finally led to its replacement by the present method of requiring clerks to be listed at specified salaries. But this has not prevented members from grafting on their clerical allowances.

Instead of getting the money directly, they now do so by circuitous means. Relatives, many of whom do not even reside in Washington, are listed on the pay-roll for the higher salaries, while non-relatives who actually do the work get the the smaller sums. By this means congressmen pilfer annually hundreds of thousands of dollars from the Treasury which they put in their own pockets.

A change of party in the national administration always

means a great fluttering in the Lame Duck cotes. The appointees of the retiring party prepare for slaughter, while the deserving needy of the victors clamor for place at the public board. When the Republicans came into power in 1920, the government services were over-run with Democratic Lame Ducks. To-day, they are as scarce as the proverbial hens' teeth, while Republican brethren fatten in their places.

A Lame Duck to be successful in getting a job must meet certain requirements. Above all else he must be a good party man. Lame duck insurgents get no jobs. Secondly, he must have influential political friends to push his interests. If he has money and is a generous campaign contributor, that always helps.

President Hoover has set up a qualification all his own for the highest posts. No man of outstanding ability is appointed to such places. The President prefers to be surrounded with inferior men. He finds he works more happily when he is not constantly under the fear that one of his subordinates or associates will contradict him or outshine him.

As a result of this personal peculiarity and the sheer lack of first-class men who are good party members, the Hoover Administration has set a new low in appointments to important offices. Under Hoover, the Cabinet, the diplomatic service, the judiciary, and the departments and commissions have been loaded down with the sorriest collection of Lame Ducks in the history of the national government.

No other President has given so much attention to, or made greater use of, discarded party hacks. The few outstanding men he has appointed were forced on him by an indignant Senate. The Senate had to reject a shabby Supreme Court selection before he would name Justice Owen J. Roberts. Only the threat of a similar spanking coerced him to appoint Justice Benjamin N. Cardozo.

Left to himself, the President always chooses the most mediocre Lame Ducks he thinks he can get by the Senate. As a result, in the three years of his administration he has built up a greater régime of Lame Ducks than any other President in twice that length of time.

As a member of the Harding and Coolidge Cabinets, Hoover frequently expressed disapproval of mediocre Lame Duck appointments by these Presidents. He successfully resisted such placements in the Department of Commerce over which he presided. As a Presidential candidate he was particularly emphatic as to what he would do if elected in rehabilitating such bodies as the International Joint Commission. Repeatedly he declared his intention of getting rid of Lame Duck hangers-on and appointing men of initiative, ability and independence. Particularly, he asserted, would he keep the judiciary and diplomatic service free from political selections.

That was all before the election. Since then he has made a mockery of these assurances as he has done in so many of his other promises and pledges. He has encrusted his Cabinet, the departments and commissions with Lame Ducks. Practically every important diplomatic post now houses a Lame Duck, and Lame Ducks constitute ninety-five per cent of his judicial appointments. The International Joint Commission, about which he once talked so often and eloquently, he has filled to the brim with needy politicians.

This commission has been a Lame Duck sinecure throughout its existence. It was created as a result of a treaty with Canada in 1909. Its purpose is to adjust waterway and related problems arising between the two countries. Its sole function on this side of the boundary has been to furnish a group of fortunate Lame Ducks with $10,000-a-year jobs, a comfortable office and a listing in the Congressional Directory.

The present Commissioners are John H. Bartlett, Chairman, P. J. McCumber and A. O. Stanley, all Lame Ducks. Bartlett and Stanley were appointed by Hoover, McCumber by Coolidge. Bartlett is a former Governor of New Hampshire and was First Assistant Postmaster General in the Harding and Coolidge Administrations. He industriously sought the Postmaster Generalship when Hoover was elected, and, although

backed in that ambition by Senator Moses, was passed over
for the more powerful and deserving Walter Brown, who in a
way is also a Lame Duck, having been soundly trounced by
Ohio voters when he aspired to the Senate in 1920.

Having powerful political backing, Bartlett had to be cared
for. He was given the chairmanship of the Joint Commission
as a consolation prize. In the spring of 1932, without resigning
from the commission, he attempted a return to active politics
by running for a vacancy in the House from his State. New
Hampshire is normally dry and rock-ribbed, but Bartlett was
overwhelmingly defeated by a wet Democrat.

When McCumber first came to the Senate in 1899, he came
with the mantle of independence about his shoulders. But in
the course of the twenty-four years that he served in the
Senate, the soft lures and wiles of Washington and New
York showed him the error of his ways. He became conservative and regular. He was chairman of the powerful Senate
Finance Committee when early in the Harding Administration the Republican machine put through the Fordney-Mc-
Cumber Tariff Act, the greatest tariff steal to be perpetrated
up to that time.

McCumber's zeal and activity in putting through this
nefarious measure won him high praise from the tariff barons
and the Republican press. But the progressive citizenry of
North Dakota didn't think so much of his operations. When
he came up for reëlection in 1924, they threw him out. But
if his home folks abandoned him, his reactionary Washington
political friends and the tariff lobbyists did not. They got him
a job on the Joint Commission. The $10,000 a year salary is
the same as that of a Congressman, and in addition, he does
not have to worry about what the folks at home think of him.

Stanley is a Kentucky Democrat. He served several terms
in the House, was Governor of the State from 1915 to 1919,
and a Senator for one term. He is a political and social wet
and had no hesitancy in saying so. Also he had strong views
about the moronic qualities of the Ku Klux Klan which he

had the courage to air. For this engaging frankness, the bigoted, night-riding hill billies decapitated him in 1924, and he set up a law office in Washington.

On the strength of the religious issue, Hoover carried Kentucky in 1928. But by 1929 the State had reverted to its normal Democratic leanings, and a Republican senatorial seat and several places in the House were in danger in the coming year's election. In an effort to stave off this serious party loss, Hoover made a number of shifts and changes in the State's Republican line-up.

It was in the course of this under-cover trading and manipulation that the rich plum on the Joint Commission fell into Stanley's eager arms. Ordinarily, such a choice prize would not be given to a Democrat. But the President's needs were great. Stanley also had the backing of a number of former Republican senatorial colleagues, with whom he is personally popular.

As the duties of the Joint Commission are insignificant, Stanley and McCumber find plenty of time to carry on private law practices on the side.

Before his election, Hoover had ambitious plans for the Joint Commission. He declared he would energize it by appointing engineers and experts, and turn over to it the long-pending negotiations with Canada on the St. Lawrence waterway project and other waterway questions.

Since then nothing whatsoever has been done about any of these grandiose plans. Instead of engineers and experts, Hoover appointed Bartlett and Stanley, two of the lamest of Lame Ducks. And when in 1931 the Canadian Government suggested the reopening of negotiations on the St. Lawrence question, he disregarded the Joint Commission entirely.

Deserving and needy as many Lame Ducks are, not all of them get well-paying sinecures. For one reason, there are not enough of these jobs to go around. A certain proportion have to be ladled out to local and State politicians, many of them Lame Ducks. Then again, not all the Washington Lame

Ducks, no matter how deserving and needy, rate juicy morsels. They all aspire to them, of course, but in the end they are glad to take what they can get.

Coming for the most part from small towns and backwood districts, they and their families never get over their Washington experience. Once they get a taste of official society and authority they would rather do anything than leave. Also, after a period of years in Congress, the average Lame Duck faces an extremely precarious situation in returning to his home town and trying to make a living by actual toil. Most of them are mediocrities, with no talent or capacity for application, and the thought of going to work throws them into a blue funk.

So they pull wires and make desperate pleas for a place on the public pay-roll. They start out by asking much and wind up by taking what they can get. This class of Lame Duck is to be found in minor positions throughout the departments and commissions, some getting as low as $2,500 a year. During the day they are ordinary government clerks, but at night, while Washington dances to the depression they shine as former members of Congress.

One of the most recent and best known of this group is Louis C. Cramton, for sixteen years a member of the House from Michigan. "Louie," as he is widely known in the capital, was the dry dictator of the House. Squat and fat, with a lop-sided jaw, and invariably disheveled, Cramton took himself with great seriousness. He was always on the alert to defend with arrogant vehemence his twin deities, prohibition and the Republican administration. Neither could err and the opposition was never right.

As chairman of the subcommittee in charge of the Interior appropriation bill, Louie ruled the department's affairs with an iron hand. He was particularly reactionary in his attitude toward the Indian bureau, whose administration until the last few years long had been a cesspool of scandal, vicious cruelty and terrorization of the helpless aborigines. Louie was a devoted supporter of this infamous Indian bureau administration. When the two present enlightened and humane commissioners, Charles Rhoades and Henry Scattergood, were appointed and sought increased appropriations for starving Indian children, Louie vigorously opposed them.

Thus for years he was one of the bullying little straw-bosses of the congressional roost, adored by the drys and esteemed by the big Republican politicians. But in 1930, much to every one's astonishment and to the secret delight of most of his colleagues in the House, Louie was soundly beaten. A wet Democrat took Cramton's measure and he was in need of a job.

A hurried search was started to find him a good berth. The drys, under the leadership of Senator Simeon D. Fess, insisted that he be well cared for. A happy solution of the problem appeared to have been found when Fess, Chairman of the George Washington Bicentennial Commission, conceived the idea of making Louie a co-commissioner of the body at $9,000 a year. It was a grand idea, but it had one great drawback.

It failed to meet the approval of Representative Sol Bloom, of New York, who held the title of Commissioner. Sol was running the George Washington carnival with dash and uproar and enjoying the attendant publicity enormously. He didn't intend sharing honors with any one, and particularly not with the meddlesome and surly Cramton.

Sol had just got rid of another commissioner. The fact that this dignitary was no less a personage than Lieutenant Colonel Ulysses S. Grant, III had not fazed Sol. He maneuvered the warrior out of the commission with such dispatch and finesse that to this day neither Grant nor the commission knows just exactly how it happened. Sol was the big shot of the show and intended to continue as such.

When Fess came gum-shoeing around with his idea of making Cramton a co-commissioner at $9,000 a year, Sol couldn't see it at all. Why should the government pay $9,000 a year for an assistant on a job which he was doing so well all by himself and not asking a penny for? he demanded. Fess had no answer except the piteous plea that Louie just had to be taken care of. Sol being a kind-hearted man had no objection to that, but he saw no reason why it should be done at the expense of his own personal publicity.

All this negotiating had been going on secretly, but somehow or other the story leaked to the press. Such matters have a way of doing that in Washington. When the story of Fess' scheme became known, considerable opposition to it was voiced in both branches of Congress. Cramton took the hint and announced that he did not want the job.

Pressure was then put on the White House to find him a place. After some search, one was made for him in the Interior Department. He was named special government agent to represent the Department at Boulder Dam, which was then just getting underway. The salary of the new job was $9,000 a year.

When Louie got to Boulder Dam he found that his work was insignificant. It consisted chiefly of signing leases with people who wanted to take up lots in the desert adjoining the great water power project. His idleness irked the officious Louie. As a member of the House, he had become so accustomed to being a straw-boss that he just couldn't keep from meddling.

So he decided that the morals of the desert construction camp needed supervising and he began to say what could and could not be done. In a short time he was known as the "Czar" of Boulder City and was the most cordially disliked man in the region.

Cramton's office was in Las Vegas, which is Nevada territory. From his window he could look down on the community's large red-light district and its numerous gambling dens, which run full blast twenty-four hours a day. The sight of all this lusty sin deeply distressed Louie's Grand Rapids soul. He made up his mind that Boulder City should be kept free of such vices and promptly issued a ukase prohibiting the use of any premise in Boulder City for "unlawful purposes" on pain of expulsion.

Louie's reforms, however, were not well taken by the construction-camp residents of Boulder City or by the citizens and merchants of the neighboring city of Las Vegas. A din of protest was raised against him in Washington, which finally became so insistent that the Interior Department called him back East for a "conference." From this he never returned.

Interior Department officials had no intention, however, of keeping him in Washington. They were taking no chances with his instinct for meddling. Three days after he had returned to the capital, Louie was again outward bound, this time for the Western Shoshone Indian Reservation, in Duck Valley, Nevada. His mission was to make a study of Indian claims to water rights on the Owahee river. His salary remained the same. The Interior Department solemnly declared that it was only a coincidence that Lame Duck Louie had been sent to Duck Valley.

*

THE diplomatic service and the Federal judiciary have long been choice havens for Lame Ducks. Hoover had plenty of precedents for playing sordid politics with these branches of the government. Despite his preëlection promises to the contrary he has lived up to the worst traditions in this regard. For mediocrity and drabness the American diplomatic corps has seldom been lower than it is to-day. Of the President's selections to the Federal bench few have escaped widespread condemnation and the bitterest opposition.

Some of his appointments to the Federal courts he made over the adverse recommendation of Attorney General Mitchell. This was particularly true in the case of Albert L. Watson, of Pennsylvania and Richard L. Hopkins, of Kansas. Mitchell considered these men incompetent to hold places on the Federal bench and so advised Hoover. But they had the militant backing of the drys, and so, disregarding his Attorney General's disapproval and the protest of many local leaders, Hoover appointed them.

His recent appointment of Judge J. H. Wilkerson, of Chicago, and Judge Kenneth Mackintosh, of Seattle, to the Federal Circuit Court of Appeals, was an even more vicious instance of political skullduggery. Both these jurists are notorious labor-haters. Wilkerson, an appointee of the besmirched Harry M. Daugherty, has the blackest labor injunction record in the country. He has repeatedly issued the most sweeping interdictions against labor unions, without giving them the slightest opportunity to defend themselves.

Mackintosh, a boyhood chum of Hoover, has a labor record only slightly less reactionary than Wilkerson's. The reason it is less vicious is because he has had fewer opportunities to attack labor. But he has more than made up for this lack by the intensity of the hatred and bias he has displayed toward labor and liberalism.

Once he wrote a public letter heartily commending ferocious atrocities that a mob of patrioteers committed on radical labor leaders in Centralia, Washington. Mackintosh is so little regarded in the State that when he ran for the Senate in 1928 he was badly defeated by Senator C. C. Dill, a Democrat, notwithstanding the fact that Hoover carried Washington by a huge majority and all the other State offices were captured by Republicans.

The Senate throughout the 1932 session refused even to act on either of these appointments. Strong protests from many quarters were heard against them by the Senate Judiciary Committee.

The use of the Federal judiciary as a Lame-Duck sanctuary is most extensive on the United States Court of Customs and Patent Appeals, the United States Customs Court, and the Court of Claims of the United States. The jobs pay high salaries and are lifetime appointments. After a certain period

MORE MERRY-GO-ROUND

of service and a certain age, a member of these courts can retire and draw full pay for the rest of his life.

They are filled to the gunwales with Lame Ducks. Of the five members of the Customs and Patent Appeals Court, four are Lame Ducks. The one vacancy that Hoover has had to fill on this tribunal he gave to Irvine L. Lenroot, former United States Senator from Wisconsin, defeated for reëlection by the La Follette Progressives in 1926.

Lenroot for many years was the elder La Follette's most loyal lieutenant. He was a leader of insurgency. But he broke with him over American entrance into the World War and from then on was one of his bitterest opponents. During his last term in the Senate, Lenroot was a leader of the reactionary Republicans. When he was thrown out of the Senate by the electorate, Lenroot became an attorney for the power trust lobby in Washington. In the 1928 campaign he was one of Hoover's most intimate political advisers. Two months after Hoover entered the White House he rewarded Lenroot with the choice political plum.

Three of the five members of the United States Court of Claims are Lame Ducks, two under appointment from Hoover. Of his two appointments to the United States Customs Court, one, David H. Kincheloe, is of the pre-Lame Duck species. Kincheloe, a Kentucky Democrat, was ranking member of the House Agricultural Committee, when Hoover was seeking support for his Federal Farm Board scheme. Kincheloe until then had been a zealous advocate of the equalization fee plan of farm relief.

Suddenly he flopped and threw his backing to the President's project. Newspaper correspondents uncovered the fact that when the Farm Board bill was being drafted in the White House, Kincheloe secretly conferred with the President at night. Shortly after the measure was maneuvered through Congress, Kincheloe was appointed to the life job on the Federal court. He indignantly denied that there was any connection between the two occurrences.

Besides following the traditional practice of loading up the diplomatic service with Lame Ducks and heavy campaign contributors, Hoover has added an innovation in this direction. In order to facilitate local political machinations in various parts of the country he created the pre-Lame-Duck class. Two of the most prominent of these he appointed to the most important diplomatic posts in Europe.

Walter E. Edge, of New Jersey, Ambassador to France, and Frederic M. Sackett, of Kentucky, Ambassador to Germany, were Republican Senators from their respective States. Both were doomed to defeat in the 1930 elections. In an effort to save their urgently needed senatorial seats for his machine, the President conceived the idea of "kicking them upstairs" and putting more likely candidates in the field for their places.

Edge and Sackett eagerly accepted. To Edge, his impending defeat was a great travail. Stodgy and lumbering, but wealthy and socially ambitious, he and his wife were heart-broken over the likelihood of having to retire to private life. Therefore, when Hoover offered him the Paris post he accepted on the spot.

In his case, the political strategy, due to the candidacy of the late Dwight Morrow, was successful. Morrow was elected and the administration retained the seat.

But in Sackett's case, the scheming failed. In place of the lugubrious Sackett, the President and his political fixers brought forward J. M. Robsion, a Kentucky hill-billy member of the House. A gangling, blatant exhorter, Robsion was even less appetizing than Sackett. At least the latter kept his mouth shut. Robsion vociferated on all occasions. When the votes were counted, he was a bad second and the Democrats captured the seat.

Walter Newton, the President's Secretary of Lame Ducks, denies that he is of the pre-Lame-Duck species. He insists that he joined the White House staff only at the urgent solicitation of the President. This may be true. But the fact remains that it was only a question of time until Newton would have been thrown for a loss by his district.

Reactionary, loud-mouthed and unctuously partisan. Newton had long been marked for defeat by the Farmer-Laborites who now control Minnesota, his home State. He knew well that sooner or later they would get him, and it was known that he was eager to land a paying appointive job. What he wanted was a judicial appointment, but nothing came his way. When the President offered him a place in his secretarial harem, it didn't take Newton long to accept. He still hopes to make the Federal bench.

✳

CONGRESSIONAL lame ducking, through the agency of padding secretarial pay-rolls with relatives, only a few of whom actually work, and many of whom do not even live in Washington, has been under fire for several years. It has been repeatedly denounced as petty graft, but no measure to put a halt to such pilfering has ever been able to obtain consideration.

The most recent attempt to curb it occurred during the 1932 session of Congress while the House was voting on the so-called "economy" bill. This measure provided sweeping wage reductions for government employees. Representative Grant E. Mouser, Jr., of Ohio, offered an amendment prohibiting members from putting relatives on the congressional clerical pay-roll, unless they actually did the work they were paid for. The House, in the process of slashing government salaries, indignantly rejected Mouser's proposal by a two-to-one vote, 88 to 44.

But the very fact that the issue had reached the House floor was a considerable advance. Never before had a bill dealing with this question got beyond a committee pigeon-hole. U. S. Stone, former Representative from Oklahoma, several years ago created a stir with charges of congressional nepotism. He introduced several bills, but could not get a hearing on them. Furthermore, he was ostracized by his colleagues. He declared that following his exposure of the names of some of the worst offenders in this grafting, the House membership cut him dead.

Stone charged that more than one hundred members of the House and thirty members of the Senate had relatives on the clerical pay-roll. He estimated that not less than one-third of the clerical pay went to this source.

In the spring of 1932 the press forced the publication of the clerical pay-roll. House leaders opposed this damaging revelation, but stories widely carried by the newspapers charging specific members with nepotism raised a storm of protests throughout the country. Authorization releasing the pay-roll was hastily voted. Many members of Congress reported that they received hundreds of letters denouncing the practice and demanding that legislation be enacted putting an end to it. It was predicted that the disclosure that they had relatives on their clerical pay-roll would cost a number of members their seats in the 1932 elections. In many districts opponents quickly seized on the fact and waged their campaigns against the incumbent on this issue.

But despite this threat of political reprisal and widespread demand for restrictive legislation, Congress refused to take any steps. Representative John R. Mitchell, of Tennessee, offered a bill flatly prohibiting the employment of relatives by members of Congress and providing a penalty of expulsion and a fine of from $1,000 to $10,000. But, like all similar measures, it was pigeon-holed. He was unable even to get a committee hearing on it.

The uncovered pay-roll revealed that more than one-fourth of the membership of the House had relatives drawing clerical salaries. These ranged from a paltry $91.66 a month to the maximum of $325 a month. Less than ten per cent of these relatives actually did any work. In a few instances, as in the case of Mrs. John Garner, wife of the Speaker, Mrs. Henry T. Rainey, wife of the Democratic floor leader, Mrs. John C.

Schafer, wife of a Republican member from Wisconsin and Mrs. W. P. Lambertson, wife of a Republican member from Kansas, all doing confidential secretarial work for their husbands, there could be no doubt that the money was well-earned. These women have reputations for being hard and able workers.

But they and a few others are the exceptions. The great bulk of relatives not only do nothing for the money they receive but many of them do not even live in Washington. While Speaker Garner's wife is a hard-working secretary in his office, his son Tully, president of his father's bank in Uvalde, Texas, and manager of his other business and real estate interests there, received $1,100 a year as a clerk on the congressional pay-roll. Young Garner visited Washington once during the 1932 session.

Representative Joseph L. Hooper, of Michigan, who resides in Washington in the swanky Hotel Carlton, was revealed as having his wife on the pay-roll for $2,500 a year. She does no work in his office. Representative William L. Nelson, Democrat of Missouri, was found to have his aged father-in-law on the pay-roll for $266 a month. This relative has never been in Washington. Nelson defended his conduct by asserting that he spent money out of his own pocket for extra clerical hire and that the check received by his father-in-law went for that purpose.

Representative Robert A. Green, Democrat of Florida, Chairman of the impressive Committee on the Disposition of Useless Executive Papers had a nephew drawing $2,700 as clerk of this committee. Repeated efforts to get in touch with this nephew failed. In addition to this relative, Green had an elderly father on his staff receiving $291.66 a month. His father is rarely in Washington. While listing his parent at $291.66 a month for doing nothing, Green pays $125 a month of his clerical allowance to a young woman who does practically all the work in his office.

Representative Thomas L. Blanton, Democrat of Texas,

who conducted a crusade during the 1932 session against government employees receiving military pensions, was found to be paying a relative $250 a month from the public till.

Representative Harold McGugin, Republican of Kansas, one of the leaders in the demand for a Federal pay-cut, carried his wife on the pay-roll for $1,400 a year.

Representative Claude Fuller, Democrat of Arkansas, the most patriotic member of the House, who at the 1932 session introduced a resolution to require all civil service applicants to be able to recite or sing the national anthem, had both his wife and a daughter on the clerical pay-roll.

The publication of the pay-roll resulted in a material reduction in the number of these Lame-Duck relatives. Speaker Garner dropped his son from the list. Fuller dropped both his wife and daughter. McGugin withdrew his wife's name. So did Representative August H. Andresen, Republican of Minnesota. He had been paying his wife $266 a month. Representative Frank P. Bohn, Republican of Michigan, struck his wife's name from the list. She had been receiving $266 a month.

The Senate is no less an offender than the House in this practice. More than a fourth of the Senators, among them leaders of both the Democratic and Republican forces, have relatives on the clerical pay-roll. Many of these do not live in Washington, and of those who do, few actually do any work.

Senator Simeon Fess, the pious and moral Chairman of the Republican National Committee, has a daughter-in-law living in Toledo, Ohio, receiving $2,220 a year as a clerk of the Senate Library Committee, of which he is chairman. Fess' justification of this graft is that his daughter-in-law takes care of clerical work in his State and when he goes to his home in Yellow Springs, Ohio, during his vacation, she helps him with such office work as may turn up.

Senator L. J. Dickinson, of Iowa, raucous keynoter at the Republican convention in Chicago in 1932, and a member of the special committee of the Senate that drafted the bill slashing the salaries of government employees, has at various times had several relatives on the congressional pay-roll. Senator Alben W. Barkley, of Kentucky, the equally leather-lunged keynoter of the Democratic convention in 1932, has a son on the pay-roll for $3,900 a year, the top senatorial clerical salary, and a daughter listed as a clerk at $1,800 a year. The son was out of the city for a long time in 1932, and the daughter, very active in the capital's young social set, rarely comes to his office.

Senator Smith Wildman Brookhart, insurgent Republican of Iowa, has five members of his family on the government pay-roll. His son receives $3,900 a year as his secretary; another son receives $5,400 a year as a Trade Commissioner in Bangkok, Siam; his daughter is down for $2,200 a year as a Senate clerk; one brother receives $2,500 a year as a referee in bankruptcy for the Iowa Federal Court; and another is paid $750 a year as bailiff of the court. Brookhart's extensive nepotism was made an issue in his campaign for renomination in 1932 and actually defeated him. Not even the massed support of his Progressive friends, led by Senator Borah, Senator La Follette and Representative La Guardia, was able to pull him through.

In his campaign for reëlection in 1932, Senator John Thomas, of Idaho, was also accused of nepotism. J. Wesley Holden, his opponent, revealed that Thomas had his daughter and sister on the Senate pay-roll as clerks at $2,200 each a year. Holden charged that Thomas's sister had never been in Washington and that she was working as an assistant cashier in a Gooding, Idaho, bank, of which Thomas is President.

Another instance similar to this is the case of Senator John C. Townsend, of Delaware. Townsend, one of the most medi-ocre Republican hacks in the Senate, is a wealthy banker and contractor. He is president of the Highway Engineering & Construction Company, of Selbyville, Delaware. This company did $244,000 worth of street paving in the District of

Columbia in 1930, $300,000 worth in 1931, and up to June, 1932, had obtained contracts for $164,000 worth of curbs and gutters.

Townsend is chairman of the Senate Committee on Audit and Control which passes on senatorial expenditures out of the contingent fund. This committee has nothing to do with highway contracts. Also, it is not illegal for a member of Congress to be interested in a company doing government work. All government construction contracts are awarded on competitive bidding.

Notwithstanding his wealth, Townsend listed his son Paul on the congressional pay-roll at the top salary of $3,900 a year. This son does no work in his office. He is vice-president of his father's construction company. Repeated inquiries for the son at Townsend's Senate office were referred to the construction firm.

Not to be outdone by the Republicans, and especially by the Chairman of the Republican National Committee, Senator Joseph T. Robinson, Democratic floor leader and vice-presidential candidate in 1928, had a whole flock of relatives on his congressional pay-roll, only one of whom actually lives in Washington and works in his office. This relative is Joe Brewer, a nephew, who is a clerk on his staff.

The other two relatives on Robinson's pay-roll were an aged mother-in-law, who received $2,580 a year as an assistant clerk of the Conference of the Minority of the Senate and lives in Little Rock, Arkansas, and H. Grady Miller, a brother-in-law, listed as assistant clerk at $2,220 a year. Miller is president of the Southwest Joint Stock Land Bank in Little Rock, and spends all his time there. He comes occasionally to Washington for brief visits.

The clerical pay-roll does not reveal the full extent of congressional nepotism. Some members craftily place their relatives on other government pay-rolls, thus avoiding the direct charge of nepotism. One such case was revealed at a social gathering recently.

Two women were introduced to each other. One expressed the opinion that she had met or seen the other somewhere in Washington.

"Yes, I remember you too," the other admitted. "I used to work in the ladies' room in the House until last December when the Democrats ousted all the Republicans." This woman is the mother-in-law of a wealthy Republican member of the House.

Another instance came to light early in 1932, also as a result of Democratic control in the House. Representative Robert G. Simmons, Republican of Nebraska, noted for his blatant attacks on government clerks and his attempts to slash the small Federal contribution to the operating expenses of the District of Columbia, was revealed as having his father-in-law on the congressional pay-roll as a messenger in the House doorkeeper's office.

When the Democrats organized the House in 1931, they fired Simmons' father-in-law, Samuel W. Weil. Simmons thereupon went to Senator Robert B. Howell, Republican of Nebraska, and asked him to get his relative a job on the Senate side, where the Republicans still held nominal control. Howell accommodated by securing the dismissal of James Reynolds, a young law student, who was working his way through college as a capital policeman.

For this work he received $1,620 a year. Reynolds had been on the force three and one-half years and had only a few months to go before completing his law studies. There was no complaint against Reynolds except that Simmons wanted his job for his aged father-in-law. When he was let out at Howell's instigation, Weil was made a doorkeeper in the men's gallery in the Senate at $1,740 a year.

Senator Norris, of Nebraska, learned of Reynold's misfortune and interested himself in his behalf. He succeeded in getting him an appointment as clerk in the Senate post office at $2,040 a year.

Several years ago it was disclosed that one member of the

House who was divorced and was required to pay his wife alimony ingeniously accomplished this by listing her as a clerk on the congressional pay-roll.

Various alibis and explanations are offered by members in justification and defense of this petty grafting. A few confidentially admit that the money goes into their own pockets. They contend they cannot afford to live in Washington and pay the social fiddler on their own salaries. The most common explanation is that the relatives perform work of a confidential nature.

One of the most ingenuous alibis ever offered was that made several years ago by Hays B. White, former Representative from Kansas. An opponent discovered White had his wife on the clerical pay-roll and he made an issue of the matter. White first tried to laugh it off, but when his opponent took to making speeches about it all over the district, he had to produce a defense.

This he did in a melodramatic manner. He admitted his wife was on the pay-roll as his secretary. But he insisted that she not only performed secretarial work, but in employing her he was upholding the sanctity of the American home.

His wife, he touchingly told his suspicious constituents, had been a devoted helpmate for many years. Together they had taken up a homestead on the Kansas prairie and side by side they had worked long and hard. Now in her old age he did not propose casting her off for a fluffy-haired sweetie.

He was true to his marriage vows and the American home, and proposed to uphold them even if he had to keep his wife on the congressional pay-roll at public expense for the rest of her days.

His constituents reëlected him by an overwhelming majority.

CHAPTER THIRTEEN

THE JANIZARIES

DURING the height of the Turkish Empire, Moham-
med II organized a body of personal soldiery attached to the
throne of the Sultan. The members of this select corps were
called Janizaries. They were ferocious and merciless fighters
and terrorized the land.

The Janizaries paid no taxes, received the best that Turkey
could offer and were a law unto themselves. Although at first
it was considered a hardship to be drafted into their corps,
eventually it became a great privilege, so that the parents of
young children sought the authorities to take them. Eventually
also the Janizaries became so powerful that no civil authority,
not even the Sultan, could touch them. They set up and de-
posed Sultans, and it was not until universal conscription was
ordered in Turkey and every citizen was taught to fight that
the Janizaries were annihilated.

There exists in Washington to-day and has existed throughout the history of the government a class which resembles, in
many respects, the Janizaries. This class is beholden only to
personal masters. It enjoys special privileges which no other
citizens enjoy. No law exisits to restrain and curb it, and none,
despite innumerable scandals and repeated effort, has ever
been enacted.

And for resourceful undermining of the nation's government, no band of mercenaries was ever more ruthless. These modern Janizaries are called Lobbyists.

Like their predecessors in Turkey, they have no respect for the Chief Executive of the nation. They play up to him when necessary, criticize him, use him, sometimes overthrow him.

Unlike the Janizaries of old, they carry no shields and cutlasses. Their arms are more subtle and insidious. The school books of children, the lecture halls of universities, the newspapers of unsuspecting readers, the practice of placing a warrior on the Republican National Committee, the disguise of another warrior as a post-office executive, the power of political pressure, the sordid ambitions of office holders—these are the weapons of the modern Janizaries.

Just as the Janizaries of the Sultan received their pay in a division of the loot, in the same way also are many modern Janizaries rewarded. And as the ancient Janizaries built up powerful independent units under an Aga, so the Janizaries of to-day have erected great buildings, paid for by their spoils and dedicated to the furtherance of their cause.

Indifferent to party strife, untouched by public responsibility, swayed only by the pay they receive and the masters they serve, these modern Janizaries have reached such proportions in Washington that they now form a super-government completely dominating the political system. They are the real rulers of the national government. They are the managers of the Washington merry-go-round. They take the tickets, turn the creaking machinery on and off. They choose the tunes to which the carousel lumbers and dangle the brass ring before the grasping riders.

But in one all-important respect they differ from their Turkish predecessors. No means has yet been found to curb them. Some of them, like the Janizaries of old, have come close to bringing about their own destruction. The investigation of the Power Lobby by the Federal Trade Commission sent it into hiding. But a year later it was back again in somewhat disguised form, sucking at the life blood of the nation. The Tariff Lobbyists who boosted the Smoot-Hawley schedules to the highest peak in history helped to bring on the depression, but two years later when there were opportunities for more tariff revision, they swarmed back to their old feeding places.

The brazenness of the modern Janizaries during the Smoot-Hawley tariff deliberations provoked such a storm of congressional indignation that after a Senate investigation, the late Senator Thaddeus H. Caraway of Arkansas offered a bill requiring lobbyists to register their names publicly. It passed the Senate but was buried in a House committee. Nothing has been heard of it since.

The Caraway Bill was the first anti-lobbying bill ever to pass a house of Congress in one hundred and forty-four years of history, despite the fact that lobbying has sapped the life of the nation ever since a swarm of speculators, who had bought up the bonds of thirteen original States, swooped down on the first Congress and secured the funding of the State debts at par.

Probably nothing ever will be done to check the power of the lobby. There are three reasons for this. One is the slow and inefficient cumbersomeness of the congressional machine through which it is difficult to pass even the most innocuous and straight-forward bill without lobbying. The second is the inefficiency of the individual Congressman and the fact that many are either so busy or so slow that they must rely on outsiders to frame and explain legislative measures for them.

Finally, and perhaps most important, the lobbying done in the halls of Congress is not nearly so insidious or so effective as the lobbying carried on behind the closed doors of the executive offices down Pennsylvania Avenue. Lobbying in the halls of Congress must influence many out of ninety-six Senators and even more out of four hundred and thirty-five representatives to be effective. But lobbying done in the Post Office or in the State Department needs to influence only one man in order to swing a million-dollar contract for a shipping line or the approval of a $100,000,000 bond issue for a foreign government. Legislation might be framed to govern the inroads of the Janizaries upon Congress but it could never frustrate their subtle approaches to government departments.

Lobbyists may be divided into two general classes: Inside Jobbers and Outside Jobbers. The latter do much of their work in the open and also they concentrate chiefly on Congress. They use the direct method of bringing pressure on a Congressman through his home district, flooding his constituents with reports on how he voted, and getting them in turn to telegraph or write to Washington. Usually there is no attempt to conceal their operations. Typical of the Outside Jobbers are the veterans, the farm lobbies, the patriotic organizations and the wets and drys.

The Inside Jobbers avoid such crude and commonplace methods. Most of them are skilled lawyers and much of their work is with the executive departments of the government, where they can sit down behind closed doors and avoid publicity. While Congress is in session they concentrate also upon Capitol Hill, but there again most of them eschew the methods of the Outside Jobbers.

In addition to these two general categories, there is a hermaphroditic group of lobbyists skilled in both inside and outside jobbing. These can, when the occasion arises, do a neat piece of fixing on the inside, or when public opinion needs to be molded to gain the ends desired, flood the country with either open or secret propaganda. Among the most skillful of these hermaphroditic Janizaries are the Power Trust, the Sugar Trust and the lobbies established for the purpose of boosting big business.

Regardless of classification or method of operation, lobbying continues to be the one industry unaffected by the depression. The Washington telephone directory lists more than five hundred associations which in one form or another, either disguised or open, function as lobbyists. Edward F. McGrady, legislative agent of the American Federation of Labor, estimates the number of professional lobbyists at around two thousand. Next to politics, bootlegging and the social racket, lobbying is the capital's most important industry.

In general, the Inside Jobbers may be divided into five groups. There are the wine-women-and-song operators, generally recognized as almost obsolete and gradually switching their form of attack to the ballroom and dinner table. There are the Lame Ducks, forced to retire from public service, and taking up lobbying as the easiest means of livelihood. There are the Close-up Men—government officials who deliberately retire from public service in order to capitalize their influence and experience in lobbying. There are the Inside Men, sometimes deliberately placed in certain key positions to use their influence for those who placed them. Finally, at the extreme poles of lobbying, as far as methods go, but getting essentially the same results, there are the super-lobbyists of the voice-from-God type and the outright hijackers.

Of these, probably the greatest degree of all around effectiveness is attained by the Close-up Men—those who once held high office and left to combine law with lobbying. Usually, when called upon to perform a specific job, they produce. Many of them receive year-round retainers from large corporations to handle all questions arising between these companies and the government. Some of this is in the nature of lobbying and some is not. It is impossible to draw a line of demarcation. Much of the work is legitimate and made necessary by the ever-present maze of government red tape. Long experience in cutting through the deviousness of government procedure has made these men worth their large retainers and many of them have no objection to being called lobbyists. They are proud of their work.

On the other hand, many prefer the more sanctimonious title of "legislative agent," "legislative representative," "legislative director," "research expert," or, best of all, just plain "attorney." In their more lyrical moments they even refer to themselves as the "Third House of Congress."

Many of the Close-up Men do not operate in Washington alone, but have bases in New York. In fact, some have done their most effective wire pulling from Paris, Geneva or South America.

No matter where they operate or what they are called, however, the principle on which they operate is the same. They are hired because of the influence they exert through the prominence of their former positions and the friends they retain in government service.

Among the more prominent Close-up Men are:

Mabel Walker Willebrandt, once in charge of the Justice Department's prohibition enforcement, who, since retirement, has worked out a plan to fill the nation's desire for wine by selling the product of her client, Fruit Industries, Inc.

Everett Sanders, former Republican Representative from Indiana, who left the White House as secretary to Calvin Coolidge, to set up a lucrative practice, and later increase his political prestige as Chairman of the Republican National Committee for Herbert Hoover's reëlection.

Ted Clarke, caustic thin-lipped personal secretary to Calvin Coolidge, who has joined Sanders in law-lobbying.

William P. MacCracken, former Assistant Secretary of Commerce for Aviation, who now represents most of the important air lines of the country and has been highly successful in feeding them fat mail contracts.

Evan Young, former Minister to the Dominican Republic, and Alan F. Winslow, son-in-law of Under-Secretary of State Castle, who have helped to secure for Pan-American Airways some of its monopolistic and highly profitable air concessions in Latin America.

J. Herbert Stabler, who resigned as chief of the Latin-American Division of the State Department to become Vice-President of All-American Cables, then securing important cable concessions in Latin America; later rejoined the State Department only to leave it in 1927 to act as Close-up Man for Andrew W. Mellon's Gulf Oil Company in Venezuela.

Joseph Patrick Tumulty, astute secretary to Woodrow Wilson, who has been an equally astute fixture among Washington's legal-lobbyists ever since.

Bascom Slemp, who slips back and forth between government service and corporation lobbying as noiselessly as he slipped in and out of the White House as first secretary to Calvin Coolidge.

John Marshall, former Assistant Attorney General in the Coolidge Administration, who now helps handle political cases for the firm of Covington, Burling and Rublee.

Frederic A. Dolbeare, former State Department official, who resigned to join the international banking firm of J. Henry Schroeder, and, now that the depression has hit the bond business, is back assisting the cause of disarmament with the American delegation in Geneva. Shortly after Dolbeare joined his firm it managed to dispel State Department objections to a $30,000,-000 loan to the Brazilian State of Sao Paulo, which, it was previously contended, would raise the price of coffee for the American consumer. The loan is now in default.

Garrard B. Winston, former Under Secretary of the Treasury, now a director of the National City Company, who figured in a credit to the Colombian Government which President Olaya linked with the Barco concession to Winston's former chief in the Treasury, Andrew W. Mellon.

A. W. Gregg, once government representative in the $10,-000,000 grudge tax suit which Mr. Mellon instituted against Senator Couzens, but who now is available to large corporations or individuals desiring advice on getting their taxes reduced.

Ellsworth C. Alvord, another Treasury expert, who, despite the fact that he has retired to the more lucrative field of aiding big tax-payers, was called in with Gregg as confidential advisers by the House Ways and Means Committee in writing the 1932 tax bill.

Stokeley W. Morgan, and Dorsey Richardson, former State Department officials, who joined the firm of Lehman Brothers, promoters of foreign bond issues which must be passed by the State Department.

H. F. Arthur Schoenfeld, former Minister to Bulgaria, and former Minister to Costa Rica, who resigned to promote the foreign contracts of the International General Electric Company, but who, when the depression hit big business, slipped quietly back to the State Department as Minister to the Dominican Republic.

Robert E. Olds, former Under Secretary of State, and Allen W. Dulles, former chief of the Near-Eastern Division, who left the State Department to join the law firm of Sullivan and Cromwell, attorneys for J. P. Morgan and Company.

S. A. Maginnis, who, after serving as Minister to Bolivia, retired to become a banking lobbyist and negotiated a $415,000 commission for the son of President Leguia of Peru, paid by the National City Bank and Seligman and Company. Maginnis' share for putting across the deal was $40,000.

With the tremendous post-war expansion of American commerce and investments, the lobby has expanded to a much broader field than Washington. The principle involved, however, remains the same and Washington is the hub around which international lobbyists rotate, though their field of operation extends from Cape Horn to Cairo.

In this new field of international lobbying, the State Department has come to play a tremendous and little realized part, both as a training school and as a happy hunting ground after graduation. It is only natural that with some twenty billions of dollars invested in foreign countries and with most of these investments under the supervision of the State Department, either through approval in the first instance, or subsequent protection, the bankers should seek out the most experienced diplomats, tempt them from government service with fat salaries and set them to work lobbying loans through the department from which they have just resigned.

Illustrative of the method used by these international Janizaries in floating loans upon the American public was the work of Allen W. Dulles, in connection with loans to Prussia. The State Department, from 1925 on, was skeptical regarding all loans to Germany. It believed that France would insist on reparation payments and that, since Germany could not pay both reparations and private loans, the latter would be defaulted. Secretary of State Kellogg warned the bankers to this effect. Furthermore, the Reich itself was opposed to further loans to German states and municipalities, which it claimed were increasing Germany's national debt, only for the purpose of building swimming pools and amusement parks. Finally, S. Parker Gilbert, agent general for reparations, not only issued an emphatic statement opposing further loans to Germany, but on November 3, 1926, wrote to Paul Cravath, attorney for various bankers, that he was "constantly amazed at the recklessness of American bankers in offering to the public the securities of German states ..." and that he could "not justify the action of the American bankers in offering securities to the public without giving the slightest hint that the German point of view (that private debts had priority over reparations) is not accepted by the Allied Governments and that, in fact the Allied point of view is diametrically opposed."

In the fall of 1927, however, Harris, Forbes and a group of associated bankers desired to float a $30,000,000 loan to the Free State of Prussia. The State Department, because of the complaints of both S. Parker Gilbert and the Reich, held up the loan. The bankers got worried. After several attempts to get the loan passed they finally sent Allen Dulles down to visit his former colleagues in Washington. Dulles is a grandson of a former Secretary of State, John W. Foster. Also he was a nephew of the late Secretary of State, Robert Lansing. He played a round of golf with Frank B. Kellogg and came back with the State Department's letter passing the loan.

To-day the State Department is doing its best to cancel $11,-000,000,000 of European war debts which the American taxpayer will have to pay, in order to save private loans made by Harris, Forbes and other bankers; and there is grave doubt, despite the State Department's efforts and despite the Hoover moratorium, whether these loans, lobbied through the State Department, ever will be repaid.

Mr. Dulles, together with his colleague, former Under Secretary Olds, also figured prominently in the award of the Barco concession to Mellon's Gulf Oil Company and to J. P. Morgan's Carib Syndicate. This concession, reputed to be worth many millions, had been in dispute in the Colombian courts for some years, and during this time the State Department took the stand that under international law the Gulf Company and the Carib Syndicate must exhaust their remedies in court before the United States could intervene.

In July, 1928, however, and before the court procedure had

been exhausted, Robert E. Olds resigned as Under Secretary of State. The same month that he resigned he wrote a letter to Francis White, Assistant Secretary in charge of Latin-American affairs, asking that the Department take up the Barco dispute with Colombia through diplomatic channels. Mr. Olds had just become a member of the firm of Sullivan and Cromwell, attorneys for J. P. Morgan and Company, twenty-five per cent owners of the Barco oil lands.

The letter was a personal one, addressed "Dear Francis," and, perhaps because of this, was subsequently removed from the files of the State Department. However, coming from a man who a few days before had virtually run the Department, it got results. Unfortunately, the results did not produce what Mr. Olds expected. Overruling the advice of Benjamin Thaw, assistant chief of the Latin-American Division, that the Barco dispute was still in the courts and therefore not a matter for diplomatic protest, Mr. White sent a note to the Colombian Government. His action aroused so much resentment that Colombia immediately declared the Barco concession null and void. The Mellons and the Morgans were in a worse fix than ever. Mr. Olds by that time had gone to Paris, and although his associate, Allen Dulles, made several trips to Washington on behalf of his clients, the State Department was able to do nothing until Enrique Olaya, for nine years Minister to the United States, became President and held his famous dinner conversation with Andrew W. Mellon, seventy-five per cent owner of the Barco. Mr. Mellon suggested that if Colombia would straighten out her oil dispute the banks would lend her money.

After that the Barco was restored.

*

EVEN more effective than the Close-up Men—although they do not operate in as great numbers—are the Inside Men. Instead of resigning their government jobs to become recognized lobbyists, they continue in key positions where their influence is even more effective. They do not, except in rare cases, work for money. While occasional instances of bribery come to light, their rewards usually are political or personal. They use their influence to repay those who got them their jobs or those from whom they expect to get more.

Typical of this class is Irving Glover, Second Assistant Postmaster General. Mr. Glover happens to owe his appointment to the Post Office Department to Walter E. Edge, former Senator from New Jersey and now Ambassador to France. Therefore, when matters arise in his department which interest Mr. Edge, Glover does not forget his patron.

Shortly after Congress passed the shipping subsidy, providing lucrative mail contracts for steamship lines, such a question apparently arose. Bids were asked by the Post Office Department on a mail route between Colombia and New Orleans. The United Fruit Company and the Colombia Steamship Company, the latter operating leased Shipping Board vessels, both bid. The United Fruit Company offered the lowest bid, but the Post Office Department indicated that the Colombia Steamship Company would get the contract. Attorneys for the United Fruit Company protested and were informed that their bid had not come up to specifications. A new bid was submitted. Still the Post Office refused to award the contract to the lowest bidder. The matter was taken to Postmaster General New and also to Comptroller General McCarl. Both remained adamant. The Colombia Steamship Line was to get the contract.

Finally, attorneys for the United Fruit Company threatened to take the dispute to court. They threatened further to expose the fact that Walter E. Edge was a heavy stockholder in the Colombia Steamship Company and that his appointee, Irving Glover, was influencing the award.

After that the United Fruit Company got its contract.

Another effective Inside Man is John Nance Garner, Democratic nominee for the Vice-Presidency. Mr. Garner plays ball with those who play ball with him and the man who really counts in his recent political life is William Randolph Hearst. Although far removed, Hearst can make Garner turn handsprings, backward and forward, and also loop the loop.

And, during the writing of the sales tax in the 1932 session of Congress, Hearst did.

Garner's first back handspring came when the House Ways and Means Committee was considering provisions of the tax bill. Its members knew that when the 1928 revenue bill was under consideration, Garner had proposed an amendment abolishing consolidated tax returns. His amendment was passed in the House, but beaten by the protectors of entrenched wealth in the Senate, and lost out in conference between the two houses. Remembering the vitriolic fight the Speaker had made for this provision of 1928, the Ways and Means Committee wrote his amendment into the tax bill in 1932.

It happened, however, that of all those affected by the abolition of the right to make consolidated tax returns, the individual probably most seriously hurt would be William Randolph Hearst. This is because consolidated tax returns allow corporations to balance losing properties against profitable ones, and Hearst long has equalized the profits of his paying newspapers and syndicates by deducting the losses of those which do not pay. With the abolition of consolidated tax returns, therefore, his profitable enterprise would have had to pay taxes, in many cases, for the first time since the war.

So Mr. Hearst's lobbyist, informed of the Ways and Means Committee's action, immediately saw John N. Garner. The next morning Mr. Garner went to the Ways and Means Committee. The measure which he had championed in 1928 came out of the bill.

Almost simultaneously Garner looped-the-loop a second time. The Ways and Means Committee, apparently not realizing that the Speaker of the House was being pushed for the Presidency by the biggest individual newspaper owner in the country, inserted a sales tax on newspaper circulation in the revenue bill.

That night John A. Kennedy got into action. Kennedy is one of Hearst's newspaper men, who in 1929 waged war on the lobbyists. For revealing that Charles L. Eyanson, of the Connecticut Manufacturers' Association, was sitting in Senator Hiram Bingham's office helping write the Smoot-Hawley Tariff, he received the Pugsley Award of $1,000 for the outstanding piece of Washington journalism during the year. Actually the story was uncovered by Edward L. Roddan. But Kennedy signed his name to it, and having proved to his employer that he could wage war on lobbyists, Mr. Hearst established him as his own personal Janizary.

So Kennedy telephoned his chief in San Simeon, California, regarding the Committee's tax on newspaper circulation.

There was a time when Mr. Hearst, discovering the popularity of waging war on lobbyists, had telegraphed from this same San Simeon the following instructions:

"Locate and corral the lobbyists and dig up the facts regarding them."

Now, however, things were different. Mr. Hearst picked up his telephone. He had a brief conversation with his candidate for the Presidency. Within two hours the sales tax on newspaper circulation was removed from the tax bill.

Garner's Democratic colleague from Georgia, Representative Charles R. Crisp, also acts as an effective Inside Man when properly approached. During the consideration of the tax bill, the Senate twice rejected a consumers' tax on electricity and placed the levy on the power companies. In its revenue bill the House enacted no tax on electricity at all. But when the bill got into conference to reconcile differences between the House and Senate provisions, Senators Reed and Smoot, ever-vigilant guardians of corporation interests, proposed reversing the Senate's stand, despite the fact that they were honor bound to insist upon the Senate's vote against the consumers' tax. They could make no headway in this, however, without the House conferees, and the House conferees were not anxious to coöperate. But while the committee was in session, Judge Crisp, chairman of the House conferees, left the committee room and held a secret meeting with Preston S. Arkwright, sanctimonious president of the Georgia Power Company. Returning to the conference room, Crisp voted with Reed and Smoot to put the tax on the consumer rather than on the power companies. The decision cost the public $60,000,000 a year.

The Power Trust also had Inside Men carefully placed in other key positions, either in the government or so close that their influence was equally effective. Among these were Joseph R. Nutt, treasurer of the Republican National Committee, and Claudius Huston, intimate of President Hoover and chosen by him to head that committee in 1929. Huston was revealed as a lobbyist for the power companies against government operation of Muscle Shoals, and this, together with certain gambling debts, forced his resignation. Nutt is one of the owners of a monopoly power group which operates in Utah, Wyoming, Idaho and Colorado.

One of the most unusual cases of an Inside Man is that of E. J. Adams, who, although drawing a salary of $4,600 a year as an employee of the Federal Trade Commission, solicited business for the P. W. Chapman Company and used stationery of the Federal Trade Commission to do so. The Federal Trade Commission at that time was exposing some of the most damaging evidence against the power companies ever revealed against the Janizaries. At the height of the investigation Adams wrote to members of the board of the municipal power plant in Eugene, Oregon, and proposed that the plant be sold to the Chapman interests. He even went so far as to promise that Pennsylvania manufacturers would set up branch works in Eugene if the plant were sold to the Chapmans. Several citizens of Eugene protested, exposed the correspondence, forced the Federal Trade Commission to investigate Adams' status, and his activities for the Chapmans were discontinued.

The most interesting thing about the case was the revelation that before joining the Federal Trade Commission, Adams had worked as assistant to A. C. Dalton, vice-president and general manager of the United States Shipping Board Merchant Fleet Corporation at the identical time that organization was selling to the P. W. Chapman Company at a ridiculously low price its prize vessels of the United States Lines and the American Merchant Lines. Immediately this deal was closed, Adams went to work for the Federal Trade Commission, then about to take up its investigation of the power companies, of which the Chapmans operate many.

One of the great lobbying battles in recent history was staged between Close-up Men on one side and Inside Men on the other. The fight was over the one commodity—sugar. The battlefield was the Seventy-first Congress, at which the Smoot-Hawley Tariff bill was being written. Each side spent a million dollars.

The National City Bank, the Hershey Chocolate Company, the United Fruit Company and American firms with investments in Cuban sugar wanted the tariff lowered. They hired Close-up Men. The Great Western Sugar Company, the Louisiana cane growers, the Mormon church and organizations interested in Western beet sugar wanted the tariff increased. They used Inside Men.

One of the Close-up Men was Edwin P. Shattuck, personal friend of Herbert Hoover, member of the war-time Sugar Equalization Board, and counsel to Mr. Hoover's Food Administration. He was paid $75,000 for "legal services," which as far as the public could see, consisted of repeated conferences with his old friend in the White House. Another Close-up Man was General Enoch H. Crowder, U.S.A. retired, former Ambassador to Cuba and intimate of President Machado.

The battle was a desperate one. Crowder even went so far as to reveal to Cuban authorities certain military plans for the defense of the United States. The Cuban Embassy, in turn, revealed them to Ira Bennett, editor of the Washington *Post,* who, according to revelations by the Caraway Committee, offered to publish editorials opposing the sugar tariff for a cash consideration. The disclosure, when brought to Bennett's attention by Carlisle Bargeron, a member of his staff, was not denied.

H. C. Lakin, president of the Cuban Company, went even further. He helped inspire a series of articles and cartoons in Latin-American papers belittling the United States, which he admitted was done for the purpose of putting diplomatic pressure on the Hoover Administration.

But despite the Close-up Men hired, and the unusual methods used, the American low-tariff sugar lobby was defeated by the Mormon Church. The Church probably has heavier investments in beet sugar than any other American organization, and protecting its interests were two competent Inside Men. One was Edgar B. Brossard, a member of the United States Tariff Commission. Brossard is a Mormon, and his family is interested financially in Utah beet sugar. Therefore, when the Tariff Commission investigated the sugar tariff in 1925, it was considered more ethical for Brossard to refrain from the discussions; and at a subsequent senatorial investigation he testified that he had nothing to do with the sugar report. When the books of the night watchman were subpœnaed, however, they showed that Brossard had come to his office every night while the sugar report was being written, on one occasion remaining as late as 2:30 A.M. Others who drafted the report testified that Brossard had sat in with them constantly.

But the key Close-up Man of the high sugar tariff lobby was Reed Smoot, chairman of the Senate Finance Committee and second in command of the Mormon Church. It took more than the revelation of military secrets, the dissemination of anti-American propaganda in Latin America, and conferences with Herbert Hoover to block Smoot, and the Mormon Church won the sugar battle.

*

THE Lame Ducks comprise a lobbying class all to themselves. They are both effective and picturesque. Having been forced by rebellious constituencies or a change in administration to leave Congress or their cozy berths in an executive department, they capitalize their terms of service for the people. The old home town is not for them. Their wives dread the thought of leaving the gossipy sessions of the Ladies of the Senate, the teas at the Congressional Country Club and the At Homes of the Cabinet ladies. Their daughters have blossomed forth as débutantes and settled down to married life in the capital. So the Lame Ducks stay on.

And they are well paid for their sojourn.

Among the most successful are:

Frank W. Mondell, of Wyoming, former Republican floor leader of the House, who is reputed to have earned a fee of $1,000,000 for putting a retroactive provision into the first Mellon tax-reduction bill, saving large estates millions of dollars in inheritance taxes.

Charles S. Thomas, former Democratic Senator from Colorado, who lobbied on the floor of the Senate for the return of $85,000,000 in inheritance taxes to the millionaire estates of Jenny Woolworth, Julia Fleishmann, James B. Duke and Senator William A. Clarke, Montana copper king.

Irvine Lenroot, who got $20,000 from the Power Trust, following his defeat as Senator from Wisconsin, but who now has retired to the more respectable security of the Federal bench.

Philip F. Campbell, who has been on the pay-roll of the Standard Oil Company as a lobbyist ever since a rebellious constituency in Kansas forced his retirement from Congress in 1922.

Senator Thomas P. Gore, the blind Democrat from Oklahoma, who also lobbied for the oil interests when he lost out in the senatorial race of 1921 and until the rebellion against Herbert Hoover restored him to the Senate in 1930.

Robert L. Owen, another Democratic Senator from Oklahoma, who since his defeat has lobbied for the oil interests.

S. Wallace Dempsey, former Republican chairman of the House Rivers and Harbors Committee, who now specializes on getting river and harbor improvement bills through Congress.

Frank H. Hitchcock, Postmaster General under Taft, who during the 1932 session of Congress parked his coat and hat in the office of David Barry, Senate sergeant-at-arms, and dined daily in the private rooms reserved for Senators, while persuading them to boost the tariff on copper—which they did.

Dempsey is a comparatively inexperienced lobbyist in point of years, but one of the most successful in point of profits. He has been operating only since his defeat in 1930, but in an expansive moment he once boasted to newspaper men of the fees he made as a river-and-harbor lobbyist and exhibited an account book listing the large sums received.

"I don't know why I ever stayed in Congress," Dempsey remarked.

His activities came to light early in 1932, when W. A. Holt, former mayor of Oconto, Wisconsin, obtained a temporary injunction restraining the city from paying a $2,000 fee to Cur-Fis, a Cleveland engineering company, of which Dempsey is reputed to be vice-president.

It happened in this way. Oconto wanted its harbor developed. Army engineers disapproved the project. So the city council sent Mayor Carl Riggins to Washington, where he engaged Dempsey to lobby the desired pork bill through Congress over the heads of the army engineers. He was to pay Dempsey $2,000 and an equal amount to the Cur-Fis service, which makes harbor surveys. When news of the deal leaked out, Holt objected and went to the courts.

*

PHIL CAMPBELL has now become a historic figure in the capital. During the many years that he represented a Kansas district in the House he was known as "the Little Napoleon" or "the Walking Pigeon-hole." The first nickname arose from the meticulous care with which he plasters a lock of hair over the center of his forehead à la Napoleon; the second from his habit, as chairman of the House Rules Committee, of stuffing important bills, opposed by the barons of big business, into his inside coat pocket where they remained until forgotten.

It was Campbell's leaning toward big business and his emulation of its social standards which eventually brought about his retirement from Congress and his present occupation of promoter of their interests.

A man of some social ambition, Campbell acquired an estate in Virginia. There he entertained occasionally and somewhat pretentiously, winning for himself among his colleagues the additional nickname of "the Gentleman from Virginia."

That was the beginning of the end. Campbell's previous campaigns had been walk-aways. But now his opponent spread the report that Phil had gone aristocratic, that he had a Virginia plantation and entertained lavishly. Close friends warned Phil that he was in danger and he rushed back to his neglected prairies.

A vigorous campaign followed, which won back some of his wavering constituents. It was to be climaxed by a big celebration the Saturday night just before election day, and for this celebration Phil hired a band. It was a big band and it played a lot. The crowds were big also. They enjoyed the band. They enjoyed the whole thing. They gave external promise of voting for Phil. Then one of Phil's henchmen arose to introduce the chief event of the evening—the candidate for reëlection. Even the presentation speech was good, and Phil rose to receive the plaudits of the crowd.

But yet as he walked toward the rostrum the band struck up "Carry Me Back to Old Virginny."

And Kansas did.

*

THERE was a day when lobbying was a he-man's game; when wine, women and blackmail were the chief stocks in trade, when Pendleton's notorious and wholly delightfully gambling den—"The Hall of the Bleeding Heart," and Sam Ward's sybaritic entertainments influenced many a vote in Congress or won many a favor in the executive departments. There was a time even during the very recent heyday of the Ku Klux

Klan when William Zumbrunn, its official agent, maintained a large yacht on the Potomac, with liquor, food and steam up, always ready for any sort of a congressional junket, once entertaining a cargo of Congressmen and Follies girls, which was the talk of the town. It was hospitality of this kind that won for Zumbrunn the title of "King of the Lobbyists."

The days of kings are now over—at least this style of kings. To-day there are super-lobbyists of the Julius H. Barnes type, and there are hijacking lobbyists of the J. A. Arnold type, and there are all kinds of successful free-lance lobbyists, but the free and easy, frank and forthright methods of the wine, women and song operators now are mostly a matter of history.

There are a lot of free-lance lobbyists who, like Gladys Moon Jones, agent for the French Line, have sometimes played their principals for suckers by sending in newspaper and magazine articles which they claim to have inspired but did not know existed in advance of publication. Their profits are nothing, however, as compared with some of the big-time hijackers. The most successful of these recently has been J. A. Arnold, receiver of retainers from large corporations anxious to reduce taxes and increase tariffs. Arnold claimed he could do both of these, and he put forward his claim so convincingly that during recent tariff and tax discussions he and his associates collected more that $1,000,000.

The sucker list which Arnold induced to come across reads like a Who's Who of American Big Business. One thousand dollars each was what the following contributed to Arnold's tax and tariff campaign: Stone & Webster, Armour & Company, Insull Utility Properties, Otis & Company, W. L. Mellon, Westinghouse Air Brake Company, O. P. and M. J. Van Sweringen, William Wrigley, Jr., Colgate-Palmolive-Peet Company, Crane Company, Byllesby Engineering & Management Corporation, and the State of Florida. Other large contributors were the Aluminum Company, Hornblower & Weeks, Illinois Central Railroad, Pillsbury Flour Mills, Carnation

Milk Products Company, Dallas Clearing House Association, American Rolling Mill Company, Minneapolis Journal, Jantzen Knitting Mills, Southern California Edison Company, and the Kellogg Company of Battle Creek, Michigan.

These contributions ostensibly went to the American Taxpayers League and the Southern Tariff Association. Both were located in the same building in adjoining offices and both were controlled by Arnold. Each year after the books of the two organizations were audited he destroyed the accounts, retaining only the auditor's report, which was drawn up by a public accountant who had served a term in prison for issuing a fraudulent certificate of solvency.

Despite exposures by the Caraway lobbying investigation, Arnold is still operating in Washington and still finding a sufficient quota of gullibles. The latest is the National Broadcasting Company which donated a number of valuable radio periods during the 1932 session of Congress to advocate wage cuts rather than higher taxes. Arnold was too clever to do the talking himself but put forward several prominent figures under the "auspices of the American Taxpayers League." Among those who spoke was Representative Harold McGugin, Republican of Kansas, then being sued by the Department of Justice for recovery of $150,000 in attorney's fees which McGugin is alleged to have collected from the estate of Jackson Barnett, a wealthy but legally incompetent Indian.

The line of demarcation between the super-lobbyist and the personal advisor to Presidents is difficult to draw. Such men as General W. W. Atterbury, President of the Pennsylvania Railroad, Owen D. Young, head of General Electric, Thomas W. Lamont, partner of J. P. Morgan and Bernard M. Baruch, all would deny that they are lobbyists. And perhaps in most cases they are not. Some of them come to Washington frequently. The door of the White House, of every Cabinet office, always is open. They advise, and they are listened to. Many of them have performed important public service and at some sacrifice. But it is exactly this that makes their influence so powerful, their position so dangerous. It is difficult, for instance, for the State Department, once having asked Mr. Lamont to perform the thankless job of heading the Bankers Consortium for China, later not to yield to his request for approval of a Morgan loan to the South Manchurian Railway, despite the fact that the United States is much opposed to strengthening the position of Japan in that area. It is also difficult, for instance, for Messrs. Hoover, Meyer and Mills, having called upon Charles G. Dawes to perform various public services, to refuse him $80,000,000 from the public treasury, despite the fact that other equally deserving banks, lacking a Dawes to plead for them, closed their doors almost at the time Mr. Dawes was getting his.

So President Hoover, having called in the Barons of Big Business and having a weather eye on campaign contributions, listens to them, yields to them as far as Congress will permit, and has made them the super-lobbyists of Washington.

*

THE SECOND great group of lobbyists, the Outside Jobbers, can be divided into two general classes: those who are out for themselves, and those who promote causes. Typical of the first are the business associations, the veterans and the farmers. Typical of the latter are the patriotic associations, the wets and drys and the pacifists.

Perhaps because they have no selfish ax to grind, because they are not out to line their own pockets, the lobbyists who promote causes are among the most effective in the capital. Furthermore, they render an important service to the nation in arousing national opinion which most of the time is as somnolent as the capital itself. Whether one believes in a big navy or in disarmament, in prohibition or the repeal of the Eighteenth Amendment, it unquestionably is healthy to provoke thought on any of these questions. Unfortunately much of the propaganda waged by these lobbyists is bitter and prejudiced. Many of the lobbyists themselves are narrow-minded—some even fanatics—unable to see any one's point of view except their own. Fortunately they are counter-balanced by equally prejudiced persons on the other side, so the net result is not an unhappy one.

Among the most important of these promoters of what they believe to be the good of the nation are:

The Anti-Saloon League, once one of the most powerful lobbies in Washington, chiefly responsible for the fact that drug stores now can get corner sites, and once able, through Wayne B. Wheeler—one of the greatest lobbyists of all time—to call upon President Harding and order him to cut down his drinking. Scott McBride, his successor, is high-minded and sincere, believes it his destiny to guide the nation between right and wrong, but lacks the League's one-time funds and power really to do any guiding.

The Methodist Board of Temperance, Prohibition and Public Morals, headed by Dr. Clarence True Wilson, who has a nice smile, a disconcerting direct gaze—makes you wish you hadn't spoken to Aunt Polly as you did—and in every way is qualified to be a fighter for the right. The Board occupies a large and ornate stone building—sometimes called the Methodist Vatican—whose proximity to the capital and the excellence of its food frequently beguiles even such ardent wets as Senator Millard Tydings of Maryland into its restaurant.

The Women's Christian Temperance Union, another member of the high tribunal for the determination of the right, whose President, Mrs. Ella Boole, is a devout drinker of water and a fervent separator of the dross from the gold.

The Association against the Prohibition Amendment, started by Captain W. H. Stayton, who operates various steamship lines out of Baltimore, and whose ever-present supply of choice beverages indicates that his advocacy of repeal is not motivated by personal thirst or selfishness. The Association draws its funds chiefly from John J. Raskob, Arthur Curtiss James, the DuPonts and other millionaire backers, undoubtedly sincere, but whose pocketbooks will profit by tax decreases made possible by the repeal of prohibition.

The Women's Organization for National Prohibition Reform, headed by Mrs. Charles Sabin, who was smart enough to surround her cause with jewels, dinner-gowns and afternoon teas, but was not strong enough to persuade the lady crusaders to drive their cars to the capital in a prohibition protest parade. Their husbands refused to let them.

The Women's International League for Peace and Freedom, headed in Washington by Miss Dorothy Detzer, a broad-gauge person of unusual ability, who was solely responsible for persuading President Hoover to appoint Miss Mary E. Wooley as an American delegate to the Geneva Disarmament Conference. Miss Detzer's effective lobbying against armament bills has caused the army and navy more heartaches than any other single civilian, and the patriots have responded by endeavoring to prevent her from renting offices near the State, War and Navy Building.

The National Council for the Prevention of War, which owns its own building and flaunts its shingle in large letters immediately opposite the windows of the Secretary of War. Frederick J. Libby, its executive, is an astute money-raiser, and a sincere but sometimes short-sighted seeker of peace. The Council resorts to educational propaganda rather than the direct methods of the Women's International League.

The Daughters of the American Revolution, who, with the support of scores of retired army and navy officers, put tremendous pressure on Congress when anything affecting the army, navy or liberalism is under discussion. Although secretly disliking President Hoover, who refuses to address their annual meetings, they were loyal enough, on the surface, to censor a speech by Representative Ham Fish, New York red-baiter, criticizing Hoover's pacific policy in Nicaragua.

The Woman Patriot, edited by Miss Mary Kilbreth, sister of a retired brigadier general, who claims Secretary Stimson is selling out the United States to Great Britain and insinuates that he showed the white feather while under fire in France. Associated with her is Ralph Burton, an attorney for patriotic organizations, who was behind publication of *The Great Mistake,* first book to expose the early business career of President Hoover.

The Navy League, founded by steel manufacturers and shipbuilders, but now boasting a wider and supposedly more patriotic membership and which wages unceasing warfare on every one daring to criticize the navy.

The Women's Joint Congressional Committee, made up of legislative agents of twenty-one women's organizations and which has played an important part in passing such measures as the Sheppard-Towner maternity act, the submission of the Child

Labor Amendment to the States, and the establishment of independent citizenship for married women.

The National Woman's Party, organized by the militants of the old suffragette days, when Alice Paul and Mabel Vernon picketed the White House, poured acid down mail boxes, and were imprisoned both in England and the United States.

The League of Women Voters, more conservative than the Woman's Party and headed by Miss Belle Sherwin, of Philadelphia's Sherwin-Paint millions.

Between the Woman's Party and the League of Women Voters there exists a rivalry such as only can exist between women. The former believes in the equality of sex. It maintains that any work that man can do also can be performed by women. The League of Women Voters believes in restricting women's rights. It claims women should not perform certain kinds of manual labor and night work. As a result, the two groups often appear before a congressional committee, each trying to persuade its bewildered male members that the opposing group has no right at all to speak for American womanhood.

The National Woman's Party maintains by far the most effective lobbying agency. Its lobbying committee includes: Miss Doris Stevens, former wife of Dudley Field Malone; Miss Maud Younger; Mrs. Iris Calderhead Walker, daughter of a former Congressman; and Miss Anita Pollitzer, daughter of a distinguished South Carolina family. They practice a policy of producing the right person to interview the right official at the right time. All Congressmen and executives are card-indexed regarding their personal tastes. If a Congressman is known to be partial to pretty women, one of them is selected to do the lobbying. If a petition is to be presented to President Hoover for a reservation in the World Court protocol safeguarding women's rights, Mrs. Stephen Pell, wealthy, socially prominent, unquestionably Republican, is summoned from New York on twenty-four hours' notice.

And at other times the Party is frequently host to influential gatherings of Congressmen, journalists and executives in the

historic colonial home which it has remodeled as its headquarters just a block from the capitol.

*

THE lobbying of cause promoters is a deadly serious thing.
They are not out for money. Many of them support themselves. They are willing to undergo hardship. Most of them
bring down upon their heads a storm of vituperation, abuse
and ridicule from the opposition. Some of them are even willing to go to jail for their cause.

The lobbying of the Outside Jobbers who are out purely for
themselves is an entirely different thing. Their financial rewards are great. Their system usually is a sure-fire proposition.
They take few risks. Their set-up is such that they usually
win, and when they lose, their losses are infinitesimal.

Take, for instance, the veteran's lobby. It is an old, old
story and it always wins. If it does not win at one session, it
wins at the next. The system never has failed since the G.A.R.
paved the way with its organized raid on the Treasury. The
Spanish War veterans followed, and the World War veterans have added a few innovations—including a bonus army
—with the result that veterans' expenditures now reach the
stupendous total of one billion dollars a year—one-fourth of
the cost of the entire Federal Government.

The weapon of the veterans' lobby is direct political action.
They threaten members of Congress that if they don't vote for
veterans' measures they will not come back to Congress; and
they make good their threats. The late Speaker Nicholas
Longworth opposed the bonus in 1930. In the campaign that
year the veterans made a house-to-house canvass of his district and came within 3,000 votes of defeating him. His previous
majority had been 18,000. After that Nick was a veterans' man.
When the bonus came up next year he bolted the President
and led the House in a revolt that passed the bill over the
Presidential veto.

The Spanish War veterans' lobby is headed by Rice W. Means, former Republican Senator from Colorado. Means now publishes a veterans' magazine in Washington and devotes much of his time to lobbying for pension measures. Elected to the Senate by a combination of veteran-Ku Klux Klan support, he was noted, during his one term for reactionary views and zeal in leading veteran raids on the Treasury. In 1930 the Spanish War veterans organized a huge drive for an increase in their pensions and Means, chief lobbyist, put it across over the Presidential veto. He and Governor Green of Michigan were even on the Senate floor when that body voted to override the veto.

The American Legion and the Veterans of Foreign Wars maintain permanent lobbying organizations in Washington headed by John Thomas Taylor for the former, and L. F. Ray for the latter. Through the influence of Hanford MacNider, past Legion president and Trubee Davison, Assistant Secretary of War, who flew out to the Detroit convention as Hoover's personal envoys, the Legion has officially pussy-footed on the bonus, but the rank and file are overwhelmingly for it and have exerted direct political pressure in support of its immediate payment. The Veterans of Foreign Wars mince no words in their demand for the bonus. They took the lead in the drive that put over the bonus loan payment in 1931, and were in the van of the bonus movement in 1932, using the Legion's inaction to support their own nation-wide membership campaign.

Equally powerful is the farm lobby. The secret of its strength, like the veterans', is direct action. If members of Congress do not vote "right" they hear about it at the next election.

The rise of the farm lobby is comparatively recent, but for a time it dominated Congress. Built up immediately after the War upon the foundation of the three great farm organizations—the National Grange, the American Farm Bureau Federation and the Farmers' Union—the lobby organized what was called the farm bloc. Gray Silver, of the Farm Bureau, directed its activities, and during the Sixty-sixth and Sixty-seventh Congress the bloc held the balance of power and enacted a long list of agricultural measures. During the past three years the farm lobby has been comparatively quiet, due partly to the increased suffering of the industrial communities but also to a clever move on the part of Herbert Hoover of giving prominent officers of the farm organization places at the public pie-counter.

Ranking along with the veterans and the farmers in power is the lobby of the American Federation of Labor and the Railroad Brotherhoods. With wage cuts being declared all over the United States, little has been heard of the labor lobby recently, but at times it has exerted powerful influence on legislation and the President. The Adamson Act, providing for an eight-hour day, and the Wagner unemployment exchange bill, owed their passage in large part to the lobby. William Nuckles Doak, former lobbyist for the Brotherhood of Railway Trainmen, also won recognition for the lobby by his appointment as Secretary of Labor, although most labor men consider this a doubtful honor. Major triumphs in recent years of the labor lobbies were the defeat of John J. Parker, North Carolina injunction jurist, whom President Hoover wanted to foist upon the Supreme Court, and the enactment in 1932 of the Norris-LaGuardia anti-injunction law. In the 1932 session the labor lobby also prevented action on the appointment by Hoover of Judge James H. Wilkerson and Judge Kenneth MacIntosh, notorious labor-baiters, to the Federal Circuit Court of Appeals.

The success of the veterans, of labor and of the farmers in lobbying what they want through Congress is chiefly due to weight of numbers. Five million veterans, most of them organized, are listened to. Nearly half the population of the United States are farmers and their families. They command attention. Four to five million union workers, plus many million others who are not organized, also exert a powerful influence. Therefore, these lobbies, and others like them, operate on comparatively little money and are open and above-board. There is no corruption, no graft, but much politics. They make no attempt to cover up what they are doing. They are frankly out for themselves; so they announce what they want and go get it.

Not so the big-business lobbies. Most of them are Outside Jobbers in that they endeavor to build up public opinion in Congress, in the home districts of Congressmen and in the country at large; but at the same time most of them pull wires that nobody is supposed to know about, while some operate the most unscrupulous and powerful undercover machines in American public life. The reason for their underground tactics is that they have money to spend but lack weight of numbers. They represent small but wealthy groups which control few votes and whose alternative to direct action is undercover work.

The only big business lobby which compares with the farmer, labor and veteran lobbies in size is the United States Chamber of Commerce. This is the giant protector of all business and has erected a $3,000,000 monument to its god on Lafayette Square, just across from the residence of the President elected on the platform of big-business promotion.

The Chamber is an open and above-board agency which honestly believes that business should come first, last and foremost and does its best to make effective that belief. Its methods for the most part also are open and above-board, verging to undercover work occasionally. It operates one of the most gigantic propaganda machines in the country. Through an endless stream of press statements, business reports, weekly and monthly bulletins, and its magazine—*Nation's Business*—it pounds home the idea that lower taxes on business, higher tariff on foreign goods, and less money to farmers and laborers are what the United States needs for prosperity. And its propaganda is convincing. It should be. The Chamber, in more prosperous days, paid to Merle Thorpe, head of the propaganda organization as editor of *Nation's Business,* a salary of $75,000—identical with that of the President.

Individual members of the United States Chamber of Commerce enrolled through local branches have little or nothing to say about the management of its affairs. Control of the organization rests in the hands of a board of directors elected at annual conventions and the almost perennial chairman of this board is Julius H. Barnes, big grain operator, super-lobbyist and the man who is credited with convincing Herbert Hoover that he was a Republican not a Democrat when the present incumbent first sought the White House in 1920.

Barnes belongs to the inner circle of advisers-to-Presidents, and is not above bringing a delegation of grain dealers to the White House to fulminate against the wheat stabilization operations of the Federal Farm Board. After the stock-market crash in 1929 he was one of the most loquacious of the President's prosperity-just-around-the-corner pronouncers, but now apparently has realized that mere Chamber-of-Commerce optimism will not improve prices, and so has slipped quietly out of the picture.

The development and expansion of the United States Chamber of Commerce in recent years has pushed into the background, the once all-powerful National Manufacturers Association which in its day was the really big shot among the business lobbies. Although the sensational Mulhall investigation of 1913 and Woodrow Wilson's charge that it was trying to frustrate reform legislation has forced it into more ethical operations, the Association still is a potent influence in the capital. The dapper Van Dyke beard of James A. Emery, chief lobbyist, is a familiar sight in congressional committee hearings, especially when labor legislation is under discussion. The Manufacturers Association is the foe of all labor reform and for years obstructed the enactment of the anti-injunction bill. Like the Chamber of Commerce, it operates chiefly in the open and uses pressure on home districts to secure results.

In 1913, however, it was a far different story. The Mulhall investigation disclosed that the Association had set up fake organizations under cover of which it conducted nation-wide legislative and political operations. One of these organizations, the National Council for Industrial Defense, was used as a propaganda agency. Another, the National Tariff Commission Association, was used to push a campaign for a permanent tariff commission. A third, the Workingmen's Protective Association, went into politics loaded with money to defeat Congressmen supported by organized labor. One of its field agents, put on the witness stand, testified that his work consisted chiefly in bribing labor leaders to double-cross their candidates.

One of the chief lobbyists of the Manufacturers Association during this period was Jim Watson, of Indiana, his principal duty being that of filling congressional committees with "right-minded" members. Among the documents uncovered by the investigators was a telegram sent by Watson to the Association in which he told of conferring with "Uncle Joe" Cannon about placing a friendly Congressman on an important committee.

Other important business lobbies are those conducted on behalf of the railroads and the bankers. Alfred P. Thom, chief lobbyist for the Association of Railway Executives, is reputed to be one of the highest paid and most effective Janizaries in the capital. The elder Senator LaFollette charged that under his guidance the railroads spent $3,000,000 in 1919-20 putting through the Esch-Cummins Act; while again in 1932 the railroad lobby was instrumental in creating the system of business doles known as the Reconstruction Finance Corporation.

*

ALTHOUGH lobbying has been rampant in the national capital ever since the Republic's founders decided to locate it off the beaten paths of populous Philadelphia and New York, and although past history has disclosed some shocking favors given to those who demanded privileged places at the public pie-counter, yet there probably never has been a time when so concerted, insistent and successful a scramble was made as during the first three years of Herbert Hoover.

Previous scrambles have been concerted and insistent; also successful. In fact, the scramble is a recognized and perhaps necessary part of every new administration in a government of the people, for the people and by the people. But probably because Herbert Hoover had advertised himself as the great engineer, the successful business man, the promoter and patron of big business, the disciples of business, both big and little, flocked to his administration in greater numbers than ever before and demanded nourishment. This was true during the hang-over days from Coolidge prosperity when the people really took seriously the Hoover prediction that the country would become still more prosperous. It was even more true after the crash, when business expected the Great Engineer to stem the tide. Then they flocked to Washington in greater numbers than ever before, and the President, pledged to a chicken in every pot and two cars in every garage, gave and gave and gave.

Those who received were not necessarily those who needed. On the contrary, they were those who asked the loudest or else who placed Close-up and Inside Men in strategic positions to exert the greatest pressure. Of these the lobbies which bagged the greatest prizes or staged the most intensive inside scrambles were the power trust, the air lines and the bankers. Their work was typical of the great hermaphroditic lobbies which both poison public opinion on the outside and pull powerful private wires on the inside.

The story of the Power Lobby is an old one, but it has a new and amazing chapter. In the last days of the Coolidge Administration the lobby's machinations were exposed with such a reverberation of public indignation that most people thought the country could be safe from its intrigues for a few years at least. But they were wrong. The tactics of the lobby in the Coolidge days was that of giving newspapers long-term credit on their paper contracts, of hiring key men on newspaper copy desks, of paying university professors fat fees for lectures and books denouncing public ownership, and of maintaining in an elaborate suite in a fashionable Washington hotel one Josiah T. Newcomb, former New York State Senator, who entertained lavishly and issued solemn pronouncements that he was not a lobbyist in any manner, shape or form. Stephen B. Davis, Assistant Secretary of Commerce, when Hoover headed that department, was hired to assist Newcomb, together with Irvine L. Lenroot of Wisconsin, a Republican, and Charles S. Thomas of Colorado, a Democrat, both Lame Duck Senators who had abandoned politics for the great game of lobbying. Their special job was to prevent the passage of the Walsh resolution calling for an investigation of the power trust. For nine months' work on this, Newcomb was paid $39,994, Davis $33,735, Lenroot and Thomas $20,000 each.

But they failed. The lobbyists succeeded in having the investigation made by the Federal Trade Commission instead of by a Senate Committee, but the former's probe was more penetrating and its revelations more amazing than a Senate Committee's ever could have been.

Having fallen down in previous lobbying, the power trust changed its tactics. It decided to concentrate on inside operations. The National Electric Light Association, one of three big power propaganda organizations, hired Hoover's former secretary, Paul Clapp, as managing director, and Major H. S. Bennion, assistant engineer of the Federal Power Commission, as one of its agents. The Niagara Falls Power Company already had hired as its vice-president Colonel William Kelly, former chief engineer of the Federal Power Commission, who for a time had been loaned by the army to the National Electric Light Association. The Pennsylvania Electric Light Company had hired Charles E. Oates, another of the Commission's former chief engineers; while the Commission's hydraulic engineer, D. L. Guy, had been hired by the Power Committee of the United States Chamber of Commerce, and O. C. Merrill, Executive Secretary of the Commission, discouraged over his failure to curb the trust, had been weaned away from government service by the World Power Conference, another propaganda agency of the Power Lobby. In addition to all this the power companies had been instrumental in the appointment of the late James W. Good as Secretary of War, which made him automatically one of the three chief executives of the Federal Power Commission. With headquarters at Chicago, Jim Good had handled the Mid-Western election campaign of Herbert Hoover, and from the now bankrupt Sam Insull and other Mid-Western utilities he had collected heavy tribute to put Hoover over the top.

Now the contributors expected to get theirs in return. They had not long to wait.

On February 28th, four days before the Coolidge Cabinet expired, Secretaries Dwight F. Davis, William A. Jardine and Roy O. West, the three executives of the Federal Power Commission, had voted into effect Order Number 28. This was one of the most controversial sections of Federal water power legislation, and had been so hotly debated that the Commission had delayed nine years before making it effective. It provided for Federal supervision of the issuing of stocks and bonds by the power companies, and was calculated to prevent just such financial catastrophes as subsequently hit the Insull interests. O. C. Merrill, Executive Secretary, for years had been trying to put the order into effect, and when he succeeded on February 28, 1929, the power companies shivered inwardly.

But they did not shiver long.

Four days later, Jim Good became Secretary of War and a member of the Federal Power Commission. Less than two months later—April 25, 1929—Good called a meeting of the Federal Power Commission and brazenly stated that so many brokerage firms handling power securities had complained to

him against Order Number 28 that he had decided to sus-
pend it.

Thus was won the first important victory in the Power
Lobby's new method of attack. Its system of Inside Men was
working.

The next major victory followed almost immediately. Merrill, who had fought the power trust for nine years, decided
it was a losing battle and accepted a lucrative position offered
by the lobby at the psychological moment to get him out of
the picture. He was replaced by F. E. Bonner, whose appointment, according to an admission by Secretary of the Interior
Wilbur, was made only after consultation with Paul Down-
ing, President of the Pacific Gas and Electric Company.
Simultaneously there was published a secret memorandum,
obviously written by a lobbyist for the National Electric Light
Association, which disclosed the lobby's method of easing
Merrill out of office by persuading him "to accept some other
more lucrative and less trying position."

The man on the Commission whom the lobby next wanted
to dispose of was William V. King, Chief Accountant, and
the secret memorandum proposed that because of Mr. King's
activity "in seeking definite information concerning charges
by our engineering and managing concerns for services billed
subsidiary companies" the accounting activities of the Commission should be "removed from the direct supervision of Mr.
King" to the Departments of War, Interior or Agriculture,
which "will not have men specifically trained for this work."

The lobby's attack on the Commission's accounting work
was inspired by two facts: First, the more the power companies
could pad their initial capital expense, the more they could
collect from the public fifty years hence, when the power
plants can be bought by municipalities; also the higher the
capital cost, the higher the rate charged to the consumer.
Illustrative of this, the Rocky Mountain Power Company, a
subsidiary of Electric Bond and Share, had charged up to the
capital expense of acquiring a power site on the Flathead

River, Montana: $140 for an Indian pow-wow, $500 to a Blackfeet Indian Chief for persuading the tribe to favor the Rocky Mountain Power Company as against a rival, $32,000 damages to a road and bridges on account of a flood, and various donations to Indians, churches, a State fair and even to a handball club in order to win the favor of Indians owning the land.

Mr. King unfortunately insisted on exposing this. He insisted also on showing that the Niagara Falls Power Company had inflated its values by $60,000,000, that the Clarion River Power Company of Pennsylvania had padded its accounts by $4,000,000, that the Conowingo project of the Philadelphia Electric Company had made unwarranted charges of nearly $3,500,000, and that the Lexington Power Company in South Carolina was inflated by $1,000,000. All of these inflation reports, although at one time sent to the Commerce Committee of the House of Representatives, had been suppressed by Inside Men working for the power lobby.

King's chief collaborator in squeezing water out of the power accounts was Charles A. Russell, solicitor of the Federal Power Commission. Russell fought even more ferociously than King in exposing the lobby's intrigue, but he fought a losing battle.

The lobby was stronger than either King or Russell. It was also stronger than the public, despite the indignation which burst forth with publication of the secret memorandum. The lobby had a friend in the White House.

After waiting a few weeks for the furore to subside, Bonner proceeded to recommend exactly what the power companies had proposed in their confidential memorandum—transfer of the Commission's accounting work "from the direct supervision of Mr. King to the Department of War, Interior or Agriculture which will not have men specially trained for this work."

Bonner not only made this recommendation, but secured the approval of Secretary Wilbur, and on one occasion confided

to the staff of the Commission that President Hoover had
given him explicit orders to favor the power companies in
this and in every other way. Bonner's recommendation, however, was blocked by the passage of legislation creating a new
Power Commission. The legislation empowered the President
to appoint five new commissioners, and after they had taken
the oath of office their first act was to discharge King and
Russell.

Congressional indignation forced the Commission to re-hire
King, but Russell was immediately snatched up by Franklin
D. Roosevelt, then about to launch his drive against the power
companies in New York State. On the whole the new tactics
of the power lobby were working admirably.

*

THE latest group of Janizaries to open an arsenal in Washington are those operating for aviation companies. Their prey is
air-mail contracts, and though infants at the game they have
been amazingly successful. Probably a large part of that success is due to the selection of William P. MacCracken, former
Assistant Secretary of Commerce in charge of Aviation, as
their chief agent. MacCracken is an able and likable operator
and knows what is going on in the aviation field down to the
last detail. It was MacCracken who first learned of a Saturday
afternoon session held by the Senate Appropriation Committee on the Post Office Bill during the Economy Drive, at which
it was decided to lop off a $7,000,000 subsidy for foreign air
mail. The Committee worked at a time when most of Washington is on the golf course. It sat in executive session and its
work presumably was secret. Newspaper men were denied all
information. But not MacCracken. Within a few hours he
knew what had happened. The next day, despite the fact that
it was Sunday, most of the executives of the big air lines
which benefited by the $7,000,000 dole had reached Washing-

ton, and under MacCracken's leadership had set down a telling barrage on members of the Appropriations Committee.

"If news of the Committee's cut leaks," the air executives wailed, "the bottom will drop out of aviation stocks to-morrow morning."

So effectively did MacCracken and his cohorts function that before Monday noon the Committee reversed itself. Mac-Cracken took no chances, however, and while the Committee met, he and his aviation men kept vigil in the Senate corridors to check its actions.

The most amazing piece of lobbying in connection with air-mail contracts—probably one of the most amazing pieces of lobbying in the history of the State Department—was accomplished by the Pan-American Airways in securing monopolistic concessions throughout Latin America. It is the policy of the State Department always to champion American companies against foreign companies wherever there is competition; but it is also the strict policy of the Department never to distinguish between American companies, and to champion them impartially. In the case of the Pan-American Airways, however, the State Department deviated from this policy with a brazen indifference that might subject it to the charge of malfeasance in office.

In some fifty-two cases the State Department made urgent diplomatic representations to Latin-American countries on behalf of Pan-American Airways. In at least six of these, the Department acted to head off other American air lines competing against Pan-American Airways. One twenty-five-year-monopoly contract sponsored by the State Department on behalf of its favorite air line was so objectionable to Guatemala that the Cabinet was forced to resign. In Nicarauga a contract which the State Department supported was considered so prejudicial to the interests of that country that Brigadier General Logan Feland, Commander of the Marines, expressed his objection to the Navy Department; while in Haiti both the American financial advisor and Brigadier General John A.

Russell, American High Commissioner, took exception to the State Department's efforts and branded the Pan-American Airways' contract "a monopoly of the most objectionable character." In Honduras a committee of Congress reported the Pan-American Airways' contract unfavorably and despite the intervention of the Honduran President, the Honduran Congress unanimously disapproved the monopolistic features of the agreement. But Pan-American Airways got the State Department's support just the same.

The chief competitor of the Pan-American Airways in South America was the New York, Rio de Janiero and Buenos Aires Line, more commonly known as Trimotors. The State Department for some unknown reason decided to discriminate against it and on almost every occasion when its interests clashed with those of the Pan-American Airways, the latter company was favored.

One clew to this discrimination was the position of Postmaster General Brown. In the summer of 1929 when the Pan-American Airways' subsidiary in Chile was experiencing difficult competition from the Curtiss Aeroplane and Motor Corporation, another American firm, Brown wrote to Secretary of State Stimson, asking him that "all practical assistance be given to the Pan-American-Grace Airways in securing operating arrangements in preference to any other American company."

Another possible clew to the support which Pan-American Airways received from the State Department was the presence of former career diplomats in its organization who carried weight with their colleagues in Washington. Evan Young, former American Minister in Santo Domingo, was one of these. He acted as Close-up Man for this privileged airways company in negotiating Latin-American monopolies. So also did Alan Winslow, son-in-law of Under Secretary of State Castle. The man in the State Department who handled most of the aviation negotiations was Hugh D. Auchincloss, who later resigned when his dual activities as a State Department official and a partner in a brokerage firm attracted public attention.

Whoever pulled the strings for Pan-American Airways pulled them well. They commanded more power in the State Department than any other company in years, with the result that Pan-American Airways is now one of the few aviation companies paying real dividends during the depression.

*

PRIOR to the Hoover depression, the bankers did not need a very active lobby in Washington. Almost everything came their way. The National City Bank and J. and W. Seligman and Company were able to get away with a $415,000 "commission" to the son of the President of Peru, and the State Department, when it heard about it, did not bat an eye, even though the loan had defaulted. Dillon, Read and Company were able to facilitate a loan to the city of Milan by dropping a lucrative "commission" in the lap of the mayor of that city, and this procedure caused not a ripple of attention in the United States, even when a Fascist court held the mayor of Milan guilty of accepting a bribe. Dillon, Read and Company also were able to secure State Department approval to a loan of $23,000,000 to Bolivia, despite the fact that $5,000,000 of the American bondholders' money went to pay for arms and munitions from the British firm of Vickers, Ltd., shortly thereafter contributing to an outbreak of hostilities between Bolivia and Paraguay. The National City Company also escaped the notice of almost every one except Herbert D. Brown, Chief of the Bureau of Efficiency, regarding loan "commissions" which Brown alleged were paid to President Arosmena of Panama.

Practically every bank and bond house in the United States had been busy floating highly precarious loans to Germany despite the repeated disapproval of the State Department, which warned the bankers that serious obligations "might arise and that they held a duty to their prospective clients fully to advise them of the circumstances." The bankers were even able to foist these loans on an unsuspecting public, despite the caustic criticism of S. Parker Gilbert, Agent General for Reparations, that their prospectus advertising the loans suppressed the truth.

The bankers had enjoyed a literal field day. When a foreign government desired a $10,000,000 loan, the bankers—with an eye to doubling their commissions—frequently insisted that the total be $20,000,000. These doubtful foreign issues were forced upon smaller member bankers under penalty of losing out on all of the issues voted by the group. And the member banks in turn, many of whose officials were acting as trust administrators for the estates of widows and children, turned the issues over to the latter's deposit vaults, where they still are—scarcely worth the paper they are printed on.

And having contributed materially to the depression by these unrestrained activities, the bankers suddenly became the most vociferous, panicky and persistent lobbyists Washington has seen in years. It was the bankers who were chiefly responsible for putting across the Hoover moratorium, aimed at the cancellation of $11,000,000,000 of Allied war debts to the United States in order to save $1,500,000,000 of highly precarious private debts, which they had loaned to Germany despite the warning of the State Department. It was the bankers who conspired with Montagu Norman, head of the Bank of England, to start the drive for universal wage cuts. It was the bankers, who sold President Hoover the scheme of setting up a national credit corporation and putting over an extension of the Hoover moratorium at the same time. They evolved their plan at a secret night conference in the Massachusetts Avenue apartment of Secretary of the Treasury Mellon. Usually conferences of this kind are held in the White House. But afraid that news of the meeting would leak out to Congress and the press, Mr. Hoover quietly left the Executive Mansion and attended the Mellon meeting.

The National Credit Corporation failed to materialize when

the bankers declined to raise the money. So the $2,000,000,000 Reconstruction Finance Corporation took its place. Almost immediately branded the "Romance Corporation," its chief function, according to the explanation Mr. Hoover gave Congressmen whose support he needed, was to make loans to productive industry, and not to refund loans which industry owed the banks. But it was too much to expect that the R.F.C. would not obey the lobby which brought it into being. One of its first doles was a $12,800,000 grant to the Missouri Pacific Railroad partly for the purpose of permitting it to pay a loan due J. P. Morgan—a loan which was severely criticized on the floor of the Senate where Senator Couzens charged that it was influenced by the Republican National Committee. There followed innumerable other loans to banks, climaxed by the record-breaking advance of $80,000,000 to Charles G. Dawes, former head of the Reconstruction Finance Corporation.

The work of the banking lobby was functioning beautifully. While it functioned, thousands of home owners, their salaries cut, were unable to meet interest payments on mortgages and were sold out. The largess of the Romance Corporation was not passed down the line.

Having provided for the biggest business dole in history, the lobby got busy saving the banking system from reform. Congress sought to remedy some of the banking practices which had led to the depression. More particularly, Senator Carter Glass, author of the Federal Reserve Act, had introduced a bill providing for far-reaching bank revisions.

The lobby swung into action. Under the tutelage of R. V. Fleming, moon-faced president of the Riggs National Bank, a night school for bankers was organized, at which banking witnesses who were to appear before congressional committees next morning were coached on exactly what to say and what not to say. No Yale freshman ever crammed for an examination more assiduously and with better success than the pupils of the banking lobby. For, with the powerful collusion of their friend in the White House, the bankers separated the reform sections from the Glass-Steagall Bill, completely shelved them, and rammed the credit inflation portions of the bill through Congress.

*

THE evils of lobbying never can be cured. The Inside Jobbers —the most dangerous and effective of all workers—will always continue to place their Close-up Men and their Inside Men in the executive departments along Pennsylvania Avenue to pull every wire possible—until they are exposed.

But in the halls of Congress lobbying can be curbed in such a way as to purge it of many of its iniquities. The remedy lies along two lines: one of them a reorganization of the committee system in Congress, the other the registration of lobbyists and the adoption of laws preventing government employees from practicing lobbying until a certain length of time after they have left government service.

The latter already has been done by the Federal Reserve Board. None of its officials now can leave it and enter the private banking field until two years after resignation. Secretary Stimson has been urged by various Senators to enforce such a rule to prevent the insidious lobbying of former State Department officials, but declines to act.

The Bureau of Internal Revenue has set a most rigorous standard for the registration of lawyers practicing before it in cases involving adjustment of tax disputes—cases in which millions of dollars sometimes are involved and from which the lobbyists once reaped hundreds of thousands when the income tax first was being interpreted. The Bureau of Internal Revenue under this system is a difficult lobbying field and no attorney would think of approaching a member of the bureau without first showing a registration card authorizing him to practice before the bureau, together with a letter empowering him to represent his client. So strict is the Bureau of Internal Revenue regarding this that when it started an investigation of alleged unethical practices on the part of William Gibbs McAdoo, former Secretary of the Treasury, with a view to disbarring him, he withdrew his right to practice.

No such regulations exist in other branches of the government nor in the halls of Congress. There any one may walk in and begin telling a Congressman how he should vote without ever being asked to show credentials as to whom he represents and what right he has to be there.

This deficiency, however, is not nearly as iniquitous as the congressional system of appointing a member on so many different committees that he has no time to follow legislation in detail and therefore accepts the explanation given him by the lobbyist. Under the present system the drain on the time and energy of any of the real figures in the Senate during a legislative session is unbelievable. Three or four committees of which he is a member may be meeting in one morning. Take, for instance, Senator McNary, one of the most intelligent and hard-working members of the upper chamber. Besides being assistant floor leader of the Senate, he is chairman of the important committee on Agriculture and Forestry which frames all farm measures. He is also a member of the committee on Commerce which deals with some of the most important business problems coming before the Senate. Almost equally important is the committee on Manufactures, of which he also is a member. He is also a member of the committee on Public Lands and Surveys, which to his State—Oregon—is perhaps more important than the other committees. Finally he is a member of the Special Committee on Conservation of Wild Life Resources—also important to Oregon. It is a physical and mental impossibility for Senator McNary to be familiar with all of the legislation before all of these committees. Therefore, when a Janizary approaches him with an explanation of a certain bill which is pending before one of these committees, Senator McNary listens. And this always will happen until Congress remedies it by limiting the membership of committees.

But the remedy probably never will be enacted. Nor will any of the others.

"The reasons why nothing has ever been done, or will be, about lobbyists," to use the words of Champ Clark, who knew his Congress, "are that members of Congress are always having favors done them by lobbyists and that they never know when they may have to turn to lobbying to make a living."

So lobbying will continue to flourish like a rank weed in the semi-tropical summer weather of Washington.